© THE BAKER & TAYLOR CO.

LOOK IT UP

Other books by Rudolf Flesch

Rudolf Flesch

LOOK IT UP

A Deskbook of American Spelling and Style

Harper & Row, Publishers

New York, Hagerstown, San Francisco, London

LOOK IT UP: A DESKBOOK OF AMERICAN SPELLING AND STYLE. Copyright © 1977 by Rudolf Flesch. All rights reserved. Printed in the United States of America. No part of this book may be used or reproduced in any manner whatsoever without written permission except in the case of brief quotations embodied in critical articles and reviews: For information address Harper & Row, Publishers, Inc., 10 East 53rd Street, New York, N.Y. 10022. Published simultaneously in Canada by Fitzhenry & Whiteside Limited, Toronto.

FIRST EDITION

Designed by C. Linda Dingler

Library of Congress Cataloging in Publication Data

Flesch, Rudolf Franz, 1911-
  Look it up.

  Bibliography: p.
  1. Americanisms. 2. English language—Orthography and spelling. 3. English language—Idioms,
corrections, errors. I. Title.
PE2817.F5   427'.9'73   75-23880
ISBN 0-06-011292-1

77 78 79 80 10 9 8 7 6 5 4 3 2 1

To my son Hugo

Please Read This First

I tried to make this book as useful and reliable as I could.

First, useful. There are over 18,000 entries, covering questions on spelling and style. Of course there's no way of knowing all the spelling and style mistakes people are apt to make, but I think I caught all the common ones. After all, I've taught people to write for over 30 years.

The book is arranged in one alphabet. This includes compounds spelled as two words. For instance you'll find *high school* between *highroad* and *high-sounding.*

Common mistakes are listed between parentheses. Naturally I didn't include every possible mistake, but I tried to include those that are most common, like (**mispell**) and (**her's**).

Some entries are longer, like **comma** and **hyphen**, but most are quite short. I want you to use this book while you're writing and don't want to hold you up with long, detailed discussions.

There are few cross-references. Since the entries are so short, I simply repeated them in the two places you might look for them. For instance you'll find the same short entry under **shall, will** and under **will, shall**.

Each entry is based on a study and comparison of the information given in the following sources: Webster's Third New International Dictionary of the English Language Unabridged (G. & C. Merriam Co., 1961); Webster's New Collegiate Dictionary (G. & C. Merriam, 1973); the Oxford English Dictionary (compact edition, 1971); A Supplement to the Oxford English Dictionary (volume 1, A-G, 1972); the latest editions of The Random House College Dictionary, Funk & Wagnalls Standard College Dictionary, Webster's New World Dictionary (college edition), The American Heritage Dictionary and the Doubleday Dictionary; the US Government Printing Office Style Manual (revised edition,

January 1973); the University of Chicago Press Manual of Style (12th edition, 1969); the New York Times Manual of Style and Usage (1976 edition); the Associated Press Stylebook (revised edition, 1970); the latest editions of the stylebooks of the Chicago Daily News, Chicago Tribune, Los Angeles Times, New York Daily News, New York Post, Philadelphia Evening Bulletin, St. Louis Post-Dispatch and Wall Street Journal; A Dictionary of Modern English Usage by H. W. Fowler (2d edition, 1965); A Dictionary of American-English Usage (based on Fowler's Modern English Usage) by Margaret Nicholson (1957); A Dictionary of Contemporary American Usage by Bergen and Cornelia Evans (1957); Modern American Usage by Wilson Follett (1966); ABC of Plain Words by Sir Ernest Gowers (1961); Current American Usage, edited by Margaret M. Bryant (1962); The Elements of Style by William Strunk Jr. and E. B. White (2d edition, 1972); The Careful Writer by Theodore M. Bernstein (1967); American Usage: The Consensus by Roy H. Copperud (1970); and The Barnhart Dictionary of New English Since 1963 (1973). Occasionally I also used other sources.

My most important source was the Unabridged Merriam-Webster dictionary, supplemented by the latest (1973) desk-size edition. To date, the Merriam-Webster company has collected 12 million quotes ("citations") from all kinds of published sources as a scientific basis for its entries. It also relies on 5 million citations collected by the Oxford English Dictionary and other scholarly dictionaries. All this adds up to 17 million citations from published sources. Because of this the spelling, style and usage listed by Merriam-Webster have the most solid scientific and statistical base. (In this book Merriam-Webster is referred to simply as Webster's.)

My second most important source was the US Government Printing Office Style Manual (called in this book the GPO Style Manual for short). It sets the style for everything published by the federal government. Surprisingly, it is very progressive in matters of spelling and style. As its preface says, it "attempts to keep abreast of and sometimes anticipate changes in orthography [spelling], grammar and type production." I used it as a correction for spellings in Webster's that seemed clearly out-of-date.

The third most important source was the monumental Oxford English Dictionary, which contains exact historical information on most words in the English language. I used it mainly to research the historical background of controversial usages.

Now let's look at a few details.

First of all, I did *not* include alternate spellings. Webster's lists the most common spelling first and the second most common second. Obviously you'll want to know and use the common, preferred form. So I didn't see any point in confusing you with spellings you may want to avoid. For the same reason, I didn't include British spellings like *jeweller* and *wilful.* This is strictly a dictionary of *American* spelling.

In a few cases I listed a spelling Webster's puts in second place. For instance, the word *subpena* is so spelled in the GPO Style Manual and many newspaper stylebooks, while Webster's puts *subpoena* first. I think the trend toward the spelling *subpena* is clear.

I listed plurals and verb forms without comment, e.g., **nostrum, nostrums; ring, rang, rung.**

The University of Chicago Style Manual says "Of ten spelling questions that arise in writing or editing, nine are probably concerned with compound words." Because of this I tried to list as many compound words as possible. To help you even more, I put in such entries as **"house-.** Almost all compounds are spelled as one word." This is followed by such entries as **houseboat, housebound** etc. I hope you'll conclude from this that less common words beginning with **house-** should also be spelled as one word. Like *houseplant* and *housewrecker,* for instance.

On controversial questions of usage, I listed what is common and standard, relying on Webster's and other sources. Most of these entries include the date of the first listing in the Oxford English Dictionary and a quotation from Shakespeare or some other classic. For example, the entry **these kind of** reads: "The idiom *these kind of* has been common since 1380. Shakespeare (King Lear, II, ii, 107) wrote 'These kind of knaves I know.' "

As a special feature, I included words you might hesitate to use because you consider them slang or too informal to be used in general writing. Take for example the word *hassle.* The entry in this book reads: **"hassle** is listed as standard usage in Webster's." Why isn't it listed as slang? Because the unabridged third edition of Webster's gives eight citations showing that *hassle* has been used by writers like S. J. Perelman and publications like the New York Times. Now since *hassle* is a useful, expressive word that may add force and clarity to your writing, I thought it was worth listing in this book to help you overcome any prejudice against it.

All experts on writing and usage agree that you should avoid pompous, bureaucratic words. There are no scientific or statistical data on this aspect of writing. So I did the next best thing and flagged such words with the modest little formula "Don't use *x* when *y* will do." For example you'll find "Don't use *subsequent* when *later* will do" and "Don't write *the undersigned* when *I* will do." I hope these brief reminders will have an effect on your style.

One more word. This is meant to be a deskbook. It won't do you any good if you don't do what the title says—look it up. Use the book over and over again until the right spelling and the right style get into your bloodstream and your nervous system—until you can't even remember the time when you didn't know that *includable* ends in *-able* but *deductible* ends in *-ible*.

R. F.

January 19, 1976

LOOK IT UP

A

a, an. Use the article *a* before words starting with a consonant *(a fork, a spoon), an* before words starting with a vowel *(an egg, an omelet).* Go by the way words are pronounced. Many words starting with *u* or *eu* are pronounced with the opening syllable *yoo*—write *a union, a used car, a eulogy.*

Use the form *an* before words starting with a silent *h*—an hour, an honor. But don't write *an hotel, an historical event* or *an hysterical outbreak,* just because the *h* in certain words used to be silent or almost silent. Stick to the current pronunciation and write *a hotel, a historical event* etc.

With abbreviations and figures stick to the pronunciation too. For instance, *f* is pronounced *ef, r* is pronounced *ar, 8* is pronounced *eight.* Write *an FBI agent, an RCA TV set, an 8-year-old girl.*

a-. There's no hyphen in such words as *abuzz, aflutter,* or *aquiver.*

aardvark starts with double *a.*

abacus, abacuses.

abate. Don't use *abate* when *drop* or *cut* will do.

abattoir. Two *t*'s, no *e.*

abbess. Double *b,* double *s.*

abbey is spelled with double *b* and *e. Abby,* the short form of *Abigail,* has no *e.*

abbot. Two *b*'s, one *t.*

abbreviate, abbreviation. Double *b.*

abbreviations. Most newspapers and book publishers no longer use periods after initials like *CBS, EDT, RFD, TWA.* With *U.S.,* periods are often used, but the form *US* without periods is getting more common. A period is *always* used after abbreviations consisting of a capital letter and one or more lowercase letters, such as *Mr., Mrs., Dr., St., Ave., Blvd.*

Don't feel you have to spell out each word at its first mention in your piece of writing. If you're sure your readers are familiar with the abbreviation, use it right away. Don't write *Young Men's Christian Association* instead of *YMCA* just because you think you have to.

ABCs. No apostrophe necessary.

abductor ends in -*or.*

aberrant, aberration. One *b,* two *r*'s.

abetter, abettor. The common spelling is *abetter,* but lawyers prefer *abettor.*

abhorrence, abhorrent end in -*ence,* -*ent.*

abjure, adjure. Don't confuse *abjure* (renounce under oath) with *adjure* (entreat).

-able, -ible. There's no reliable rule to follow when you're in doubt whether a word ends in -*able* or -*ible.* The -*ible* words are rarer, so chances are if you spell it -*able* you'll be right.

ablebodied. One word.

ablutions. Don't use *ablutions* when *wash* will do.

abode. Don't use *abode* when *house* or *home* will do.

A-bomb. Capital *A,* hyphen, lowercase *b.*

abominable ends in -*able.*

aborigine, aborigines. Single *e.*

aborning. No hyphen.

about-face. Hyphenated.

above. You can use this word as an adverb *(as specified above),* an adjective *(the above specifications)* or a noun *(we refer to the above).* You can use it to refer to something on the same page or a previous page.

aboveboard. One word.

above-captioned, above-cited. Hyphened.

aboveground. One word.

above-mentioned, above-named, above-said. Hyphened.

abridgeable ends in -*eable* because of the soft *g.*

abridgment. No *e* after *g.*

abscess is spelled with a *c* after the first *s.*

abscissa, abscissas. Spelled with a *c* after the first *s.*

abscission. Spelled with a *c* after the first *s.*

absence. No *c* after the *s.*

absent. Don't use *absent* when *without* will do.

absentminded, absentmindedly, absentmindedness. No hyphen.

abstention ends in -*tion.*

abstinence, abstinent end in *-ence, -ent.*

abundance, abundant end in *-ance, -ant.*

abut, abutted, abutting, abutment. One *t* in *abut* and *abutment,* two *t*'s in *abutted* and *abutting.*

abysmal, abyss are spelled with *y.* One *s* in *abysmal.*

ac-. If you can't find the word you're looking for under *ac-,* try *acc-.*

academy. Two *a*'s followed by *e.*

Acadia, Arcadia. *Acadia* means Nova Scotia, *Arcadia* is a land of peace and harmony.

a cappella. Two words. Spell it with two *p*'s and two *l*'s.

accede, exceed. *Accede* (spelled with *-ede*) means yield, *exceed* (spelled with *-eed*) means surpass. Don't use *accede* when *give in* or *yield* will do.

accelerate, exhilarate. *Accelerate* means speed up, *exhilarate* means cheer up. Don't use *accelerate* when *speed up* will do.

accelerator ends in *-or.*

accents. Follow the practice of most newspapers and the GPO Style Manual and forget about accents in most English words taken from French, Spanish or other foreign languages. Write *apropos, boutonniere, cabana, cafe, coupe, facade, melee, role, smorgasbord, soiree, vicuna.* There are only a few foreign words that are never spelled without accents, e.g. *attaché, chargé d'affaires, mañana, outré, passé, pâté, père, touché.*

accentuate. *U* after the first *t.*

accept, except. *Accept* means take, *except* means exclude.

acceptable, acceptability end in *-able, -ability.*

acceptance ends in *-ance.*

accepter, acceptor. Spell it *accepter* in everyday writing, *acceptor* as a legal term.

access, excess. *Access* means approach, entry, *excess* means superfluity, intemperance.

accessible, accessibility end in *-ible, -ibility.*

accessory ends in *-ory.*

accidentally ends in *-ally.* Reminder: "It *all* happened *accidentally.*"

accidentprone. No hyphen.

acclaim, acclamation. Two *c*'s.

accolade. Two *c*'s, one *l.*

accommodate, accommodation. Double *c and* double *m.* Think of "hotel accommodations with *two double* beds."

accompany, accompanies, accompanied, accompanying, accompaniment, accompanist. Spelled with *y* in *accompany, i* in *accompanies, accompanied, accompaniment, accompanist,* and *yi* in *accompanying.*

accomplice. Two *c*'s.

accomplish. Two *c*'s. Don't use *accomplish* when *do* will do.

accord. Don't use *accord* when *give* will do.

accordion ends in *-ion.*

accost. Two *c*'s.

account. Don't use *on account of* when *because* or *because of* will do.

accouter, accouterments. Spell with *-er.*

accredit. Two *c*'s.

accrual, accrue. Two *c*'s.

accumulate, accumulation. Two *c*'s. Don't use *accumulate* when *gather* or *collect* will do.

accurate, accurately, accuracy. Two *c*'s followed by *u.* Remember "Ac*cu*racy is the only *cure* for mistakes."

accursed. Spell with *-ed.*

accusatory. Double *c.* Ends in *-ory.*

accustom, accustomed. Two *c*'s.

acetic, ascetic. *Acetic* means acid, *ascetic* means austere.

acetylene. Watch the *y* after the *t.*

ache, ached, aching. There's no *e* in *aching.*

-ache. Use no hyphen in words ending in *-ache* like *headache, toothache.*

achieve, achievement. *I* before *e.* Don't write *achieve* when *get, reach* or *do* will do.

Achilles heel. You don't need an apostrophe.

aching. No *e.*

achromatic is spelled with *ch.*

acidophilus ends in *-us.*

acidproof. One word.

ack-ack is spelled with a hyphen.

acknowledge, acknowledged, acknowledging contain the words *know* and *ledge.* There's no *e* after the *g* in *acknowledging.*

acknowledgeable ends in *-eable.*

acknowledgment. No *e* after the *g.*

acme ends in *e.*

acne ends in *e.*

aco-. If you can't find the word you're looking for under *aco-,* try *acco-.*

acolyte has only one *c.*

acoustic, acoustically, acoustics. Spelled with *ou.*

acqu-. If you can't find the word you're looking for under *acqu-,* try *aqu-.*

acquaint, acquaintance. Don't forget the *c. Acquaintance* ends in *-ance.*

acquaintanceship. You don't need the ending *-ship.* Write *acquaintance.*

acquiesce, acquiescence, acquiescent. Two silent *c*'s to remember —one after the *a,* a second one after the *s.*

acquire. *C* before *q.* Don't write *acquire* when *get* or *gain* will do.

acquisition. *C* before *q.*

acquit, acquitted, acquitting, acquittal. *C* before the *q.* Two *t*'s in all forms except *acquit.*

acre is spelled with *-re.*

acreage. Don't leave out the *e.*

acrid. One *c.*

acrimonious, acrimony. One *c.*

acrobat, acrobatic, acrobatics. All start with *ac-.*

acronym. Spelled with *y.*

acrophobia means fear of heights, *agoraphobia* means fear of open spaces.

acropolis. One *c*

across. *A* plus *cross.*

across-the-board (adjective). Two hyphens.

acrostic. Starts with *ac.*

acrylic is spelled with *y* and one *l.*

actionable ends in *-able.*

active voice. The verb *love* in *John loves Mary* is in the active voice, in *Mary is loved by John* it's in the passive voice. It's a basic rule of good style that the active voice is better than the passive voice. Don't use the passive voice unless it's essential, as in *he was murdered.*

actor ends in *-or.*

actually. Two *l*'s. You don't need a comma in such a sentence as *actually I was quite surprised.*

acu-. If you can't find the word you're looking for under *acu-,* try *accu-.*

acumen. One *c.*

acute. One *c*.

ad, short for advertisement, is standard usage.

A.D., as in *A.D. 1776.* Use capitals followed by periods. *A.D.* comes before the date.

adagio, adagios.

adamant. Three *a*'s.

adapt, adopt. *Adapt* means make fit, *adopt* means take or take up.

adaptable ends in *-able.*

adapter ends in *-er.*

(adaption). The standard word is *adaptation.*

addendum, addenda.

addible ends in *-ible.*

addition. Don't use *in addition* when *besides, also, too* will do.

additional. Don't use *additional* when *more* will do.

additionally. Don't use *additionally* when *besides, also, too* will do.

addlebrained, addlepated. No hyphen.

address. Two *d*'s. Reminder: *"Add* an *address."*

I recommend the following simple forms of address for letters, on the envelope and inside:

Normally, write *Mr., Mrs., Miss* or *Ms.* (or *Dr., Capt., Lt.* etc.) followed by the full name. Address officials of corporations as

> Mr. John Doe, Vice President (or whatever)
> XYZ Corporation

Address lawyers as *Mr. John Doe* or, more old-fashioned, as *John Doe, Esq.*

Use these special forms of address:

President of the US
> Name: *The President* (Don't give his name.)
> Salutation: *Dear Mr. President:*

Vice President of the US
> Name: *The Vice President* (Don't give his name.)
> Salutation: *Dear Mr. Vice President:*

Cabinet Member
> Name: *Hon.* (full name), *Secretary of State*
> Salutation: *Dear Mr. Secretary:*

US or State Senator
>   Name: *Hon.* (full name)
>   Salutation: *Dear Senator* (last name):

Member of Congress or State Legislature
>   Name: *Hon.* (full name)
>   Salutation: *Dear Mr.* (last name):

Chief Justice of the US
>   Name: *The Chief Justice* (Don't give his name.)
>   *Supreme Court of the United States*
>   Salutation: *Dear Mr. Chief Justice:*

Justice of the US Supreme Court
>   Name: *Hon.* (full name), *Associate Justice*
>   *Supreme Court of the United States*
>   Salutation: *Dear Mr. Justice:*

Judge
>   Name: *Hon.* (full name)
>   Salutation: *Dear Judge* (last name):

Governor
>   Name: *Hon.* (full name)
>   *Governor of* ——
>   Salutation: *Dear Governor* (last name):

Mayor
>   Name: *Hon.* (full name)
>   *Mayor of* ——
>   Salutation: *Dear Mayor* (last name):

American Ambassador
>   Name: *Hon.* (full name)
>   Salutation: *Dear Mr. Ambassador:*

American Consul
>   Name: (full name), *Esq.*
>   *American Consul*
>   Salutation: *Dear Mr.* (last name):

Foreign Ambassador
 Name: *His Excellency* (full name)
   Ambassador of ——
 Salutation: *Your Excellency:*

Foreign Minister
 Name: *Hon.* (full name)
   Minister of ——
 Salutation: *Dear Mr. Minister:*

Foreign Consul
 Name: (full name), *Esq.*
   Consul of ——
 Salutation: *Dear Mr. Consul:*

Episcopal Bishop
 Name: *The Right Reverend* (full name)
   Bishop of ——
 Salutation: *Dear Bishop* (last name):

Methodist Bishop
 Name: *Bishop* (full name)
 Salutation: *Dear Bishop* (last name):

Cardinal
 Name: *His Eminence* (first name) *Cardinal* (last name)
   Archbishop of ——
 Salutation: *Your Eminence:*

Monsignor
 Name: *The Right Reverend Msgr.* (full name)
 Salutation: *Dear Msgr.* (last name):

Catholic Archbishop or Bishop
 Name: *The Most Reverend* (full name)
   Archbishop (or *Bishop*) *of* ——
 Salutation: *Most Reverend Sir:*

Protestant Minister
 Name: *Rev. (Dr.)* (full name)
 Salutation: *Dear Mr.* (or *Dr.*) (last name):

Catholic Priest
>Name: *Rev.* (full name)
>Salutation: *Dear Father* (last name):

Rabbi
>Name: *Rabbi* (full name)
>Salutation: *Dear Rabbi* (last name):

The forms of address for foreign rulers and aristocrats are too complex to list here.

addressee. Two *d*'s, two *s*'s, two *e*'s.

adducible ends in *-ible.*

adequate, adequacy. The *d* is followed by an *e.* Don't use *adequate* when *enough* will do.

adherence, adherent end in *-ence* and *-ent.*

adherence, adhesion. Use *adherence* when you mean following an idea, *adhesion* when you mean sticking to a material.

ad hoc. Never hyphenated.

adieu, adieus.

ad infinitum ends in *-um.*

ad interim. No hyphen.

adjacent. Don't use *adjacent* when *next* will do.

adjoin, adjourn. *Adjoin* means lie next to, *adjourn* means suspend.

adjudicator ends in *-or.*

adjunct. Don't leave out the *d.*

adjure, abjure. *Adjure* means entreat, *abjure* means renounce.

adjustable ends in *-able.*

adjuster ends in *-er.*

adjutant general, adjutants general.

ad-lib, ad-libbed, ad-libbing. An *ad-lib* remark. Hyphened.

adman. No hyphen.

administer. Don't use *administer* when *give, run* or *manage* will do.

(administrate). The shorter form *administer* is better.

Administration. Use a capital *A* only when you mean a specific administration. Otherwise start the word with a small *a.*

administrator ends in *-or.*

admirable ends in *-able.*

admissible ends in *-ible.*

admission, admittance. You can use either word when you mean permitted entry.

admit of. Don't use *admit of* when *allow* will do.

ad nauseam ends in *-eam*.

adolescent, adolescence. Don't forget the *c* after the *s*.

adopt, adapt. *Adopt* means take or take up, *adapt* means make fit.

adopted, adoptive. Children are *adopted* by *adoptive* parents.

adorable ends in *-able*.

adrenaline has an *e* at the end.

(adress). Misspelling of *address*.

adscititious. Watch the *sc*. Ends in *-itious*.

adulterous, adultery. Be sure to put in the *e*.

adumbrate, adumbration. Don't use these stilted words when you mean *foreshadow* or *foreshadowing*.

ad valorem. No hyphen.

advance. Don't write *thank you in advance*. The phrase implies that the addressee of your letter *must* do what you ask him.

advance man. No hyphen.

advance planning says the same thing twice. Write *planning*.

advantageous. The *e* is needed to mark the soft *g* sound.

adventitious ends in *-itious*. It doesn't mean advantageous but accidental.

adversary ends in *-ary*.

adverse, averse. *Adverse* means unfavorable, *averse* means disinclined to.

advertise, advertisement. Spelled with *-ise*.

advertiser ends in *-er*.

advice, advise. *Advice* is the noun *(give advice)*, *advise* is the verb *(advise me)*. *Advice* also means notice in business and bank English and *advise* means notify or tell. Don't use *advise* when *write* or *tell* will do.

advisable ends in *-able*.

advise. The phrases *please be advised* and *we wish to advise* are usually unnecessary.

adviser, advisor. Follow newspaper style and spell it *adviser*.

advisory ends in *-ory*.

adz, adze. Spell it without the *e*.

-ae, -as. The plural of words with the Latin ending *-a* may be either *-ae* or *-as*. The practice varies. Look for the specific word.

-ae-, -e-. Most words that used to be spelled with *-ae-* are now commonly spelled with *-e-*, like *anesthesia, archeology, hemoglobin, medieval.*

aegis, egis. This is an exception to the rule just given. The form *aegis* is more common.

(aeon), eon. Spell it *eon.*

aerate is spelled with *ae-.*

aerial is spelled with *ae-.*

aerie, aery. The most common spelling of this word for an eagle's nest is *aerie.*

aero-. Words starting with *aero-* are spelled as one word without a hyphen, unless the next letter is *o.* Examples: *aerodynamics, aeronautics, aeronautical, aerosol.* But: *aero-otitis.*

(aeroplane). The US word is *airplane.*

(aesthetic). Spell it *esthetic.*

afar. No hyphen.

affable ends in *-able.*

affair. Spell it without an *e* at the end in all senses.

affect, effect. To *affect* means to influence, to *effect* means to bring about. "If you *affect* someone, you *a*lter his *a*ttitude; if you *effect* something, you *e*stablish an *e*nd result."

affectation. Two *f*'s.

affection, affectionate, affectionately. Two *f*'s.

affidavit. Two *f*'s.

affiliate, affiliated, affiliation. Two *f*'s.

affinity. Some grammarians insist that *affinity* should only be used with *between* or *with,* but you've plenty of authorities behind you if you write about an *affinity for* or *to.*

affirmative. Don't use *affirmative* when *yes* will do.

affix. Two *f*'s.

afflatus, afflatuses.

afflict, inflict. You are *afflicted with* or *by* something painful someone has *inflicted on* you.

afford. Don't use *afford* when *give* will do.

afforest, afforestation. Two *f*'s.

affranchise ends in *-ise.*

affray, affright, affront. Two *f*'s.

afghan is spelled with *gh.*

aficionado, aficionados. One *f.*

A-flat. Use a hyphen.

AFL-CIO is now the usual abbreviated form. Don't spell it out.

afoot. No hyphen.

aforegoing, aforementioned, aforesaid. No hyphen.

aforethought. Alive only in the phrase *with malice aforethought.*

a fortiori. No hyphen in this Latin phrase.

afresh. No hyphen.

Afro. You can say *an Afro haircut* or simply *an Afro.* Use a capital *A.*

after-. Some compounds are spelled as one word, but some are hyphened, particularly those with the accent on the second part.

afterbeat, afterdeck. One word.

after-dinner. Hyphened.

aftereffect. One word.

after-hours. Hyphened.

aftermath, aftertaste, aftertax. One word.

after-theater. Hyphened.

afterthought. One word

afterward, afterwards. Usage is divided. Use the form that comes naturally to you. The King James version of the Bible has *afterwards:* "Thou canst not follow me now; but thou shall follow me afterwards." (John 13:36.)

ag-. If you can't find the word you're looking for under *ag-,* try *agg-.*

age, aged. These words are often superfluous, as in the phrases *at the age of 27, aged 9, 65 years of age.* Write *27, 9, 65.*

(ageing). Follow the trend and spell it *aging.* Remember "Drinking *gin* speeds a*ging.*"

ageless. No hyphen.

agencywide. No hyphen.

agenda is now usually treated as a singular. There *is* a word *agendum,* meaning an item on an agenda, but for the plural of this word you can use *agendums.*

age-old, age-stricken, age-weary. Hyphened.

agglomerate, agglomeration; agglutinate, agglutination; aggrandize, aggrandizement. All spelled with two *g*'s.

aggravate, aggravation. Some grammarians insist you shouldn't use *aggravate* in the sense of irritate rather than make worse. But this so-called mistake has been made by famous writers since 1611. Thackeray wrote "Threats only served to aggravate people." So if you want to use *aggravate* or *aggravation* in this way, go right ahead.

aggregate (verb) in the sense of *total* is now standard English. But don't use *aggregate* when *total* will do.

aggression, aggressive. Two *g*'s.

aggressor ends in *-or*.

aggrieve. Two *g*'s.

aghast is spelled with an *h*.

aging. Spell it without *e*.

agitator ends in *-or*.

a-go-go. Two hyphens.

agonize ends in *-ize*.

agoraphobia means fear of open spaces, *acrophobia* means fear of heights.

(ago since). Instead of "It's 12 years *ago since* he died," write either "It's 12 years since he died" or "It's 12 years ago that he died."

agree, agreed, agreeing, agreement. One *g*.

agreeable ends in *-able*.

aground. No hyphen.

ague ends in *-ue*.

agueproof. No hyphen.

ah well needs no comma.

aide, aid. *Aide* is the more common spelling for an assistant or helper.

aide-de-camp, aides-de-camp.

aide-mémoire, aides-mémoire. Accent.

aigrette, egret. *Aigrette* means plume or spray, *egret* means a heron.

ain't is "used orally in most parts of the US by many educated speakers" (Webster). But not in writing.

air-. Most compounds are spelled without a hyphen.

airbag, airbase, airborne, airbus, aircargo, aircoach. One word.

air-condition, air-conditioned, air-conditioning, air-conditioner. All hyphened.

air-conscious. Hyphened.

air-cool, air-cooled. Hyphened.

aircraft, aircrew, airdrome, airdrop. One word.

air express. Two words, no hyphen.

airfield, airflow. One word.

air force. Two words.

airfreight, airlift. One word.

airline, air line. One word when you mean a company, two words when you mean a beeline.

airliner, airmail, airman, airmass, airminded, airphoto, airplane, airport, airpower. One word.

air raid. Two words, no hyphen.

airship, airshow, airsick, airsickness, airspace, airspeed, airstream, airstrike, airstrip, airtight. One word.

air time. Two words, no hyphen.

airward, airwave, airway, airwise, airworthy. One word.

aisle, isle. *Aisle* in a theater, *isle* in the sea.

a la. Write *a la* (without accent) in such expressions as *a la carte* or *a la king. Alamode* is now often spelled as one word.

Aladdin has one *l* and two *d*'s.

albatross ends in double *s.*

albeit. So spelled. Don't use *albeit* when *though* will do.

albino, albinos.

albumen, albumin. *Albumen* means the white of an egg, *albumin* the protein it contains.

alderman, alderwoman. No hyphen.

alehouse. No hyphen.

alfresco. One word.

alga, algae.

alibi, meaning excuse, is now standard usage. You can also use *alibi* as a verb—*to alibi, alibied, alibiing.*

alight, alighted. The past tense *alit* is poetical.

align, alignment; aline, alinement. The spellings *align* and *alignment* are more common.

A-line. Hyphened.

alkali, alkalis.

all-. Most words starting with *all-* are hyphened. Write *all-absorbing, all-clear, all-fired, all-inclusive, all-out, all-around, all-seeing, all-star.* But it's *all in* (two words), and *alltime* and *allwise* (no hyphen).

(Alladin). Misspelling of *Aladdin.*

allay, allayed, allaying.

all but. Don't write *all but* when *almost* will do.

all but one takes a singular verb. *All but one was killed.*

all-clear. Hyphened.

allege, alleged, alleging, allegedly. No *d* before *g.*

allegiance ends in *-ance.*

allegro, allegros.

allergic, allergy. It's standard usage to say *he's allergic to marriage.*

alleviate, alleviation. Two *l*'s.

alley, alleys; ally, allies. An *alley* is a lane, an *ally* is an associate.

alleyway has no hyphen.

all-fired. Hyphen.

alliance ends in *-ance.*

all-inclusive. Hyphened.

alliteration, allocate, allocation. Two *l*'s.

all of. In a sentence like *all of the members were present* you can leave out *of,* but there's no rule that says you have to.

allot, allotted, allotting, allottee, allotment. It's one *t* in *allot* and *allotment* and two *t*'s in the other forms.

all-out. Hyphened.

allowance ends in *-ance.*

alloy has two *l*'s.

all ready, already. *All ready* means prepared, *already* means previously.

all right, alright. *All right* is the established spelling, but see ALRIGHT. Webster's lists both forms as standard usage.

all-seeing. Hyphened.

allspice. One word.

all-star. Hyphened.

all the time is idiomatic American English.

alltime. One word.

all together, altogether. *All together* means collectively, *altogether* means wholly.

allude, elude. *Allude* means hint, *elude* means avoid.

allure, allurement. Two *l*'s.

allusion, illusion. *Allusion* means hint, *illusion* means false image. Don't write *allusion* when you mean a direct reference.

allwise. One word.

ally, allies; alley, alleys. An *ally* is an associate, an *alley* is a lane.

-ally, -ly. It's *accidentally, incidentally, practically, politically, sarcastically, statistically* etc. The only word that ends in *-icly* is *publicly.*

alma mater, alma maters.

almanac no longer has a *k* at the end.

almighty. One *l.*

almond. Don't forget the silent *l.*

alms is the singular *(an alms)* and the plural.

almsgiver, almsgiving, almshouse. No hyphen.

alongship, alongshore. No hyphen.

along with can be used with the plural verb, as in *the mental suffering, along with the physical pain, were intolerable.*

alpenstock. German spelling.

alpha ray. Two words.

already, all ready. *Already* means previously, *all ready* means prepared.

already existing. Cut out *already.*

alright, all right. *All right* is the established spelling, but *alright* has been used by good writers since 1893. Webster's lists *alright* as standard usage and quotes Gertrude Stein: "The first two years of the medical school were *alright.*" The 1972 Supplement to the Oxford English Dictionary calls *alright* "a frequent spelling."

also. You need no comma before or after *also.*

also-ran, also-rans.

altar, alter. Distinguish *altar* (in a church) from *alter* (change).

altar boy. Two words.

altarpiece. One word.

altar rail. Two words.

alter. Don't use *alter* when *change* will do.

altercation. Don't write *altercation* when *quarrel* or *row* will do.

alternately, alternatively. *Alternately* means by turns, *alternatively* means as a possible choice.

alternative. Conservative grammarians say that *alternative* can refer only to a choice between two things. But Gladstone in 1848 said "I prefer the fourth and last of these *alternatives.*" Anyway, don't use *alternative* when *choice* will do.

(altho). Spell it *although.*

alto, altos.

altogether, all together. *Altogether* means wholly, *all together* means collectively.

aluminum is the American word, *aluminium* is British and Canadian.

alumnus, alumna. The plural of *alumnus* is *alumni,* that of *alumna alumnae.*

always. One *l.*

a.m. Follow newspaper style and the GPO Style Manual and use lowercase letters with periods.

amanuensis, amanuenses.

amaryllis. Spelled with *y.*

amateur ends in -*eur*.

ambassador ends in -*or*.

amber-colored. Hyphen.

ambi-. All words with this prefix are spelled as one word.

ambidextrous. No *e* after the *t*.

ambience, ambiance. Use the ending -*ence*.

ambiguous, ambiguity. Watch the *u* after the *g*.

ambition, ambitious are spelled with *t*.

ambulance ends in -*ance*.

ameba, amoeba. The trend is away from the old-fashioned spelling *amoeba*.

ameliorate, amelioration. Don't use these words when *improve, improvement* will do.

amenable ends in -*able*.

amend, emend. *Amend* is the general word, *emend* means to correct by making changes in a text.

amethyst ends in -*yst*.

amicus curiae, amici curiae.

amid, amidst. Follow the New York Times and use only the form *amid*.

amidships has no hyphen.

amigo, amigos.

amino-. Spell words beginning with *amino-* as one word without a hyphen. But it's *amino acid* (two words).

ammo, short for *ammunition,* is listed as a standard word in Webster's.

ammonia has two *m*'s.

(amoeba). Spell it *ameba*.

amok, amuck. To run *amuck* sounds less pretentious.

among, amongst. The New York Times uses only the form *among*.

amoral, immoral. *Amoral* means indifferent to moral standards, *immoral* means wicked.

amount, number. *Amount* refers to bulk, weight, quantity, *number* refers to things or people that can be counted. The phrase *in the amount of* is often superfluous.

amour ends -*our*.

amour propre. No hyphen.

amperehour, amperemeter, ampereturn. No hyphen.

ampersand is the name of the sign &. Use it only in company names like *A&P*. Otherwise write *and*.

amphi- forms words without a hyphen.

amphitheater ends in -*er*.

ampul, ampule, ampoule. Spell it *ampul.*

amuck, amok. The spelling *amuck* is less pretentious.

amulet ends in *-et.*

an-. If you can't find the word you're looking for under *an-,* try *ann-.*

an, a. See A, AN. Briefly, go by the pronunciation. Write *an egg, an hour, an FBI agent,* but *a union, a hotel.*

anachronism, anachronistic. Don't forget the *h.*

(anaemia, anaemic). Now generally spelled *anemia, anemic.*

(anaesthesia, anaesthetic). Now generally spelled *anesthesia, anesthetic.*

analogue, analog. Spell it *analogue.*

analogy. It's *-alogy,* not *-ology.*

analysis, analyses.

analyst, annalist. *Analyst* means psychiatrist or researcher, *annalist* means historian.

analyze ends in *-yze, analyzable* ends in *-able.*

anatomize ends in *-ize.*

ancestor ends in *-or.*

anchor ends in *-or.*

anchor light. Two words.

anchorman. One word.

ancient. Spelled with *c.*

ancillary has two *l*'s.

and. Since the King James version of the Bible and before, *and* has been used at the beginning of sentences, e.g. "And God said, Let there be light; and there was light." (Genesis 1:1.)

Follow newspaper style and put no comma before *and* in a series. Write *tall, dark and handsome.*

See also AMPERSAND.

and etc. Strike out *and.* The *et* in *etc.* is a built-in Latin *and.*

and I, and he, and she. People often say *and I, and he, and she,* when traditional grammar would call for *and me, and him, and her.* For instance, people say *between you and I, let's you and I go, what with Jack and he being friends, I want both you and she to know.* Shakespeare wrote "All debts are cleared between you and I" (Merchant of Venice, III, ii, 319). The idiom has been in use since 1596.

and/or is a useful shortcut. Instead of writing "one year in jail or a $500 fine or both" you can write "one year in jail and/or a $500 fine."

and which, and who. One of the two words is usually superfluous. Strike out *and*. If that doesn't work, strike out *which* or *who*.

anecdotage ends in *-age*.

anemia, anemic are now generally spelled with *e* instead of *ae*.

anemone ends in *-e*.

anent is an antique. Avoid.

anesthesia, anesthetic, anesthetize are now commonly spelled with *e* instead of *ae*.

anesthesiologist, anesthetist. An *anesthesiologist* is an M.D., an *anesthetist* isn't.

aneurysm with *y* is now the established spelling.

angel, meaning financial backer, is now listed as standard usage in Webster's.

angel, angle. An *angel* has wings, an *angle* is a corner.

angelcake, angelfish, angelfood, angelfood cake. No hyphen.

angle iron. Two words.

angleworm. One word.

anglicize. Spell with a small *a* and a *z*.

Anglo-. It's *Anglo-American, Anglo-Catholic, Anglo-Saxon,* but *Anglomania, Anglophile* and *Anglophobia*.

angular ends in *-ar*.

aniline is spelled with an *e* at the end.

animus ends in *-us*.

anise has an *e* at the end.

anisette ends in *-ette*.

anklebone. No hyphen.

ankle-deep. Hyphened.

annex, annexe. Spell it *annex*.

annihilate, annihilation. Double *n*.

anniversary. Double *n,* ends in *-ary*.

(annoint). Misspelling of *anoint*.

annotate, annotated, annotator. Two *n*'s.

announce, announcement, announcer. All start with *ann-*.

annoyance ends in *-ance*.

annual. Two *n*'s.

annually. Two *l*'s.

annuity, annuitant. Two *n*'s. *Annuitant* ends in *-ant*.

annul, annulled, annulling, annulment. *Annul* and *annulment* have one *l,* but the other two forms have two *l*'s. Remember "An annulment happens normally only once in a lifetime."

anoint, anointment. One *n* after the *a*. "To *anoint* someone, you use *an oint*ment."

anomalous, anomaly. One *n*. The vowels are *a—o—a*.

anon. Archaic. Don't use. Say *soon*.

anonymous, anonymity. Two single *n*'s.

anorak ends in *-ak*.

answer. Don't forget the *w*.

antagonize ends in *-ize*.

antarctic. It's up to you whether you pronounce this word *ant-ARKtic* or *antARTic*, but be sure to spell it with a *c* between the *r* and the *t*.

ante-, anti-. *Ante* means before, *anti* means against. Words beginning with *ante-* are spelled as one word without a hyphen, except when the second part starts with a capital or with an *e* (*ante-Victorian, ante-examination*).

anteater. One word.

antebellum. One word.

antecede. The common word now is *precede*. Both end in *-ede*.

antecedent ends in *-ent*.

antechamber, antedate start with *ante-*.

antediluvian. In spite of the fact that it means before the *deluge*, the letter after the *d* is *i*.

antelope. The vowels are *a—e—o—e*.

antemortem, antenatal. No hyphen.

antenna. Insects have *antennae*, TV sets *antennas*.

antenuptial, antepenult, anteroom. No hyphen.

ante up is listed as standard usage in Webster's.

anthill. One word.

Anthony is always spelled with *th*, even though many people pronounce it with a *t*.

anthropo-. No hyphen in compound words.

anti-, ante-. *Anti* means against, *ante* means before. Spell all words starting with *anti-* as one word without a hyphen, except when the second part starts with a capital or an *i* (*anti-American, anti-inflation*).

antiaircraft, antibiotic, antibody. One word.

Antichrist. Capital *A*, one word.

anticipate. Don't use *anticipate* when *expect* will do.

anticlimax, anticoagulant, antidepressant, antidote, antifreeze, antihero, antiknock, antilabor. One word.

antimacassar. One of those spelling demons. One *c*, two *s*'s.

antipollution, antipoverty. One word.

anti-Semitic, anti-Semitism. Hyphen and capital *S*.

antiseptic, antislavery, antisocial. One word.

antithesis, antitheses.

antitoxin, antitrust, antiwar. One word.

anxious. If you believe in the old superstition that you shouldn't write *anxious* when you mean eager, forget it. The word has been so used since 1742. Anthony Trollope wrote of "a kind-hearted landlord ever anxious to ameliorate the condition of the poor."

any, anybody, anyone. The use of *they, their* and the plural verb with these words is listed as standard usage in Webster's. John Ruskin wrote "I am never angry with anyone unless they deserve it." The usage dates back to 1526.

anymore. One word.

anyplace (one word) is listed in Webster's as standard usage.

anytime (one word) is listed in Webster's as standard usage.

anyway, anywhere, anywise. One word, no hyphen.

A 1. No hyphen.

ap-. If you can't find the word you're looking for under *ap-*, try *app-*.

apartheid (pronounced *aPARTite*) is the spelling of the word for the racial segregation system in South Africa.

apartment. One *p*.

aperitif. No accent.

aperture. Don't use *aperture* when *opening* will do.

apex, apexes.

apiary, aviary. An *apiary* houses bees, an *aviary* birds.

apiece. One word as in *I paid $3 apiece.*

aplenty sounds old-fashioned. Use with care if at all.

aplomb has a *b* at the end.

apocalypse ends in *-ypse*.

apocryphal. No *h* after *c*.

apogee. Don't write *apogee* when *peak* will do.

apologetically ends in *-ally*.

apologize. *O* after *l*. Ends in *-ize*.

apologue ends in *-ogue*.

apology ends in *-ology*.

apostasy. There's no *c*.

a posteriori. Two words.

apostle. Don't forget the *t*.

apostrophe, apostrophes. The plural ends in *-es*—no *i*. Use apostrophes in contractions like *we've, he's, don't, she'll.*

Use *s* and no apostrophe for the plural of letters, or letter-combinations, figures and hyphened nouns like *the 1970s, ABCs, two-by-fours.* But use an apostrophe for the plural of capital-letter abbreviations with periods, lowercase letters and capital letters that would otherwise look confusing, like *Ph.D.'s, g's, A's.*

Use an apostrophe when you leave out the century in a date, like *the spirit of '76.* But not in decades, like *the 70s.*

Put an apostrophe before the *s* in the possessive case of singular nouns, like *the boy's jacket, Mary's aunt.* Do the same with nouns ending in *s, x, z, ch* or *sh,* e.g. *the boss's daughter, Max's coat, Dr. Fitch's office, Liz's husband, Trish's hat, Dickens's novels, Papadopoulos's fall.* But use an apostrophe only (no *s*) with nouns that have two sibilant sounds, e.g. *Jesus' sayings, Grandma Moses' paintings, Onassis' yacht, Lipchitz' sculptures, Alexis' clothes, Aziz' name.* And add no *s* in such expressions as *for goodness' sake, for appearance' sake.*

Put an apostrophe after the *s* in the possessive case of plural nouns like *the boys' team, the teachers' union, the Joneses' house* except for plurals that don't end in *s* like *men's wear, children's games.* Never put an apostrophe before the *s* to form the plural of a name. Write *the Browns, the Smiths, the Robinsons.*

Don't put an apostrophe into names that don't have it, like *Doctors Hospital, Teachers College.*

apostrophize ends in *-ize.*

apothecary. There's an *e* after the *h.*

apothegm. Don't overlook the silent *g.*

appall, appalled, appalling. Double *p* and double *l* in all forms.

apparatus, apparatuses.

apparel, appareled, appareling. One *l* in all forms.

apparent, apparently. You don't need a comma before or after *apparently.* Write *he had apparently forgotten it.*

appearance ends in *-ance.*

appear on the scene. Leave out *on the scene.*

appease, appeasement. Two *p*'s.

appellant, appellate, appellee. Two *p*'s and two *l*'s.

appellation. Don't use *appellation* when *name* will do.

appendix, appendixes. The operation is spelled *appendectomy.*

appetite. Two *p*'s.

appetizer, appetizing. Spelled with *z.*

applaud, applause. Two *p*'s.

applecart, applegrower, applejack, applejuice, applesauce. One word. It's *apple pie* (two words), but *apple-pie order. Apple-polish* and *apple-polisher* are hyphened.

appliance ends in *-ance.*

applicable ends in *-able.*

applicant, application, applicator, applied. Two *p*'s.

appliqué. Spell it with the accent.

appoint, appointment; apportion, apportionment; appraise, appraiser. Two *p*'s.

appreciable ends in *-able.*

apprehend, apprehension, apprehensive. Two *p*'s.

apprehensible ends in *-ible.*

apprentice, apprenticeship. Two *p*'s.

apprise, apprize. *Apprise* means inform, *apprize* means appraise.

approach, approaching. Two *p*'s.

approbation. Two *p*'s.

appropriate. Don't use *appropriate* when *proper* will do.

approval, approve. Two *p*'s.

approximately. Don't use *approximately* when *about* will do.

appurtenance is spelled with *u* after two *p*'s.

après-ski. Spell with accent and hyphen.

a priori. Two words.

apropos. One word, no hyphen, no accent.

apse has an *e* at the end.

aqu-. If you can't find the word you're looking for under *aqu-,* try *acqu-.*

aqualung, aquamarine, aquatint. One word.

aquarium, aquariums. No *c.*

aquatic. No *c* before the *q.*

aqueduct has an *e* in the middle.

(aquittal). Misspelling of *acquittal.*

Arab, Arabian, Arabic. *Arab* refers to Arabs (the people), *Arabian* to Arabia (the country) and *Arabic* to language and writing. The only exception is *gum arabic.*

arable ends in *-able.*

arbiter, arbitrator. An *arbiter* pronounces his judgments on taste and fashion. An *arbitrator* decides legal disputes. An *arbitrator* makes a decision that is binding, in contrast to a *mediator* who tries for a settlement by the parties.

arbor ends in *-or.*

arboretum, arboretums.

arc, ark. An *arc* is a curve, an *ark* is a boat. Spell the verb *arc, arced, arcing.*

Arcadia, Acadia. *Arcadia* is a land of peace and harmony, *Acadia* is Nova Scotia.

arcanum, arcana.

arch-. Spell compounds without a hyphen except when the second part starts with a capital, e.g. *arch-Freudian.*

archangel, archbishop, archdiocese, archduke, archenemy. One word.

archeology, archeologist, archeological. The modern spelling with *e* is listed in the New York Times Manual of Style and Usage and the GPO Style Manual.

archfiend. One word.

archipelago, archipelagoes.

architect, architecture. Spelled with *ch.*

archpriest, archrival, archrogue, archway. One word.

arctic. Whether you pronounce the first *c* or not, put it in when you write the word.

ardor ends in *-or.*

arduous. Don't forget the *u* after the *d.*

are, is. When there's a question whether to write *are* or *is,* go by the noun that comes first. Write *the children are my only concern,* but *my only concern is the children.* But in a question go by the real subject: *what kind of collateral are these shares?*

areaway. One word.

areawide. One word.

aren't. Common contraction of *are not* or *am not.*

argue, argued, arguing, argument, arguable. No *e* after the *u* in *arguing, argument, arguable.*

argyle. Spell it this way. No capital *A* necessary.

arise, arose, arisen can now be used only for situations, but not for people. Too poetic.

aristocratically ends in *-ally.*

arithmetic, arithmetical. No vowel between *th* and *m.*

ark, arc. An *ark* is a boat, an *arc* is a curve.

arm-. Spell compounds as one word.

armadillo, armadillos.

armband, armchair, armful, armfuls. One word.

armistice ends in -*ce.*
armor ends in -*or.* Makes *armorial, armorplate.*
armpit, armrest. One word.
arm's-length. Spell with apostrophe and hyphen.
arm-twisting. Hyphened.
around in all senses is now standard American English. Don't
 think you have to say *about.*
arouse, rouse. You *arouse* curiosity, but you *rouse* a sleeper.
 One *r.*
arpeggio, arpeggios.
arraign, arraignment (charge of a prisoner). Two *r*'s, *ai, gn.*
arrange, arrangement. Two *r*'s.
arrant, errant. *Arrant* means outright, *errant* means wandering.
array, arrears. Two *r*'s.
arrester ends in -*er.*
arrière-pensée needs the two accents.
arrive, arrival. Two *r*'s.
arrogance, arrogant end in -*ance,* -*ant.*
arrow-. Don't hyphen *arrowhead, arrowroot, arrowwood, arrow-
 worm.*
arroyo, arroyos.
(artefact). Spell it *artifact.*
arterio-. Write all words starting with *arterio-* as one word, e.g.
 arteriosclerosis.
artery ends in -*ery.*
arthritis. No vowel between *th* and *r.*
(artic). Misspelling of *arctic.*
articles. See A, AN; THE.
artifact. Spell it with *i.*
artillery, artilleryman. Two *l*'s.
artisan ends in -*san.*
artist, artiste. *Artiste* with an *e* means a male or female professional performer, but the trend is toward using *artist* without
 the *e* in all senses.
artistically ends in -*ally.*
artsy, artsy-craftsy are established variations of *arty, arty-crafty.*
artwork. One word.
arty, arty-crafty. Standard usage.
asafetida. The spelling *asafoetida* is old-fashioned.
as a matter of fact. You don't need a comma after this. Write *as
 a matter of fact I was disappointed.*
asbestos ends in -*os.*

ascend. Don't write *ascend* when *go up* will do.

ascendancy, ascendant. Spelled with *sc* and *an.*

ascent, assent. *Ascent* means go up, *assent* means say yes.

ascertain. Don't write *ascertain* when *find out* will do.

ascetic, acetic. *Ascetic* means austere, *acetic* means vinegary.

as follows must have an *s* at the end.

as good or better than. Don't worry about this idiom. It's now standard usage.

ash-. Noun compounds are usually spelled as one word, modifiers are hyphened.

A-sharp. Capital *A,* hyphen, lowercase *s.*

ash-blond. Hyphened.

ashcan. One word.

ash-colored, ash-gray. Hyphened.

ash heap. Two words.

ashpile, ashpit, ashtray. One word.

Asian flu.

asinine. This word comes from the Latin *asinus,* which means *donkey* or *ass.* It has only one *s.*

(asma). Misspelling of *asthma.*

as of. Don't use *as of* when *on, at, by* will do.

asparagus. Three *a*'s. Ends in *-us.*

as per. Commercial jargon. Instead of *as per our agreement* write *under our agreement.*

asphalt is spelled with *ph.*

asphyxia, asphyxiate. Spelled with *ph* and *y.*

aspidistra, aspidistras.

ass-. If you can't find the word you're looking for under *ass-,* try *as-.*

assail, assailant. Double *s.*

assassin, assassinate, assassination. Two double *s*'s.

assault. Double *s.*

assay, essay (verb). *Assay* means test, *essay* means try.

assegai. Spell it with *e* in the middle.

assemblage, assembly. *Assemblage* means a gathering of things or people, *assembly* means a formal meeting.

assemble. Double *s.*

assembly makes *assemblyman* (one word), but *assembly line* and *assembly room* (two words).

assent, ascent. *Assent* means saying yes, *ascent* means going up. Don't use *assent* when *agree* will do.

assert. Don't use *assert* when *say* will do.

assess, assessment, assessor. Two double *s*'s. *Assessor* ends in *-or.*

asset. Two *s*'s.

assiduous, assiduity. Don't leave out the *u* after the *d.*

assigner is the regular spelling, but most lawyers prefer *assignor.*

assimilable ends in *-able.*

assimilate, assimilation. Double *s.*

(assinine). Misspelling of *asinine.* Think of "asinine *as* a donkey."

assist, assistance, assistant. Don't use when *help* or *helper* will do.

assistant cashier, assistant manager, assistant professor. No hyphen in these titles.

associate, association. Two *s*'s.

associate professor. No hyphen.

assuage. Two *s*'s followed by *u.*

assume, presume. If you *presume* something to be true, it means you've good reason to think so ("Dr. Livingstone, I presume?"), but you can freely *assume* whatever you feel like ("Let's assume your annual income is a million dollars").

assurance ends in *-ance.* In England it can be used to mean *insurance,* but not in the US.

asterisk ends in *-isk.* Asterisks are now out of style in writing. To show that something was left out of a sentence, don't use asterisks, but three periods (four at the end of a sentence). For footnote references use numbers.

asthma, asthmatic. The words are pronounced *azma* and *azmatic* but they're spelled with *sth.*

as though. Don't hesitate to use *as though* instead of *as if.*

as to whether is two words too long. Write *whether.*

astro-. Write words beginning with *astro-* as one word, e.g. *astrodome, astronaut, astrophotography.*

as well as. You don't need commas around phrases beginning with *as well as.* Write *faculty as well as students were represented.* Or, better still, replace *as well as* by *and.*

as yet. Except at the beginning of a sentence, leave out *as.*

asylum. Spelled with *y.*

asymmetric, asymmetrical. Spell it with *y* and double *m.*

at, in. Use *in* with names of cities, no matter how small—*in New York, in Podunk.*

at about has been criticized by conservative grammarians, but there's no reason why you shouldn't use this idiom.

atheneum. Spell it like this.

athlete, athletic, athletics. Nothing between the *h* and the *l.*

athlete's foot. Apostrophe before the *s.* It's *one* athlete's foot.

-ation. Beware of the *-ation* style. Don't write sentences like *there were many indications of rapid deterioration in the organization.*

atlas ends with one *s.* The plural is *atlases.*

atmosphere, atmospheric. Spelled with *ph.*

atrocious ends in *-cious.*

attach. Two *t*'s.

attaché, attaché case. Don't forget the accent on the *e.*

attached hereto. Strike out *hereto.*

attacked ends in *-cked.*

attain. Don't use *attain* when *get* or *gain* will do.

attar is spelled with two *t*'s.

attempt. Don't use *attempt* when *try* will do.

attendance, attendant end in *-ance* and *-ant.*

attention line. If you want your letter to go to a specific person in the organization you're writing to, you can add an attention line after the inside address that says *Attention: Mr. George B. Smith, Personnel Manager.* If you do that, stick to the regular salutation *Gentlemen.* But if you address your letter to *Mr. George B. Smith, Personnel Manager, Wondrous Widget Company,* make your salutation *Dear Mr. Smith.*

attenuate has a double *t.*

attester ends in *-er.*

attitude. Double *t.*

attorney-at-law, attorneys-at-law. Use hyphens.

attorney general, attorneys general.

attrition starts with *att-.*

attune starts with *att-.*

audible ends in *-ible.*

audience ends in *-ence.*

audio-. Write words starting with *audio-* as one word, e.g. *audiovisual.*

auditor ends in *-or.*

auditory ends in *-ory.*

auger, augur. An *auger* bores holes, to *augur* means to predict.

aught sounds quaint today. Say either *zero* or *anything.*

augment. Don't say *augment* when *add to* will do.

augur, augury. The vowel after the *g* is *u.*

auntie. Spell it with *-ie.*

aural, oral. *Aural* means by ear, *oral* means by mouth.

auspicious ends in *-ious.*

autarchy, autarky. *Autarchy* means absolute sovereignty, *autarky* means national self-sufficiency and economic independence.

author. It sounds self-important rather than modest when you refer to yourself as *the author.* Say *I.*

author (verb). Don't say *he authored the book* when you mean he wrote it.

authoress. Women authors are apt to resent being called *authoresses.* Call them authors.

authoritative ends in *-tative.*

authorize ends in *-ize.*

auto-. Spell compounds as one word, except for such words as *auto-observation,* which are hyphened.

auto, autos.

autochthonous is spelled with *chth.*

auto-da-fé, autos-da-fé. Spell it with the accent.

autointoxication, automaker. One word.

automatically ends in *-ally.*

automaton, automatons.

autosuggestion. One word.

autumn ends in *-mn.* Don't capitalize.

auxiliary ends in *-ary.*

available ends in *-able.*

avant-garde. Hyphen, no *u* after the *g, e* at the end.

avaricious ends in *-icious.*

avenge, revenge. You *avenge* a wrong done to someone else, but you *revenge* yourself to even up a score.

Avenue in addresses is spelled with a capital *A.*

averse. The idiom is *averse to.*

avertible ends in *-ible.*

aviary, apiary. An *aviary* houses birds, an *apiary* bees.

aviator ends in *-or.*

aviatrix, aviatrixes. The trend is toward using *aviator* or *pilot* for men and women.

avocado, avocados.

avocation, vocation. An *avocation* is a hobby, a *vocation* is a regular job.

avoidable ends in *-able.*

avoidance, evasion. Tax *avoidance* is legal, but tax *evasion* is not.

awake, awoke, awakened. These forms are often used when the word is used figuratively, e.g. *She awoke* (or *was awakened*) *to the danger.* When you mean rouse from sleep, write *wake, woke, waked.*

award, reward. An *award* is a prize, a *reward* is a compensation.

away in the sense of far is standard usage, e.g. *away back in the 1940s.* The form *way* (without apostrophe) is also standard.

-away. Don't use a hyphen in words ending in *-away*, e.g. *giveaway, runaway.*

awe, awed, awing.

aweigh is the right spelling in the phrase *anchors aweigh.*

awesome has an *e* in the middle.

awestruck, awestricken. No hyphen.

awfully, meaning very, is standard usage. Webster's also lists *awful* with the same meaning and quotes Willa Cather "You were an awful smart boy." The Oxford English Dictionary quotes Anthony Trollope "It is awful lonely here, too."

awhile, a while. *Awhile* means briefly, e.g. *He stayed awhile, a while* means a short time, e.g. *It took a while to sink in.*

awkward is spelled with *-wkw-*.

AWOL, awol. No periods needed.

ax. The spelling without *e* is now standard.

ax-. Most compound words are spelled as one word.

ax-grinding. Hyphened.

axhead. One word.

axis, axes.

axletree. One word.

ax-shaped. Hyphened.

aye. Spell it with *e—The ayes have it. Aye, aye, sir.*

(azma). Misspelling of *asthma.*

B

-b, -bb-. A *b* at the end of a one-syllable word is doubled before the suffixes *-ed, -er, -ing, -ery, -y, -ie, -est, -ish* etc., if there's only one vowel immediately before the *b*. Examples: *rub, rubbed; rob, robber; web, webbing; shrub, shrubbery; grub, grubby; cab, cabbie; glib, glibbest; snob, snobbish.*

baboon. Only one *b* in the middle.

baby-. Spell most compounds as one word.

baby, babied, babying.

babyface, babyfaced. One word.

baby food. Two words.

babysit, babysitter, babysitting. One word.

baccalaureate. Two *c*'s, one *l*.

baccarat. Two *c*'s.

bacchanalia, bacchanalian. Spelled with *cch*.

bachelor ends in *-or*. There's no *t*.

bacillus, bacilli.

back-, -back. Most compounds starting with *back-* are spelled as one word. Compounds ending in *-back* are always spelled as one word, e.g. *comeback, flareback, halfback, setback, switchback, throwback.*

backache, backbite, backbiting, backboard, backbone, backboned, backbreaker, backbreaking, backcountry, backdate (verb), **backdated, backdoor** (adjective), **backdown** (noun), **backdrop.** One word.

back end. Two words, no hyphen.

backer-down, backer-up. Hyphened.

backfield, backfire, backflap, background, backhand, backhanded, backhaul, backhauled. One word.

back-in (noun). Hyphened.

backlash, backlist, backlog. One word.

back of meaning *behind* is standard usage.

backpack, backpacker, backpay. One word.

backpedal, backpedaled, backpedaling.

backrest, backroad, backroom, backseat. One word.

(backsheesh). Spell it *baksheesh.*

backslap, backslapper, backslide, backstage, backstop, backstrap. One word.

back street. Two words, no hyphen.

backstretch, backstroke, backswept, backswing, backtalk, backtrack, backup (adj., noun). One word.

backward, backwards. For the adverb, use either form *(looking backward* or *looking backwards).* For the adjective, use *backward—a backward glance, a backward child.*

backwash, backwater, backwoods, backyard. One word.

bacterium, bacteria.

bade is the past tense of *bid,* as in the phrase *we bade him farewell.*

badly. To *feel badly* or *need something badly* are both listed in Webster's as standard usage.

bad-mouth. Hyphen.

bag-. Most compounds are spelled as one word.

bagel ends in *-el.*

baggagemaster. One word.

baggage rack, baggage train. Two words, no hyphen.

bagman. Standard usage. No hyphen.

bagnio, bagnios.

bagpipe. No hyphen.

bag-shaped. Hyphen.

baguette ends in *-ette.*

bail, bale. You *bail* out water or a prisoner, but it's a *bale* of hay.

bailiwick. Spell it with three *i*'s.

bailor. Spell it with *-or.*

bailout (noun), **bailsman.** No hyphen.

baited, bated. A *baited* hook, but with *bated* breath.

baked goods. Don't leave out the *d.*

bakehouse, bakepan. One word.

baker's dozen. Apostrophe before *s.* It's *one* baker's dozen.

bakeshop. One word.

baksheesh. Spelled with *ee.*

balalaika. *A* before *i.*

balance. Standard usage in the sense of *rest* or *remainder.*

balconied ends in -*ied.*
baldfaced, baldhead, baldheaded. One word.
balding. Standard usage.
baldpate. One word.
bale, bail. A *bale* of hay, but *bail* for a prisoner.
baleful ends in -*ful.*
balk, balky. Spell without *u.*
ball-. Spell compounds as one word except for *ball-like, bell-like.*
ballad, ballade. A *ballad* is a sentimental song, a *ballade* is a verse
 form or a piano composition.
ball bearing. Two words.
ballfield. One word.
ballgame. One word if used figuratively, two if used literally.
ballistic, ballistics. Two *l*'s.
ball-like. Hyphened.
balloon. Two *l*'s. It's a blown-up *ball.*
ballot, balloted, balloting. One *t* in all forms.
ballplayer, ballpoint, ballroom. One word.
ballyhoo.
baloney, bologna. *Baloney* means nonsense, *bologna* means a sausage.
bamboozle. Standard usage.
banana. No double *n*'s.
band-. Almost all compounds are spelled as one word.
bandanna ends in -*anna* with double *n.*
bandbox. One word.
bandeau, bandeaux.
bandit, bandits. The plural *banditti* is old-fashioned.
bandmaster. One word.
bandolier. Spell it with -*ier.*
bandsaw, bandsawed, bandsawing, bandstand, bandwagon. One
 word.
bandy-legged. Hyphened.
bangup. One word, e.g. *a bangup job.*
banister. Spell it with one *n.*
banjo, banjos.
banknote, banknote, bankroll. One word.
bankruptcy. Don't leave out the *t.*
bankside. One word.
banneret. Spell it with -*et.*
banquet, banqueted, banqueting, banqueter. One *t* in all forms.

banquet, banquette. A *banquet* is a meal, a *banquette* is a raised walk, sidewalk or bench.

bantamweight. One word.

baptistery. Spell it with the *e*.

baptize ends in *-ize*.

bar-. Most compounds are spelled as one word.

Barabbas. One *r*, two *b*'s.

barbarian, barbaric, barbarous. There's no clear distinction between the three forms. They all mean savage, crude, uncivilized.

barbecue, barbecued, barbecuing. Spell like this. No *q*.

barbed wire. Two words.

barbershop. One word.

barbiturate ends in *-rate*.

barcarole. Spell with one *l*.

bare, bared, baring; bear, bore, borne. To *bare* means to expose, to *bear* means to carry or suffer.

bareback, barebacked, barefaced, barefoot, barehanded, bareheaded, bareknuckle, bareknuckled, barelegged. One word.

barely . . . than, as in *we had barely taken off than they started serving dinner* is listed as standard usage in Webster's.

barfly. One word.

bargainer, bargainor. A *bargainer* is one who bargains, a *bargainor* is the vendor in a bargain and sale.

bargeman, bargemaster. One word.

baritone. Spell it with *i*.

bark, meaning boat, is now spelled like this. *Barque* is old-fashioned.

barkeeper. One word.

barleycorn. One word.

barley water. Two words.

barmaid, barman. One word.

bar mitzvah, bar mitzvahed, bar mitzvahing. Two words, no hyphen.

barn dance. Two words.

barnstorm, barnstormed, barnstorming, barnstormer, barnyard. One word.

baronetcy ends in *-etcy*.

(barque). Outmoded spelling of *bark*.

baroque is spelled with *que*.

barouche. Spelled with *ou*.

barracks is a plural. *Barracks are.*

barrage. Two *r*'s.

barratry. Two *r*'s.

barrel, barreled, barreling. One *l* in all forms.

barrelful, barrelfuls.

barrelhead. One word.

barrenness. Double *n*.

barrette ends in *-ette*.

barricade. Two *r*'s.

barring in the sense of excepting. Two *r*'s.

barroom, bartender. One word.

(barytone). The established spelling is *baritone*.

basal, basic. There's no real difference in meaning, but *basal metabolism* and *basic principles* are fixed phrases.

base-. Most compounds are one word.

baseball, baseboard. One word.

based on. Commonly used as a preposition, e.g. *Based on future prices today for October delivery, Cuba will pay around $1.5 million for the shipment* (New York Times).

baseline, base line. *Baseline* has to do with baseball, *base line* with surveying.

baseload, baseman. One word.

base metal, base pay. Two words.

basically ends in *-ally*.

basis, bases. *Basis* often makes for wordiness. Instead of *on a once-a-week basis* write *once a week*.

basket case. Two words.

basketmaker, basketware. One word.

basket weave. Two words.

bas mitzvah. For a girl.

bas-relief. Hyphen.

bass drum. Two words.

basset hound. Two words.

bass fiddle, bass horn. Two words.

bassinet ends in *-et*.

basso, bassos.

bassoon. Two *s*'s, two *o*'s.

bass viol. Two words.

Bastille. Spell with two *l*'s.

bat-. Most compounds are spelled as one word.

(batchelor). Misspelling of *bachelor*.

bateau, bateaux.

bated, baited. With *bated* breath, but a *baited* hook.

bath-. Most compounds are spelled as one word.

bathhouse. One word.

bathinette ends in *-ette.*

bathmat, bathrobe, bathroom. One word.

bath towel. Two words.

bathtub. One word.

bathyscaphe. Spelled with *y* and *e* at the end.

batiste has an *e* at the end.

batman. One word.

battalion. Two *t*'s, one *l.* Remember "The *battalion* fought in a *battle.*"

battercake. One word.

battle-. Spell most compounds as one word.

battleax. One word.

battle cruiser, battle cry. Two words.

battlefield, battlefront, battleground. One word.

battle jacket. Two words.

battleline, battleship. One word.

battle star. Two words.

battlewagon. One word.

batty is listed in Webster's as standard usage.

batwing. One word.

(baulk, baulky). Spell the words *balk, balky.*

bayonet, bayoneted, bayoneting. One *t* in all forms.

bay rum. Two words.

bazaar, bizarre. *Bazaar* means an oriental market, *bizarre* means odd.

-bb-. See -B, -BB-.

BB gun. Two capital *B*'s.

B.C., as in *202 B.C.* Use capitals followed by periods.

beach, beech. A *beach* is sandy, a *beech* is a tree.

beachcomber, beachhead. One word.

beadwork. One word.

bean-. Most compounds are spelled as one word.

beanbag, beanfield, beanpicker, beanpole, beanpot, beanstalk. One word.

bear-. All compound words are spelled as one word.

bear, bare. To *bear* means to carry or suffer, to *bare* means to expose.

bearbaiting, bearskin, beartrap. One word.

beat, beet. *Beat* means strike, defeat etc., *beet* means a vegetable.

beau, beaux.

Beaujolais, the French wine, is spelled like this, with a capital *B*.

beauteous is too poetic for ordinary writing. Write *beautiful.*

beautician ends in *-ician.*

beautifully. Two *l*'s.

beauty shop. Two words.

beaverboard, beaverpelt. One word.

because. Conservative grammarians oppose the construction *the reason is because,* but good writers have used it since 1656. George Eliot wrote "The reason Adam was walking along the lanes at this time was because his work for the rest of the day lay at a country house about three miles off."

bed, bedded, bedding. Most compounds with *bed-* are written as one word.

bedboard, bedbug, bedchamber, bedclothes. One word.

bed check. Two words.

bedevil, bedeviled, bedeviling. One *l* in all forms.

bedfast, bedfellow, bedframe. One word.

bedimmed. Two *m*'s.

bed jacket. Two words.

bedlamp. One word.

bed linen. Two words.

bedmate. One word.

Bedouin, Bedouins. Spell with *ou.*

bedpan, bedpost. One word.

bed rest. Two words.

bedridden, bedrock, bedroll, bedroom, bedsheet, bedside, bedsore, bedspace, bedspread, bedspring, bedstead, bedstraw, bedtime. One word.

bed-wetter, bed-wetting. Hyphenated.

beech, beach. A *beech* is a tree, a *beach* is sandy.

beef, beefs.

beef, meaning complain or complaint, is listed as standard usage in Webster's.

beefeater, beefsteak, beeftongue. One word.

beef up is listed as standard usage in Webster's.

beehive, beekeeper, beekeeping, beeline, beeswax. One word.

beet, beat. A *beet* is a vegetable, to *beat* is to strike.

beetfield. One word.

beetle-browed. Hyphenated.

before-cited. Hyphened.

beforehand. One word.

before-mentioned, before-named, before-tax. All hyphened.

befriend. *I* before *e.*

beg. Avoid old-fashioned business letter phrases like *I beg to advise* or *we beg to remain.*

beggar. Two *g*'s, ends in *-ar.*

beggarman, beggarwoman. One word.

begin, began, begun; beginner, beginning.

beguile, beguiling. Don't leave out the *u.*

behalf. *In behalf of* and *on behalf of* are both standard usage.

behavior ends in *-or.*

behoove, behooved, behooving. Spell with two *o*'s.

beige is spelled with *e* before *i* like other words with the sound of *AY.* Think of *"eight neighbors* dressed in *beige."*

being as, being that. These conjunctions are not standard usage. Say *since* or *because.*

bejeweled. One *l.*

belabor is standard usage in the phrase *belabor a point.*

beleaguer, beleaguered. Contains the word *league.*

belie, belied, belying.

belief, beliefs. *I* before *e.*

believable ends in *-able.*

believe. *I* before *e.*

bell-. Almost all compounds are spelled as one word.

bell-bottomed. Hyphened.

bellboy. One word.

bell buoy. Two words.

belle, as in *the belle of the ball,* has an *e* at the end.

bellhop. One word.

belligerence, belligerent. Two *l*'s. End in *-ence* and *-ent.*

bell-like. Hyphen.

bellringer, bellringing, bellweather. One word.

bellyache, bellyaching. One word. Standard usage for *complain.*

bellybutton. One word.

below may mean lower on the same page or on a later page.

belowstairs. One word.

beltmaker. One word.

bemedaled. One *l.*

benchmark, benchwarmer, benchwork. One word.

benefactor. Spell with a second *e* after the *n.* Ends in *-or.*

beneficent, beneficence end in *-ent, -ence.*

beneficial, beneficiary. Spelled with a second *e* after the *n.* Don't use *beneficial* when *helpful* will do.

(beneficient). Misspelling of *beneficent.*

benefit, benefited, benefiting. One *t* in all forms. The thing to remember is "Keep fit."

benevolent, benevolence end in *-ent, -ence.*

benign, benignant. There's no clear distinction in meaning. Doctors in speaking of a tumor or growth always use the word *benign* (or *malignant*).

bentwood. One word.

bequeath. Although usually pronounced to rhyme with *breathe,* this word has no *e* at the end. Don't use *bequeath* when *give* will do.

beret ends in *et.*

-berry. Spell words ending in *-berry* as one word.

berrypicker, berrypicking. One word.

berth, birth. A *berth* is a space, a *birth* is an event.

beryllium is spelled with *y* and two *l*'s.

beseech, besought, besought. Standard forms.

(beseige). Misspelling of *besiege.*

beside, besides. *Beside* means next to, e.g. *Sit beside me; besides* means in addition, e.g. *Besides, he's out of town.*

besiege. *I* before *e.* Think of "the *s*iege of *S*ingapore."

best-. Spell compound adjectives with a hyphen when you use them before a noun, e.g. *the best-dressed woman, the best-liked candidate.* But *among the reporters, he was the best informed.*

best man. Two words.

bestseller, bestselling. Follow the trend and spell as one word.

bet. The more common form of the past tense is *bet* rather than *betted,* e.g. *I bet $10 and I lost.* The phrase *you bet* is standard usage.

bête noire. Be sure to spell it with the accent and the *e* at the end of *noire.*

better. In the common idiom *had better* (in the sense of *ought to*) the word *had* is often shortened to *'d (you'd better do it)* or left out altogether *(we better leave).* There's a trend toward leaving it out.

better-. Hyphen when used before a noun, otherwise two words, e.g. *a better-known remedy, he was better off where he was.*

bettor is more widely used than *better* for a person who bets.

between. The idea that you should say *among* instead of *between* when you're referring to more than two persons or things is pure superstition. The Oxford English Dictionary says "In all senses *between* has been, from its earliest appearance, extended to more than two. . . ." and traces the usage back to 971. Dr. Samuel Johnson said "I hope that between publick business, improving studies, and domestick pleasures, neither melancholy nor caprice will find any place for entrance."

betweendecks. One word.

between you and I. This common idiom is disapproved by conservative grammarians, but Shakespeare wrote "All debts are cleared between you and I." (Merchant of Venice, III, ii. 319)

bevel, beveled, beveling. One *l* in all forms.

bewigged. Two *g*'s.

B-flat. Capital *B,* hyphen.

bi-. Spell all compounds as one word.

biannual, biennial. *Biannual* means twice a year, *biennial* means every two years.

bias, biased, biasing, biases. One *s* in all forms.

Bible, bible. Use a capital *B* when you mean scripture and a small *b* when you mean a standard authority, like *the coin collector's bible.*

bibliographies. Here are a few simple rules for typing bibliographies:

1. Put the bibliography at the end of your paper, article or manuscript.

2. Start each bibliography item flush at the left margin. If it runs to two or more lines, indent each line except the first. Single-space each item, use double space between items.

3. For a book, give the author's name (last name first), the exact title of the book (underlined), place of publication, publisher (shortened name), date of publication, volume number if any (use the abbreviation *vol.*). Also, if needed, number of page or pages quoted (use the abbreviation *p.* or *pp.*).

4. For another book by the same author, don't repeat the name but use a long dash.

5. For a scholarly magazine article, give the author's name (last name first), the title of the article (in quotes), the name of the periodical (underlined, shortened), volume number (underlined, don't use *vol.*), page number or numbers (don't use *p.* or *pp.*), year.

6. For a newspaper or popular magazine article, leave out the volume number but give the exact date.

7. Arrange the items alphabetically.

Examples:

Chall, Jeanne. *Learning to Read: The Great Debate,* New York: McGraw-Hill, 1967.

Flesch, R. *Why Johnny Can't Read,* New York: Harper & Row, 1955.

Reinhold, R. "Johnny Still Can't Read Very Well," *N.Y. Times,* 16 June 1974, sec. 4, 9.

Rosner, S. L. "Dyslexia: A Problem in Definition," *Am. Orthopt. J., 18:* 94, 1968.

bicameral, bicentennial. One word.

biceps, bicepses.

bicycle. It's *bi-* and *cycle.*

bid, bade (pronounded *bad*), **bidden** (e.g. farewell).

bid, bid, bid (e.g. at an auction).

biennial, biannual. *Biennial* means every two years, *biannual* means twice a year.

bier, beer. You have a *bier* at a funeral, a *beer* at a bar.

big-. Most compounds are spelled as one word.

big-eared. Hyphened.

bighearted. One word.

big league. Two words.

bigmouthed, bigname. One word.

bigot, bigoted. One *t.*

big shot. Two words.

bigtime, bigwig. One word.

bijou, bijous.

bike, biked, biking. Standard usage.

bilateral, bilingual. One word.

bilious. One *l.*

bill-. All compounds are spelled as one word.

billboard. One word.

billet-doux, billets-doux.

billfold. One word.

billiard, billiards. It's *billiard ball,* but a game of *billiards.*

billion. A US billion is a thousand millions, but a British billion is a million millions.

billionaire. One *n.*

bimetallism. One *t,* two *l*'s.

bimonthly. Use *bimonthly* when you mean every other month, and *semimonthly* when you mean twice a month.

binary ends in -*ary*.

binoculars. One *n.*

bio- compounds are spelled as one word.

bipartisan, biplane, biracial. One word.

birchwood. One word.

bird-. Compounds are spelled as one word, except for *bird dog* and *bird song.*

birdbander, birdbanding, birdbath, birdbrain, birdcage. One word.

bird dog. Two words.

birdie, birdied, birdieing. So spelled.

birdlife, birdseed. One word.

bird's-eye. Apostrophe, *s,* hyphen.

bird song. Two words.

birth-. Compounds are spelled as one word or two words, but not hyphened.

birth, berth. A *birth* is an event, a *berth* is a space.

birth certificate, birth control, birth date. Two words.

birthday, birthmark. One word.

birth pang. Two words.

birthplace, birthrate, birthright, birthstone. One word.

biscuit.

biscuitmaker, biscuitmaking. One word.

bison. The plural is *bison.*

bisque. Spelled with -*que* in all senses.

bistate. One word.

bitch, meaning a woman or a complaint, is listed as standard usage in Webster's.

bittersweet. One word.

bivalve. Don't call an oyster a *succulent bivalve.* It's a famous example of long-worn-out humor.

bivouac, bivouacked, bivouacking, bivouacker. One of those spelling-bee words.

biweekly means every other week.

bizarre, bazaar. *Bizarre* means odd, *bazaar* means an oriental market.

bizonal. One word.

black. The trend is toward using the word *black* rather than *Negro.* Spell it with a small *b* (like the GOP Style Manual).

black-. Most compounds are spelled as one word.

black-and-blue, black-and-white. Hyphened.

blackball, blackberry, blackbird, blackboard. One word.

black-eyed. Hyphened.

blackface, blackfaced. One word.

black flag. Two words.

blackguard. So spelled, even though it's pronounced *blaggard.*

blackhead, blackhearted, blackjack, blackleg. One word.

black-letter (adjective). Hyphened.

blacklist. One word.

black lung. Two words.

blackmail. One word.

black market (noun), **black-market** (verb), **black-marketeer.**

blackout. One word.

black sheep. Two words.

blacksmith, blackstrap, blacktop. One word.

blah, blahs. Listed as standard usage in Webster's.

blamable. No *e* after the *m.*

blame on. Listed in Webster's and Oxford English Dictionary as standard usage. Rudyard Kipling wrote "If you can keep your head when all about you are losing theirs and blaming it on you."

blameworthy. One word.

blancmange. French spelling, one word.

blasé. Spell it with the accent.

blasphemous, blasphemy. Spelled with *ph.*

blastoff. One word.

blatant, blatancy end in *-ant, -ancy.*

bleachhouse, bleachyard. One word.

blear-eyed. (Not *bleary-.*)

blessed is the established spelling.

(bleu cheese). The usual spelling is *blue cheese.*

blind date. Standard usage.

blindfold, blindspot. One word.

blintze. Spell it with an *e* at the end.

blithely, blithesome. Don't drop the *e* in the middle.

blitzkrieg. *I* before *e.* Small *b.*

blizzard. Two *z*'s.

blob, blobbed, blobbing. Standard usage.

bloc, block. A *bloc* is a group of people, a *block* is a thing.

blockbuster, blockbusting, blockhead, blockhouse. One word.

blond, blonde. The GPO Style Manual and many newspapers have dropped the final *e* in all uses. But *a blonde* (with an *e*) is commonly used for a woman.

blood-. Compounds are mostly spelled as one word.

blood bank. Two words.

bloodbath. One word.

blood count. Two words.

bloodcurdling. One word.

blood group. Two words.

bloodhound, bloodletting, bloodline, bloodmobile. One word.

blood poisoning, blood pressure. Two words.

bloodshed, bloodstain, bloodstone, bloodstream, bloodthirsty. One word.

blood-type (verb). Hyphened.

bloody-minded, bloody-mindedness. Hyphened.

-blossom. Spell words ending in *-blossom* as one word.

blouse is spelled with *ou.*

(blousy). Misspelling of *blowzy.*

blow-. All compounds are spelled as one word.

blowby (noun). One word.

blow-by-blow. Hyphened.

blowdown (noun), **blowfish, blowgun, blowhard, blowhole, blowoff** (noun), **blowout** (noun), **blowtorch, blowup** (noun). One word.

blowzy. Spell it with *w* and *z.*

bludgeon must have the *e* after the *g.*

blue-. Most compounds are spelled as one word.

blueblood, blueberry, bluebird. One word.

blue cheese, blue chip. Two words.

blue-collar, blue-eyed. Hyphened.

bluegrass. One word.

(blueing). Spell it *bluing.*

bluejacket. One word.

blue jay, blue jeans, blue movie. Two words.

bluenose. One word.

blue-pencil, blue-penciled, blue-penciling. One *l* in all forms. Hyphened.

bluepoint, blueprint. One word.

blue-ribbon (adj.). Hyphened.

blues. Plural used with singular verb.

bluestocking, bluestreak. One word.

bluey is spelled with an *e.*

bluing. Spell it without *e.*

bluish. No *e*.

blunderbuss ends in double *s*.

blur, blurred, blurring, blurry. Double *r* except in *blur*.

blvd. Standard abbreviation of *boulevard*. Use capital *B* in addresses.

board foot, board game. Two words.

boardinghouse. One word.

boarding school. Two words.

boardroom, boardwalk. Two words.

boat. Webster's says it's standard usage to use the word *boat* in referring to a large ship. The word has been so used since 1572.

-boat. Spell all compounds as one word, e.g. *rowboat, lifeboat*.

boat-. Most compounds are spelled as one word.

boatbuilder, boatbuilding, boathook, boathouse, boatload, boatman, boatowner. One word.

boat race. Two words.

boatside. One word.

boatswain (pronounced *bosn*). Spelled the long way.

boat train. Two words.

boatwright, boatyard. Two words.

bobby pin. Two words.

bobtail, bobwhite. One word.

body-. Most compounds are spelled as one word.

bodybending, bodybuilder, bodybuilding, bodyguard. One word.

body shop, body stocking. Two words.

bodywork. One word.

bogey, bogeys, bogeyed, bogeying, bogeyman. Spell with *ey* whether you refer to a bugbear or to golf.

bogus. Standard usage.

bohemian. Spell it with a small *b* when you mean the lifestyle.

boilermaker, boilerplate, boilerroom. One word.

boisterous. Don't leave out the *e*.

bolero, boleros.

bolivar, bolivars. Venezuelan currency.

bologna, baloney. A *bologna* is a sausage, *baloney* is nonsense.

bombazine.

bona fide, bona fides. *Bona fide* is an adjective and means genuine, in good faith, like a *bona fide* offer, a *bona fide* antique. *Bona fides* is a noun and means good faith, as in *I don't question his bona fides*. Never use a hyphen with either expression.

(boney). Misspelling of *bony*.

bondholder. One word.

bond paper. Two words.

bone-. Most compounds are spelled as one word.

bone china. Two words.

bone-dry. Hyphened.

bonehead, bonesetter, boneyard. One word.

bonfire. No *e* in the middle.

bonhomie. Spelled with *h* and one *m*.

bonny ends in *-y.*

bonus, bonuses.

bon vivant, bons vivants. No hyphen.

bon voyage. No hyphen.

bony. No *e.*

boobytrap. One word.

boogie-woogie. Hyphened.

-book. Spell compounds ending in *-book* as one word, e.g. *bank-book, notebook, pocketbook.*

book-. Almost all compound words starting with *book-* are spelled as one word.

bookbinder, bookbindery, bookcase. One word. ·

book club. Two words.

bookdealer, bookend, bookfair. One word.

bookie ends in *-ie.*

book jacket. Two words.

bookkeeper, bookkeeping. Two *o*'s, two *k*'s, two *e*'s.

book-learned. Hyphened.

book learning. Two words.

book-lined. Hyphened.

booklist, booklover, bookmaker, bookmaking, bookmark. One word.

book matches. Two words.

bookmobile, bookplate, bookrack, bookrest. One word.

book review. Two words.

booksale, bookseller, bookselling, bookshelf, bookshop, book-stack, bookstall, bookstand, bookstore. One word.

book trade, book value. Two words.

bookworm. One word.

boomtown. One word.

boondoggle, boondoggling. Standard usage in the sense of busy-work.

boost is standard usage in all senses.

boot-. Spell compounds as one word.

bootblack. One word.

bootee. Spell it with double *e*.

bootjack, bootlace, bootleg, bootlegger, bootlick, bootmaker, bootmaking, bootstrap. One word.

boot tree. Two words.

booze, boozer, boozy. Listed as standard usage in Webster's.

(boquet). Misspelling of *bouquet.*

bordello, bordellos.

borderline, borehole. One word.

-born. Compounds ending in *-born* are usually spelled as one word, e.g. *inborn, stillborn, reborn.* But *American-born, German-born* etc. are hyphened.

born, borne. *Born* means brought into the world, *borne* means carried.

-borne. Compounds ending in *-borne* are spelled as one word, e.g. *airborne, seaborne.*

(boro). Spell out *borough.*

borscht. Spell the Russian soup with a *t* at the end.

boss. Standard usage.

both is often unnecessary, as in *(both) Smith and Jones agreed.* Strike it out whenever you can.

bottle-. Compounds are mostly spelled as one word.

bottle-fed. Hyphened.

bottleneck, bottletight. One word.

bottle washer. Two words.

bottomland, bottommost. One word.

bouffant. Spelled with *ou* and *-ant.*

bougainvillea ends in *-ea.*

bough, bow. Spell it *bough* when you mean the branch of a tree. In all other senses spell it *bow.*

boughten is dialect and not standard usage.

bouillabaisse. Two *l*'s, two *s*'s.

bouillon, bullion. *Bouillon* is clear soup, *bullion* is gold or silver.

boulder is spelled with *ou.*

boulevard. In addresses, spell it with a capital *B* or abbreviate it *Blvd.*

bounceable ends in *-eable.*

-bound. Spell compounds ending in *-bound* as one word *(eastbound, earthbound)* except if the first part is a proper name *(Boston-bound).*

boundary ends in *-ary*.

bounteous ends in *-eous*.

bountiful is spelled with an *i*.

bouquet. There are two *u*'s.

bourbon. Small *b* when you mean the whiskey.

bourgeois, bourgeoisie. Don't leave out the *e* after the *g*.

(bourn, bourne). Archaic words meaning either brook or boundary. Avoid. Don't use mistakenly for *born* or *borne*.

boutique is spelled with *ou*.

boutonniere. Two *n*'s, no accent.

bovine. Don't use as a substitute word for *cow*. Use a pronoun or repeat *cow*.

bow-. Almost all compounds are spelled as one word.

bow, bough. Spell it *bough* only when you mean the branch of a tree.

bowdlerize, bowdlerization. Spelled with *ow* and *z*.

bowfront. One word.

bowie knife. Small *b*.

bowknot, bowlegged. One word.

bowline. One word.

bow-shaped. Two words.

bowsprit, bowstring. One word.

bow tie. Two words.

bowwow.

box-. Some compounds are spelled as one word, some as two words, some are hyphened.

boxcar, boxkite, boxlike. One word.

box lunch. Two words.

box office (noun). Two words.

box-office (adjective) Hyphened, e.g. *box-office receipts*.

box score, box seat, box spring (noun). Two words.

box-spring (adj.). Hyphened.

boy may be offensive when used in referring to a man.

boycott.

boyfriend. One word.

boyish.

boysenberry. One word.

bra for *brassiere* is standard usage.

brackets. Use brackets to enclose inserted words of your own in quoted matter, e.g. *the practice began during the* [*Theodore*] *Roosevelt Administration.*

Brackets are also sometimes used to mark parentheses within parentheses, but it's simpler—and common—to use regular parentheses for this purpose.

braggadocio. Two *g*'s, one *c*.

braggart. Two *g*'s.

Brahman, Brahmin. Use *Brahman* for Hindus, *Brahmin* for Bostonians.

braille. Spell with a small *b* and double *l*.

brain-. Most compounds are spelled as one word.

brainchild. One word.

-brained. Compounds ending in *-brained* are usually spelled as one word, e.g. *harebrained, featherbrained.*

brain fever. Two words.

brainpan. One word.

brain-picking. Hyphened.

brainpower, brainsick, brainstorm, brainwash, brainwashed, brainwashing. One word.

brake-. Most compounds are spelled as one word.

brake, break. Spell it *brake* for slowing or stopping. Otherwise spell it *break.*

brakedrum. One word.

brake lining. Two words.

brakeman, brakeshoe. One word.

braless. One word.

brandnew. Follow the GPO Style Manual and spell it without a hyphen.

brass in the sense of impudence and in the sense of brass hats is listed as standard usage in Webster's.

brass band. Two words.

brass hat. Two words. Standard usage.

brassiere. Spell it without accent.

brass tacks. Listed in Webster's as standard usage.

brassware. One word.

bravado, bravadoes.

bravo, bravos.

brazenfaced. One word.

brazenness. Two *n*'s.

brazil nut. Two words, small *b*.

breach, breech. *Breach* means break, *breech* means rump.

bread-. Almost all compounds are spelled as one word.

bread-and-butter (adjective). Hyphened.

breadbasket, breadbox, breadcrumb, breadfruit. One word.

bread knife. Two words.

breadline. One word.

breadth ends in -*dth*.

bread tray. Two words.

breadwinner, breadwinning. One word.

break-. Most compounds are spelled as one word.

breakable ends in -*able*.

breakaway, breakdown. One word.

break-even. Hyphened.

breakfront. One word.

break-in (noun). Hyphened.

breakneck, breakoff (noun), **breakout** (noun), **breakover** (noun), **breakstone, breakthrough** (noun), **breakup** (noun), **breakwater.** One word.

breast-. Noun compounds are spelled as one word, modifiers are hyphened.

breastbone. One word.

breast-deep, breast-fed, breast-high. Hyphened.

breastplate, breaststroke, breastwork. One word.

breath, breathe. *Breath* is the noun, *breathe* the verb.

breathtaking. One word.

breeches is so spelled even though it's pronounced *britches*.

breechloader, breechloading. One word.

breezeway. One word.

brewer's yeast. Small *b,* apostrophe, two words.

brewmaster. One word.

briar, brier. Spell the pipe wood *briar* and the thorny bush *brier*.

bribetaker, bribetaking. One word.

bric-a-brac. Two hyphens, no accent.

brick-. Spell noun compounds as one word, adjectives with a hyphen.

brickbat. One word.

brick-colored. Hyphened.

brickkiln, bricklayer, bricklaying, brickmason. One word.

brick-red. Hyphened.

brickwork, brickyard. One word.

bridal, bridle. *Bridal* refers to a bride, *bridle* to a horse.

bridechamber, bridegroom, bridesmaid. One word.

bride-to-be. Two hyphens.

bridgeable ends in -*eable*.

bridgebuilder, bridgehead, bridgework. One word.

bridle, bridal. *Bridle* refers to a horse, *bridal* to a bride.

briefcase. One word.

brier, briar. Spell the thorny bush *brier,* the pipe wood *briar.*

brigadier general. Two words.

brilliant, brilliance, brilliancy. Spelled with *-ant, -ance, -ancy.*

bring, take. You *bring* something or someone *to* a place, but you *take* something or someone *away.*

briny. No *e.*

brioche. ends in *-oche.*

briquette. The ending *-ette* is more common than *-et.*

brisling. Spell the fish without *t.*

bristle, bristling. Spelled with *t.*

Britain ends in *-ain.* Remember "Brit*ain* cont*ain*s England, Scotland and Wales."

Britannia, Britannica. One *t,* two *n*'s.

(britches). Misspelling of *breeches.*

Briton sounds too poetic nowadays. The normal word is *Englishman.*

Brittany (in France). Two *t*'s, one *n.*

broach, brooch. You *broach* a subject, but you wear a *brooch.*

broad-. Most compounds are spelled as one word.

broadax, broadbrim. One word.

broadcast. Use *broadcast* rather than *broadcasted.*

broadcloth. One word.

broad gauge, broad jump. Two words.

broadleaf, broadminded. One word.

broad-shouldered. Hyphened.

broadside. One word.

broad-spectrum. Hyphened.

broadsword, broadtail. One word.

brocatelle. One *c.*

broccoli. Two *c*'s, one *l,* ends in *-i.*

brochette ends in *-ette.*

brogue ends in *-ue.*

broke in the sense of penniless has been standard usage for centuries. Samuel Pepys wrote "Being newly broke by running in debt."

broken-down. Hyphened.

brokenhearted. One word.

brokenness. Two *n*'s.

bromo, bromos.

bronchial, bronchitis. Spelled with *ch*.

bronco, broncos.

broncobuster. One word.

brooch, broach. A *brooch* (rhymes with *coach*) is an ornament to wear, but you *broach* a question.

broom handle. Two words.

broomstick. One word.

brother-in-law, brothers-in-law.

brougham (a carriage or car, rhymes with *groom*). So spelled.

brouhaha.

browbeat, browbeaten, browbeating. One word.

brown-. Some compounds are spelled as one word, some as two.

brown bread. Two words.

brownie ends in *-ie*.

brownness. Two *n*'s.

brownout, brownstone. One word.

browse, browsing. Spelled with *ow*.

brucellosis, brucelloses. Two *l*'s.

bruise, bruiser. Spelled with *ui*. *Big bruiser* is standard usage.

bruit, brute. Spell *bruit* with *ui* in *bruited about*. Otherwise write *brute*.

brunch. Standard usage.

brunet, brunette. Many newspapers and the GPO Style Manual spell it always *brunet*. But *a brunette* (with *-ette*) is commonly used for a woman.

brush-. Most compounds are spelled as one word.

brushfire, brushland, brushoff, brushwood, brushwork. One word.

brusque. Spell it with *que*.

brussels sprouts. Spell it with a small *b*.

brutalize ends in *-ize*.

brutish. No *e*.

bubble gum. Two words.

buccaneer. Two *c*'s, one *n*.

buck-. Compounds are spelled as one word.

buckaroo. Spell it with an *a*.

bucketful, bucketfuls.

bucket seat. Two words.

bucketshop. One word.

buckpasser, buckpassing, buckshot, buckskin, bucktooth, buckwheat. One word.

Buddha, Buddhism, Buddhist. Spelled with *ddh.*

budgerigar ends in *-ar.*

buff in the sense of fan, enthusiast, is standard usage, going back to around 1920.

buffalo, buffaloes.

buffoon. Two *f*'s, two *o*'s.

bug, bugged, bugging. Standard usage in referring to a hidden microphone.

bugbear. One word.

bug-eyed. Hyphened.

buildup. One word.

built-in, built-up. Hyphened.

(buisness). Misspelling of *business.*

bulkhead, bulkheaded. One word.

bull-. Almost all compounds are spelled as one word.

bulldog, bulldoze, bulldozer. One word.

bulletin is spelled with two *l*'s and an *e.* Remember "It starts with a *bullet.*"

bulletproof. One word.

bullfight, bullfighter, bullfighting, bullfinch, bullfrog, bullheaded, bullhorn. One word.

bullion, bouillon. *Bullion* is gold or silver, *bouillon* is clear soup.

bullpen, bullring, bullseye, bullterrier, bullwhip. One word.

bulwark. One *l* and *a.*

bum. Webster's lists all common American usages as standard.

bumblebee. One word.

bump, meaning to displace someone on a plane or in a job, is standard usage.

bumpersticker. One word.

bumpkin, bumptious. Spelled with *p.*

bunch, meaning a group of people, has been standard usage since 1622. George Bernard Shaw wrote "He will be the best of the bunch, like all new converts."

bunco, buncos. Spell it with *c.*

(buncombe). Spell it *bunkum* or use the shorter form *bunk.*

bunion. Only one *n* in the middle.

bunk, bunkum. Both forms are standard usage. W. Somerset Maugham wrote "It's all bunk what they're saying to you, about honor and patriotism and glory, bunk, bunk, bunk."

bunkhouse. One word.

bunsen burner. Spell it with a small *b.*

buoy, buoyant, buoyancy. Spelled with *uoy.*

bur, burr. Spell it *bur* when you mean a prickly seed pod and *burr* when you mean a dentist's burr or a Scotch burr.

bureau, bureaus; bureaucrat, bureaucracy. The first syllable has the vowel *u,* the second has *eau. Bureaucracy* ends in *-acy.*

burgeon.

-burger, burgher. A *burgher* with an *h* lives in a borough, but a *hamburger* or *cheeseburger* is spelled without an *h.*

burglar ends in *-ar.*

burglarize, burgle. Both forms are now standard usage.

burlesque ends in *-esque.*

burned, burnt. Spell it *burned.*

burnoose, burnous. Spell it *burnoose.*

burr, bur. Two *r*'s when you mean a dentist's burr or a Scotch burr, but one *r* when you mean a prickly seed pod.

burro, burros.

bursar ends in *-ar.*

burst. In the past tense the form *burst* is more common than *bursted.*

bury, buried.

burying is spelled with *-yi-.*

bus, buses, bused, busing. When you write about transport, use one *s* in all forms. *Buss, busses, bussed, bussing* refers to kissing.

bus-. Most compounds are spelled as one word.

busboy, busdriver, busfare. One word.

bush-. Most compounds are spelled as one word.

bushed in the sense of exhausted is listed as standard usage in Webster's.

bushelful, bushelfuls.

bush league, bush leaguer. Two words.

bushranger, bushranging. One word.

bush shirt. Two words.

bushwhack, bushwhacker, bushwhacking. One word.

busied, busier, busiest, busily. Spelled with an *i* after the *s.*

business, busyness. The spelling with *y* means being busy.

businesslike, businessman, businesswise, businesswoman. One word.

busline, busload, busman. One word.

(bussing). Don't use this spelling when you mean transport.

bust, busted, busting is standard usage in the sense of breaking or breaking up, e.g. *trust busting.* Also in the sense of taming, e.g.

broncobusting. Bust is also standard usage in the sense of flop, but *busted* in the sense of raided or arrested is listed in Webster's as slang.

bustle. Don't forget the silent *t.*

bustup. One word.

busybody, busywork. One word.

but. The idea that *but* shouldn't be used at the beginning of a sentence is pure superstition. Follow the example of the Bible, which says "But Jesus gave him no answer" (John 19:9). Be sure not to put a comma after *But.*

But doesn't fit where there's no logical contrast, as in "The bell seemed to be out of order, but no amount of banging at the door evoked any reaction." Avoid this mistake. Also don't write sentences that contain both *but* and *however.*

Webster's lists *but* with *me, him, her, us* as standard usage and quotes Robert Louis Stevenson "There was no one left but me."

See also BUT WHAT, BUT WHICH, BUT WHO.

butadiene ends in *-iene.*

butter-. Most compounds are spelled as one word.

butterball. One word.

butter dish. Two words.

butterfat, butterfingered, butterfingers. One word.

butter knife. Two words.

buttermilk, butternut, butterscotch. One word.

button-down in the sense of conventional is listed in Webster's as standard usage. Hyphened.

buttonhole, buttonholed, buttonholing, buttonholer, buttonhook. All one word.

but what in such a sentence as *I don't know but what I will go* is listed in Webster's as standard usage.

but which, but who. One of the two words is usually superfluous. Strike out *but.* If that doesn't work, strike out *which* or *who.*

butyraceous. This spelling demon means buttery.

buy, as in *he didn't buy the idea* or *it's a good buy.* Both usages are listed as standard in Webster's.

buzz is spelled with double *z.*

buzz bomb, buzz saw. Two words.

-by. Spell compounds ending in *-by* as one word, e.g. *standby, passerby.*

by-. Spell all compounds as one word except *by-election, by-and-by* (noun), *by-your-leave* (noun).

by, bye. Spell without *e* in *by and by.* But *bye-bye* is more common with two *e*'s.

by-and-by (noun), as in *the sweet by-and-by.* Hyphened.

by-election. Hyphened.

bygone, bylaw, byline, bypass, bypath, byplay, byproduct, byroad, bystander, bystreet, byway, byword. One word.

by-your-leave (noun). Hyphened.

Byzantine. Spelled with capital *B* and *y*.

C

c-. If you can't find the word you're looking for under *c-,* try *ch-* or *s-.*

-c, -ck-. A *c* at the end of a word is changed to *ck* before the suffixes *-ed, -er, -ing, -y.* Examples: *shellac, shellacked; picnic, picnicker; panic, panicked; colic, colicky.*

ca. Standard abbreviation of *circa* (about), e.g. *ca. 1910.*

cab-. Spell compounds as one word.

cabal, caballed, caballing.

cabala (Jewish mysticism). Spell with one *b.*

cabana. No Spanish accent mark on the *n* necessary.

cabaret ends in *-et.*

cabbagehead. One word.

cabby, cabbies. Spell the singular with *y.*

cabdriver, cabdriving, cabfare. One word.

cabin boy, cabin car, cabin class, cabin cruiser. Spelled as two words.

cabinetmaker, cabinetmaking, cabinetwork. One word.

cabin fever. Two words.

cable car, cable stitch, cable TV. Spelled as two words.

caboodle. Standard usage.

cabstand. One word.

cacao means the cacao bean cocoa is made from.

cache, cash. A *cache* is a hiding place, *cash* is money.

cachet ends in *-et.*

cachinnate, cachinnation. Spelled with *ch* and double *n.*

cacophonous, cacophony. Spelled *ca-co-pho-.*

cactus, cactuses. This plural, rather than *cacti,* is listed in the GPO Style Manual.

caddie, caddy. It's a golf *caddie* but a tea *caddy.* But the golf *caddie* is *caddying.*

cadet ends in *-et.*

cadre ends in *-re.*

caduceus, the symbol of medicine, ends in *-eus.*

(Caesarian). Now rare spelling of *cesarean* (operation).

caesura, caesuras.

cafe needs no accent.

cafeteria. One *f.*

caffeine. Two *f*'s, *ei, e* at the end.

cagey is standard usage, spelled with *e.*

cajole, cajolery.

cake mix. Two words.

cakewalk. One word.

calcareous ends in *-eous.*

calcimine. Spelled with *ci.*

calculate. Don't use *calculate* when *figure* will do.

calculus, calculi.

caldron. This spelling, rather than *cauldron,* is common in the US.

calendar, calender, colander. A *calendar* (ending in *-ar*) lists dates, a *calender* (with *-er*) is a paper-finishing machine and a *colander* is a sieve.

calf, calves.

calf love. Two words.

calfskin. One word.

caliber. Spell it with *-er.*

calico, calicoes.

caliper. Spell it with one *l.*

caliph. Spell it with *ph.*

calisthenics is spelled with one *l* and *sth.*

calix, calices.

calk. This rather than *caulk* is the common US spelling.

call-. Most compounds are spelled as one word.

callback (noun)**, callbox, callboy.** One word.

call girl, call house. Two words.

calligraphy. Double *l.*

call-in (noun)**.** Hyphened.

calliope. Two *l*'s.

callous, callus. *Callous* (with *-ous*) means insensitive, a *callus* (with *-us*) is an area of hardened skin. In the same way, *calloused* means insensitive, *callused* means hardened (skin).

callup (noun)**.** One word.

calorie. Spell it with *-ie.*

calvary, cavalry. *Calvary* refers to the suffering of Christ, *cavalry* to horsemen. *Cavalry* has *val* in it, so maybe Tennyson's famous lines "Into the *valley* of Death rode the six hundred" will help you.

camaraderie has three *a*'s followed by *e* and ending in *-ie.*

cameldriver. One word.

(cameleon). Misspelling of *chameleon.*

camellia is spelled with double *l* even though it's pronounced with a long *ee.*

camel's hair. No hyphen.

cameo, cameos.

cameraman, cameramen. One word.

camomile. Spell it with *c,* not *ch.*

camouflage is spelled with *ou.*

camp, campy in the sense of homosexual or amusingly tasteless is listed in Webster's (1973) as standard usage.

campaign ends in *-aign.*

campcraft, campfire, campground. One word.

camphor. Spelled with *ph.*

campsite. One word.

can, may. The idea that you should use *can* only for physical ability and *may* for legal permission has long been discredited. *Can* for permission has been in use since 1542. The Bible (I Cor. 10:21) says "Ye cannot drink the cup of the Lord, and the cup of devils."

canal, canalled, canalling.

canapé. Spell it with the accent.

cancel, canceled, canceling, cancelable, canceler are all spelled commonly with one *l.*

cancellation is commonly spelled with two *l*'s. Remember "He was *l*ucky to get a *l*ate cance*ll*ation for the trip to Chicago."

candelabra, candelabras. The word is really the plural of *candelabrum,* but current usage treats it as a singular.

candle-. Most compounds are spelled as one word.

candleholder, candlelight, candlelighter, candlelit, candlepower, candlestick. All one word.

candor ends in *-or.*

candystick. One word.

candy striper. Two words.

canebrake. One word.

cane chair. Two words.

canecutter, canefield. One word.

cane sugar. Two words.

canine. Don't use *canine* as a substitute word for *dog.* Use a pronoun or repeat *dog.*

canister. One *n.*

cannel coal. Two *n*'s. Two words.

cannibalize ends in *-ize.*

cannon, canon. A *cannon* is a big gun, a *canon* is a rule, law or clergyman.

cannonade. First a double *n,* then a single one.

cannonball. One word.

cannoneer. First two *n*'s, then one.

cannot. It's common to spell it as one word.

canoe, canoed, canoeing, canoeist. The *e* must be kept in all forms.

canon, cannon. A *canon* is a rule, law or clergyman, a *cannon* is a big gun.

(cañon). Spell it *canyon.*

canonical. Two single *n*'s.

canonize ends in *-ize.*

can opener. Two words.

can't. This contraction of *cannot* is standard usage.

cantaloupe. Commonly spelled with *e* at the end.

cantankerous. Originally a humorous word, now standard usage.

can't help but, cannot help but is a long-established idiom. Stephen Vincent Benét wrote "And cannot help but see him, day after day."

canto, cantos.

can't seem to, cannot seem to is a common idiom, listed as standard usage in Webster's, e.g. *I can't seem to solve this problem.*

canvas, canvass. *Canvas* (with one *s*) means a cloth, *canvass* (with two *s*'s) means to solicit.

canvass, canvassed, canvassing, canvasser. Two *s*'s in all forms.

canyon. Spell it with *y.*

caoutchouc. A famous spelling demon. First *aou,* then *ou.*

capable ends in *-able.*

capacious ends in *-cious.*

capful, capfuls.

capillary. Two *l*'s.

capital, capitol. A *capital* is a city, a *capitol* is a building.

capitalize ends in *-ize.*

capitals. Here's a set of simple rules for capitalizing, based on Webster's, the GPO Style Manual, the New York Times Manual of Style and Usage and other authoritative sources. In general, the trend is away from using capitals, so if you're in doubt it's better to use a small letter.

1. Capitalize the first word of a sentence or sentence fragment, e.g. *The weather forecast for tomorrow is encouraging. Sunny and mild.* Capitalize the first word of each line of poetry and the first word of a direct quotation within a sentence, e.g. *He said "This will surprise you."* But don't capitalize a partial quotation, e.g. *He predicted "a stunning surprise."*

2. Capitalize the first word of a direct question within a sentence, e.g. *The question is, Did the witness tell the truth?*

3. Capitalize the first word after a colon only if it starts a direct quotation or question. Otherwise follow Webster's and don't capitalize the first word after a colon, e.g. *In the end he never made his prepared speech: the meeting was canceled.* Or *Result: inflation and unemployment.*

4. Capitalize all words in headings, titles and headlines, including parts of hyphened compounds except for these 15 words: *a, an, and, as, at, but, by, for, if, in, of, on, or, the, to.* But capitalize these too if they are the first or last word of a line. Don't capitalize the second part of hyphened numbers and fractions. Examples:

> *Don't Be Afraid to Be Laughed At*
> *How to Figure the Tax-Free Part of an Annuity*
> *Priest Reading Twenty-third Psalm at Ex-Con's Funeral*

5. Capitalize the first word of the salutation of a letter and the first word of the complimentary close, e.g. *Dear Otto, Sincerely yours.*

6. Capitalize single letters used as syllables, e.g. the interjection *O*, the pronoun *I*, *X*-ray, vitamin *B*.

7. Capitalize the names of persons, places, geographical features, organizations, congresses, councils, committees, historical periods and events, ships, aircraft, spacecraft, days of the week, months, holidays, holy days, courts, treaties, trademarks, planets, constellations and stars (except for the sun, the earth and the moon). Examples: *Johann Sebastian Bach, London, Hawaii, the League of Women Voters, The Diet of Worms, the Ways and Means Committee, the Congress of Vienna, the Middle Ages, the Battle of Gettysburg, the Queen Elizabeth 2, Air Force*

1, Apollo 11, Wednesday, October, Christmas, Yom Kippur, the Tax Court, the Treaty of Utrecht, Pepsi-Cola, American Express, Venus, Cassiopeia. But don't capitalize names used as common nouns, e.g. *diesel engine, plaster of paris, brussels sprouts.*

Don't capitalize the article *the* in referring to newspapers and magazines, e.g. *the New Yorker, the Wall Street Journal.*

Don't capitalize the words *de, du, van, von* etc. in foreign names, e.g. *Charles de Gaulle, Roger Martin du Gard, Otto von Bismarck, Ludwig van Beethoven,* but capitalize them in American names, e.g. *Cecil B. De Mille, W. E. B. Du Bois, Martin Van Buren.*

Don't capitalize the names of the four seasons, *spring, summer, fall and winter.*

8. Capitalize derivatives of proper names and words referring to peoples and languages, e.g. *Canadian, Czech, Finnish, Sioux, Victorian, Pre-Raphaelite.* But don't capitalize words that have become common nouns, e.g. *pasteurize, cashmere, jeremiad.*

9. Capitalize common nouns used as titles preceding the names of persons or as part of the name of a geographical feature, e.g. *Captain Robert Smith, Judge William Keenan, the Missouri River, the Tappan Zee Bridge, Belden Avenue, Elm Street, the Rocky Mountains.* But don't capitalize such words otherwise. Also don't capitalize "false" titles, e.g. *trapeze artist Tony Cavalla, skillful negotiator Francis Klein.*

10. Capitalize compass directions referring to a specific region, e.g. *the South, the Far East,* but don't capitalize them otherwise, e.g. *then we turned north.*

11. Capitalize words of family relationship preceding a person's name, e.g. *Uncle Henry, Aunt Martha.*

12. Capitalize words of respect used in directly addressing a person, e.g. *Your Honor, Dear Senator Portland, Mr. Chairman.*

13. Capitalize the word *God* meaning the one supreme being. But capitalization of the pronouns *he, his, him* referring to God is now rare.

14. *Don't* capitalize such words as *presidential, federal, congressional, constitutional, state, governor, board, county, city, commission, bureau* unless they form part of a name like *Federal Reserve Board, Congressional Medal of Honor, New York State Motor Vehicle Bureau.*

15. Don't capitalize *a.m.* and *p.m.*

capriccio, capriccios.

caprice ends in *-ice*.

capricious ends in *-cious*.

capsize ends in *-ize*.

capstone. One word.

car-. Almost all compounds are spelled as one word.

(caracter). Misspelling of *character*.

caracul, karakul. Spell it *caracul* for the fur, *karakul* for the lamb.

carafe. One *r*, one *f*.

caramel. *A* after *r*.

carat, caret, karat. A *carat* is a unit of weight for diamonds, a *caret* is a proofreader's mark, a *karat* is a unit of fineness for gold.

caravansary, caravansaries. Spell it this way.

carbarn. One word.

carbo-. All compounds are spelled as one word, e.g. *carbohydrate*.

carbon paper. Two words.

carburetor, carbureted, carbureting. *Carburetor* is spelled with *bur,* one *t* and *-or*. It's one of the few English words where *e* stands for the sound of *ay*. To remember the *e,* think of the *e*ngine.

carcass ends in double *s*.

carcino-. Spell all compounds as one word.

card-. Most compounds are spelled as one word.

cardboard, cardcase. One word.

card-carrying. Hyphened.

card index. Two words.

cardio-. Spell compounds as one word.

cardplayer, cardsharp. One word.

careen, career. To *careen* means to sway from side to side, to *career* means to go at top speed.

carefree, careful. One word.

caress. One *r*.

caret, carat, karat. A *caret* is a proofreader's mark, a *carat* is a unit of weight for diamonds, a *karat* is a unit of fineness for gold.

caretaker, caretaking, careworn. One word.

carfare. One word.

cargo, cargoes.

carhop. One word.

Caribbean. One *r*, two *b*'s, ends in *-ean*.

caribou. Spelled with *ou*.

caries. The plural is also *caries.*

carillon. Two *l*'s, ends in *-on.*

(carisma). Misspelling of *charisma.*

carload, carlot, carmaker. One word.

carny, carnies. Standard usage for people who work at a carnival.

carol, caroled, caroling, caroler. One *l* in all forms.

carom, caromed, caroming. One *r.*

carotene ends in *-ene.*

carousal, carrousel. A *carousal* is a drunken revel, a *carrousel* (usually spelled with two *r*'s) is a merry-go-round.

carpet-. Compounds are one word, two words or hyphenated.

carpetbag, carpetbagger, carpetbagging. One word.

carpet sweeper, carpet tack. Two words.

car pool. Two words, but *carpool* is also common.

carport. One word.

carrel (in a library). Two *r*'s, ends in *-el.*

carriagemaker. One word.

carriage trade. Two words.

carriageway. One word.

carrousel, carousal. A *carrousel* is a merry-go-round, a *carousal* is a drunken revel.

carry-. Spell all compounds as one word.

carryall, carryback (noun), **carryon** (noun, adj.), **carryout** (noun), **carryover** (pronoun, adj.). One word.

carsick. One word.

carte blanche. No hyphen.

cartilage. Spelled with an *i* in the middle.

cartload, cartwheel, cartwright. One word.

carwash. One word.

case. If you're overusing the word *case,* try to kick the habit. Instead of *this is not the case* write *this is not so;* instead of *in many cases,* write *often;* and so on.

case-. Most compounds are spelled as one word.

casebook, caseharden, casehardened. One word.

casein ends in *-ein.*

case history, case law. Spelled as two words.

caseload. One word.

case study, case system. Spelled as two words.

casework, caseworker. One word.

cashbook, cashbox. One word.

cashier ends in *-ier.*

cashmere. Small *c.*

casino, casinos.

casket. At the New York Times, *casket* for *coffin* is taboo.

(casm). Misspelling of *chasm.*

cassette. Two *s*'s, ends in *-ette.*

cast, caste. Spell it *caste* with an *e* when you mean a social class or rank. Otherwise spell it *cast.*

castanets. Think of "cast a net."

castaway. One word.

caster, castor. Spell it *caster* when you mean a roller, *castor* when you mean castor oil.

castoff (noun, adj.). One word.

castor, caster. Spell it *castor* in *castor oil,* but *caster* when you mean a roller.

casual, causal. *Casual* means offhand, *causal* refers to a cause.

casualty, casualties. Nothing between the *l* and the *t.*

cat-. Almost all compounds are spelled as one word, e.g. *catnap.*

cataclysm, cataclysmic. Spelled with *y.*

catafalque ends in *-que.*

(catagory). Misspelling of *category.*

catalog, cataloged, cataloging, cataloger. The spelling *catalogue* is beginning to look old-fashioned.

catalyst, catalytic, catalyze. Spelled with *y.*

catarrh ends in *-rrh.*

catastrophe, catastrophes. The plural ends in *-es.*

catbird, catcall. One word.

catchall. One word.

catch-as-catch-can. Three hyphens.

catchpenny. One word.

catchup, catsup, ketchup. The most common spelling is *ketchup.*

catechism, catechist, catechize, catechumen. Spelled with *ch. Catechize* ends in *-ize.*

category is spelled with *e* after the *t.* Don't use *category* when *class* will do.

cater-cornered, catty-cornered, kitty-cornered. All three words are common, *cater-cornered* seems to have a slight edge.

caterpillar ends in *-ar.*

catfish. One word.

catharsis, catharses.

catholicize ends in *-ize.*

catnap, catnip. One word.

cat-o'-nine-tails. Three hyphens.

cat's-eye, cat's-paw. Apostrophe and hyphen.

catsup, catchup, ketchup. The most common spelling is *ketchup*.

cattleman. One word.

catty-cornered. *Cater-cornered* seems the most common of the variations.

catwalk. One word.

Caucasian is the police term for white. In everyday writing, use *white* with a small *w*.

(cauldron). The common US spelling is *caldron*.

cauliflower is spelled with *au* and ends in *-flower*.

(caulk). The common US spelling is *calk*.

causal, casual. *Causal* refers to a cause, *casual* means offhand.

cause célèbre. Spelled with two accents.

causerie. Spelled with *au*.

cauterize ends in *-ize*.

cautious ends in *-tious*.

cavalry, calvary. *Cavalry* means horsemen, *calvary* refers to the suffering of Christ. *Cavalry* has *val* in it, so maybe Tennyson's famous lines "Into the *valley* of Death rode the six hundred" will help you.

cavalryman. One word.

caveat is spelled with *e*.

cavedweller. One word.

cave-in (noun). Hyphened.

caveman. One word.

caviar. Spell it without an *e* at the end.

cavil, caviled, caviling, caviler. One *l* in all forms.

-ce, -cy. If in doubt whether a word should end in *-ce* or *-cy* (e.g. *inadvertence* or *inadvertency*), use the *-ce* ending when writing of the idea in general and the *-cy* ending when writing of specific instances. E.g. *The mistake happened through inadvertence,* but *It was an inadvertency that caused the mistake.*

cease. Don't use *cease* or *cease and desist* when *stop* will do.

ceasefire. Follow the trend and spell it as one word.

cecum, ceca. This, rather than *caecum,* is now the more common spelling.

cedar ends in *-ar*.

cede, ceded, ceding. Spelled with *c* and one *e*.

-cede, -ceed, -sede. There are eight words ending in *-cede—accede, antecede, cede, concede, intercede, precede, recede, secede.*

There are three words ending in -*ceed*—*exceed, proceed, succeed*. And there's one word ending in -*sede*—*supersede*.

ceiling. The spelling follows the rule "*I* before *e* except after *c.*"

cellar ends in -*ar*.

cellarette, cellaret. The spelling *cellarette* is more common.

cellmate. One word.

cello, cellos, cellist. The apostrophe in front is now old-fashioned.

cellophane. Two *l*'s.

cellulose. Two *l*'s, followed by *u*.

Celtic. Now always spelled with *C*.

cembalo. The plural *cembali* is more common than *cembalos*.

cemetery ends in -*ery*. Think of "a parking *meter* at the cemetery."

cenotaph. The second vowel is an *o*.

censer, censor. A *censer* is an incense burner, a *censor* checks the contents of movies, books etc.

censor, censure. To *censor* means to suppress, to *censure* means to condemn.

census starts with *c* and ends with -*us*.

census taker. Two words.

cent, scent. A *cent* is a coin, a *scent* is a smell.

centaur ends in -*aur*.

centennial. Two *n*'s.

center ends in -*er*.

center around. The idiom is standard usage.

centerboard. One word.

center field. Two words.

centerpiece. One word.

centi-. Spell compounds as one word.

centigrade, centigram, centiliter, centimeter, centipede. One word.

central Asia, central Europe etc. Spell with a small *c*.

centralize ends in -*ize*.

centripetal. The vowel after the *p* is *e*.

centuries. Spell out the numbers through the ninth, then use figures, e.g. *the sixth century, the 17th century.* Hyphen modifiers, e.g. *a 19th-century sculptor.* Remember that the 1500s are the 16th century, the 1900s the 20th century etc.

cereal, serial. A *cereal* with *c* (ends in -*eal*) is a breakfast food, a *serial* with *s* (ends in -*ial*) is a continued story.

cerebrospinal, cerebrovascular. One word.

ceremonial, ceremonious. *Ceremonial* means marked by ceremony, *ceremonious* means given to ceremony, e.g. *ceremonial occasions, a ceremonious old courtier.*

certainty, certitude. *Certainty* means being certain, but *certitude* means absolute freedom from doubt. So don't write *certitude* when all you mean is *certainty.*

certificate ends in *-ate.*

cesarean with a small *c* is now the common spelling of the operation.

cessation. Two *s*'s.

cession, session. *Cession* means yielding, *session* means sitting.

cesspit, cesspool. One word.

chafe, chaff. To *chafe* means to irritate, to *chaff* means to tease.

chagrin, chagrined, chagrining. One *n* in all forms.

chain-. Some compounds are spelled as one word, some as two.

chain bag, chain belt, chain gang, chain letter, chain mail, chain reaction, chain saw. Two words.

chain-smoke, chain-smoking, chain-smoker. Hyphened.

chainstitch, chainstore, chainwork. One word.

chair-. Most compounds are spelled as one word.

chairborne. One word.

chair lift. Two words.

chairman, chairmaned, chairmaning. One *n* in all forms. Small *c,* except when used as a title, e.g. *Mr. Chairman.*

chairperson, chairwoman. One word.

chaise, meaning carriage, is spelled with *ai.*

chaise longue ends in *-gue.* The most commonly used plural is *chaise longues.*

chaise lounge, a misspelling and mispronunciation of *chaise longue,* is listed in Webster's and Random House as standard usage.

chalkboard, chalkline. One word.

chalk-white. Hyphened.

challis ends in *-is.*

chambermaid. One word.

chamber music, chamber orchestra. Two words.

chameleon. Starts with *ch,* ends in *-eon.*

chamois, shammy. The spelling *chamois* is more common, although the word meaning leather is pronounced *shammy.*

(chamomile). Spell it *camomile.*

champagne ends in *-agne.*

chancellor, chancellery. Two *l*'s in both words. The more common spelling of *chancellery* ends in *-ery*.

chancre, chancrous end in *-cre, -crous.*

chancy has no *e*.

chandelier ends in *-ier*.

changeable ends in *-eable*.

changeover. One word.

channel, channeled, channeling. One *l* in all forms.

chantey, shanty. *Chantey* with *ch* and *ey* is the common spelling for the sailors' song, *shanty* for the hut.

Chanukah. Another common spelling is *Hanukkah.*

chaos, chaotic. Spelled with *ch* and *ao*.

chapeau, chapeaus.

chapel ends in *-el*.

chaperon. Spell the noun and the verb without a final *e*.

char, charred, charring.

character, characteristic, characterize, characterization. Spelled with *ch*. Don't use *character* when a simpler word will do. For instance, instead of *a price change of this character* write *such a price change.*

charcoal. One word.

chargeable ends in *-eable*.

charge account. Two words.

chargé d'affairs, chargés d'affaires. Always spelled with the accent.

chargeoff (noun), **chargeout** (noun). One word.

charisma, charismatic. Spelled with *ch*.

(charivari). Spell it *shivaree*.

charlatan. Spelled with *ch* and three *a*'s.

charley horse. Spelled with a small *c* and *-ey*. Two words.

Charlie. The usual spelling of the name ends in *-ie*.

charted, chartered. *Charted* means mapped out, *chartered* means leased.

chartreuse ends in *-euse*.

chasm starts with *ch*.

chassis. The plural is also *chassis*.

chasten. Watch the silent *t*.

chastise ends in *-ise*.

chasuble ends in *-uble*.

chateau, chateaus. Follow the trend and leave out the accent. The common plural ends in *s*.

chatelaine ends in *-aine.* No accent.

chattel ends in *-el.*

chauffeur, chauffeured, chauffeuring. Spelled with double *f,* ends in *-eur.*

chautauqua has two *au*'s.

chauvinism, chauvinist. Spelled with *ch* and *au.*

cheapskate. One word.

check. So spelled in all senses. *Check into* and *check up on* are common idioms.

check-. All compounds except *check-in* are spelled as one word.

checkbook. One word.

checkerboard. One word.

checkers. So spelled in the US.

check-in (noun and modifier). Hyphened.

checklist, checkmark, checkmate, checkoff (noun), **checkout** (noun), **checkpoint, checkrein, checkroom, checkup** (noun), **checkwriter, checkwriting.** One word.

Cheddar. Capital *C,* two *d*'s, ends in *-ar.*

cheekbone, cheerleader. One word.

cheese. Spell with a small *c* after a capitalized specific name, e.g. *Cheddar cheese, Camembert cheese, Roquefort cheese.*

cheese-. Except for *cheese knife,* spell compounds as one word.

cheeseburger, cheesecake, cheesecloth. One word.

cheese knife. Two words.

cheesemaker, cheeseparing. One word.

cheetah ends in *-ah.*

chef, chefs.

chef d'oeuvre, chefs d'oeuvre.

chemisette ends in *-ette.*

chemo-. Spell all compounds as one word, e.g. *chemotherapy.*

chenille ends in *-ille.*

(cheque, chequers). British spellings of US *check* and *checkers.*

cheroot.

cherrystone. One word.

cherub, cherubs.

chessboard, chessman. One word.

chesterfield (coat). Small *c.*

chestnut. Don't leave out the silent *t.*

chevron. No *e* between the *v* and the *r.*

chew out. Listed as standard usage in Webster's.

chew the rag, chew the fat. Listed as slang in Webster's.

Chianti. Capital *C.*

chiaroscuro, chiaroscuros.

chic, sheik. *Chic* means elegant or elegance, *sheik* means an Arab ruler. The pronunciation is the same, although *sheik* is sometimes pronounced *shake.*

chicanery. Spelled with *ch.*

Chicano, Chicanos. Capital *C.*

chicken in the sense of scared is listed as slang in Webster's.

chickenfeed is spelled as one word. In the sense of a small amount of money it is listed as slang in Webster's.

chickenhearted, chickenpox. One word.

chicken wire. Two words.

chicory. So spelled.

chide, chided, chided.

chief, chiefs. Follows the rule "*i* before *e* except after *c.*"

chief executive. Don't use this when *president* will do.

chieftain ends in *-ain.*

chiffon. Spelled with *ch* and two *f*'s.

chiffonier ends in *-ier.*

Chihuahua. Spelled with capital *C.* There's no *w* in this word.

chilblains. One *l* in *chil-.*

childbearing, childbed, childbirth. One word.

childish, childlike. *Childish* means unpleasantly like a child, *childlike* pleasantly so.

Chile, the country. Ends in *e.*

chili, chili con carne. Spelled in the US with one *l* and ending in *i.*

chill, chilly. The commonly used adjective is *chilly. Chill* now sounds bookish, e.g. *A chill reception.*

chimera, chimerical. *E* (not *ae*) is the common spelling.

chimney. Nothing between the *m* and the *n.*

chimp for *chimpanzee* is listed in Webster's as standard usage.

Chinaman is an offensive word. Write *Chinese.*

chinaware. One word.

chin-high. Hyphenated.

chino, chinos.

chinstrap. One word.

chintzy. Listed in Webster's as standard usage in both senses. Spelled with *tz.*

chip in. Listed in Webster's as standard usage.

chipmunk. One word.

chiro-. Spell all compounds as one word.

chiromancer, chiromancy, chiropodist, chiropody, chiropractic. One word.

chiropractor ends in *-or.*

chisel, chiseled, chiseling. One *l* in all forms. *Chisel* in the sense of cheat is listed as standard usage in Webster's. It has been so used since 1808.

chitchat. One word.

chivalry, chivalrous. Spelled with *al.*

chloro-. Spell all compounds as one word.

chloroform, chlorophyll. One word.

chlorpromazine.

chockablock. One word.

chock-full. Hyphened. Two *l*'s.

chocolate. *O* between *c* and *l.*

choir, quire. A *choir* is a group of singers, a *quire* is 24 sheets of paper. The pronunciation of the two words is the same.

choirboy, choirmaster. One word.

cholera, choleric, cholesterol. All spelled with *ch.*

choose, chose, chosen.

choosy. No *e.*

chopstick. One word.

choral, chorale. *Choral* is an adjective referring to a chorus, a *chorale* (with the accent on the second syllable and an *e* at the end) is a hymn.

chord, cord. It's a musical *chord,* but a *cord* for tying things together, a *cord* of wood, an electric *cord,* a spinal *cord,* a vocal *cord.* Remember, the *chord* with *h* is the one you *h*ear.

chorea, the disease, is spelled with *ch.*

chortle is standard usage, meaning chuckle.

chorus, chorused, chorusing. One *s* in all forms.

chowchow, chowline. One word.

chow mein. Two words.

christen, christened, christening.

Christianize ends in *-ize.*

Christian name. *First name* is now more common.

Christlike. One word.

Christmas. Watch the silent *t.* The form *Xmas* is standard usage.

chrome is spelled with *ch.*

chromo-. Spell compounds as one word.

chronic means habitual or recurring. It doesn't mean severe.

chrono-. Spell compounds as one word.

chronological, chronology, chronometer. Spelled with *ch* and as one word.

chrysanthemum. A famous spelling demon. Spelled with *ch, y* and *mum* at the end.

chrysoprase ends in *-ase.*

(chrystal). Misspelling of *crystal.*

chuckwagon. One word.

chukker (polo). Spell it with *-er.*

chunk, chunky. Standard usage.

churchgoer, churchgoing, churchyard. One word.

chute, chutist. So spelled in all meanings (fall, rapids, slide, parachute). No apostrophe.

chutzpah. Spell it with *h* at the end. Listed as standard usage for nerve or gall in Webster's.

cigarbox, cigarcase. One word.

cigarette. Webster's, the GPO Style Manual and most newspapers spell it *cigarette* rather than *cigaret.*

cigarette case, cigarette holder, cigarette maker, cigarette paper. Two words.

cigarholder, cigarmaker, cigarstore. One word.

cinch. *A cinch* in the sense of something sure and easy is listed as standard usage in Webster's and the Oxford English Dictionary. The word has been so used since 1888.

Cincinnati is spelled with two *n*'s and one *t.*

cine-. Spell compounds as one word.

cinema has an *e* after the *n.*

cinnamon is spelled with a double *n.*

cinquecento. Remember it means the 1500s, that is, the 16th century.

cion, scion. The spelling varies. In the sense of a shoot or twig, the common spelling is *cion,* but for a descendant or child it's always *scion.*

cipher. Spell it with *i.*

circa means *about;* used with dates. The standard abbreviation is *ca.,* e.g. *ca. 1910.* It's now more common to write *about 1910.*

circuit ends in *-uit.*

circuit breaker, circuit court, circuit judge. All spelled as two words.

circuitous. The *i* comes before the *t.* Don't use *circuitous* when *roundabout* will do.

circuit rider. Two words.

circular ends in *-ar.*

circulatory ends in *-ory.*

circum-. Spell compounds as one word.

circumcise ends in *-ise.*

circumference ends in *-ence.*

circumlocution, circumnavigate, circumnavigation, circumnavigator, circumscribe, circumspect. One word.

circumstance ends in *-ance.* The idiom *under the circumstances* is standard usage.

circumstantial evidence is indirect in contrast to direct evidence, *not* in contrast to eyewitnesses.

circumvention ends in *-tion.*

circus, circuses.

cirrhosis is spelled with *rrh.*

cis-. Spell compounds as one word, e.g. *cisalpine.*

citable. No *e* after the *t.*

cite, site. *Cite* means summon or quote, *site* means a place.

city-born. Hyphened.

citybound. One word.

city-bred. Hyphened.

cityfolk, citylike, cityscape. One word.

city-state. Hyphened.

citywide. One word.

civil defense. Small *c.*

civilize, civilized, civilization. Spell with *z.*

civilly. Two *l*'s.

civil service. Small *c.*

Civil War (US). In the South, the term *War Between the States* is common.

-ck-. A *c* at the end of a word is changed to *-ck-* before the suffixes *-ed, -er, -ing, -y,* e.g. *shellacked, picnicker, panicking, colicky.*

clad is now poetic or archaic. Avoid.

claim, in the sense of say or assert, is standard usage, as in *he claimed he hadn't been there.*

clambake. One word.

clamor ends in *-or.*

clam up is listed as standard usage in Webster's.

clangor ends in *-or.*

clannish. Double *n.*

clap for gonorrhea is listed as standard usage in Webster's. Used since 1587.

clapboard, claptrap. One word.

clarinet ends in *-et.*

clarinetist. One *t* after the *e.*

class-. Some compounds are spelled as one word, some as two, some are hyphened.

class action. Two words.

classbook. One word.

class-conscious. Hyphened.

class consciousness, class day. Two words.

classic, classical. As a rule, use *classical* only when you're referring to Greek and Roman literature; otherwise say *classic.*

classifiable ends in *-able.*

classify, classified, classifying, classifier.

classless, classmate, classroom, classwork. One word.

clayey ends in *-ey.*

clean-. Some compounds are hyphened, some are spelled as one word.

clean-cut. Hyphened.

cleanhanded. One word.

clean-limbed. Hyphened.

cleanness. Two *n*'s.

cleanout (noun). One word.

cleanse, cleanser. Spelled with *ea.*

clean-shaven. Hyphened.

cleanup (noun). One word.

clear-. Most compounds are spelled as one word.

clearance ends in *-ance.*

clear-cut, clear-eyed. Hyphened.

clearheaded. One word.

clearinghouse. One word.

clear-minded, clear-sighted. Hyphened.

clearup (noun). One word.

clef.

clerestory. Spell it with *ere.*

clew, clue. Spell it *clew* in the nautical sense and *clue* when you mean a piece of evidence.

cliché is usually spelled with the accent. Clichés are trite phrases and expressions like *strong as an ox* or *a fly in the ointment.* Try to avoid them in your writing.

client. A lawyer, accountant or consultant sells his professional services to *clients,* a doctor has *patients,* a bank or store has *customers,* a hotel has *guests.*

clientele. No accent.

cliffdweller, cliffhanger. One word.

climactic, climatic, climacteric. *Climactic* has to do with a climax, *climatic* with the climate, *climacteric* with the menopause.

climax as a verb (to reach or bring to a climax) is standard usage, even though at the New York Times it's taboo.

climb, clime. You *climb* a ladder, but you speak of a tropical *clime* or climate.

climb down is standard usage.

climbout. One word.

clinician ends in *-cian*.

clinker in the sense of boner or flop is listed as standard usage in Webster's.

clipboard. One word.

clip joint. Listed in Webster's as slang.

clique, cliquey.

cloak-and-dagger. Two hyphens.

cloakroom. One word.

clock-. Spell all compounds except *clock tower* as one word.

clocklike. One word.

clock tower. Two words.

clockwatcher, clockwise, clockwork. One word.

clodhopper, clodhopping. One word.

cloisonné. Spell with the accent.

close-. Some compounds are hyphened, some spelled as one word, some as two.

close corporation. This form of the word is more common than *closed corporation.*

close-cropped, close-cut. Hyphened.

closed-door, closed-end. Hyphened.

closedown (noun), **closefisted.** One word.

close-grained, close-hauled, close-knit, close-lipped. Hyphened.

closemouthed, closeout. One word.

close-shaven. Hyphened.

closeup. One word.

closure, cloture. The parliamentary procedure is spelled *cloture.*

clothbound. One word.

clothes-. Spell all compounds except *clothes closet* as one word.

clothes, cloths. *Clothes* are what you wear, *cloths* are pieces of cloth.

clothesbag, clothesbasket, clothesbrush. One word.

clothes closet. Two words.

clotheshorse, clothesline, clothespin, clothesrack. One word.

cloture, closure. The parliamentary procedure is spelled *cloture.*

cloudburst, cloudcapped. One word.

cloud nine is listed as standard usage in Webster's.

clout in the sense of pull or influence is listed as standard usage in Webster's.

cloverleaf, cloverleafs. One word.

club-. Compounds are spelled as one word or two.

club car, club chair, club coupe. Two words.

clubfoot, clubfooted, clubhouse, clubman. One word.

club sandwich, club soda, club steak. Two words.

clubwoman. One word.

clue, clew. Spell it *clue* when you mean the piece of evidence, but *clew* in the nautical sense.

CO, in capitals and with no periods, is the standard abbreviation of *Commanding Officer.*

co. with a period is the standard abbreviation of *company* or *county.* In names spell it with a capital *C.*

c/o is the standard abbreviation of *care of.*

co-. Write all compounds except *co-op, co-owner, co-worker* as one word.

coadjutor is spelled with *dj.*

coagulant, coagulate, coagulation. No hyphen.

coal-. Compounds are spelled as one word or two. A few are hyphened.

coalbag, coalbin. One word.

coal-black. Hyphened.

coalbox. One word.

coal car. Two words.

coalesce, coalescing, coalescent. Spelled with *sc.*

coalfield. One word.

coal gas, coal hole, coal loader. Two words.

coalmine, coalminer. One word.

coal seam, coal tar, coal truck. Two words.

coalyard. One word.

coarse, course. Spell it *coarse* when you mean rough or crude. Otherwise it's *course.*

Coast Guard. Two words, capitalized.

coastguardsman, coastline. One word.

coatdress, coathanger, coatrack, coatroom, coattail. One word.

coat tree. Two words.

coauthor, coaxial. One word, no hyphen.

cobblestone. One word.

cobelligerent. One word.

cocaine ends in -*e.*

cocaptain. One word.

coccyx is spelled with two *c*'s and a *y.* The common plural is *coccyges.*

cochair, cochairman. One word.

cock-. Spell all compounds except *cock robin* as one word.

cockeyed, cocksure. One word.

coco, cocoa. *Coco* for the coconut, *cocoa* for the beverage.

coconut. Spell it without *a.*

cocoon. There's only one *c* in the middle.

c.o.d. Abbreviation of *cash on delivery.* The GPO Style Manual and most newspapers spell it with lowercase letters and periods.

codebook. One word.

codefendant. One word, no hyphen. Ends in -*ant.*

codeine is spelled with an *e* at the end.

codex, codices.

codicil ends in -*cil.*

cod-liver oil. Hyphened.

coed, coeditor, coeducation, coeducational, coefficient, coequal, coerce. One word, no hyphen.

coercible ends in -*ible.*

coercion ends in -*cion.* There's no *s.*

coercive, coeval, coexecutor, coexist, coexistence, coexistent, co-extensive, cofeature. One word, no hyphen.

coffee-. Most compounds are spelled as one word.

coffeebreak, coffeecake. One word.

coffee cup. Two words.

coffeehouse, coffeepot. One word.

coffee shop. Two words.

coffee-table book. Hyphened.

cognizant, cognizance. Don't leave out the *g.*

cognoscenti. Spelled with *gn, sc,* and *i* at the end.

cogwheel. One word.

coheir, coheiress. One word, no hyphen.

coherent, coherence end in -*ent* and -*ence.*

cohort in the sense of companion or associate is standard usage.

coiffeur, coiffeuse, coiffure. Spelled with *oiff.*

coinbox. One word.

coincidence, coincident end in *-ence* and *-ent.*

coincidentally, coincidently. The spelling *coincidentally* is more common. Think of "It *all* happened coincident*all*y."

coined words. See NEW WORDS.

coin-op, coin-operated. Hyphened.

coinsurance. One word, no hyphen.

coke oven. Two words.

col-, coll-. If you can't find the word you're looking for under *col-,* try *coll-.*

colander is the right spelling for the sieve.

cold-. Compounds are spelled as one word, two words, or hyphened.

coldblooded. One word.

cold cream, cold cuts, cold duck, cold front. Two words.

coldhearted. One word.

cold-shoulder (verb). Hyphened.

cold type, cold war, cold wave. Two words.

coleslaw. One word. No *d.*

colic, colicky.

coliseum, Colosseum. Spell it *coliseum* with a small *c,* one *l,* an *i* and one *s* when you mean a modern building, but spell it *Colosseum* with a capital *C,* two *o*'s, one *l* and two *s*'s when you're writing about ancient Rome. Of course when *Coliseum* is used as a proper name, the *C* is capitalized.

colitis. One *l.*

collaborate, collaborator, collaboration. Two *l*'s.

collaborate together says the same thing twice. Strike out *together.*

collapse. Two *l*'s.

collapsible ends in *-ible.*

collar ends in *-ar.*

collarbone. One word.

collateral. Double *l.*

collation. Don't use *collation* when *meal* will do.

colleague. Two *l*'s, ends in *-eague.*

collectible. Commonly spelled with *-ible.*

collector ends in *-or.*

college, collegiate. No *d.*

collide has two *l*'s.

collie ends in *-ie.*

collision. Two *l*'s.

(collonnade). Misspelling of *colonnade.*

colloquium, colloquiums.

colloquy, colloquies.

(collossal, collossus). Misspellings of *colossal, colossus.*

cologne ends in *-gne.*

colon. Here's a set of simple rules for using a colon, based mainly on Webster's and the GPO Style Manual.

1. The traditional use of the colon is before a phrase or clause that explains, specifies or emphasizes what has gone before, e.g. *He was famished: he hadn't eaten for two days.—The house was completely sold out: word of mouth had done its work.—He had only one aim in life: to make money.—We considered three factors: time, cost and feasibility.* This use of the colon is no longer common. The trend is toward using periods or dashes in the first two examples, dashes in the last two.

Don't capitalize the next word after this type of colon.

2. Use a colon after a sentence introducing a new paragraph. For example:

> *The following resolution was adopted:*
>   *Whereas . . .*
> Or:
> *The committee issued the following statement:*
>   *"After an exhaustive investigation . . ."*

Use a comma rather than a colon for a question or quotation on the same line, e.g. *The question is,·Where is the money coming from? The witness answered, "To the best of my recollection . . ."*

3. Use a colon after a written or spoken salutation, e.g. *Dear Sir:—Gentlemen:—My Fellow Americans:.* But use a comma after the salutation of an informal personal or business letter, e.g. *Dear Mary,—Dear Mr. Hansen,.*

4. Use a colon in clock time, bibliographical and biblical references, and between book titles and subtitles, e.g. *8:45 a.m.—Journal of Sociology 4: 354–376—New York: Harper & Row—Luke 4:3—The Book of Surprises: An Anthology of the Unusual.*

5. Don't use a colon and a dash together. Strike out the dash.

colonel. So spelled even though it's pronounced *kernel.*

colonist. One *l.*

colonize, colonization. Spelled with *z.*

colonnade. One *l,* two *n*'s.

colony. One *l.*

colophon. One *l* and *ph.*

color ends in *-or.*

color-. Most compounds are spelled as two words.

colorable ends in *-able.*

color bar. Two words.

colorbearer. One word.

color-blind. Hyphened.

color blindness. Two words.

colorfast. One word.

color guard, color line. Two words.

colossal. One *l,* two *s*'s. Think of *"colossal losses."*

Colosseum. The one in Rome. Capital *C,* one *l,* two *s*'s.

colossus. One *l,* two *s*'s, ends in *-us.*

column, columnist. Don't leave out the *n.*

com-, comm-. If you can't find the word you're looking for under *com-,* look under *comm-.*

coma, comma. A *coma* is a state of unconsciousness, a *comma* is a punctuation mark.

comaker. One word.

comatose. One *m.*

comb. Be sure to write the silent *b.*

combat, combated, combating, combatant, combative. One *t* in all forms.

combo, combos. Standard usage.

combustible ends in *-ible.*

comeback. One word.

comedian ends in *-ian.*

comedienne ends in *-ienne.* No accent.

comedown. One word.

comely. Spelled so even though it's usually pronounced *kumly.*

come-on (noun). Hyphened.

comeuppance. One word.

comfortable ends in *-able.*

comfy. Listed as standard usage in Webster's.

comic book. Two words.

comity, meaning courtesy, is spelled with one *m.*

comma, coma. A *comma* is a punctuation mark, a *coma* is a state of unconsciousness.

comma. The following rules are based mainly on Webster's and common newspaper usage. The trend is toward using fewer and fewer commas.

1. Don't use a comma before the last item in a series, e.g. *He was tall, dark and handsome.—Is it animal, vegetable or mineral?*

2. Don't use a comma before *and, but, or, nor* in a compound sentence, e.g. *She was preparing for an audition and I heard her practicing many hours a day.—Is this a legitimate defense or are we confronted here by a self-serving argument?—We don't agree with the proposition as stated nor are we willing to enter into negotiations.—Be sure to visit the public library but remember it isn't open on Sundays.*

3. Don't use a comma before or after short interjections, adverbs or adverbial clauses or phrases, e.g. *Ah well.—The sooner the better.—Of course he couldn't have foreseen that.—Indeed this was exactly what he expected to happen.—I therefore urge all of you to vote for the amendment.—Obviously that wasn't what he meant.—Her second piece of advice was very useful too.—Before her accident she had been an ardent skier.* But use a comma or commas to mark what would be a noticeable pause or change in pitch in speaking, e.g. *He was, politically speaking, a babe in the woods.—That, however, was more than he could bear.—After having lived in the same house for 27 years, he suddenly pulled up stakes and moved to a community 2000 miles away.*

4. Use a comma before and after parenthetical, commenting or contrasting phrases or clauses, e.g. *Governor McIver, it is reported, has decided to run for a second term.—The audience, which was in a generous mood, applauded at every occasion.— We visited Salzburg, the city where the famous festivals are held. —His mother-in-law, Mrs. Robertson, was not present.—Greece, not Italy, was what he wanted to see.* But use no commas before and after phrases or clauses that are essential to the sentence, e.g. *The day that had been set for the meeting finally arrived.— Her brother Dennis was with her when she came in.* (She had more than one brother.)

See also WHICH, THAT.

5. Use a comma between independent but closely connected clauses, e.g. *I came, I saw, I conquered.—Joe is right, we can't finish the job today.—He could hardly stand up, he was so tired. —There was nobody there, so I turned around and went straight* *home.—She went out of the room, she didn't want to witness his embarrassment.—Terrible weather, isn't it?—The theater was dark, the second show was over.* (Thomas Wolfe)—*Chic means elegant or elegance,* sheik *means an Arab ruler.*—But don't use a comma but a period between longer, not closely connected sentences, e.g. *Two persons were killed and seven injured in the plane crash. The authorities are investigating the causes of the accident.* (Period, not comma, after *crash.*)

6. Don't use a comma between two or more adjectives referring to unrelated features, e.g. *A dirty old man.—A used 1972 four-door sedan.* But use a comma between adjectives referring to related features, e.g. *His testimony was a string of muddled, ambiguous, impenetrable sentences.*

7. Use a comma to prevent misreading, e.g. *To Jack, Morton was someone who could do no wrong.—He was sincerely grateful, for the opportunity to go home on a weekend didn't come very often.*

8. Don't use a comma in inverted sentences, e.g. *A great technician he was not.—Out of the ghetto came a great new playwright.*

9. Don't use a comma to mark the omission of a verb, e.g. *Mrs. Black gave $1000, Dr. White $500.* (No comma after *White.*)

10. Don't use a comma before *of,* Roman numerals, *Jr., Sr., &* or in street addresses, e.g. *Philip Jones of 10 Maple Street, Philadelphia, Louis XIV, Joseph Brown Jr., Edward Smith Sr., Roberts & Cunningham, 24 Maple Street.* But use a comma before a title following a name, e.g. *Charles Fox, M.D.,* or a country, state or county following a place name, e.g. *Portland, Maine.*

11. In dates, don't use a comma between the month and the year, e.g. *April 1974* or (military style) *6 October 1968.* But use a comma after the day of the month, e.g. *May 8, 1972.*

12. Use a comma—instead of a more formal colon—before a quoted statement, e.g. *He said, "It's too late."* But there's a trend toward using no punctuation, e.g. *He said "It's too late."* Use commas to set off a quotation within a sentence, e.g. *"The Russians," he said, "are crazy about blue jeans."* Remember "comma quote"—put the comma inside the quotation marks.

13. Use commas to group numbers in units of three, e.g. *19,684, $6,485,843.* But don't use commas in four-digit numbers, street numbers, dates or pagination, e.g. *$3500, 1600 Pennsylvania Avenue, 1974, page 1284.*

14. Use a comma after the complimentary close of a letter, e.g. *Affectionately,—Sincerely yours,.*

15. Use a comma to set off a name in a sentence, e.g. *I tell you, John, it is too late.—Dick, come here.*

16. Don't use a comma after *And, But, Or, So, Also* at the beginning of a sentence.

17. Don't use a comma between the subject and the verb of a sentence, e.g. *Mr. Arthur Turner and five other men allegedly associated with him in the stock swindle were indicted.* (No comma after *swindle.*)

18. Use a comma after the salutation in informal personal and business letters, e.g. *Dear Mary,—Dear Mr. Hansen,.*

19. Don't use a comma and a dash together. Strike out the comma.

commandant. Two *m*'s, ends in *-ant.*

commander in chief, commanders in chief. No hyphens.

commando, commandos.

commemorate, commemoration, commemorative. Double *m.*

commence. Don't use *commence* when *begin* or *start* will do.

commend. Two *m*'s.

commendable ends in *-able.*

commensurate. Two *m*'s.

commentary. Two *m*'s, ends in *-ary.*

(commentate). Use *comment.*

commentator ends in *-or.*

commingle. Two *m*'s.

commiserate with is listed in Webster's as standard usage.

commission, commissioner. Two *m*'s, two *s*'s.

commit, committed, committing, committal.

commitment. One *t* after the *i.*

committee. Two *m*'s, two *t*'s, two *e*'s.

committeeman, committeewoman. One word.

commodity. Two *m*'s.

common-law marriage, common-law wife. Hyphened.

commonness. Double *n.*

commonplace. One word.

common sense, commonsense. Two words as noun, one word as adjective, e.g. *a commonsense attitude.*

commonsensible, commonsensical. One word.

commonweal, commonwealth. One word.

commotion. Two *m*'s.

communicate. Don't use *communicate* when *write* or *tell* will do.

communiqué. Spell it with the accent.

companionable ends in *-able*.

companionway. One word.

companywide. One word.

comparable ends in *-able*.

comparative is spelled with *a* after the *r*.

comparison is spelled with *i* after the *r*. Remember "The *comparison* shopper went to *Paris.*"

compatible ends in *-ible*.

compel, compelled, compelling.

compendious, compendium, compendiums. The words refer to a brief summary or digest, not a large work.

compensate, compensation. Don't use these words when *pay* will do.

competent, competence end in *-ent, -ence*.

competition, competitive. The *p* is followed by *e*. Think of *compete*.

competitor ends in *-or*.

complacency, complacence. *Complacency* is the more common form.

complacent, complaisant. *Complacent* (ending in *-ent*) means self-satisfied or unconcerned, *complaisant* (ending in *-ant*) means eager to please.

complainant ends in *-ant*.

complected is listed in Webster's as standard usage, e.g. *a tall, thin man, fairly dark complected* (E. J. Kahn Jr.).

(complection). Misspelling of *complexion*.

complement, compliment. A *complement* makes complete, a *compliment* is flattering. Remember "Compl*i*ments are good for the ego—the *I.*"

complementary, complimentary. Something *complementary* supplies a balance, something *complimentary* is a courtesy or favor.

complete. Don't use *complete* when you mean fill out a form.

complexion is spelled with *x*.

compliance, compliant end in *-ance, -ant*.

compliment, complimentary. When you mean a favor or flattery, spell it with *i*.

complimentary close. In business letters and formal personal letters the most common forms are *Sincerely, Sincerely yours, Very truly yours, Yours sincerely, Yours very truly.* There's a trend toward the more informal *Sincerely yours, Sincerely,* or *Yours sincerely. Faithfully yours* and *Yours truly* are no longer common. *Cordially yours* and *Cordially* are getting more common.

In letters to high officials *Respectfully yours* is common.

In informal personal letters the most common forms are *Sincerely yours, Sincerely, Yours, As ever,* or various expressions of personal sentiment.

Start the complimentary close with a capital and end it with a comma.

Don't tie it into the letter with an old-fashioned phrase like *I am* or *We remain.*

comportment. No *e* before the last *m.*

compote ends in *e.*

compound words. The trend is toward using no hyphen but writing a compound word as one word, e.g. *antiaircraft, byproduct, ceasefire, takeover, tipoff.* Some two-word compounds never take a hyphen, e.g. *blue jay, civil rights, high school, income tax.*
See also HYPHEN.

comprehensible ends in *-ible.*

comprehension ends in *-sion.*

compressible ends in *-ible.*

comprise in the sense of make up (rather than contain) is listed in Webster's as standard usage, but it's simpler and clearer to say *make up, form* or *compose.*

compromise ends in *-ise.*

comptroller, controller. The simpler spelling *controller* is more common.

compulsive, compulsory. *Compulsive* acts are caused by an obsession, *compulsory* acts are enforced by someone else.

compute. Don't use *compute* when *figure* will do.

comrade is spelled with an *e* at the end.

(comradery). Misspelling of *camaraderie.*

con-. If you can't find the word you're looking for under *con-,* try *conn-.*

conceal. Don't use *conceal* when *hide* will do.

concede ends in *-ede.*

conceit, conceited. The spelling follows the rule "*i* before *e* except after *c.*"

conceivable ends in *-able.*

conceive. *E* before *i* after *c.*

(concensus). Misspelling of *consensus.*

conceptualize ends in *-ize.*

concertize ends in *-ize.* Standard usage.

concertmaster. One word.

concerto, concertos. (Musicians may prefer *concerti.*)

concessionaire. One *n* before *-aire.*

conciliatory ends in *-ory.*

concomitant. One *m,* ends in *-ant.*

concretize ends in *-ize.* Standard usage.

concubinage. No *e* after *n.*

concupiscence, concupiscent ends in *-ence, -ent.* Watch the *sc.*

concur, concurred, concurring, concurrent, concurrence. Double *r* in all forms except *concur.*

condemn, contemn. You *condemn* something as wrong or evil, but when you *contemn* it, you express contempt.

condenser ends in *-er.*

condescend, condescension are spelled with *sc.*

condign (as in *condign punishment*) ends in *-ign.*

condition. The phrase *a serious heart condition* is listed as standard usage in Webster's.

condolence ends in *-ence.*

condominium, condominiums.

conducive. Write *conducive to* (not *of* or *with*).

conductor ends in *-or.*

conduit ends in *-uit.*

confectionery ends in *-ery.*

confederacy ends in *-acy.*

confer, conferred, conferring, conferrable, conferrer. Double *r* in all forms except *confer, conferee* and *conference.*

conferee. One *r.*

conference. One *r.*

conference call, conference room. Two words.

confessor ends in *-or.*

confess to (a crime) is standard usage.

confetti ends in *i.*

confidant, confidante. Webster's and the GPO Style Manual say you can use *confidant* for either sex, but *confidante* for a woman is common usage.

confident, confidence end in *-ent, -ence.*

confluence ends in *-ence.*

conform. Both *conform with* and *conform to* are commonly used. But don't use *conform* when *match* will do.

confound, confuse. Both mean to perplex, mix up.

confrere. Commonly spelled without accent.

congeries, congeries. So spelled, singular and plural.

conglomerate. One *m.*

congratulate, congratulation, congratulatory. There's no *d.* Remember "hear*t*fel*t* congra*t*ulations."

Congress. Capitalize when you mean the US Congress. The word *the* is usually left out.

congressional. Capitalize only if part of a title.

Congressional Medal of Honor. Capital *C, M* and *H.*

Congressman, Congresswoman. Capitalize.

congruent, congruence end in *-ent, -ence.*

conifer. One *n.*

conjecture. Don't use *conjecture* when *guess* will do.

conjurer. Spell it with *-er.*

conk out is listed as standard usage in Webster's.

conn-, con-. If you can't find the word you're looking for under *conn-,* try under *con-.*

connectable. Spell it with *-able.*

Connecticut.

connector. Spell it with *-or.*

(connexion). Spelled *connection* in the US.

conniptions. Listed as standard in Webster's.

connivance. Spell it with *-ance.*

connive. Two *n*'s.

connoisseur. A famous spelling demon. Two *n*'s, *oi,* two *s*'s, ends in *-eur.*

connote, denote. *Connote* means suggest or imply, *denote* means signify.

conqueror ends in *-or.*

consanguineous ends in *-eous.*

conscience. Spelled with *sc* and *ie.*

conscientious ends in *-tious.*

conscientiousness, consciousness. *Conscientiousness* means scrupulousn*e*ss, *consciousness* means awareness.

conscious ends in *-scious.*

-conscious. Compounds are hyphened, e.g. *class-conscious.*

consecrator ends in *-or.*

consensus. Spelled with *s* after *con-.* Remember "It makes *sense* to get a consensus." *Consensus of opinion* says the same thing twice—strike out *of opinion.*

consequence, consequent end in *-ence, -ent.* Don't use *consequence* when *result* will do.

consequently. Don't use *consequently* when *so* will do. Don't set it off by commas.

consh-. Try *consci-.*

consider doesn't need *as* in such expressions as *consider it done.*

considerable. Don't use *considerable* when you mean *considerably.* It's dialect, not standard usage.

consistency, consistence. *Consistency* with *y* is the common form of the word.

consistent ends in *-ent.*

consistory ends in *-ory.*

consommé is usually spelled with the accent.

consonant ends in *-ant.*

consortium, consortia. The Latin plural with *a* is common.

conspicuous. Don't forget the *u* before the ending *-ous.*

conspiracy ends in *-acy.*

conspirator ends in *-or.*

constant, constancy end in *-ant, -ancy.*

constellation. Two *l*'s.

constituency, constituent end in *-ency, -ent.*

constitute. Don't use *constitute* when *be* will do.

constitution. Small *c,* except when you refer to the US Constitution.

constitutional. Small *c,* except when part of a title.

constructive criticism. A call for *constructive criticism* always has a ring of hypocrisy. Avoid.

constructor ends in *-or.*

consul, counsel, council. A *consul* is a representative of a foreign country, a *counsel* is a lawyer, a *council* is a group.

consulate. Small *c.*

consulter ends in *-er,* except for the Roman Catholic office of *consultor.*

consummate, consummation. Two *m*'s.

consumption is spelled with *p.*

contact in the sense of *get in touch with* is standard usage.

contagious ends in *-ious.*

contemn, condemn. To *contemn* means to express contempt, to *condemn* means to criticize as bad.

contemplate. Don't use *contemplate* when *plan* will do.

contemporaneous ends in *-eous.*

contemptible, contemptuous. Contemptible (ends in *-ible*) means mean, *contemptuous* means scornful.

contention ends in *-tion*.

contiguous, contiguity. Watch the *u* after the *g*. *Contiguous* means touching along a line or at one point.

continent, continence end in *-ent, -ence*.

continental. Small *c* except when part of a title, e.g. *Continental Congress*.

continual, continuous. *Continual* used to mean intermittent, *continuous* incessant. Now listed in Webster's as interchangeable.

continuum, continua.

contra-. Write all compounds as one word.

contractible ends in *-ible*.

contractions like *don't, hasn't, that's, we'll* are now standard usage in writing.

contractor ends in *-or*.

contractual ends in *-ual*.

contradicter. Spell it with *-er*.

contradistinction, contraindicate, contraindication. One word.

contralto, contraltos.

contraption. Standard usage.

contrariwise. *I* before *w*.

contravention ends in *-tion*.

contretemps. So spelled. The plural is *contretemps* too.

contributor, contributory end in *-or, -ory*.

contrivance ends in *-ance*.

control, controlled, controlling, controller, controllable. One *l* in *control*, two *l*'s in all other forms.

controller. Don't use the old-fashioned form *comptroller*.

controversial ends in *-sial*.

controversy is spelled with *o* before the *v*. Remember "a *controversy over* something."

controvertible ends in *-ible*.

contumacy, contumely. *Contumacy* means stubbornness, *contumely* means scorn.

contusions. Don't say *contusions* when you mean bruises.

conundrum, conundrums. There's no double *n*.

convalesce, convalesced, convalescing, convalescent. Watch the *sc*.

convenience, convenient end in *-ence, ent*.

convenience, earliest. *At your earliest convenience* is a roundabout way of saying *soon*.

convention ends in *-tion*.

conversationalist is the common form. The word *conversationist* is not standard.

converter. Spell it with *-er* in all meanings.

convertible ends in *-ible*.

conveyor. Spell it with *or* in all senses.

convince to, as in *she convinced him to do it,* is listed as standard usage in Webster's.

convincible ends in *-ible*.

convocation is spelled with *c* in the middle even though *convoke* is spelled with *k*.

convolvulus, convolvuluses.

coo, cooed, cooing.

(coockoo). Misspelling of *cuckoo*.

cook-. Spell all compounds as one word.

cookbook, cookhouse. One word.

cookie. Spell it with *-ie*.

cookout, cookstove. One word.

cool, as in *he lost his cool,* is listed as standard usage in Webster's.

coolheaded. One word.

coolie (Oriental laborer). So spelled.

cool it. Listed as standard usage in Webster's.

coolly. Two *o*'s, two *l*'s.

coonskin. One word.

co-op. Hyphened.

cooped-up (modifier). Hyphened.

cooperate, cooperation, cooperative. No hyphen.

cooperate together says the same thing twice. Strike out *together*.

coopt. No hyphen.

coordinate, coordination. No hyphen.

co-owner. Hyphened.

cop (policeman) is listed as standard usage in Webster's, but *cop* (steal) is listed as slang.

cop a plea. Standard usage.

copartner. One word.

cope, without *with,* as in *I can't cope,* is listed as standard usage in Webster's.

copied, copies, copier.

copilot. One word.

copout (noun). One word. Listed as standard usage in Webster's.

copperplate. One word.

copter. No apostrophe.

copy, copies, copied, copying, copier.

copy-. Spell all compounds as one word.

copybook, copycat, copydesk, copyeditor, copyholder, copyhold-ing, copyreader, copyright, copywriter. One word.

coquette (verb and noun), **coquetted, coquetting, coquettish.** Two *t*'s in all forms.

cor-. If you can't find the word you're looking for under *cor-,* try *corr-.*

coral, corral. A *coral* is red, a *corral* means an enclosure.

coralline. Two *l*'s.

coral pink, coral red. Two words.

cord, chord. It's a *cord* for tying things together, a *cord* of wood, an electric *cord,* a vocal *cord,* but it's a musical *chord.* Remember, the *chord* with *h* is the one you *h*ear.

cordially. As a complimentary close of business letters, *Cordially yours* and *Cordially* are in fairly common use. *Sincerely yours, Sincerely, Very truly yours, Yours sincerely, Yours very truly* are the most common forms.

cordovan (leather). Small *c.*

corduroy. The vowel after the *d* is *u.*

cordwood. One word.

core, corps. A *core* is a center, a *corps* is a group.

coreligionist. One word, no hyphen.

(corellate). Misspelling of *correlate.*

(corespond). Misspelling of *correspond.*

corespondent, correspondent. A *corespondent* with one *r* is an adulterer named in a divorce suit, a *correspondent* with two *r*'s is a letter writer.

corgi, corgis.

Corinne. One *r.*

corkscrew. One word.

corn-. Almost all compounds are spelled as one word.

cornball. Listed as standard usage in Webster's.

corn bread. Two words.

corncob, corncrib. One word.

corned beef. Two words.

cornerstone. One word.

cornetist. Spell it with one *t* after the *e.*

cornfed, cornfield, cornflakes, cornhusk, cornhusking, cornmeal. One word.

corn pone. Two words.

cornstalk, cornstarch. One word.

cornucopia, cornucopias. *U* in the middle.

corny, in the sense of trite, old-fashioned, is listed in Webster's as standard usage.

corolla. One *r.*

corollary. One *r,* two *l*'s.

coronary. One *r.*

coronation. One *r.*

coroner. One *r.*

coronet. One *r.*

corporal, corporeal. It's *corporal* punishment, but *corporeal* when you mean tangible, substantial.

corps, as in Corps of Engineers, is pronounced *kore* but spelled with *-ps.*

corpse, with *e* at the end, is pronounced *korps* and means a dead body.

corpsman. One word.

corpulent, corpulence end in *-ent, ence.* Don't use the rare form *corpulency.*

corpuscle. Watch the *sc.*

corpus delicti, corpora delicti. Many people think that *corpus delicti* means the body of a murder victim, but the phrase means the basic fact of any crime, e.g. a breaking and entering.

corr-, cor-. If you can't find the word you're looking for under *corr-,* try *cor-.*

corral, corralled, corralling. Two *l*'s in all forms except the present tense.

correct. Two *r*'s.

correctable ends in *-able.*

correction, corrector, corrective. Two *r*'s.

correlate, correlation, correlative. Two *r*'s.

correspondence ends in *-ence.*

correspondent, corespondent. A *correspondent* is a letter writer, a *corespondent* is an adulterer named in a divorce suit.

corridor. Two *r*'s.

corroborate, corroboration, corroborative. Double *r*'s. Don't use *corroborate* when *confirm* will do.

corrode, corroded, corroding. Two *r*'s.

corrodible ends in *-ible.*

corrosive. Two *r*'s.

corrugated. Two *r*'s.

corrupter. Spell it with *-er.*

corruptible ends in *-ible.*

(corruscate). Misspelling of *coruscate.*

corseted. One *t.*

cortege. Spell it without accent.

cortex, cortices.

coruscate, coruscating. One *r.*

corvette ends in *-ette.*

(cosey). Misspelling of *cozy.*

cosigner. cosponsor. No hyphen.

cosseted. One *t.*

co-star. Hyphened.

costive means constipated.

cost of living. No hyphen except when used as a modifier, e.g. *cost-of-living index.*

costume, custom. *Costume* refers to clothing, *custom* to usage or import duties.

costwise. One word.

(cosy). The common spelling is *cozy.*

cotenant. One word.

coterie ends in *-ie.*

coterminous. One word.

cotillion. One *t,* two *l*'s, ends in *-ion.*

cotrustee. One word.

cotter pin. Two words.

cottonfield, cottongrower. One word.

cotton mill. Two words.

cottonpicker. One word.

cottonpicking, in the sense of *damned,* is listed in Webster's as standard usage. One word.

cottonseed, cottontail. One word.

cough up is listed in Webster's as standard usage.

couldn't. Standard contraction of *could not.*

could've. Contraction of *could have.*

coulee. No accent.

council, counsel. A *council* is a group, a *counsel* is a lawyer.

councilman, councilmanic. One word.

councilor, counselor. A *councilor* is a member of a council, a *counselor* is an adviser. Only one *l* in each word.

councilwoman. One word.

counsel, counseled, counseling, counselor. One *l* in all forms.

countdown. One word.

countenance ends in *-ance*.

counter-. Spell all compounds as one word.

counteract, counteralliance, counterargument, counterattack, counterbalance, counterchange, countercharge. One word.

countercheck, counter check. Spell as one word when you mean counteract, but as two words when you mean a bank check.

counterclaim, counterclockwise, countercoup, counterculture, countercurrent, counterdemonstration, counterespionage, counterexample. One word.

counterfeit. Spelled with *ei*.

counterforce, counterguerrilla, counterinsurgency, counterintelligence, counterirritant, countermarch, countermeasure, countermove, counteroffense, counteroffer, counterpart, counterplan, counterplot, counterpoint, counterproductive, counterprogramming, counterpropaganda, counterproposal, counterreformation, counterrevolution, counterrevolutionary, counterspy, counterterrorism, countertrend, counterview. One word.

countinghouse. One word.

countrified. Spell it with *i* after *r*.

country-. Most compounds are spelled as one word.

country-born, country-bred. Hyphened.

country club. Two words.

countryman, countryseat, countryside, countrywide, countrywoman. One word.

county seat. Two words.

countywide. One word.

coup, coups.

coup de grace, coups de grace. Spell it without accent.

coup d'etat, coups d'etat. Spell it without accent.

coupe. Spell it without accent.

couple of, in the sense of a few, is listed as standard usage in Webster's.

coupon is spelled with *ou*.

courageous ends in *-eous*.

course, coarse. It's *coarse* when you mean rough, crude. Otherwise spell it *course*.

court-. Almost all compounds are spelled as one word.

courteous begins with *court-* and ends with *-eous*.

courtesan ends in *-san*.

courtesy, curtsy. *Courtesy* means politeness, a *curtsy* means a bow.

courthouse. One word.

court-martial, courts-martial. Hyphened.

Court of St. James's. The British court.

courtplaster, courtroom, courtyard. One word.

cousin-german, cousins-german. Hyphened.

couturiere. No accent.

covenanter, covenantor. Spell it ordinarily with *-er* but with *-or* as a legal term. Capital *C* when you mean Scottish history.

coveralls, coverup. One word.

covet, coveted, coveting, covetous. One *t* in all forms.

covey, coveys.

cow-. Spell all compounds except for *cow-eyed* and *cow pony* as one word.

cowbarn, cowbell, cowboy, cowcatcher. One word.

cow-eyed. Hyphened.

cowgirl, cowhand, cowherd, cowhide, cowlick. One word.

co-worker. Hyphened.

cowpath. One word.

cow pony. Two words.

cowpuncher. One word.

cowrie shell. Spell with *-ie.*

cowshed, cowtail. One word.

coxcomb. Spelled with *x.*

coxswain. So spelled even though pronounced *koxn.*

coy, coyer, coyest, coyly, coyness.

coyote ends in *-ote.*

cozy, cozier, coziest, cozily, coziness. Spell all forms with *z.*

CPA. No periods necessary.

cr-. If you can't find the word you're looking for under *cr-,* try *chr-.*

crabgrass, crabmeat, crabwise. One word.

crack-. Spell all compounds as one word.

(crackajack). The spelling *crackerjack* is more common.

crackbrained, crackdown, crackerjack, crackpot, crackup (noun). One word. All listed in Webster's as standard usage.

cradlesong. One word.

cranberry.

crank. Listed in Webster's as standard usage in all senses (eccentric, grouch etc.).

crankcase, crankshaft. One word.

cranky. Standard usage.

crape, crepe. Write *crape* with *a* when you mean mourning, otherwise spell it *crepe*.

crapehanger. One word.

crappy. Listed as slang in Webster's.

crapshooter. One word.

crash dive (noun), **crash-dive** (verb). Two words as a noun, hyphenated as a verb.

crash-land (verb). Hyphenated.

crash landing. Two words.

cravenness. Two *n*'s.

crawfish, crayfish. Both variants are common.

craziness. Spelled with *i.*

crazy quilt. Two words.

creak, creek. *Creak* refers to sound, *creek* is a small stream.

cream cheese, cream puff, cream soda. Two words.

crèche. Spelled with the accent.

credence ends in *-ence.*

credible ends in *-ible.*

credo, credos.

credulous, credible, creditable. *Credulous* means willing to believe, *credible* means believable, *creditable* means creditworthy.

creep, as in *he is a creep* or *he gives me the creeps,* is listed as standard usage in Webster's.

crème. Spell it with the accent.

crenel, creneled, creneling. One *l* in all forms.

crenelate, crenelated, crenelating, crenelation. One *l* in all forms.

crepe, crepe de chine, crepe paper, crepe suzette. No accent.

crescendo, crescendos. Spelled with *sc.*

crescent. Spelled with *sc.*

crestfallen. One word.

cretin. The vowels are *e* and *i.*

cretonne. One *t,* two *n*'s.

crevasse, crevice. A *crevice* is a small crack or fissure, a *crevasse* is a deep cleft in a glacier or levee.

crew cut, crew neck. Two words.

crier, as in *town crier,* is spelled with *-ier.*

crimebuster, crimebusting. One word.

crime wave. Two words.

crisis, crises.

crisp, crispy. Both variants are standard usage.

crisscross. One word.

criterion, criteria.

critical, as in *his condition is critical,* is standard usage.

criticize ends in *-ize.*

critique. So spelled. Don't use the verb or noun *critique* when *review* will do.

croak, meaning to die, is slang.

crochet, crocheted, crocheting.

(crochety). Misspelling of *crotchety.*

crocus, crocuses.

crony, cronyism.

(croop). Misspelling of *croup.*

croquet, croquette. *Croquet* is the game, *croquette* is the fried food.

cross-. There's no general rule for compounds with *cross-.*

crossbar, crossbeam, crossbearer. One word.

cross-bill (law). Hyphened.

crossbones, crossbow, crossbred, crossbreed. One word.

cross-check, cross-country, cross-cultural. Hyphened.

crosscurrent, crosscut. One word.

cross-examination, cross-examine, cross-examiner, cross-eyed, cross-fertilization, cross-fertilize, cross-file. Hyphened.

cross fire. Two words.

cross-grained. Hyphened.

cross-hair. Two words.

crosshatch, crosshatching, crosshead, crosshaul. One word.

cross-index, cross-legged, cross-link, cross-national. Hyphened.

crossover (noun), **crosspatch, crosspiece.** One word.

cross-pollinate, cross-pollination, cross-purpose, cross-question, cross-refer, cross-reference. Hyphened.

crossroad. One word.

cross section. Two words.

cross-stitch. Hyphened.

crosstalk, crosstown, crosswalk, crossway, crosswise, crossword. One word.

crotchety is spelled with *tch.*

croup is spelled with *ou.*

croupier ends in *-ier.*

croupy. Spelled with *ou.*

crouton. Spelled with *ou.*

crowbar. One word.

crow's-feet. Spelled with apostrophe and hyphen.

cruel, crueler, cruelest, cruelly, cruelty. Spell only *cruelly* with double *l,* all other words with single *l.*

cruise, cruse. A *cruise* is a voyage, a *cruse* is a jar.

crummy is the common spelling (no *b*). Listed in Webster's as standard usage meaning wretched, cheap, worthless.

crustacean ends in *-ean.*

crux, cruxes.

cruzeiro, cruzeiros. Brazilian currency, so spelled.

crybaby. One word.

crypt-, crypto-. Spell all compounds as one word, except for compounds with proper nouns, e.g. *crypto-Communist.*

cryptic. Spelled with *y.*

(crysanthemum). Misspelling of *chrysanthemum.*

crystal. One *l,* starts with *cr.*

crystal ball. Two words.

crystal-clear. Hyphened.

crystal gazing. Two words.

crystalline, crystallize. Two *l*'s.

C-sharp. Capital *C* and hyphen.

cubbyhole. One word.

cubmaster. One word.

cub scout. Two words.

cuckoo. The first vowel is a *u.*

cudgel, cudgeled, cudgeling. One *l* in all forms.

cue, queue. Spell it *cue* in all senses except braid. In England people *queue* up, but in America they *stand in* (or *on*) *line.* The verb forms are *cue, cued, cuing* and *queue, queued, queuing.*

cuff links. Two words.

cui bono is Latin and means *who stood to gain from this?* No hyphen.

cuisine.

cul-de-sac, culs-de-sac.

culinary ends in *-ary.* Don't use *culinary* where *kitchen* or *cooking* will do.

culpable ends in *-able.*

cum is Latin and means *with.* Always used with two hyphens, e.g. *breakfast-cum-work.* Don't use *cum* where *and* will do.

cumbrous. No *e.*

cummerbund. Two *m*'s.

cumulus, cumuli.

cuneiform. Spelled with *ei*.

cupbearer, cupboard, cupcake. One word.

cupful, cupfuls.

cup hook. Two words.

curaçao. Always spelled with a cedilla under the second *c*.

curator ends in *-or*.

curb, kerb. Spell it *curb* in all senses.

curbstone. One word.

cure-all. Hyphened.

curette, curetted, curetting, curettage. Double *t* in all forms.

curio, curios.

curlicue. Spell it with *i*.

curly. No *e*.

curlyhead, curlylocks, curlytop. One word.

curmudgeon ends in *-dgeon*.

currant, current. A *currant* is a fruit, a *current* flows.

currency is spelled with *e*.

currently. Don't use *currently* where *now* will do.

curriculum, curriculums or curricula. The plural *curriculums* is the only one listed in the GPO Style Manual and the New York Times Manual of Style and Usage.

currycomb. One word.

curtain ends in *-ain*.

curtain call, curtain lecture, curtain raiser. Two words.

curtsy, courtesy. A *curtsy* means a bow, *courtesy* means politeness. Spell *curtsy* without *e*.

curvaceous ends in *-eous*.

cushion is spelled with *sh* and *i*.

custody. The vowel after *t* is *o*.

custom, costume. *Custom* refers to usage or import duties, *costume* refers to clothing.

customary ends in *-ary*. Don't use *customary* when *usual* will do.

custom-built. Hyphen.

customer. A *customer* buys goods or general services, a *client* buys professional services from a lawyer, accountant or consultant.

customhouse. One word.

custom-made, custom-tailored. Hyphened.

cut-. Most compounds are spelled as one word.

cut-and-dried. Two hyphens.

cutaway, cutback, cutdown. One word.

cute. Listed as standard usage in Webster's.

cutesy. Listed as standard usage in Webster's.

cut glass. Two words.

cut-in (noun, adjective). Hyphened.

cutlass. Spell it with double *s.*

cutoff, cutout, cutover. One word.

cut-rate. Hyphened.

cutthroat. One word.

cutup. One word.

cyano-. Spell all compounds as one word.

cyclamen ends in *-en.*

cycle, cycled, cycling.

cyclo-. Spell all compounds as one word.

cyclopedia, cyclopedic. Spell with *e.*

cygnet. Spelled with *cy.*

cylinder, cylindrical. The *y* comes first.

cymbal, symbol. *Cymbals* make a clashing sound, *symbols* are signs.

cynic, cynical. Use *cynic* for the noun, *cynical* for the adjective.

cynosure starts with *cy,* ends in *-sure.*

(cypher). Spell it *cipher.*

cypress, Cyprus. *Cypress* is the tree, *Cyprus* is the island.

Cypriot. Spell it without an *e* at the end.

cyst. Spelled with *y.*

czar, czarevitch, czarevna, czarina. These are the commonly used spellings.

czardas. Spelling of the Hungarian dance. The plural is also *czardas.*

Czech, Czechoslovak, Czechoslovakia, Commonly used spellings.

D

-d, -dd-. A *d* at the end of a one-syllable word is doubled before the suffixes *-ed, -er, -ing, -able, -y, -ie, -en, -est, -ish* etc. if there's only one vowel before the *d*. Examples: *wed, wedded; plod, plodder; bed, bedding; bid, biddable; mud, muddy; glad, gladden; red, reddest; fad, faddish.* The same rule applies to two-syllable words ending in *d* and accented on the second syllable, e.g. *embed, embedded; forbid, forbidding.*

'd. Contraction of *had* or *would,* e.g. *he'd said so, they'd return later.*

d'. In names, the French or Italian preposition *d'* is usually lower-cased in foreign names, e.g. *Jean d'Alembert,* but capitalized in English and American names, e.g. *Isaac D'Israeli.*

da. Spelled with a small *d* in such foreign names as *Leonardo da Vinci.*

DA. Abbreviation of *district attorney.* No periods necessary.

dab, in the sense of fingerprint, is slang.

dachshund, dachshunds. This spelling demon is spelled with *chsh* and no *o.*

Dacron is a trademark and should be capitalized.

(daemon). Spell it *demon.*

daffodil. Two *f*'s.

daguerreotype. A spelling bee word. It's *-rre-* before the *o.*

dahlia. Watch the *h.*

daiquiri has three *i*'s.

dairy, diary. A *dairy* has to do with milk, butter and cheese, a *diary* is a journal.

dairy farm. Two words.

dairymaid, dairyman. One word.

dais is spelled with *-ais.*

dally, dallied, dallying.

Dalmatian. Capital *D*, ends in -*tian*.

damageable ends in -*eable*.

damask ends in -*k*.

dammed, damned. *Dammed* means blocked, *damned* means condemned.

damnedest. Standard usage, so spelled.

damsel. Spell it without *o*.

damsite. One word.

dance hall. Two words.

dandelion. *E* in the middle.

Dandie Dinmont. Spelled with two capital *D*'s and -*ie*.

danger line, danger point. Two words.

dangling words and phrases. A classic example of a dangling phrase appeared in Life magazine after President Kennedy's assassination: "Mr. Zapruder, filming the Presidential motorcade, recorded the exact instant the President was shot. *Then, sobbing, his fingers slipped from the camera.*"

The word *sobbing* in the second sentence is a dangling participle. What the writer meant was that Mr. Zapruder was sobbing. But what he wrote, by letting the participle dangle, was that his fingers were.

This kind of construction is extremely common in writing. Sometimes it wrecks the sentence, as in the *sobbing* example. Sometimes it's completely harmless and fully established, as in *speaking of Mary, I saw her at the supermarket the other day*. Sometimes it's just slightly awkward, as in *once known as an "Uncle Tom," his career is over*.

So be careful. It may comfort you to know that many great writers occasionally wrote dangling phrases. Lord Byron wrote "Awakening with a start, the waters heave around me."

daredevil, daredeviltry, daresay. One word.

Dark Ages. Two words, both capitalized.

dark-eyed, dark-haired. Hyphened.

dark horse. Two words.

darkroom. One word.

dash. Use a dash to mark a sudden shift in the sentence, e.g. *It all started because of Hitler—but of course you know all about that.* Or use two dashes to mark a parenthesis where two commas wouldn't be enough, e.g. *The afternoon TV audience—children doing their homework, housewives doing nothing in particular, hospital patients fighting boredom—watched it with a minimum* *of interest.* Or use a dash to set off a summarizing, amplifying or explanatory statement, e.g. *The result was easy to predict— it was a complete flop.—Wine, women and song—this was the sum total of his aims in life.* Or use a dash to mark an unfinished sentence, e.g. *Well, I'll be—.*

Use two hyphens to write a dash on the typewriter. Use no space before or after it.

Don't use a dash together with a comma, semicolon or colon.

dashboard. One word.

data. Webster's lists the use of *data* with a singular verb (e.g. *the data is plentiful*) as standard usage. Of course you can also use *data* with a plural verb. Write it the way it comes naturally to you.

datable ends in *-able.*

date, in the sense of *person of the opposite sex with whom one has a social engagement* is standard usage.

dateline. One word.

dates. The standard American form is *March 7, 1974* with a comma between the day of the month and the year. The form *7 March 1974* is military and British usage. If you don't give the day of the month, use no comma, e.g. *March 1974.*

datum. The regular plural is *data* (which can also be used as a singular) but in surveying and engineering the plural *datums* is common.

daughter-in-law, daughters-in-law. Spelled with two hyphens.

day-. Most compounds are spelled as one word.

daybed, daybook, daybreak. One word.

day-care (adjective). Hyphened.

day coach. Two words.

daydream, daydreamer, daydreaming. One word.

day in court. Three separate words.

day laborer, day letter. Two words.

daylight. One word.

daylight saving time. Three separate words.

daylong. One word.

day nurse, day nursery. Two words.

day room, day school, day student. Two words.

daytime, daywork. One word.

-dd-. See -D, -DD-.

D-day. Capital *D* and hyphen.

de. In names, the French preposition *de* is usually lowercased in foreign names, e.g. *Charles de Gaulle,* but capitalized in American names, e.g. *Cecil B. De Mille.*

de-. Spell all compounds as one word except when *de-* is prefixed to a word beginning with *e,* e.g. *de-emphasize.*

Don't form or use words with *de-* that can't be found in a desk dictionary, like *deideologize* or *detrivialization.* Stick to the common way of expressing your thought.

deactivate. One word.

dead-. Compounds are spelled as one word, two words or with a hyphen.

deadbeat. One word.

dead center, dead end. Two words.

deadfall, deadhead. One word.

dead heat, dead horse, dead letter. Two words.

deadlight, deadline, deadlock, deadpan. One word.

dead set. Two words.

deadweight, deadwood. One word.

deaerate, deaeration. Spelled with *eae.*

deaf-mute, deaf-muteness. Hyphened.

deal in the sense of transaction or bargain is listed in Webster's as standard usage.

dealt is spelled with *ea.*

Dear, My dear. The standard salutation is *Dear (Mr. Smith). My dear* is more formal and rarely used. In England *My dear* is considered less formal than *Dear.*

Dear Madam, Dear Sir. Don't use these salutations when you know the addressee's name. It's a slight discourtesy.

(Dear Sirs). The standard salutation in letters to business firms and organizations is *Gentlemen.*

dearth. Don't use *dearth* where *little* will do, e.g. *there is a dearth of information* instead of *there is little information.*

deary is more common than *dearie.*

deathbed. One word.

death benefit. Two words.

deathblow. One word.

death-dealing, death-defying. Hyphened.

death house, death knell. Two words.

deathlike. One word.

death mask, death rate, death rattle. Two words.

death's-head. Apostrophe, *s,* hyphen.

deathtrap, deathwatch. One word.

deb, short for *debutante,* is listed in Webster's as standard usage.

debacle. No accent.

debark, debarkation are shorter variants of *disembark, disembarkation.* They're standard usage.

debatable. No *e* after the *t.*

debate. You debate a question, you don't *debate about* a question.

debater ends in *-er.*

debonair. Spell without *e* at the end.

debrief means to interrogate someone *after* he's returned from a mission. *Before* the mission he is *briefed.*

debris. Spell it without accent.

debug. Listed as standard usage in Webster's.

debunk, debunker. Listed as standard usage in Webster's.

debut, debutant, debutante. Spell without accent.

deca-, deci-. The prefix *deca-* means ten times, the prefix *deci-* means one-tenth.

decades. Don't spell out four-digit historical decades, but use figures, e.g. *the 1970s* (without apostrophe). But two-digit decades are commonly either spelled out, e.g. *the seventies,* or written as figures, e.g. *the 70s* (without an apostrophe in front of or before the *s*).

Decalogue. Spell it with a capital *D* and *-ue.*

decanter ends in *-er.*

deceit, deceitful, deceive. These words follow the rule "*i* before *e* except after *c.*"

decent is spelled with *c.*

deci-, deca-. *Deci-* means one-tenth, *deca-* means ten times.

decibel ends in *-bel.* Named after Alexander Graham Bell.

decide is spelled with a *c.*

deciduous ends in *-uous.*

decimate now means destroy a large part of. Originally it meant to kill every tenth man, but there's no point in going back to the ancient Romans for the meaning of a word.

decision, decisive. Start with *dec-.*

deck chair. Two words.

deckhand, deckhouse. One word.

declare. Don't use *declare* when *say* will do.

déclassé. Two accents.

declension ends in *-sion.*

decolletage, decolleté. The first is a noun and means a low neckline, the second is an adjective and means with a low neckline.

Spell both words without an accent on the first *e,* but keep the accent on the last *é* of *decolleté.*

decor. Spell it without accent.

decorator ends in *-or.*

decoupage. Spell it without accent.

decreed, decreer. There's never a triple *e* in English.

decrescendo, decrescendos. Spelled with *sc.*

decry, descry. *Decry* means disparage, *descry* means detect. Often confused, so you'd better stay away from both words.

deduce, deduct. *Deduce* means infer, *deduct* means subtract.

deducible ends in *-ible.*

deductible ends in *-ible.*

deejay (for *disk jockey*) is listed in Webster's as standard usage.

deem. Don't use *deem* when *think* will do.

de-emphasize ends in *-ize.* It's one of the few words with *de-* that is hyphened.

-deep. Words ending in *-deep* are hyphened, e.g. *ankle-deep, knee-deep.*

deep-. Most compounds are hyphened.

deep-dish, deep-freeze, deep-freezing, deep-going, deep-rooted, deep-sea, deep-seated. All hyphened.

deep-six is listed in Webster's as slang.

deepwater. One word.

deerskin, deerstalker. One word.

de-escalate, de-escalation. Hyphened.

de facto. Never hyphened.

defective, deficient. *Defective* implies a flaw or imperfection, *deficient* implies a lack or shortcoming.

defendant ends in *-ant.*

defense. The American spelling ends in *-se.*

defensible ends in *-ible.*

defer, deferred, deferring. You *defer* to someone else, you *delay* until some other time.

deference. One *r.*

deferrable. Two *r*'s, ends in *-able.*

deferred means postponed.

defiance, defiant end in *-ance, -ant.*

deficiency. Don't use *deficiency* when *lack* will do.

deficient, defective. *Deficient* implies a lack or shortcoming, *defective* implies a flaw or imperfection.

defier. So spelled.

definable ends in *-able*.

definite, definitive. *Definite* means clear, precise, *definitive* means final, complete. Watch the *i* before the *t* in *definite*. Remember "that's definitely *it.*"

deflection. The American spelling is with *ct*.

defy, defied, defying.

dégagé. Two accents.

degree-day. Hyphened.

deice, deicer. Spell it without a hyphen.

deign is spelled with *-eign*.

déjà vu. Spell it with both accents.

de jure. Never hyphened.

delay, defer. You *delay* until later, you *defer* to someone else.

delectable ends in *-able*.

delegate. *E* after the *l*.

deleterious. *E* after *l*, ends in *-ious*. Don't use *deleterious* when *harmful* will do.

deli, short for *delicatessen,* is listed in Webster's as standard usage.

delicacy ends in *-cy*.

delicatessen.

delicious ends in *-cious*. Now standard usage for things other than food.

delimitate can always be shortened to *delimit*.

deliquesce, deliquescent. Spelled with *sc*.

deliverance ends in *-ance*.

deliveryman. One word.

delusion, illusion. A *delusion* comes from a state of mind, an *illusion* from a deceptive appearance.

deluxe. One word.

demagogic. No *u* before *-ic*.

demagogue, demagoguery. Common spellings.

demarcation. Commonly spelled with *c*.

demean in the sense of degrade or debase is standard usage.

demeanor ends in *-or*.

demesne is spelled with *es*.

demi-. Spell compounds as one word, except for words like *demi-Christian, demi-incognito*.

demigod, demijohn, demimondaine, demimonde, demirelievo, demirep. One word.

demise. Don't use *demise* when *death* or *lease* will do.

demitasse. One word.

demo, demos. *Demo,* short for *demonstration* or *demonstrator,* is listed in Webster's as standard usage.

democracy ends in *-acy.*

demon. Spell it with *e* (not *ae*).

demoniac, demoniacal. Both forms are common, but in the sense of fiendish the more common form is *demoniacal.*

demonstrable ends in *-able.*

demonstrate. Don't use *demonstrate* when *show* will do.

demoralize, demoralization. Spelled with *z.*

demote is standard usage.

demur, demurred, demurring, demurrage, demurral, demurrer. Double *r* in all forms except *demur.*

dengue ends in *-ue.*

deniable ends in *-able.*

denominator ends in *-or.* (Below the line.)

denote, connote. *Denote* means signify, *connote* means suggest or imply.

denouement. Spell it without accent.

de novo. Never hyphened.

dentifrice.

denunciation. No *o* after the first *n.*

deny, denies, denied, denying, deniable.

deodorant ends in *-ant.*

deodorize ends in *-ize.*

department store. Never hyphened.

dependable ends in *-able.*

dependence, dependency, dependent. Spell these words with *-ence, -ency, -ent.* Memorize "take your depen*dent*s to your *dent*ist once a year."

depilatory ends in *-ory.*

deplorable ends in *-able.*

depositor ends in *-or.*

deprecate, depreciate. Conservative grammarians insist that *deprecate* means disapprove and you should use *depreciate* when you mean disparage. But everybody uses *deprecate* in both senses and Webster's lists *deprecate* in the sense of disparage as standard usage. It quotes the English writer Robert Graves, "He insisted that he was merely a private citizen and *deprecated* any public honors paid to him."

depth charge. No hyphen.

deputize ends in *-ize.*

deputy. No hyphen in *deputy commissioner, deputy mayor* etc.

Derby, derby. Capitalize when you mean a specific race like the Kentucky Derby, but use a small *d* when you mean a race or a hat.

derelict. *E* after the *r*.

de rigueur. Two words.

derisive, derisory. Commonly *derisive* is used to mean mocking, *derisory* to mean ridiculous.

derivative. *A* after the first *v*.

derogatory ends in *-ory*.

derriere. Spell it without accent.

derring-do. Double *r* and hyphen.

des-. If you can't find the word you're looking for, try under *dis-*.

descend. Watch the *sc*.

descendant. Spell both noun and adjective with *-ant*. Memorize "We are all descend*a*nts of *A*dam."

descent is spelled with *sc*.

describable ends in *-able*.

describe, description start with *desc-*. To remind yourself, think of writing a *description* sitting at a *desk*.

descry, decry. *Descry* means detect, *decry* means disparage. The two words are often confused, so you'd better stay away from them.

desecrater. Spell it with *-er*.

desert, dessert. Spell it with double *s* when you mean the sweet course at the end of a meal. In all other senses spell it *desert*. Remember that a *dessert* with two *s*'s is "*s*weet and *s*ugary."

deserter ends in *-er*.

deshabille. No accent. The more common form is *dishabille* with *i*.

desiccated. One *s*, two *c*'s.

desiderate. Don't use *desiderate* when *want* or *wish* will do.

desideratum, desiderata.

designate. Don't use *designate* when *name* will do.

-designate. Hyphened as a suffix, e.g. *the Secretary-designate*.

desirable ends in *-able*. There's no *e* after the *r*.

desire. Don't use *desire* when *want* or *wish* will do.

desist. Don't use *desist* when *stop* will do.

deskbook, deskman, deskwork. One word.

desolate, desolation. One *s*.

despair starts with *des-*. Remember when you're *despairing*, you're *desperate*.

(despatch). The common spelling is *dispatch* with an *i*.

desperado, desperadoes.

desperate, desperation. Two *e*'s, after the *d* and after the *p*.

despicable ends in *-able*.

despise ends in *-ise*.

despite the fact that. Don't use this phrase when *although* or *though* will do.

despoil starts with *des-*.

despondent, despondency end in *-ent, -ency*.

dessert, desert. Spell it with double *s* when you mean the sweet course at the end of a meal. In all other senses spell it *desert*. Remember that a *dessert* with two *s*'s is "*s*weet and *s*ugary."

dessert fork, dessert knife. Two words.

dessertspoon, dessertspoonful. One word.

dessert wine. Two words.

destroy, destroyed, destroying, destroyer.

destructible ends in *-ible*.

destruction starts with *des-*.

desuetude is spelled with *sue* in it.

desultory ends in *-ory*.

detail man. Two words.

detectable ends in *-able*.

détente. Spell with accent.

detention ends in *-tion*.

deter, deterred, deterring, deterrent. Two *r*'s in all forms except *deter*.

detergent is spelled with three *e*'s. ·

deteriorate. Don't use *deteriorate* when *get worse* or *worsen* will do.

determinative. Don't use *be determinative of* when *fix, find, settle, decide* etc. will do.

determine. Don't use *determine* when *fix, find, settle, decide* etc. will do.

deterrence, deterrent. Two *r*'s. The words end in *-ence, -ent*.

detestable ends in *-able*.

detour. No accent.

detractor ends in *-or*.

detrimental. Don't use *detrimental* when *harmful* will do.

detritus ends in *-us*.

deuce is spelled with *eu*.

deus ex machina. So spelled; never hyphened.

Deuteronomy is spelled with *eu*.

deutsche mark. Currency of West Germany. Spell with small *d* and small *m*. Abbreviation: *DM*.

development. No *e* after the *p*. Don't use *development* when *growth* will do.

device, devise. A *device* is a contrivance, to *devise* means to form. *Devise* ends in *-ise*. Don't use *devise* when *give* will do.

deviser, devisor. A *deviser* with *-er* is anyone who devises, a *devisor* with *-or* is someone who devises property in a will.

devotee is spelled with double *e*.

dewdrop, dewlap, dewlapped. One word.

dew point. Two words.

dewy, dewier, dewiest.

dexterous is more common than *dextrous*.

dextro-. Spell compounds as one word.

di, The Italian preposition *di* is usually lowercased in foreign names, e.g. *Salvatore di Giacomo,* but capitalized in English and American names like *Joe Di Maggio.*

diabetes ends in *-es.*

diacritical marks. See ACCENTS.

(diaeresis). The form *dieresis* is more common.

diagnosis, diagnoses.

diagram, diagramed, diagraming, diagrammatic. Spell all forms with one *m* except *diagrammatic.*

dial, dialed, dialing. One *l* in all forms.

dialogue. Spell it with *-gue.*

dialysis, dialytic, dialyze. *Y* after the *l.*

diametrically ends in *-ally.*

diamondback. One word.

diaper. Don't leave out the *a.*

diaphanous. *A* after *ph.*

diaphragm. Watch the silent *g.*

diarrhea is now the common spelling. Watch the *rrh.*

diary, dairy. A *diary* is a journal, a *dairy* has to do with milk, butter and cheese. "In a diary the *I* comes first."

dice box, dice cup, dice play. Two words.

dicey, dicier, diciest. Listed as standard usage in Webster's.

dichotomy is spelled with *ch.*

dickey. Spell it with *-ey.*

dictator ends in *-or.*

dictionary ends in *-ary.*

dictum, dicta.

didn't. Common contraction of *did not.*

dido, didoes.

die, died, dies, dying. Only *dying* (no *e*) has a *y.*

die from is listed in Webster's as a standard idiom. So is *die of.*

diehard. One word.

dieresis. A *dieresis* means the two dots placed over a vowel to show it's pronounced as a separate syllable, e.g. *naïve, preëminent.* Diereses are no longer commonly used. The common forms now are *naive, preeminent.*

diesel engine, diesel fuel. Small *d.*

dietitian. Ends in *-tian* like the painter Titian. The spelling is whimsical but standard.

difference ends in *-ence.*

different than is now standard usage. The idiom has been used by such classic English writers as Samuel Richardson ("A very different Pamela than I used to leave all company and pleasure for") and Oliver Goldsmith ("Elected for very different merits than those of skill in war.").

diffidence, diffident end in *-ence, -ent.*

diffuser ends in *-er.*

diffusible ends in *-ible.*

dig, dug, dug.

digester ends in *-er.*

digestible ends in *-ible.*

dignitary ends in *-ary.*

dike is spelled with *i.*

dilapidated starts with *di-.*

dilatory ends in *-ory.*

dilemma. One *l,* two *m*'s. A *dilemma* originally meant a difficult choice between two alternatives, but the use of the word for a general difficulty or problem is now standard usage.

dilettante, dilettantes. One *l,* two *t*'s.

diligent, diligence end in *-ent, -ence.*

dillydally, dillydallied, dillydallying.

dimension. *I* after *d,* ends in *-ension.*

dime's worth. No hyphen.

diminuendo, diminuendos.

diminution. The vowels are *i—i—u—io.*

dimout. One word.

dimwit. One word.

dim-witted. Hyphened.

dinar, dinars. Currency of Yugoslavia, Iraq etc.

diner-out, diners-out.

dinette ends in *-ette.*

dingbat, dingdong. One word.

dinghy, dingy. A *dinghy* is a boat, *dingy* means shabby.

dinginess. The *y* changes to *i.*

dining car, dining hall, dining room. Two words.

dinner bell, dinner dance, dinner hour, dinner jacket. Two words.

dinnertime, dinnerware. One word.

diocese, diocesan.

diphtheria. Watch the *h* after the *p.*

diphthong. Watch the *h* after the *p.*

dipstick. One word.

director ends in *-or.*

dirigible ends in *-ible.*

dirndl. No *e.*

dirt-cheap. Hyphened.

dirt farmer, dirt road. Two words.

dirty work. Two words.

dis-. If you can't find the word you're looking for under *dis-,* try *diss-* or *dys-.* All words starting with the prefix *dis-* are spelled as one word.

   Don't form or use words with *dis-* that can't be found in a desk dictionary, like *disenjoy, disenable* or *disenthusiastic.* Stick to the common way of expressing your thoughts.

disagree, disagreeable, disagreement. One *g.*

(disapate). Misspelling of *dissipate.*

disappear, disappearance. One *s—dis* plus *appear, appearance.*

disappoint, disappointed, disappointment. One *s—dis* plus *appoint, appointed, appointment.*

disapprove, disapproval. One *s—dis* plus *approve, approval.*

disarmament has *mam* in it.

disarray. One *s—dis* plus *array.*

disassemble. First one *s,* then two—*dis* plus *assemble.*

disassociate, dissociate. Both words mean exactly the same thing and *dissociate* is one syllable shorter. But *disassociate* is commonly used and perhaps more emphatic.

disastrous. No *e* between the *t* and the *r.*

disbar, disbarred, disbarring, disbarment. One *r* in *disbar* and *disbarment.*

disbelief, disbeliefs.

disc, disk. *Disk* with *k* is now the more common spelling in all senses, including *slipped disk* and *disk jockey.* This is the style of most newspapers, the New York Times Manual of Style and Usage, the GPO Style Manual and Webster's.

discern. Spelled with *sc.*

discernible ends in *-ible.*

disciple. Watch the *sc.*

discipline, disciplinary, disciplinarian. All spelled with *sc. Disciplinary* ends in *-ary.*

(disc jockey). Spell it *disk jockey.*

disclose. Don't use *disclose* when *show* will do.

discombobulate. *U* after the second *b.*

discomfit, discomfited, discomfiting, discomfiture. One *t* in all forms. Because *discomfit* sounds so much like *discomfort,* most people use *discomfit* and *discomfiture* in the sense of mild perplexity or embarrassment. Originally *discomfit* meant to overwhelm or utterly defeat, but that meaning is now rare.

discontinue. Don't use *discontinue* when *stop* will do.

discotheque. So spelled. No accent.

discountenance ends in *-ance.*

discourageable ends in *-eable.*

discourteous ends in *-eous.*

discourtesy ends in *-esy.*

discover, invent. To *discover* means to find something that's there, to *invent* means to think up something new.

discreditable ends in *-able.*

discreet, discrete. *Discreet* with double *e* means prudent, quiet, able to keep a secret. *Discrete,* ending in *-ete,* means distinct, separate.

discretionary ends in *-ary.*

(discribe). Misspelling of *describe.*

discriminatory ends in *-ory.*

(discription). Misspelling of *description.*

discus, discuses.

discussable. Spell it with *-able.*

discuss about. Leave out *about.* You discuss an issue, not about an issue.

disease. Remember it's *dis-* plus *ease.*

(disect). Misspelling of *dissect.*

disembark, disembarkation. Common forms. *Debark* and *debarkation* are rare.

disenfranchise, disenfranchisement. The shorter forms *disfranchise* and *disfranchisement* are also common, but *disenfranchise* and *disenfranchisement* are more emphatic.

disengageable ends in *-eable.*

disentangle. One *s.*

disequilibrium. Don't use *disequilibrium* when *imbalance* will do.

disfavor ends in *-or.*

disfranchise, disfranchisement. See DISENFRANCHISE.

(disfunction). Misspelling of *dysfunction.*

disgruntle, disgruntled, disgruntling, disgruntlement are all standard usage.

disguise ends in *-ise.*

dishabille. Spell it like this. No accent.

dishboard, dishcloth. One word.

dishevel, disheveled, disheveling, dishevelment. One *l* in all forms.

dishonor, dishonorable. Spelled with *-or.*

dishpan, dishrag. One word.

dish towel. Two words.

dishwasher, dishwashing, dishwater. One word.

disillusioned. One *s—dis* plus *illusioned.*

disingenuous. Watch the *u* before *-ous.*

disintegrate. One *s—dis* plus *integrate.*

disinterest, disinterested. Listed as standard usage in Webster's and the Oxford English Dictionary in the sense of lack of interest, uninterested. *Disinterested* has been so used since 1612, *disinterest* since 1889.

disk, disc. Disk with *k* is now the more common spelling in all senses, including *slipped disk* and *disk jockey.* This is the style of most newspapers, the New York Times Manual of Style and Usage, the GPO Style Manual and Webster's.

disk jockey. Two words.

dislodgment. No *e* after the *g.*

dismissible ends in *-ible.*

disobedience, disobedient end in *-ence, -ent.*

(disorientate). Use the shorter word *disorient.*

(dispair). Misspelling of *despair.*

disparate means distinct, *desperate* means in despair.

dispatch, despatch. *Dispatch* with an *i* is the more common spelling.

dispatcher, despatcher. The spelling with *i* is more common.

dispel, dispelled, dispelling. Double *l* in all forms except *dispel.*

dispensable ends in *-able.*

dispensary ends in *-ary.*

dispense. Don't use *dispense* when *give out* will do.

dispenser ends in *-er.*

display. Don't use *display* when *show* will do.

dispositive. Don't use *dispositive* when *dispose of* will do.

dispossess, dispossessed. There are five *s*'s.

disproved, disproven. *Disproven* is rare. Use *disproved.*

disputatious ends in *-atious.*

disrobe. Don't use *disrobe* when *undress* will do.

(dissapate). Misspelling of *dissipate.*

dissatisfy, dissatisfied, dissatisfying, dissatisfaction. All with double *s.*

dissect, dissection. Two *s*'s, even though often pronounced with a long *i.*

dissemble. Two *s*'s.

disseminate, dissemination. Two *s*'s.

dissension. Double *s,* ends in *-sion.*

dissent. Double *s.*

dissenter ends in *-er.*

dissertation, disservice, dissever. All double *s.*

dissident, dissidence end in *-ent, -ence.*

dissimilar, dissimulate, dissimulation, dissipate, dissipation. All double *s.*

dissociate, dissociation. *Disassociate* and *disassociation* are more common and perhaps more emphatic.

dissolute, dissolution. Double *s.*

dissolvable ends in *-able. Dissoluble* is the more common form.

dissonant, dissonance end in *-ant, -ance.*

dissuade, dissuasion. Double *s.*

dissymmetry. Double *s,* followed by *y.*

distant. Don't say *in the not too distant future* when *fairly soon* will do.

distensible ends in *-ible.*

distention ends in *-tion.*

distich is spelled with *ch.*

distill, distilled, distillate, distillation, distiller. Double *l* in all forms.

distillery ends in *-ery.*

distinct, distinctive. *Distinct* means separate or evident, *distinctive* means characteristic. Don't use *distinctive* when you mean *distinct.*

distingué. Spell it with the accent.

distractible ends in *-ible.*

distrait means absentminded. Use it without an *e* at the end for both sexes.

distraught is stronger than *distrait*—it means deeply agitated.

distributor ends in *-or.*

district attorney. No hyphen.

districtwide. One word.

disturbance ends in *-ance.*

ditchdigger. One word.

ditto, dittos (noun); **ditto, dittoes, dittoed, dittoing** (verb).

diva, divas.

dive. The past tense is *dived* or *dove.* Both forms are common.

divers, diverse. *Divers* (without an *e* at the end) means several, *diverse* means various.

(divice). Misspelling of *device.*

divide, divine start with *di-.*

divisible ends in *-ible.*

division of words. Try to avoid dividing words at the end of a line. If you have to, follow these rules:

    1. Don't mislead the reader as to the pronunciation of the whole word, e.g. *dec-orative,* not *de-corative; lep-rous,* not *le-prous; mys-tery,* not *my-stery; prop-erty,* not *pro-perty; re-fuse* (decline) but *ref-use* (garbage).

    2. Divide between double consonants, except when the first part is the simple form of the word, *com-mit-tee, trot-ting,* but *bluff-ing, tell-ing.*

    3. Don't divide a one-syllable word, including words ending in *-ed,* e.g. *hurled, matched, roared.*

    4. Don't divide so that only one or two letters are left at the end or the beginning of the line, e.g. don't divide words like *aside, before, enough, many, trial, maniac.*

    5. Don't divide words of six letters or less, e.g. *consul, lethal, martyr.*

    6. Don't divide so that only a suffix is left for the next line, e.g. don't divide before *-able, -ceous, -cial, -cion, -cious, -geous, -gion, -ible, -sial, -sion, -tial, -tion, -tious.*

    7. Divide hyphened words at the hyphen, e.g. *daughter-in-law, ill-favored.*

divorcee. Use the word for both sexes. No accent.

divulge Don't use *divulge* when *tell* will do.

D-major. Capital *D,* hyphen, small *m.*

docile, docilely.

dock, pier. Now interchangeable in standard usage.

dock-. Spell all compounds as one word.

dockhand, dockmaster, dockside, dockyard. One word.

doctor ends in *-or.*

doctrinaire ends in *-aire.*

documentary ends in *-ary.*

dodo, dodoes.

-doer. Compounds are spelled as one word, e.g. *evildoer, wrong-doer.*

doeskin. One word.

doesn't. Standard contraction of *does not.*

dog-. Compounds are spelled as one word, as two words, or hyphened.

dogbane, dogberry. One word.

dog biscuit. Two words.

dogbite, dogcart, dogcatcher. One word.

dog collar, dog days. Two words.

dog-ear, dog-eared. Hyphened.

dogface, dogfight, dogfish, dogfood. One word.

doggerel.

doggie bag. Two words. Spelled with *-ie.*

doggo. *To lie doggo* is listed in Webster's as standard usage.

doggone. One word.

doggy. Spell it with *y* except in *doggie bag.*

doghouse, dogleg, dognap. One word.

do-gooder. Hyphened.

dog owner, dog paddle. Two words.

dograce, dogracing. One word.

dog show. Two words.

dogsled. One word.

dog tag. Two words.

dog-tired. Hyphened.

dogtrot, dogwatch. One word.

do . . . have, as in *do you have a match?* is standard American usage.

doily. No *e.*

dollar, dollars. Use *$* and figures for sums of money, e.g. *$1, $2, $3.25, $10.* But spell out *dollar* or *dollars* with *the* or *a,* e.g. *Pay the two dollars.—He gave me a dollar.*

dollar's worth. Spelled with an apostrophe.

dollhouse. One word.

dolor, dolorous. Spelled with *or.*

dominance, dominant end in *-ance, -ant.*

dominie ends in *-ie.*

domino, dominoes.

donate, donation. Don't use *donate* or *donation* when *give* or *gift* will do.

done in the sense of *through* or in the sense of *socially correct* is standard usage.

donor ends in *-or.*

do-nothing. Hyphened.

don't is the standard contraction of *do not.* It is also listed in Webster's as a contraction of *does not* "often used by educated speakers though the construction is sometimes objected to." The Oxford English Dictionary quotes Samuel Richardson "He don't know you" and Aldous Huxley "I only hope that this letter will reach you, though your loss will not be very great if it don't."

don't-know (noun), **don't-knows.** Hyphened.

donut. Common variant of *doughnut.*

doohickey ends in *-ey.* Listed in Webster's as standard usage.

doomsday. One word.

door-. Spell most compounds as one word.

doorbell. One word.

door chain, door check. Two words.

doorframe. One word.

door hinge. Two words.

doorjamb, doorkeeper. One word.

door key. Two words.

doorknob. One word.

door lock. Two words.

doorman, doormat, doornail, doorplate, doorpost. One word.

door prize. Two words.

doorsill, doorstep, doorstop, doorway, dooryard. One word.

dope. Listed in Webster's as standard usage for a narcotic drug, information or a stupid person.

dope fiend. Two words.

dope out. Listed as standard usage in Webster's.

dope pusher. Two words.

dopesheet. One word.

dopester. Standard usage.

dopey, dopier, dopiest. Spelled with *-ey, -ier, -iest.*

dormitory ends in *-ory.*

dorso-. Spell compounds as one word, e.g. *dorsolateral.*

dory. No *e.*

(dos-à-dos). The common spelling of the square dance figure is *do-si-do.*

do's and don'ts. One apostrophe before the *s* in *do's* and one before the *t* in *don'ts.*

do-si-do, do-si-dos. Common spelling of the square dance figure.

dossier ends in *-ier.*

Dostoyevsky, Fyodor. Common English transliteration of the Russian novelist's name. But *Dostoevski, Dostoevsky, Dostoyevski, Dostoievski* are also used.

dotted swiss. Small *s.*

double-. Compounds are one word, two words or hyphened.

double-barreled, double-breasted. Hyphened.

doublecheck, doublecross, doublecrosser, doublecrossing. One word.

double-dealer, double-dealing, double-decker, double-duty, double-dyed, double-edged. Hyphened.

double entry. Two words.

double-faced. Hyphened.

doubleheader, doubleknit. One word.

double negative. Some types of double negatives, e.g. *I don't know nothing about it,* are not standard usage, but some other types, e.g. *I shouldn't wonder if it didn't rain* or *She is not sure she won't make the trip* are idiomatic and commonly used. Shakespeare wrote "I will not budge for no man's pleasure." (*Romeo and Juliet,* III, i, 58) and Jane Austen wrote "There was none too poor or too remote not to feel an interest."

double-park, double-quick. Hyphened.

double take. Two words.

double-talk. Hyphened.

(doubtlessly). Cumbersome and unnecessary. Use *doubtless* as the adjective and the adverb.

doughboy, doughnut. One word.

dour is spelled with *ou.*

dove, past tense of the verb *dive,* is standard usage.

dovecote, dovetail. One word.

dowdy is spelled with *ow.*

dowel, doweled, doweling. One *l* in all forms.

dower, dowry. A *dower* is the widow's life share in her husband's estate, a *dowry* is the portion brought by a bride to her husband.

-down. Spell compounds as one word, e.g. *breakdown, comedown, hoedown, letdown, putdown, rundown, turndown.*

down-. Spell all compounds as one word.

down-and-out. Two hyphens.

downbeat, downcast, downfall, downfield, downgrade, down-hearted, downhill. One word.

down payment. Two words.

downpour, downrange, downriver, downstage, downstairs, down-state, downstream, downstroke, downswing, downtime. One word.

down-to-earth. Two hyphens.

downtown, downtrodden, downturn. One word.

downward, downwards. Use *downward* without *s* as the adjective, e.g. *a downward glance.* As an adverb, e.g. *He looked downward,* the form without *s* is more common.

downwind. One word.

dowry. Spell it without *e.*

Dr. It is customary in addresses and salutations of letters to use *Dr.* in writing to a doctor of medicine or a dentist. It is less common, but by no means rare, to use the *Dr.* title in addressing a doctor of philosophy, veterinarian, etc. At any rate, never use *Dr.* and *M.D.* or *Ph.D.* both.

drachma, drachmas. Greek unit of currency.

draft. Use the spelling *draft* (rather than *draught*) for all meanings.

draft-exempt. Hyphen.

draftsman. So spelled.

dragline, dragnet. One word.

dragoman, dragomans.

dragonfly. One word.

dragon's teeth. Two words and apostrophe.

drainboard, drainpipe. One word.

dramatically ends in *-ally.*

dramatis personae. No hyphen. Ends in *-ae.*

dramatize ends in *-ize.*

(draught). Spell it *draft* in all senses.

draw-. Spell all compounds as one word.

drawback (noun), **drawbridge, drawdown** (noun). One word.

drawing board, drawing room. Two words.

drawstring. One word.

dray horse. Two words.

dreadnought. One word.

(dreamt). The common American form is *dreamed.*

dress circle, dress goods. Two words.

dressing gown, dressing room. Two words.

dressmaker, dressmaking. One word.

dress rehearsal, dress shirt, dress suit, dress uniform. Two words.

driblet. One *b.*

dries, dried. Spelled with *i.*

drier, dryer. Spell it *drier* when you mean more dry, *dryer* for the appliance.

driest is spelled with *i.*

driftwood. One word.

drillbook, drillmaster, drillyard. One word.

(drily). The common US spelling is *dryly.*

drink, drank, drunk.

drinkable ends in *-able.*

drip-dry. Hyphened.

drive, drove, driven.

driveaway. One word.

drive-in (noun, adj.). Hyphened.

drivel, driveled, driveling. One *l* in all forms.

drive shaft. Two words.

driveway. One word.

droll. Spelled with double *l.*

droopy. No *e.*

drop-. Almost all compounds are spelled as one word.

drop cloth, drop curtain. Two words.

drop-forge (verb). Hyphened.

dropkick, droplight, dropoff (noun), **dropout** (noun), **dropstitch.** One word.

drought, droughty. Common spellings.

drowsy. Spelled with *w* and *s.*

drugstore. One word.

drumbeat, drumfire, drumhead, drumroll, drumstick. One word.

drunk, drunken. The noun is always *drunk,* e.g. *He was a drunk.* The adjective before the noun is usually *drunken,* e.g. *a drunken brawl, drunken driving.* But the common form *after* the noun is *drunk,* e.g. *He was drunk.*

drunkenness. Two *n*'s.

dry, drier, driest, dries, dried, dryer (appliance), **drying, dryly, dryness.**

dry-. Compounds are one word, two words or hyphened.

dryasdust. One word.

dry cell. Two words.

dryclean, drycleaner, drycleaning. One word.

drydock, drydocked. One word.

dryer. The appliance is spelled with *y.*

dry-eyed. Hyphened.

dry goods, dry ice. Two words.

dryly. Common US spelling.

dryness. Spelled with *y.*

drypoint. One word.

dry rot, dry run. Two words.

du. In French names, the preposition *du* is usually spelled with a small *d,* e.g. the French writer *Roger Martin du Gard.* In American names the *Du* is usually capitalized, e.g. *W.E.B. Du Bois.* But there are exceptions, such as the *du Pont* family, who prefer to spell their name with a small *d.* The name of the company is *E. I. du Pont de Nemours & Company,* but it is commonly shortened to *Du Pont.*

dual, duel. *Dual* means double, a *duel* is a formal fight between two persons.

dubiety. Don't write *dubiety* when *doubt* will do.

duckbill, duckboard, duckfooted, duckpin. One word.

duck soup. Listed as standard usage in Webster's.

dudgeon ends in *-geon.*

duel, dueled, dueling, duelist, dueler. One *l* in all forms.

duet, duetted, duetting.

due to, in the sense of *because of,* is listed as standard usage in Webster's.

due to the fact that. Don't use this phrase when *because* or *since* will do.

duffelbag is spelled with *el.* One word.

dugout. One word.

dullness. Two *l*'s.

dull-witted. Hyphened.

dully (in a dull manner). Two *l*'s.

duly (properly). No *e.*

dumb, in the sense of *stupid,* is listed as standard usage in Webster's.

dumbbell. One word.

dumbfounded, dumfounded. The spelling with *b* is more common.

dumbwaiter. One word.

dumdum. One word.

dummy, in the sense of *stupid person,* is listed as standard usage in Webster's.

dump truck. Two words.

dunghill. One word.

duodecimo, duodecimos.

duplicate. Don't use *duplicate* when *copy* will do.

duplicator ends in *-or.*

durable ends in *-able.*

during the course of. Don't use this phrase when *during* will do.

during the time that. Don't use this phrase when *while* will do.

dust-. Most compounds are spelled as one word.

dustbin, dustcloth, dustcover, dustheap, dustpan, duststorm, dustup. All one word.

duteous ends in *-eous.*

dutiable is spelled with *i.*

dutiful is spelled with *i.*

dutybound. One word, spelled with *y.*

duty-free. Hyphened.

dwarf, dwarfs.

dwell, dwelt, dwelling, dweller. Don't use *dwell* when *live* will do.

dye, dyed, dyeing. *Dyeing* means coloring, *dying* means expiring.

dyestuff. One word.

(dyke). Spell it *dike.*

dynamo, dynamos.

dynamo-. Spell compounds as one word.

dynasty is spelled with *a* after the *n.*

dys-, dis-. The Greek prefix *dys-* means bad, abnormal, impaired, the prefix *dis-* means not, apart, opposite etc. Compounds with *dys-* are spelled as one word.

dysentery, dysfunction, dyspepsia, dyspeptic, dystrophy. One word.

E

each with *their* is standard usage, e.g. *each contributed their share.*

each other is standard usage when referring to more than two, e.g. *people looked at each other in surprise.*

ear-. Most compounds are spelled as one word.

earache, eardrop, eardrum. One word.

earliest convenience. Don't write *at your earliest convenience* when *soon* will do.

earmark, earmuff, earphone, earplug, earring, earshot, earsplitting. One word.

earth-. Most compounds are spelled as one word.

earthbound, earthenware, earthquake, earthshaking, earthworm. One word.

earwax, earwitness. One word.

east, the East. Small *e* for the point of the compass, capital *E* for the region.

eastbound. One word.

eastward, eastwards. The adjective is *eastward.* For the adverb, usage is divided. Use the form that comes naturally to you.

easygoing. One word.

eatable ends in *-able.* Means not spoiled. *Edible* means fit to be eaten.

eavesdrop, eavesdropper, eavesdropping.

ebb tide. Two words.

ebullience, ebullient end in *-ence, -ent.* Two *l*'s.

eccentric, eccentricity start with *ecc-.*

echelon is spelled with *ch.*

echo, echoes, echoed, echoing.

éclair, éclat. Spell both words with the accent.

economic, economical. *Economic* has to do with economics, *economical* means thrifty.

economize ends in *-ize*.

ecstasy, ecstasies ends in *-asy, -asies*. (No *x*.)

ecstatically ends in *-ally*. (No *x*.)

eczema is spelled with *cz*.

edelweiss.

edema.

edgeways, edgewise. One word.

edible ends in *-ible*. Means fit to be eaten. *Eatable* means not spoiled.

edifice. Don't use *edifice* when *building* will do.

editorial we. The pronoun *we*, referring to yourself alone, is no longer common usage. When you write of yourself, say *I*.

editor in chief. No hyphens.

educable ends in *-able*.

educationist, educator. An *educationist* is an educational theorist, an *educator* is a teacher or school administrator.

eerie. The common spelling of the word, meaning uncanny, ends in *-ie*.

eerily ends in *-ily*.

effect, affect. To *effect* means to bring about, to *affect* means to influence. "If you *affect* someone, you *a*lter his *a*ttitude. If you *effect* something, you *e*stablish an *e*nd result."

effective, effectual, efficacious, efficient. *Effective* means producing a result, *effectual* means producing the desired result, *efficacious* refers usually to a drug or medicine and *efficient* to a thing or person that produces a result without loss or waste of energy.

effectuate. Don't use *effectuate* when *bring about* will do.

effervescent, effervescence are spelled with *sc*.

effete in the sense of decadent, effeminate is standard usage.

efficacy ends in *-cy*.

efficient. See EFFECTIVE.

efflorescent, efflorescence end in *-ent, -ence*.

effluvia is the plural of *effluvium*, but is also commonly used with a singular verb.

effort. Don't use *in an effort to* when the simple preposition *to* will do.

e.g. means *for example*. Don't confuse it with *i.e.*, which means *that is*. No comma after *e.g.* No italics or underlining.

eggbeater, eggcup, egghead, eggnog, eggplant. One word.

egg-shaped. Hyphened.

eggshell. One word.

egis, aegis. The spelling *aegis* is more common.

ego, egos.

egoism, egoist, egotism, egotist, egotistical. In the sense of self-centered, selfish, selfishness, the forms with *t*—*egotist, egotism, egotistical*—are more common. *Egoism* and *egoist* are technical philosophical terms.

ego trip is listed as standard usage in Webster's.

egregious means glaringly bad. In the sense of *distinguished* the word is obsolete.

egress. Don't use *egress* when *exit* will do.

egret, aigrette. *Egret* means a heron, *aigrette* means plume or spray.

(egzema). Misspelling of *eczema.*

ei, ie. The basic rule is

> Write *i* before *e*
> Except after *c*
> Or when sounded like *ay*
> As in *neighbor* and *weigh.*

But there are a few exceptions, like *either, neither, leisure, seize, seizure, weird, height, sleight* and *stein.*

eiderdown starts with *ei.*

eight ball. Two words.

18th century. Don't spell it out. It means the 1700s.

eightfold. One word.

eighth ends in *-hth.*

eighties or **80s,** without apostrophe.

Eire. Former name of Republic of Ireland. No longer used.

eisteddfod. Watch the spelling of this Welsh word.

either. The singular or plural verb after *either* or *either . . . or* is listed as standard usage in Webster's, e.g. *Either of them are satisfactory.* Don't use a comma before *either* in such a sentence as *I don't believe it either.* Sir Walter Scott wrote "If you do not go I will not go either."

ejaculate. Don't use *ejaculate* when *say* will do.

ejector ends in *-or.*

eke out. You *eke out* a meager income, but it's also standard usage to *eke out a living.*

élan. Spell it with the accent.

elapse. Don't use *elapse* when *pass* will do.

elbow grease. Two words.

elbowroom. One word.

elder, eldest. The commonly used forms are *older* and *oldest.*

El Dorado. Capital *E,* capital *D.*

elect, election. Don't use *elect* or *election* when *choose* or *choice* will do.

-elect. Always hyphened, e.g. *president-elect, governor-elect.*

Election Day. Capitalized.

elector ends in *-or.*

electric, electrical. The form *electrical* is now rarely used. It is *electric chair, electric guitar, electric effect, electric shock* etc.

electro-. Spell all compounds as one word.

electrolysis, electrolyze. Watch the *y.*

electronic. Don't confuse *electronic* with *electric. Electronics* has to do with electrons, e.g. in tubes or transistors.

electronically ends in *-ally.*

eleemosynary. A famous spelling bee word. Double *e* after the *l* and *y* after the *s.*

elegant, elegance end in *-ant, -ance.*

elegy, eulogy. An *elegy* is a mournful poem, a *eulogy* is a funeral oration or a statement of high praise.

elementary ends in *-ary.*

elevator ends in *-or.*

elf, elves.

elicit, illicit. *Elicit* means to draw or bring out, *illicit* means illegal.

eligibility has four *i*'s.

eligible ends in *-ible.*

eliminate. Don't use *eliminate* when *get rid of, drop, wipe out* or *cut out* will do.

elite. Spell it without accent.

ellipse. Two *l*'s.

ellipsis means the omission of words. Mark it by three periods in the middle of a sentence and four periods at the end of a sentence, with the first of the four periods immediately following the last word. Don't use asterisks. Use ellipsis marks only in quotations from important documents where it is necessary to show the reader that words were left out.

eloquent, eloquence end in *-ent, -ence.*

else, else's. The standard idiom is *somebody else's, everyone else's* etc.

elucidate. Don't use *elucidate* when *explain* will do.

elude, allude. *Elude* means avoid, *allude* means hint.

'em, meaning *them,* is listed as standard usage in Webster's. Shakespeare wrote "Some are born great, some achieve greatness, and some have greatness thrust upon 'em." (Twelfth Night, II, v, 158).

emanate. Don't use *emanate* when *come* will do.

embargo, embargoes, embargoed, embargoing.

embarkation is spelled with *k.*

embarrass, embarrassment. Two *r*'s, two *s*'s. Remember "*R*ichard *R*oe was embarrassed by *S*ister *S*ue."

embed, embedded, embedding. Spell with *em-.*

embonpoint is spelled with an *n* before the *p.*

embowel, emboweled, emboweling. One *l* in all forms.

embrace. Don't use *embrace* when *include* or *hold* will do.

embraceable ends in *-eable.*

embryo, embryos.

embryo-. Spell all compounds as one word.

emcee, for *MC,* is listed in Webster's as standard usage. Other forms are spelled *emceed, emceeing.*

emend, amend. To *emend* means to correct a text, to *amend* means to improve in general.

emerge. Don't use *emerge* when *come out* will do.

emigrant, immigrant. An *emigrant* leaves a country to settle elsewhere, an *immigrant* enters a country to settle there.

émigré, emigré. The spelling with two accents is more common.

eminent, eminence end in *-ent, -ence.*

eminent, imminent. *Eminent* means outstanding, *imminent* means threatening.

emolument. Don't use *emolument* when *salary, fee* or *wages* will do.

emote. Standard usage.

(empanel). Spell it *impanel.*

emperor ends in *-or.*

emphasize ends in *-ize.* Don't use *emphasize* when *stress* will do.

emphatically ends in *-ally.*

employ. Don't use *employ* when *use* will do.

employee, employe. The spelling *employee* is almost universal, although some newspapers insist on *employe.*

employment. Don't use *employment* when *job* or *work* will do.

emporium, emporiums. Don't use *emporium* when *store* will do.

emprise ends in *-ise.*

empty, emptied, emptying.

empty-handed, empty-headed. Hyphened.

empyrean is spelled with *y* and ends in *-ean.*

enable can be used for people or things. Webster's quotes "legislation *enabling* the admission of a state."

enamel, enameled, enameling. One *l* in all forms.

enamelware. One word.

enamor ends in *-or.*

en banc. Two words.

encage starts with *en-.*

encamp starts with *en-.*

encase, incase. The spelling *encase* is more common.

enceinte is spelled with *ei.*

encephalo-. Spell compounds as one word.

enchilada. One *l.*

encipher, enclasp start with *en-.*

enclose, inclose. The spelling *enclose* is more common.

enclosed herewith. The word *herewith* is unnecessary. Leave it out.

enclosure, inclosure. The spelling *enclosure* is more common.

encomium, encomiums.

encourage, encourageable, encouragement start with *en-.*

(encrust). The common US spelling is *incrust.*

encumbrance. No *e* between *b* and *r.* Don't use *encumbrance* when *burden* will do.

encyclical. There's a *cycle* hidden in this word.

encyclopedia, encyclopedic. The modern spelling is with *e* after *p,* not *ae.*

endeavor ends in *-or.* Don't use *endeavor* when *try* will do.

endemic, epidemic. *Endemic* means locally prevalant, *epidemic* means excessively prevalent, contagious.

end game. Two words.

endmost. One word.

endo-. Spell compounds as one word.

endorsable ends in *-able.*

endorse, endorsement, indorse, indorsement. The *en-* forms are far more common.

end paper. Two words.

endue, indue. The spelling with *en-* is more common.

endurance ends in *-ance.*

endure, indure. The spelling with *en-* is more common.
endways, endwise. One word.
enema, enemas.
enemy, enemies. The second vowel is *e.*
energize ends in *-ize.*
enervate, enervating. One *n.*
enfold, infold. The spelling *enfold* is more common.
enforce starts with *en-.*
enforceable ends in *-eable.*
enfranchise ends in *-ise.*
engageable ends in *-eable.*
engine house, engine room. Two words.
engraft, ingraft. The spelling *engraft* is more common.
(engrained). Spell it *ingrained.*
engrave starts with *en-.*
engulf, ingulf. The spelling *engulf* is more common.
enhance. Only things and qualities can be *enhanced,* not people.
en masse. Two words.
enmesh starts with *en-.*
ennui. So spelled.
enormity in the sense of vast size as well as outrage is listed as
    standard usage in Webster's, which quotes Harvard president J.
    B. Conant, "the *enormity* of the task of teachers in slum
    schools." The usage dates back to 1846.
(enquire, enquiry). The common spellings are *inquire, inquiry.*
enroll, enrolled, enrolling, enrollment. Double *l* in all forms.
en route. Two words.
ensconce ends in *-ce.*
ensheathe starts with *en-.*
enshrine starts with *en-.*
ensign ends in *-sign.*
ensnare starts with *en-.*
ensue. Don't use *ensue* when *follow* will do.
(ensurance). Always spelled *insurance.*
ensure, insure. Use either form when you mean make sure, but use
    only *insure* when you mean guarantee against loss.
entangle starts with *en-.*
entero-. Spell compounds as one word.
(enterpreneur). Misspelling of *entrepreneur.*
enterprise ends in *-ise.*
enthrall, enthralled, enthralling, enthrallment. Two *l*'s in all
    forms.

enthrone. Spell it with *en-*.

enthuse. Standard usage.

enthusiastically ends in *-ally*.

entomb starts with *en-*.

entomology, etymology. *Entomology* has to do with insects, *etymology* with words.

entr'acte. Spelled with an apostrophe.

entreat starts with *en-*.

entree. Spell without accent.

entrepôt. Spell with accent.

entrepreneur is spelled with *-re-*.

entrust, intrust. The common spelling is *entrust*.

entryway. One word.

entwine starts with *en-*.

(enure). Spell it *inure*.

envelop (verb), **enveloped, enveloping, envelopment, envelope** (noun).

enviable ends in *-able*.

environment, environmental. Watch the *-nm-*.

envisage, envision. Don't use *envision* (see as in a vision) when you mean *envisage* (contemplate).

envoi, envoy. Spell the postscript or concluding stanza of a poem with *i*. The diplomatic agent is always spelled with *y*.

enwrap, enwrapped, enwrapping.

enzyme. Spelled with *y*.

eon. The spelling *aeon* is going out of style.

epaulet. Spell it with *-et*.

épée. Accents on the first and second *e*.

ephemeral. So spelled.

epi-. Spell compounds as one word.

epigram. One *m*.

epigrammatic. Two *m*'s.

epilogue. The shortened form *epilog* is rarely used.

epistle. Spelled with *t*.

epitome means embodiment, not high point.

epitomize ends in *-ize*.

epoch ends in *-och*.

equal, equaled, equaling. One *l* in all forms.

equalize, equalization. Spelled with *z*.

equally as says the same thing twice. Leave out *equally*.

equal to. Don't use *equal to* when *of* will do.

equanimity. First *n,* then *m*.

equator ends in *-or.*

equerry. Two *r*'s.

equestrian. Male rider.

equestrienne. Female rider.

equi-. Spell compounds as one word, e.g. *equidistant.*

equilibrium, equilibriums.

equine. Don't use *equine* when *horse* will do.

equip, equipped, equipping, equipment. Two *p*'s in *equipped* and *equipping,* one *p* in *equip, equipment.*

equipage. One *p.*

equitable ends in *-able.*

equivalence, equivalent end in *-ence, -ent.*

eradicate Don't use *eradicate* when *wipe out* will do.

eraser ends in *-er.*

ere. Don't use the poetic word *ere* when *before* will do.

erelong. Don't use *erelong* when *before long* or *soon* will do.

ergo. Don't use the Latin word *ergo* when *therefore* or *so* will do.

err, erred, erring. Two *r*'s in all forms.

errant, errand, arrant. *Errant* means wandering, *errand* means a brief trip for some purpose. *Arrant* means thoroughly bad.

erratic. Two *r*'s.

erratum, errata. Webster's lists *errata* with the singular verb as standard usage.

erroneous ends in *-eous.*

erstwhile. Don't use *erstwhile* when *former* or *formerly* will do.

eruption, irruption. *Eruption* means bursting out, *irruption* means bursting in.

erysipelas. First *y,* then *i.*

escalator ends in *-or.*

escapable ends in *-able.*

escapee is standard usage.

eschew. Don't use *eschew* when *avoid* or *shun* will do.

escudo, escudos. Chilean and Portuguese currency.

escutcheon ends in *-eon.*

Eskimo, Eskimos.

esophagus, esophagi.

especial, especially; special, specially. There used to be a fine distinction between *especial, especially,* meaning to an exceptional degree, and *special, specially,* meaning for a particular purpose. But *special* and *specially* are now commonly used in both senses.

espouse, espousal. Don't use *espouse, espousal* when *marry* or *take up* will do.

Esq., an abbreviation of *Esquire,* is old-fashioned but still fairly common on the inside and outside address of letters addressed to lawyers, e.g. *Jonathan Smith, Esq.* If you use *Esq.* after the name, don't use *Mr., Dr.* etc. before the name.

-ess. Long-established words like *actress* or *waitress* are OK, but many others like *authoress* and *poetess* may be resented.

essay, assay. *Essay* means try, *assay* means test.

essence ends in *-ence.*

Establishment. Standard usage (with capital *E*) in the sense of controlling group, power structure.

esthetic, esthete. Follow the trend and spell these words with *e,* not *ae.*

estimable ends in *-able.*

estivate, estivation. Follow the trend and spell with *e,* not *ae.*

Estonia. Spell without *h.*

estop. Don't use *estop* when *stop* will do.

estoppel ends in *-el.*

et al., an abbreviation for the Latin *et alii* (and others), is commonly used in legal documents and bibliographies. Don't use it elsewhere, when *and others* will do. It refers to people only, not things. It's *et* (no period) *al.* (period).

etc., an abbreviation of the Latin *et cetera,* means *and so forth.* Don't spell out *et cetera.* Don't use *etc.* when you started your list with *such as, for example* or the like. Don't write *and etc.* (the *et* in *etc.* means *and*). Don't use a comma before *etc.* Don't use *etc.* at the end of a list if you couldn't name any additions.

ethereal ends in *-eal.*

ethics, ethic. *Ethics* means rules of conduct, moral principles, a branch of philosophy, *ethic* means a set of moral values, e.g. *the Puritan work ethic.*

etiology. The modern spelling starts with *e,* not *ae.*

etiquette ends in *-ette.*

et seq. Latin abbreviation of *et sequentes* or *et sequentia* (and the following). Don't italicize (underline). The trend is toward using the English abbreviation *ff.*

étude. Spell it with the accent.

etymologist, entomologist. An *etymologist* studies words, an *entomologist* insects.

etymology, entomology. *Etymology* deals with the origin of words, *entomology* with insects.

eu-. If you can't find the word you're looking for under *eu-*, try under *u-*.

eucharist. Spelled with *ch*.

euchre, euchred, euchring. No *e* after the *h*.

eugenics, genetics. *Eugenics* deals with race improvement, *genetics* with heredity.

eulogize ends in *-ize*.

eulogy, elegy. A *eulogy* is a funeral oration or a statement of high praise, an *elegy* is a mournful poem.

eunuch ends in *-uch*.

eupeptic means having good digestion, but Webster's lists it also as standard usage in the sense of cheerful in general.

euphemism, euphuism. A *euphemism* is a substitute word for one that is offensive or unpleasant (e.g. *underprivileged* for *poor*), *euphuism* is a highly artificial, ornate 16th-century literary style.

euphoria is spelled with *eu* and *ph*.

euthanasia has an *a* after the *th*.

evacuee is standard usage.

evanescent, evanescence. Spelled with *sc*.

evangelize ends in *-ize*.

evasion, avoidance. Tax *evasion* is illegal, but tax *avoidance* is legal.

evenhanded. One word.

evenness. Two *n*'s.

even-numbered. Hyphened.

evensong. One word.

event. Don't write *in the event that* when *if* will do.

even-tempered. Hyphened.

eventide. One word.

eventuate. Don't use *eventuate* when *happen* or *result* will do.

ever-. Compounds are hyphened before a noun, spelled as two words otherwise, e.g. *his ever-growing fame,* but *His fame was ever growing.*

everblooming. One word.

ever-faithful. Hyphened.

evergreen, everlasting, evermore. One word.

ever-normal, ever-present, ever-ready. Hyphened.

ever so is listed in Webster's as standard usage.

ever so often, every so often. *Ever so often* means very often, *every so often* means now and then.

every, everybody, everyone. The use of *they, their* or the plural verb with these words is listed as standard usage in Webster's. Henry Fielding wrote "Everyone in the house were in their beds." The usage dates back to 1526.

everyday, every day. Write as one word when you mean ordinary, two words when you mean each day.

everyone, every one. Write as one word when you mean everybody, two words when you mean each one.

everyplace. One word. Standard usage.

every so often, ever so often. *Every so often* means now and then, *ever so often* means very often.

every time. Two words.

everywhere. One word. No *s* at the end.

evidence. Don't use the verb *evidence* when *show* will do.

evidently. Nothing between the *t* and the *l*.

evildoer, evildoing. One word.

evilly. Two *l*'s.

evince. Don't use *evince* when *show* will do.

eviscerate is spelled with *sc*.

evocation is spelled with *c*.

evolutionary ends in *-ary*.

ewe, yew. A *ewe* is a female sheep, a *yew* is a tree.

ex-. Hyphened when used in the sense of *former*, e.g. *ex-convict, ex-governor, ex-queen, ex-tennis champion*.

exaggerate, exaggeration. Two *g*'s.

exalt, exult. To *exalt* means to raise or praise, to *exult* means to rejoice.

exam for *examination* is standard usage.

examiner ends in *-er*.

ex cathedra. No hyphen.

exceed is spelled with double *e*. Don't use *not to exceed* when *up to* or *no more than* will do.

exceedingly, excessively. *Exceedingly* means extremely, *excessively* means overly, too much.

excel, excelled, excelling. One *l* in *excel*, two *l*'s in the other forms.

excellence, excellency. Use *excellence* for high quality, *excellency* for the title of ambassadors etc.

excellent is spelled with *xc,* double *l* and *-ent.* There's a *cell* hidden in the word.

except, accept. *Except* means exclude, *accept* means take.

excepting. Don't use *excepting* when *except* will do.

exception. Don't use *with the exception of* when *except* will do.

exceptionable, exceptional. *Exceptionable* means objectionable, *exceptional* means rare.

excerpt is spelled with *xc.*

excess. Don't use *in excess of* when *over* or *more than* will do.

exchangeable ends in *-eable.*

exchequer is spelled with *qu.*

excisable ends in *-able.*

excise ends in *-ise.*

excitable ends in *-able.*

exclamation point. Exclamation points are sometimes necessary after incomplete sentences, e.g. *What a man! How nice of you! All aboard!* to mark surprise, admiration, incredulity or commands. But more often exclamation points are unnecessary and better left out, e.g. *Oh dear. Don't tell me. You don't say.*

excludable, excludible. Both spellings are used, but *excludable* is more common.

excrescence is spelled with *xc* and *sc.*

excusable ends in *-able.*

exec (without abbreviation period) is listed as standard usage in Webster's.

execrable ends in *-able.*

execute. Don't use *execute* when *sign* will do.

executor ends in *-or.*

executrix, executrices.

exegesis, exegeses.

exemplary ends in *-ary.*

exercise, exorcise. To *exercise* means to use, practice, to *exorcise* means to expel an evil spirit. Both words end in *-ise.*

exercise care. Don't write *exercise care* when *take care* will do.

(exerpt). Misspelling of *excerpt.*

exeunt. Stage direction when two or more characters leave. Plural of *exit.*

exhale, exhalation. Spelled with *h.*

exhaust, exhausted, exhausting. Don't leave out the *h.* Remember you pant and ex*h*ale when you're ex*h*austed.

exhaustible ends in *-ible.*

exhausting, exhaustive. *Exhausting* means tiring, *exhaustive* means thorough.

exhibit. Don't use *exhibit* when *show* will do.

exhibitor ends in *-or.*

exhilarate, accelerate. *Exhilarate* means cheer up, *accelerate* means speed up. Watch the *h* in *exhilarate.*

(exhorbitant). Misspelling of *exorbitant.*

exhort, exhortation. Spelled with *h.*

exigence, exigent end in *-ence, -ent.*

exiguous (very small) ends in *-uous.*

existence ends in *-ence.* Think of the crowded *existence* of "t*en* m*en* in a d*en.*"

ex libris. Two words.

ex officio. Always two words.

exonerate. No *h.*

exorbitant. No *h.*

exorcise, exercise. To *exorcise* means to expel an evil spirit, to *exercise* means to use or practice. Both words are spelled with *-ise.*

expansible ends in *-ible.*

expatriate ends in *-ate.* An *expatriate* is someone who lives abroad.

expect in the sense of suppose or think is listed as standard usage in Webster's.

expectable ends in *-able.*

(expectance). *Expectancy* is the common word.

expectorate is an old-fashioned euphemism for *spit.* Write *spit.*

expedient, expediency end in *-ent, -ency.*

expedite. Don't use *expedite* when *speed* or *speed up* will do.

expediter ends in *-er.*

expeditionary ends in *-ary.*

expel, expelled, expelling. Double *l* in all forms except *expel.*

expendable ends in *-able.*

expenditure. Don't use *expenditure* when *expense* will do.

expense. No *c.*

expensive. Only goods are *expensive,* not prices.

experience (verb). Don't use *experience* when *have* will do.

experimentally ends in *-ally.*

expertise ends in *-ise.*

explanatory ends in *-ory.*

explicable ends in *-able.*

explicit, implicit. *Explicit* means expressed, *implicit* means unexpressed but implied.

exposé. Spell it with the accent.

ex post facto. Never hyphened.

expound. Don't use *expound* when *explain* will do.

expressible ends in *-ible.*

expressman, expressway. One word.

exsiccate. Spelled with *xs* and double *c.*

extant, extent. *Extant* means still in existence, *extent* means range.

(extasy). Misspelling of *ecstasy.*

extemporaneous ends in *-eous.*

extemporize ends in *-ize.*

extend. Don't use *extend* when *give* will do.

extended, extensive. *Extended* means prolonged, *extensive* means wide, broad, large. Don't use either word when a simple word will do.

extension ends in *-sion.*

extent, extant. *Extent* means range, *extant* means still existing.

extern. Spell without final *e.*

extinguish. Don't use *extinguish* when *put out* will do.

extol, extoll. The spelling with one *l* is more common. The other forms have two *l*'s: *extolled, extolling.*

extra, noun and adjective, is standard usage.

extra-. Spell compounds as one word except for such words as *extra-alimentary, extra-large, extra-long.*

extra-artistic. Hyphened.

extracurricular, extrahazardous, extrajudicial. One word.

extra-large, extra-long. Hyphened.

extramarital, extramural, extraordinary, extraordinarily, extraordinariness, extrasensory, extraterritorial, extraterritoriality. One word.

extravagance, extravagant end in *-ance, -ant.*

extravaganza ends in *-za.*

extravert, extrovert. Spell it *extravert,* following Webster's.

exuberance, exuberant end in *-ance, -ant.*

exult, exalt. *Exult* means rejoice, *exalt* means raise or praise.

eye-. Most compounds are spelled as one word.

eyeball, eyebank, eyebrow. One word.

eye-catching. Hyphened.

eyecup. One word.

-eyed. *Cross-eyed, one-eyed, open-eyed* etc. are hyphened but *cock-eyed* and *walleyed* are spelled as one word.

eyedropper, eyeful, eyeglasses, eyehole. One word.

eyeing. Spell it like this, following Webster's.

eyelash, eyelid. One word.

eye-liner, eye-opener, eye-opening. Hyphened.

eyepiece, eyepopper, eyeshade. One word.

eye shadow. Two words.

eyesight, eyesore, eyestrain, eyetooth, eyewash, eyewitness, eye-witnessing. One word.

eyrie, aerie, aery. The most common spelling of the word for eagle's nest is *aerie.*

F

f-. If you can't find the word you're looking for, try under *ph*.
fabricator ends in *-or*.
facade. Spell it without a cedilla under the *c*.
face-. Most compounds are spelled as one word.
face card. Two words.
facecloth. One word.
-faced. Most compounds are hyphened, e.g. *grim-faced*.
facedown, facelift, facelifting, faceplate. One word.
face powder. Two words.
face-saver, face-saving. Hyphened.
facetious ends in *-tious*.
face up to is standard usage.
facial ends in *-cial*.
facilely ends in *-lely*.
facilitate. Don't use *facilitate* when *make easier* will do.
facility. Don't use *facility* when *plant, airport* etc. will do.
facing. No *e*.
facsimile is spelled with *cs*.
fact. Don't write *the fact that* when a simple *that* will do, e.g. *I admit* (the fact) *that I was at home.*
fact finder. Two words.
fact-finding. Hyphened.
factitious, fictitious. *Factitious* means sham, *fictitious* means imaginary. Both words end in *-tious*.
factotum, factotums.
facts are defined in Webster's as "information presented as having objective reality." So there's nothing wrong with the phrase *the true facts* or *the real facts*.
fadeaway. One word.
fade-in. Hyphened.

fadeout. One word.

(faecal, faeces). Now commonly spelled *fecal, feces.*

(faerie, faery). Rare variants of *fairy.*

fag, faggot, fagot. *Fag* and *faggot* are listed in Webster's as standard usage for homosexual. *Fagot* with one *g* is the more common spelling when you mean a bundle of sticks.

Fahrenheit ends in *-eit.* Spelled with a capital *F.*

faience. Spell it without dieresis.

fail. Don't use *fails to, failed to* when *doesn't, didn't* will do.

failing. Don't use *failing* when *without* will do.

faille ends in *-ille.*

fail-safe. Hyphened.

failure. Don't use *failure to* (do) when *not* (doing) will do.

faint, feint. *Faint* means weak, *feint* means something feigned.

fainthearted. One word.

fair, fare. *Fair* means pleasing, clean, just, *fare* means the price of a trip.

fairground. One word.

fair-haired, fair-minded. Hyphened.

fair play, fair trade. Two words.

fairway. One word.

fair-weather. Hyphened.

fairyland. One word.

fairy tale (noun). Two words.

fairy-tale (adj.). Hyphened.

fait accompli, faits accomplis.

faith cure. Two words.

faithfully. *Faithfully yours* and *Yours faithfully* are no longer common at the end of American letters. They are considered highly formal.

fake is standard usage.

faker, fakir. A *faker* is someone who fakes, a *fakir* is an Indian ascetic or wonder-worker.

(falderal). The common spelling is *folderol.*

fall. The common American term for what the British call *autumn.* Don't capitalize.

fallacy ends in *-acy.*

fallback. One word.

fall for. Webster's lists this phrase as standard usage.

fall guy. Two words. Listed in Webster's as standard usage.

fallible ends in *-ible.*

falling-out, fallings-out.

fallout (noun). One word.

false titles, e.g. *grocer* Anthony Lotta, *insurance agent* Joe Farley, were originally invented by *Time* magazine and are now commonly used by the press. Don't capitalize.

falsetto, falsettos.

famed in the sense of famous is standard usage.

familiarize ends in *-ize.*

fan in the sense of enthusiast is standard usage.

fanatic, fanatical. *Fanatical* is getting more common.

fanatically ends in *-ally.*

fan belt. Two words.

fancy dress. Two words.

fancy-free. Hyphened.

fan dance. Two words.

fandango, fandangos.

fan-jet. Hyphened.

fan letter. Two words.

fanlight, fantail. One word.

fantastically ends in *-ally.*

fantasy. Spell it with *f.*

fantoccini is spelled with *o* and two *c*'s.

far-. Compounds are spelled as one word or two words or hyphened.

far-advanced. Hyphened.

faraway. One word.

fare, fair. *Fare* means the price of a trip, *fair* means pleasing, clean, just.

farfetched, farflung. One word.

far-gone. Hyphened.

farinaceous ends in *-eous.*

farm-. Most compounds are spelled as one word.

farm bloc. Two words.

farm-bred. Hyphened.

farmerette ends in *-ette.*

farmhand, farmhouse, farmland, farmowner, farmstead, farmyard. One word.

far-off, far-out. Hyphened.

farrago, farragoes. Two *r*'s.

far-reaching. Hyphened.

farseeing, farsighted. One word.

farther, farthest, farthermost; further, furthest, furthermost. *Farther* etc. is commonly used in the sense of *at a greater distance* or *to a greater degree. Further* etc. is commonly used in these two senses and also in the sense of *in addition.*

fascinate, fascinating, fascination are spelled with *sc.*

fascism, fascist are spelled with *sc.* Use a small *f.*

fashionable ends in *-able.*

fashion plate. Two words.

fast-. Most compounds are hyphened.

fastback, fastball. One word.

fasten. Watch the silent *t.*

fast-flowing, fast-food, fast-moving, fast-talk. Hyphened.

fatal, fateful. *Fatal* in the sense of *fateful* or momentous is standard usage.

fatback. One word.

fat cat. Two words.

fateful, fatal. *Fateful* refers to destiny. But it is also standard usage in the sense of *fatal* or deadly.

fat-free. Hyphened.

fathead. One word.

Father. Capitalize when used as a title for a priest or minister.

father confessor. Two words.

father-in-law, fathers-in-law. Hyphened.

fatherland, fatherlike. One word.

fatigue ends in *-gue.*

fatso, fatsoes. Standard usage in derogatory sense.

fatuous. *U* before *-ous.*

faucet is spelled with *au.*

fault (verb) in the sense of blame is standard usage. But don't use *fault* when *blame* will do.

faultfinder, faultfinding. One word.

faun, fawn. A *faun* is a rural god, a *fawn* is a young deer.

fauna, faunas.

faux pas. The plural is also spelled *faux pas.*

favor ends in *-or. Favor* in the sense of business letter is obsolete.

fawn, faun. A *fawn* is a young deer, a *faun* is a rural god.

faze, phase. *Faze* is standard usage for disturb, *phase* means aspect.

feasible ends in *-ible.* In the sense of probable or likely it is standard usage.

featherbed, featherbedding, featherbrained. One word.

-feathered. Compounds are hyphened, e.g. *fine-feathered, soft-feathered.*

featherweight. One word.

feature (verb) is standard usage.

-featured. Compounds are hyphened, e.g. *ill-featured.*

February. Don't leave out the first *r.*

fecal, feces. Spell with *e.*

federal. Don't capitalize except in titles.

fedora. Small *f.*

fed up. Listed in Webster's as standard usage. No hyphen.

feebleminded. One word.

feedback, feedbag, feedbox, feedlot, feedstock, feedstore, feedstuff. One word.

feel in the sense of think, believe is standard usage. Shakespeare wrote "garlands, Griffith, which I feel I am not worthy yet to wear." (*Henry VIII,* IV, ii, 91)

feel badly is listed as standard usage in Webster's.

feet. Plural of *foot,* as in *6 feet tall.* But it's a *10-foot pole.*

feign ends in *-eign.*

feint, faint. *Feint* means something feigned, *faint* means weak.

feisty is spelled with *ei.*

felicitate. Don't use *felicitate* when *congratulate* will do.

felicity. Don't use *felicity* when *happiness* will do.

feline. Don't use *feline* when *cat* will do.

fellow. Write all compounds except *fellowman* and *fellowship* as two words.

fellow American, fellow citizen, fellow employee, fellow feeling. Two words.

fellowman. One word.

fellowship. One word.

fellow traveler, fellow worker. Two words.

felon, felony. One *l.*

female (noun) sounds contemptuous. Say *woman.*

feminine. Don't use *feminine* when *a woman* will do.

femur, femurs.

fence in the sense of receiver of stolen goods is standard English.

fencepost. One word.

ferment, foment. In the sense of incite the two words are interchangeable.

fernleaf. One word.

ferocious ends in *-cious.*

ferrule, ferule. A *ferrule* (two *r*'s) is a metal cap on a cane, a *ferule* (one *r*) is a ruler to punish children with.

ferry, ferried, ferrying.

ferryboat, ferryman. One word.

fertile, fertilely, fertilize, fertilizer.

fetal. Spell with *e*.

fete. Spell it without accent.

fetid. Spell with *e*.

fetish. Spell with *sh*.

fetus. Spell with *e*.

feud, feudal. Spelled with *eu*.

fever heat, fever pitch. Two words.

few in number. Strike out *in number*. Say *few*.

fey in the sense of enchanted, strange is spelled with *ey*.

fez, fezzes.

fiancé, fiancée. A *fiancé*, ending in one *e* with an accent, is an engaged man, a *fiancée*, with an accented *e* plus another *e*, is an engaged woman.

fiasco, fiascoes.

fiber ends in *-er*.

fiberboard, fiberglass. One word. Small *f* in *fiberglass*.

fibrillation. Two *l*'s.

fibula, fibulae.

fickle ends in *-le*.

fiction ends in *-tion*.

fictitious ends in *-itious*.

fiddle is no longer used seriously for *violin* except among musicians.

fiddle-de-dee.

fiddle-faddle. Hyphened.

fiddlesticks. One word.

fidget, fidgeted, fidgeting. One *t* in all forms.

field-. Most compounds are spelled as two words.

field glasses, field house, field marshal. Two words.

fieldstone. One word.

field test, field trip. Two words.

fieldwork, fieldworker. One word.

fiend in the senses of fan, addict, wizard or mischievous person is listed as standard usage in Webster's.

fierce is spelled with *ie*.

fiery, fierier, fieriest. Spelled with *ie*.

fife, fifes.

15th century. Don't spell it out. It means the 1400s.

fifties or **50s,** without apostrophe.

fifty-one etc. Hyphened.

fig bar, fig leaf. Two words.

figure (verb) in the sense of think, conclude is listed as standard usage in Webster's.

figurehead. One word.

figure out is listed as standard usage in Webster's.

figures. See NUMBERS.

(filagree). Misspelling of *filigree.*

filch. Standard usage.

filecard. One word.

file clerk. Two words.

filet, fillet. The word is spelled with one *l* when you mean lace and in *filet mignon.* Otherwise the common spelling is with two *l*'s regardless of the pronunciation.

filet mignon, filets mignons.

filibuster. One *l.*

Filipino, Filipinos. Spelled with *F* and one *p* even though the *Philippines* are spelled with *Ph* and two *p*'s.

fillet, filet. Spell with double *l* except when you mean lace and in *filet mignon.*

fill-in. Hyphened.

fillip, filliped. Two *l*'s.

fillout. One word.

fill-up. Hyphened.

filmdom. Standard usage.

filmmaker, filmmaking, filmstrip. One word.

filterable. Spell it with *e* after *t.*

filter tip. Two words.

filter-tipped. Hyphened.

filtrate. Don't use *filtrate* when *filter* will do.

finable. No *e.*

finagle is listed in Webster's as standard usage. Spelled with *i.*

finale ends in *-le.*

finalize ends in *-ize.* Don't use *finalize* when *complete, finish, end* will do.

finally, finely. *Finally* means at the end, *finely* means in a fine way.

financier is spelled with *ie.*

fine as an adverb, as in *you did fine,* is listed as standard usage in Webster's.

fine art. Two words.

fine-cut, fine-drawn. Hyphened.

fineness. *E* between the two *n*'s. Quality of being fine.

fine print. Two words.

finespun. One word.

finesse ends in *-esse.*

fine-tooth comb. Hyphened.

fingerboard. One word.

finger bowl. Two words.

fingernail, fingerprint, fingertip. One word.

finger wave. Two words.

finicky, finical, finicking. The commonly used form is *finicky.*

fink, meaning informer or strikebreaker, or used as a general term of disapproval, is listed as standard usage in Webster's.

finnan haddie. Double *n,* double *d.*

fiord, fjord. The GPO Style Manual lists *fiord,* except in proper names that use *Fjord.*

fire in the sense of dismiss from a job is standard usage.

fire-. Most compounds are spelled as one word.

fire alarm. Two words.

firearms, fireball, firebird, fireboat, firebomb, firebox, firebrand, firebreak, firebrick. One word.

fire brigade. Two words.

firebug, firecracker. One word.

fire department. Two words.

firedog. One word.

fire drill. Two words.

fire-eater, fire-eating. Hyphened.

fire engine, fire escape, fire extinguisher. Two words.

firefighter, firefly, fireguard, firehouse. One word.

fire insurance, fire irons. Two words.

firelight, fireman, fireplace, fireplug, firepower, fireproof. One word.

fire sale, fire screen, fire ship. Two words.

fireside. One word.

fire station. Two words.

firestone, firestorm, firetrap, firetruck. One word.

fire wall. Two words.

firewood, fireworks. One word.

firm, strictly speaking, means a partnership rather than a corporation. When you want a short word for *corporation,* say *company* rather than *firm.*

first-. Most compounds are hyphened.

first, firstly. The common form of the adverb is *first*. In enumerations write *first . . . second . . . third . . .* etc.

first aid. Two words.

firstborn. One word.

first-class, first-degree. Hyphened.

firstfruits, firsthand. One word.

first lady, first lieutenant. Two words.

firstly is rare. The common form of the adverb is *first.*

first magnitude. Don't use *of the first magnitude* when *big* will do.

first mate, first night. Two words.

first-rate, first-string. Hyphened.

first two. Standard usage.

fish. The plural *fish* is much more common than *fishes.*

-fish. Compounds are spelled as one word, e.g. *goldfish.*

fish-. Most compounds are spelled as one word.

fish-and-chips. Two hyphens.

fishbone, fishbowl, fishcake, fishhook, fishmonger, fishnet, fishpond. One word.

fish stick. Two words.

fishtail, fishwife. One word.

fishy, meaning dubious, is listed as standard usage in Webster's.

fission ends in *-ssion.*

fistfight, fistful. One word.

fisticuffs. *I* in the middle.

fitted, fit. *Fitted* is more common than *fit* as the past tense of *fit.*

five-and-ten. Two hyphens.

fivefold, fivescore. One word.

fix is listed as standard usage in Webster's in all senses, including fix a jury, castrate, predicament, shot of narcotic etc.

fixer. Standard usage.

fizz. Two *z*'s.

fjord. The GPO Style Manual lists *fiord* with *i* for the common noun, *Fjord* for names.

flabbergast. Listed in Webster's as standard usage.

flack. Listed in Webster's as standard usage for press agent, publicity.

flag-. Most compounds are spelled as one word.

flagbearer. One word.

flagellate, flagellation. Two *l*'s.

flageolet is spelled with *eo.*

flagitious ends in *-itious.*

flagman, flagpole. One word.

flagrant ends in *-ant.*

flagship, flagstaff, flagstick, flagstone. One word.

flag-waving. Hyphened.

flair, flare. *Flair* means talent, bent, knack, *flare* means flame.

flak (no *c*) means antiaircraft fire or opposition in general.

flambé, flambéed. Both forms are common.

flambeau, flambeaux.

flamenco, flamencos.

flameout, flameproof, flamethrower. One word.

flamingo, flamingos.

flammable ends in *-able.* Now more common than *inflammable,* which means the same.

flannel, flannelette. Two *n*'s, one *l.*

flare, flair. *Flare* means flame, *flair* means talent, bent, knack.

flareback, flareout, flareup. One word.

flashback, flashboard, flashbulb. One word.

flash card. Two words.

flashcube, flashgun, flashlight, flashover. One word.

flash point. Two words.

flashtube. One word.

flatbed, flatboat. One word.

flat-bottomed. Hyphened.

flatcar. One word.

flat-chested. Hyphened.

flatfoot, flatfeet. But *flatfoot, flatfoots* is listed in Webster's as slang for policeman or sailor.

flat-footed. Hyphened.

flatiron. One word.

flat-out. Hyphened.

flat silver. Two words.

flattop. One word.

flatulence, flatulent end in *-ence, -ent.*

flatware, flatwork, flatworm. One word.

flaunt, flout. *Flaunt* means show off, *flout* means scorn.

flautist, flutist. *Flutist* is more common.

flavor ends in *-or.*

fleabag, fleabite. One word.

flea-bitten. Hyphened.

flea market. Two words.

flection, flexion. *Flection* is more common in the US.

fledgling. No *e* between *g* and *l*.

flee, fly. In the sense of escape or run away both words are now rare.

fleshpot. One word.

fleur-de-lis. Two hyphens. The spelling with *i* is more common.

flew, flue. *Flew* is the past tense of *fly,* but it's a chimney *flue.*

flexible ends in *-ible.*

flibbertigibbet. Two double *b*'s.

flick for movie is listed as standard usage in Webster's.

flier, flyer. Spell it *flyer* when you mean a crack train or a handbill, *flier* in all other senses.

flight. Most compounds are spelled as two words.

flight bag, flight control, flight crew, flight deck, flight line, flight path, flight pay, flight plan, flight strip. Two words.

flimflam, flimflammed, flimflamming. Double *m* except in *flimflam.*

flimsy, flimsier, flimsiest, flimsily, flimsies.

flip, in the sense of losing one's mind, is listed in Webster's and elsewhere as slang.

flip-flop. Hyphened.

flippant, flippancy end in *-ant, -ancy.*

flirtatious ends in *-atious.*

flood-. Most compounds are spelled as one word.

flood control. Two words.

floodgate, floodlight, floodplain, floodtide, floodwall. One word.

floor, story. In the US there's no difference between a *floor* and a *story* of a building. The more common spelling of *story* in this sense is without *e—story, stories.*

floorboard. One word.

floor lamp, floor leader. Two words.

floor-length. Hyphened.

floor manager, floor model, floor sample, floor show. Two words.

floorspace, floorwalker. One word.

floozy, floozies. Listed as standard usage in Webster's.

flophouse. One word.

florescence, fluorescence. *Florescence* means flourishing, *fluorescence* means emitting radiation.

flossy in the sense of slick, stylish is listed as standard usage in Webster's.

flotage, flotation both mean floating. The word *floatage* is common for the charge for shipping railroad cars on a barge.

flotsam and jetsam aren't the same. *Flotsam* means floating debris, *jetsam* means what is thrown overboard and is found floating or washed ashore.

flounder, founder. To *flounder* means to stumble violently as in a mire, to *founder* means to sink.

(flourescence, flourescent). Misspellings of *fluorescence, fluorescent.*

flour mill, flour sack. Two words.

flout, flaunt. *Flout* means scorn, *flaunt* means show off.

flowchart. One word.

flowed, flown. *Flowed* is the past participle of *flow, flown* is the past participle of *fly.*

-flower. Compounds are usually spelled as one word, e.g. *wallflower.*

flower-. Compounds are spelled as one word, as two words, or hyphened.

flowerbed. One word.

flower child, flower girl. Two words.

flowerpot. One word.

flower shop, flower show. Two words.

flown, flowed. *Flown* is the past participle of *fly, flowed* is the past participle of *flow.*

flowoff. One word.

flu, short for *influenza,* is listed in Webster's as standard usage.

flue, flew. *Flue* is what you find in a chimney, *flew* is the past tense of *fly.*

fluent, fluency end in *-ent, -ency.*

fluky. No *e.*

flummox is listed as standard usage in Webster's.

flunk is listed as standard usage in Webster's.

flunky. No *e.*

fluorescence, florescence. *Fluorescence* means emitting radiation, *florescence* means flourishing. Spell *fluorescence, fluorescent* with *uo* and *sc.*

fluoridation, fluorine. Spelled with *uo.*

fluoro-. Spell compounds as one word.

flutist, flautist. The common US spelling is *flutist.*

fluty. No *e.*

fly, flew, flown. Rare in the US in the sense of flee, escape. In baseball the forms are *fly, flied, flying.*

fly-. Most compounds are spelled as one word.

flyable. Spelled with *y.*

flyaway, flyblown, flyby. One word.

fly-by-night. Two hyphens.

flycatcher. One word.

flyer, flier. Spell it *flyer* in the sense of crack train or handbill, otherwise *flier.*

flying buttress, flying fish, flying saucer, flying squad. Two words.

flyleaf, flyover, flypaper, flyspeck, flyswatter, flyweight, flywheel. One word.

foam rubber. Two words.

FOB (free on board). Capitals and no periods.

focalize ends in *-ize.*

fo'c'sle. Common variant spelling of *forecastle.* Two apostrophes, not three.

focus, focuses, focused, focusing.

(foetal, foetus, foetid). The common modern spellings are *fetal, fetus, fetid.*

fogbound, foghorn. One word.

fogy. Spell without *e.*

-fold. Compounds are spelled as one word, e.g. *twofold, threefold, manifold, manyfold, twentyfold.*

foldaway, foldboat. One word.

folderol. Spell *o—e—o.*

fold-in (adj.). Hyphenated.

foldout (noun), **foldup** (noun, adj.). One word.

folio, folios.

folk dance. Two words.

folklore. One word.

folk mass, folk medicine. Two words.

folks, in the sense of relatives or parents, is listed as standard usage in Webster's.

folksinger, folksong, folktale, folkway. One word.

following. Don't use *following* when *after* will do.

follows. *As follows* is always in the singular.

follow-through (noun). Hyphenated.

followup (noun, adj.). One word.

fondue. Spell it with *e* at the end.

food chain, food poisoning, food stamp. Two words.

foodstuff. One word.

foolhardy, foolproof, foolscap. One word.

fool's errand. Two words.

foot, feet. It's *6 feet tall,* but a *10-foot pole.*

foot-. Most compounds are spelled as one word.

foot-and-mouth. Two hyphens.

footbath, footboard, footboy, footbrake, footbridge, footcandle. One word.

foot-dragging. Hyphened.

-footed. Compounds are hyphened, e.g. *light-footed, heavy-footed.*

footgear, foothill, foothold, footlights, footlocker, footloose, footman. One word.

footnotes. Here are a few simple rules for writing footnotes:

1. Footnotes are standard in scholarly, technical or legal writing. In ordinary writing try to avoid them. If you refer to sources, do it casually in the text.

2. Number the footnotes in your report, paper or article consecutively. Put a raised number immediately after the word, sentence or quote footnoted. Then put the same number, with a period, at the beginning of the footnote.

3. Put footnotes at the bottom of the page. Use a line to separate your text from the footnotes.

4. Indent each footnote. Single-space footnotes that run to more than one line. (But double-space a book manuscript.) Double-space between footnotes.

5. In the first reference to a book, give the author's name (first name first), the shortened title of the book (underlined), place of publication, publisher (shortened name), date of publication, volume number if any (use the abbreviation *vol.*), number of page or pages quoted (use the abbreviations *p.* or *pp.*).

Examples:

1. Rudolf Flesch, *Say What You Mean,* New York, Harper & Row, 1972, p. 93.

2. *Webster's New Collegiate Dictionary,* Springfield, Mass., Merriam, 1973, pp. 1527–1528.

6. In the first reference to a scholarly magazine article, give the author's name (first name first), the title of the article (in quotes), the name of the periodical (underlined, shortened form), volume number (underlined, don't use *vol.*), issue number, date, page number or numbers (don't use *p.* or *pp.*)

In the first reference to a newspaper or popular magazine article, leave out the volume and issue numbers. Give the date in military style, e.g. *23 May 1973.*

Examples:

> 1. Rudolf Flesch, "A New Readability Yardstick," *J. of Applied Psychology,* 32, no. 3, June 1948, 222–223.
> 2. Richard Harris, "Reflections," *New Yorker,* 10 June 1974, 46–63.
> 3. Louis Harris, "Majority Want Nixon Out," *N.Y. Post,* 13 June 1974.

7. In later references to the same source, use the author's last name and the page number. (*Ibid.* and *op. cit.* are old-fashioned.)

Example:

> 1. Flesch, p. 86.

footpad, footpath, footprint, footrace, footrest. One word.

foot rule, foot soldier. Two words.

footsore, footstep, footstool, footwear, footwork. One word.

for-, fore-. There's no easy-to-remember rule when to spell compounds with *for-* and when with *fore-*. You just have to memorize the words one by one.

forbade, the past tense of *forbid,* is commonly spelled with *e* at the end. However, the pronunciation always rhymes with *mad.*

forbear, forebear. To *forbear* means to endure or avoid, a *forebear* is an ancestor.

forbearance ends in *-ance.*

forbid, forbade, forbidden.

forbore is the past tense of *forbear.*

forceful, forcible. *Forceful* means effective, *forcible* means by force.

forceps, forceps. The plural form is the same as the singular.

forcible ends in *-ible.*

fore-, for-. There's no easy-to-remember rule when to spell compounds with *fore-* and when with *for-*. You just have to memorize the words one by one.

fore-and-aft. Two hyphens.

forearm, forebear (ancestor), **forebode, foreboding, forecast, forecastle** (also spelled *fo'c'sle*), **foreclose, foreclosure, foredeck, foredo, forefather, forefinger, forefoot, forefront.** One word, spelled with *fore-.*

(foregather). Commonly spelled *forgather.*

forego, forgo. *Forego* means precede, *forgo* (commonly spelled without *e*) means relinquish.

foregoing. Don't use *the foregoing* when *this* will do.

foregone (conclusion). Starts with *fore*.

foreground, forehand, forehead. One word, spelled with *fore*.

foreign, foreigner. Spelled with *eign*.

foreignness. Two *n*'s.

foreign words may baffle your reader. If in doubt, say it in English.

foreknowledge, forelady, foreleg, forelock, foreman, foremost, forenoon, foreordain, forepart, forepaw, foreplay, forerunner, foresail, foresee, foreshadow, foreshorten, foresight, foreskin, forestall. One word, spelled with *fore*.

(foreswear). Commonly spelled *forswear*.

foretaste, foretell, forethought, foretold. One word, spelled with *fore*.

forever. One word.

forewarn, forewoman. One word, spelled with *fore-*.

foreword. *Preface* is more common.

forfeit, forfeiture. Spelled with *ei*.

forfend. Spell it with no *e* between *r* and *f*.

for free is listed as standard usage in Webster's.

forgather. Commonly spelled without *e* between *r* and *g*. Don't use *forgather* when *assemble* or *meet* will do.

forgave. Past tense of *forgive*.

forgeable is spelled with *ea*.

forgettable has two *t*'s and ends in *-able*.

forgivable. No *e* after the *v*.

forgive, forgiveness start with *for-*.

forgo, forego. *Forgo* (no *e*) means give up, *forego* means precede.

(forgone). Spell it *foregone,* as in *foregone conclusion*.

forklift. One word.

forlorn. No *e*.

formally, formerly. *Formally* means in a formal way, *formerly* means previously.

former, latter. Don't use *the former* and *the latter,* since they force the reader to go back to see which is which. It is better to repeat the noun or nouns. Boswell wrote of Dr. Samuel Johnson "He never used the phrases the former and the latter, having observed that they often occasioned obscurity; he therefore contrived to construct his sentences so as not to have occasion for them, and would even rather repeat the same words, in order to avoid them."

formerly, formally. *Formerly* means previously, *formally* means in a formal way.

formfitting. One word.

formidable ends in *-able*.

form letter. Two words.

forms of address. See ADDRESS.

formula, formulas.

formulate. Don't use *formulate* when *form* will do.

forsake, forsook, forsaken, forsaking. No *e* after *for*.

forsooth is listed as archaic in the Random House Dictionary.

forswear, forswore, forsworn. No *e* after *for*.

forsythia. Spelled with *y*.

forte, in the sense of strong point, is spelled with a silent *e* at the end.

forth, fourth. *Forth* means forward, *fourth* means 4th.

for the period of. Change to *for*.

for the purpose of. Change to *for* or *to* with the infinitive.

for the reason that. Change to *because, since*.

forthright. One word.

forthwith. The more common words are *at once* or *immediately*.

forties or **40s,** without apostrophe. No *u*.

fortieth. No *u*.

fortissimo, fortissimos.

fortnight, fortnightly. British usage, rare in US.

fortuitous, fortunate. *Fortuitous* means accidental, *fortunate* means lucky. But *fortuitous* in the sense of lucky is also listed as standard usage in Webster's.

fortune cookie, fortune hunter, fortune hunting. Two words.

fortuneteller, fortunetelling. One word.

forty. No *u*. Remember *"Forty* soldiers held the *fort."*

forty-one, forty-two etc. Hyphened.

forty-niner. Hyphened.

forum, forums.

forward. Don't use *forward* when *send* will do.

forward, forwards. For the adverb, use the form that comes naturally to you.

fossil. Two *s*'s, ends in *-il*.

fossilize ends in *-ize*.

foul, fowl. *Foul* means dirty, *fowl* means a bird.

foul line. Two words.

foulmouthed. One word.

foul play. When you mean murder, say murder.

foulup. One word.

founder, flounder. To *founder* means to sink, to *flounder* means to stumble violently as in mire.

foundry. No *e*.

fountainhead. One word.

fountain pen. Two words.

four-flush, four-flusher. Hyphened.

fourfold. One word.

four-in-hand. Two hyphens.

fourpenny, fourposter, foursome, foursquare. One word.

fourteen. Don't leave out the *u*.

14th century. Don't spell it out. It means the 1300s.

fourth, forth. *Fourth* means 4th, *forth* means forward.

fourthly. It's simpler to write *fourth*.

(fourty). Misspelling of *forty*.

fowl, foul. *Fowl* means a bird, *foul* means dirty.

foxhole. One word.

fox hunting. Two words.

foxtail. One word.

fox terrier. Two words.

fox-trot. Hyphened.

fracas, fracases.

fraction in the sense of a small part is standard usage.

fractions are always hyphened, e.g. *one-tenth, two-thirds, four-fifths*. But use only one hyphen, not two, e.g. *one twenty-fourth*.

fragmentary ends in *-ary*.

fragmentize. Don't use *fragmentize* instead of *fragment*.

fragrant, fragrance end in *-ant, -ance*.

frame house. Two words.

frameup. One word.

franc. French and Swiss currency.

franchise, franchisee, franchisor. The *franchisee* is the one who is granted a franchise, the *franchisor* is the one who grants it. (Don't use *franchiser* because it may mean *franchisee* or *franchisor*.)

Frankenstein. In Mary Shelley's novel *Frankenstein* was the man who made the monster, not the monster itself. But the word *Frankenstein* has been so often misused for the monster itself that dictionaries list this as standard usage.

frankincense. First *c*, then *s*.

frantically, franticly. Both forms are standard usage, but *frantically* is more common.

frappé. Spell it with the accent.

frat, short for *fraternity,* is listed as standard usage in Webster's.

fraternize ends in *-ize.*

fraudulent, fraudulence end in *-ent, -ence.*

fraught. Don't use the semi-archaic *fraught with* when *full of* will do.

frazzle is listed as standard usage in Webster's.

freak in the sense of *fan* is listed as standard usage in Webster's.

free, freer, freest. Never more than two *e*'s.

free-. Most compounds are spelled as one word.

free, for. *For free* is listed as standard usage in Webster's.

freebie ends in *-ie.* Listed in Webster's as standard usage.

freebooter, freeborn. One word.

free-fall, free-floating, free-for-all. Hyphened.

freehand, freehanded, freehearted, freehold, freelance, freelancer, freeload, freeloader, freeloading, freeman. One word.

Freemason. Capital *F,* one word.

Freemasonry, freemasonry. Capitalize when you mean the Freemasons. Use small *f* when you mean natural fellowship and sympathy.

freer, freest. Two *e*'s.

freestanding, freestone, freestyle, freethinker, freethinking, free-trader, freeway, freewheel, freewheeler, freewheeling, freewill (adj.). One word.

freeze, frieze. *Freeze* means congeal into ice, *frieze* means a decorative band.

freight, freighter. Spelled with *eigh.*

(freind). Misspelling of *friend.*

French bulldog. Capital *F.*

french chalk, french cuff, french door, french dressing, french-fried, french fries, french fry. Small *f*'s.

French words. Don't use a French word when an English word will do just as well.

frenetic, phrenetic. The spelling with *f* is far more common.

frequently. Don't use *frequently* when *often* will do.

fresco, frescoes.

friable, fryable. *Friable* means what can be crumbled, *fryable* means what can be fried.

friar ends in *-ar.*

fricassee. One *c,* two *s*'s. Think of "*c*hicken *s*tew in a *s*auce."

fridge. Standard usage, mainly British, for *refrigerator.*

friedcake. One word.

friend, friendly, friendship. Often misspelled, Think of "the *end* of a beautiful *friendship.*"

friendlily sounds so awkward that the adverb *friendly* is listed as standard usage in most dictionaries.

friendliness. Spelled with *i,* not *y.*

friends with. *I am friends with Bill* is idiomatic English.

(frier). The common spelling is *fryer.*

frieze, freeze. A *frieze* is a decorative band, *freeze* means congeal into ice.

frijoles.

frisbee. Spell with small *f* and *ee.*

fritillary. One *t,* two *l*'s.

fritz. *On the fritz* and *fritz out* are listed in dictionaries as slang.

frivolous. *O* after *v.*

frizz, frizzed, frizzes, frizzle, frizzled, frizzles. Two *z*'s in all forms.

frock coat. Two words.

frogman. One word.

frolic, frolicked, frolicking. Spelled with *ck* in all forms except *frolic.*

frolicsome. Spelled with *cs.*

from whence sounds archaic. The common form is *where . . . from.*

front-end. Hyphened.

frontier ends in *-ier.*

frontispiece. Two *i*'s.

fronto-. Spell compounds as one word, e.g. *frontogenesis.*

front page. Two words.

frontrunner. One word.

froufrou. One word.

froward, forward. *Froward* means contrary, *forward* means ahead.

frowzy, frowsy. The spelling with *z* is more common.

frozenness. Two *n*'s.

fruitcake. One word.

fruit fly. Two words.

fruition. The meaning *realization, bearing fruit* is now listed as standard in most dictionaries.

fryable, friable. *Fryable* means what can be fried, *friable* means what can be crumbled.

fryer, frier. Commonly spelled with *y.*

frying pan. Two words.

F-sharp. Capital *F* and hyphen.

fuchsia. Spelled with *chs.*

(fued, fuedal). Misspellings of *feud, feudal.*

fuel, fueled, fueling. One *l* in all forms.

fugitive. Two *i*'s.

fugue ends in -*ue.*

Führer, Fuehrer. Both spellings are correct.

-ful. The plural of *cupful, handful, spoonful* etc. is *cupfuls, handfuls, spoonfuls* etc.

fulcrum, fulcrums.

fulfill, fulfilled, fulfilling, fulfillment. First one *l,* then two.

full-. Compounds are spelled as one word, as two words, or hyphened.

fullback. One word.

full-blooded, full-blown, full-bodied, full-dress, full-fashioned, full-fledged, full-grown, full-length. All hyphened.

fullmouthed. One word.

fullness. Two *l*'s.

full-scale, full-size. Hyphened.

fulltime. One word.

fully. Two *l*'s.

fulsome means gross, excessive, disgustingly overdone. If you use it to mean copious or lavish, you may puzzle your reader.

fun. The adjective *fun,* as in *fun city,* is listed as standard usage in Webster's.

fundamentally ends in -*ally.*

fundraiser, fundraising. One word.

funds. Don't use *funds* when *cash* or *money* will do.

funereal ends in -*eal.*

fungous (adj.). Related to fungi.

fungus, fungi.

funk, funky are listed as standard usage in Webster's.

funlover, funloving. One word.

funnel, funneled, funneling. One *l* in all forms.

funny in the sense of peculiar is listed as standard usage in Webster's.

funny bone, funny paper. Two words.

furbelow ends in -*ow.*

fur coat. Two words.

fur-lined. Hyphened.

furlough. The common word is *leave.*

furnish. Don't use *furnish* when *give* will do.

furor, rather than *furore,* is the common US word.

furred, furry. Two *r*'s.

further, furthest, furthermost; farther, farthest, farthermost. *Farther* etc. is commonly used in the sense of *at a greater distance* or *to a greater degree; further* etc. is commonly used in these two senses and also in the sense of *in addition.*

furtherance ends in *-ance.*

furthermore. Don't use *furthermore* when *also* will do or when no connective is needed.

fury. No *e.*

(fuschia). Misspelling of *fuchsia.*

fuse is the common spelling, but *fuze* with *z* is often used in military writing.

fuselage. The middle vowel is *e.*

fuseplug. One word.

fusillade is spelled with *i* and two *l*'s.

fussbudget, fusspot. One word.

futilely. Two *l*'s.

future. Don't say *in the near future* when *soon* will do. Don't say *in the not-too-distant future* when *before long* will do.

fuze, fuse. The common spelling is *fuse* but *fuze* is often used in military writing.

fuzz for police is listed as standard usage in Webster's.

G

g-. If you can't find the word you're looking for under *g-*, try under *gh-*.

-g-, -gg-. A *g* at the end of a word is doubled before the suffixes *-ed, -er, -able, -ing, -y, -ie, -est, -ish* etc. if there's only one vowel before the *g*. Examples: *drag, dragged; big, bigger, biggest; hug, huggable; zigzag, zigzagging; bag, baggy; prig, priggish.*

gabardine, gaberdine. Spell the modern fabric *gabardine*, the medieval cloak *gaberdine.*

gadget is standard usage.

gaffe in the sense of social blunder is spelled with an *e* at the end.

gaga is standard usage.

gage, gauge. The spelling *gauge* is so odd and so often misspelled that you're much better off always spelling the word *gage*. In technical writing, the regular spelling is *gage* anyway.

gagman. One word.

gag rule. Two words.

gaiety. Spelled with *aie.*

gaily. Spelled with *ai.*

gainfully employed. Don't write *gainfully employed* when *working* will do.

gainsay. Don't use *gainsay* when *deny* will do.

gait, gate. *Gait* means a way of walking, *gate* means an entrance.

(galavant). The common spelling is *gallivant.*

Galilean. So spelled. Two single *l*'s.

gall in the sense of impudence is standard usage.

gallant, gallantry. Spelled with *-ant.*

gallbladder. One word.

galleon ends in *-eon.*

gallerygoer. One word.

galley, galleys. Spelled with *ey.*

galley proof, galley slave. Two words.

gallimaufry. Spelled with two *l*'s and *au*.

gallivant is spelled with two *l*'s and *i*.

gallon. A US gallon is 231 cubic inches, an imperial gallon, used also in Canada, is 5 US quarts.

gallop, galloped, galloping. One *p* in all forms.

gallows, gallowses.

gallstone. One word.

galore. Standard usage.

galosh.

galumph is standard usage.

galvanize ends in *-ize*.

galvano-. Spell compounds as one word.

gambit, gamut. *Gambit* means a chess move, *gamut* means range.

gamble, gambol. To *gamble* means to wager, to *gambol* means to frolic.

gambol, gamboled, gamboling. One *l* in all forms.

gamekeeper, gamekeeping. One word.

gamut, gantlet. You can run a *gamut* (a whole range) or a *gantlet* (a flogging ordeal), but they're not the same thing.

gamy. No *e*.

ganglion, ganglia.

gangplank. One word.

gangrene, gangrenous. Single *e* after *gr*.

gangway. One word.

gantlet, gauntlet. There are two words, both spelled either way. Commonly the flogging ordeal you run is spelled *gantlet* and the glove you throw down as a challenge is spelled *gauntlet*.

(gaol). British spelling of *jail*.

garb. Don't use *garb* when *clothing* or *dress* will do.

garbage can, garbage truck. Two words.

garçon. Spell it with the cedilla under the *c*.

gargantuan. Small *g*.

garments. Don't use *garments* when *clothes* will do.

garrote, garroted, garroting. Spell it with two *r*'s and one *t* in all forms.

garrulous. Two *r*'s, followed by *u*.

gas, gases. No double *s* in the plural. Listed in Webster's as standard usage in the sense of gasoline. Slang in the sense of pleasure ("a gas").

gas, gassed, gassing. Two *s*'s in all forms except *gas*.

gas-. Some compounds are hyphened, some are one word, some two.

gasbag. One word.

gaseous ends in *-eous.*

gashouse. One word.

gasify, gasified. *I* after the *s.*

gaslight. One word.

gas mask. Two words.

gasmeter. One word.

gasoline ends in *-ine.*

gassy. Double *s.*

gate, gait. A *gate* is an opening, *gait* is a manner of walking.

gatekeeper, gateleg, gatepost, gateway. One word.

gauche, gaucherie are spelled with *auch.*

gaucho, gauchos.

gauge, gage. The spelling *gauge* is so odd and so apt to be misspelled that you're much better off always spelling the word *gage.* In technical writing *gage* is the regular spelling anyway.

gauntlet, gantlet. There are two words, both spelled either way. Commonly the flogging ordeal is spelled *gantlet* and the glove you throw down as a challenge is spelled *gauntlet.*

gavel, gaveled, gaveling. One *l* in all forms.

gawk, gawky are spelled with *aw.*

gay, gayer, gayest are spelled with *y,* but *gaily* and *gaiety* are spelled with *i. Gay* in the sense of homosexual is listed in Webster's as standard usage.

(gayly). The more common spelling is *gaily.*

gazelle. Spelled with *z* and double *l.*

gazetteer. One *z,* two *t*'s, followed by two *e*'s.

gearbox, gearshift, gearwheel. One word.

gee-whiz. Listed in Webster's as standard usage. Hyphened.

geezer. Listed in Webster's as standard usage.

Geiger counter starts with a capital *G.*

gelatin. Spell it without an *e* at the end.

gemcutter, gemstone. One word.

gendarme, gendarmerie.

gender. Don't write *gender* when you mean *sex,* even as a joke.

genealogy. Watch the *a* after the second *e.*

general. In such nouns as *attorney general, postmaster general, surgeon general,* the plural is *attorneys general, postmasters general, surgeons general.*

general consensus. Leave out *general.* It's unnecessary.

generalissimo, generalissimos.

generalize, generalization are spelled with *z.*

general public. Leave out *general.* It's unnecessary.

generator ends in *-or.*

genesis, geneses.

genie. A *genie,* in or out of a bottle, is spelled this way.

genitive. See APOSTROPHE.

genius, geniuses.

genre. Spell it like this. Don't underline.

genteel, genteelly. Two *l*'s in *genteelly.*

gentile. Small *g.*

gentleman. In general references to a person of the male sex, say *man* rather than *gentleman,* e.g. *I saw a man entering the house.* But use *gentlemen* in addressing a group and *gentleman* for courtesy, e.g. *This gentleman is next in line.*

gentlewoman is old-fashioned. Use *lady.*

genus. The plural is *genera.*

geo-. Spell compounds as one word.

geographic, geographical. The longer form is more common.

gerbil ends in *-il.*

German words. Don't use a German word when an English word will do just as well.

Germany, Germanys. The two *Germanys,* East and West, are spelled with *y.*

germ cell. Two words.

germfree, germproof. One word.

gerrymander, gerrymandering start with *g.*

gerund. See -ING.

get is natural, standard English. Don't use words like *become* or *obtain* when *get* will do.

getatable. One word.

getaway. One word.

get-together (noun). Hyphened.

getup. One word.

get with it is listed in Webster's as standard usage.

gewgaw. Spelled with *ew* and *aw.*

geyser is spelled with *ey* and *s.*

-gg-. See -G-, -GG-.

gh-. If you can't find the word you're looking for under *gh-,* try *g-.*

ghastly. Spelled with *gh*.

gherkin. Spelled with *gh*.

ghetto, ghettos.

ghost, ghostlike, ghostly. Spelled with *gh*.

ghost town. Two words.

ghostwrite, ghostwriter. One word.

ghoul, ghoulish. Spelled with *gh* and *ou*.

GI is listed in Webster's as standard usage. Use no periods. The plural is *GI's* or *GIs*.

gibberish starts with *g*.

gibe, jibe. *Gibe* means taut, to *jibe* means to match.

gift. Don't use *gift* as a verb when the simple word *give* will do.

giftware. One word.

gift-wrap, gift-wrapped. Hyphened.

giftwrapping. One word.

gigolo, gigolos.

gild, guild. *Gild* means cover with gold, *guild* with *u* means a union or group.

(gilder). Misspelling of *guilder*.

gilt, guilt. *Gilt* means a gold covering, *guilt* means culpability.

gilt-edge, gilt-edged. Hyphened.

gimmick is listed in Webster's as standard usage.

gingerbread, gingersnap. One word.

gingham. Watch the *gh*.

(gipsy). The common spelling is *gypsy*.

giraffe ends in *-ffe*.

gird. The more common past tense is *girded,* not *girt.*

girlfriend. One word.

girlie ends in *-ie*.

(gismo). The more common spelling is *gizmo*.

give (noun), capacity to yield, is standard usage.

give-and-take. Hyphened.

giveaway (noun). One word.

giveup (noun). One word.

gizmo, gizmos. Listed in Webster's as standard usage.

glacé. Spell it with the accent.

gladhand (verb). One word.

glad hand (noun). Two words.

gladiator ends in *-or*.

gladiolus, gladioluses. The plural *gladioluses* is more common than *gladioli* or *gladiolus*.

(glamor). The common spelling is *glamour* with *ou*.

glamorize, glamorous are spelled with *-or-*.

glamour. This is the common spelling.

glassblower, glassblowing, glasscutter, glasscutting. One word.

glassful, glassfuls.

glasshouse, glassmaker, glassmaking, glassware. One word.

glazier is spelled with *zi*.

glimpse ends in *e*.

glob is standard usage.

globetrotter, globetrotting. One word.

glockenspiel. Spelled as in German.

glop is listed in Webster's as slang.

glower is spelled with *ower*.

glowworm. One word.

gluco-. Spell compounds as one word, e.g. *glucoside*.

glue, gluing. Spell *gluing* without *e*.

gluepot. One word.

gluey is spelled with *e*.

glycerin. Commonly spelled without *e* at the end.

glycero-. Spell compounds as one word.

G-man, G-men. Capital *G* and hyphen.

gnarled, gnash, gnaw start with silent *g*.

gneiss. A famous spelling-bee word. Silent *g*, *ei* and double *s*.

gnome, gnomic. Silent *g*.

GNP. Abbreviation of Gross National Product. Use no periods.

gnu. The animal. Silent *g*.

go (noun). The plural is *goes*, e.g. *I had several goes at it*.

go-ahead. Hyphened.

goalie ends in *-ie*.

goalkeeper, goalpost. One word.

go-around. Hyphened.

goatherd, goatskin. One word.

gob, gobs. Listed as standard usage in Webster's.

gobbledygook. Commonly so spelled.

go-between. Hyphened.

go-by. Hyphened. Standard usage.

go-cart. Hyphened.

God, the one supreme being, is always spelled with a capital *G*. In compounds the word is often spelled with a small *g*.

god-awful. Listed as standard usage in Webster's. Small *g* and hyphened.

godchild, goddamn, goddamned, goddaughter. Small *g,* one word.

goddess. Two *d*'s, two *s*'s.

godfather. Small *g,* one word.

God-fearing. Capital *G,* hyphened.

godforsaken. Small *g,* one word.

God-given. Capital *G,* hyphened.

godhead, godless, godlike. Small *g,* one word.

God-loving. Capital *G,* hyphened.

godmother. One word.

godown (noun). One word.

godparent, godsend, godson, godspeed. One word.

-goer. Spell as one word such words as *moviegoer, operagoer, theatergoer.*

gofer, meaning errand boy, is slang.

go-getter, go-getting. Hyphened.

go-go. Hyphened.

going-over, goings-over. Hyphened.

goings-on. Hyphened.

gold-. Most compounds are spelled as one word.

goldbrick (used figuratively), **goldbug, golddigger.** One word.

golden rule. Small *g,* small *r.*

goldfish, goldfish (plural). One word.

gold mine, gold rush, gold standard. Two words.

golf-. Spell all compounds as two words.

golliwog. One *g* at the end.

goner is listed as standard usage in Webster's.

gonorrhea is spelled with *rrh.*

goo, gooey are listed as standard usage in Webster's.

good, as an adverb in the sense of *well,* is listed as standard usage in Webster's. Walt Whitman wrote "I hope you are well and getting along good."

goodby. Most newspapers and the GPO Style Manual spell it without a hyphen and without an *e* at the end.

good-for-nothing, good-humored, good-looking, good-natured, good-sized, good-tempered. Hyphened.

goodwill. One word.

goody, goodies. Standard usage.

goody-goody. Standard usage.

gooey. Spelled with *e.* Standard usage.

goof, goof-off (noun), **goofy.** Listed in Webster's as standard usage.

gook. Listed in Webster's as standard usage.

goose, geese.

gooseneck, goosepimples, goosestep. One word.

gorgeous ends in *-eous.*

gorilla, guerrilla. A *gorilla (o* and one *r)* is an ape, a *guerrilla* (*ue* and two *r*'s) is an underground fighter.

gormandize, gormandizing has no *u.*

gospel. Spell it with one *l.*

gossip, gossiped, gossiping, gossipy. One *p* in all forms.

got, gotten. Both past tenses of *get* are standard usage. So is the phrase *have got,* meaning *have,* and *have gotten,* meaning *have received.*

gouache. Spelled with *oua.*

goulash is spelled with *ou.*

gourmand, gourmet. A *gourmand* is a hearty eater, a *gourmet* is a connoisseur of fine food.

government. Watch the· *n* before the *m.* Small *g* except when *Government* is part of a title.

governor ends in *-or.*

grab, as in *how does that grab you?* is listed in Webster's (1973) as standard usage.

grab bag. Two words.

grabhook. One word.

graduate. The common usage is active, not passive: "He *graduated* from college." Don't leave out *from.*

graffiti. Two *f*'s, one *t.* The singular is *graffito.*

graham crackers, graham flour. Small *g.*

gram. Common spelling.

grammar ends in *-ar.* Remember "The study of grammar *mars* the enjoyment of English."

grammatical, grammatically. Watch the ending *-ally.*

granary. No *i.*

grand-. Spell all family compounds as one word, others as two.

grandchild, granddad, granddaughter. One word.

grand duchess, grand duke. Two words.

grandeur ends in *-eur.*

grandfather. One word.

grandiloquent, grandiloquence end in *-ent, -ence.*

grandma. One word.

grand master. Two words.

grandmother, grandnephew, grandniece, grandparent, grandson, granduncle. One word.

granny. No *e*.

grant-in-aid. Hyphened.

grantor ends in *-or*.

grapefruit. One word.

grape juice. Two words.

grapeshot, grapevine. Two words.

grapho-. Spell compounds as one word.

grass in the sense of marijuana is listed in Webster's as standard usage.

grassroots. One word.

grateful is spelled with *-ate*.

gratis. Don't write *gratis* when *free* will do.

gratuitous means free, uncalled-for. Don't use it in any other sense.

gratuity. Don't say *gratuity* when *tip* will do.

gravamen. The common plural is *gravamens*. Don't use *gravamen* when *burden* or *grievance* will do.

gravedigger. One word.

gravel, graveled, graveling. One *l* in all forms.

gravelly. Two *l*'s.

graveside, gravesite, gravestone, graveyard. One word.

gray, grey. Spelled with *a* in the US, with *e* in Britain.

(grayhound). Always spelled *greyhound*.

greasepaint, greaseproof. One word.

greasy ends in *-sy*.

great-. Hyphened in family compounds.

great-aunt. Hyphened.

Great Britain ends in *-ain*. Remember "Great Bri*tain* con*tain*s England, Scotland and Wales."

greatcoat. One word.

(greatful). Misspelling of *grateful*.

great-grandchild, great-granddaughter, great-grandfather, great-grandmother. All hyphened.

greathearted. One word.

great-nephew, great-niece, great-uncle. All hyphened.

Grecian, Greek. *Grecian* refers to ancient Greece, *Greek* is the general word.

Greco-. The spelling with *e* is common.

greenback, greenbelt. One word.

green-eyed. Hyphened.

greengage, greengrocer, greenhouse. One word.

greenness. Two *n*'s.

greenroom. One word.

(grewsome). Spell it *gruesome*.

(grey). The common US spelling is *gray*.

greyhound is spelled with *e*.

griddlecake. One word.

gridiron. One word.

grief, griefs. *I* before *e* except after *c*.

griefstricken. One word.

grievance ends in *-ance*.

grieve, grieved, grieving. *I* before *e* except after *c*.

grievous, grievously. No *i* after the *v*.

griffin. The common spelling ends in *-in*.

grill, grille. A *grill* (without an *e* at the end) is a cooking utensil or a restaurant, a *grille* (with the *e*) is a grating or ornamental screen. The verb *grill* in the sense of question is listed in Webster's as standard usage.

grillroom, grillwork. One word.

grimy. No *e*.

gringo, gringoes.

gripe in the sense of complain is listed in Webster's as standard usage.

grippe, meaning flu, ends in *-ppe*.

grisly, grizzly. *Grisly* means horrible, gruesome, *grizzly* means grayish like a *grizzly beard* or a *grizzly bear*.

gristle is spelled with a silent *t*.

gristmill. One word.

grocery store. Two words.

groggy. Standard usage.

groovy in the sense of wonderful is listed in Webster's as standard usage.

grosgrain. Spelled with an *s* between the *o* and the *g*.

gross national product. No capitals. Commonly abbreviated GNP.

grotto, grottoes.

grouch, grouchy. Listed in Webster's as standard usage.

ground crew, ground floor, ground swell. Two words.

grouse. The plural is *grouse*.

grouse in the sense of complain is listed in Webster's as standard usage.

grovel, groveled, groveling. One *l* in all forms.

-grower. Spell words ending in *-grower* as one word.

grownup. One word.

grueling. One *l.*

gruesome. *E* after *u.*

Gruyère. Capital *G* and accent on the *e.*

G-sharp. Capital *G* and hyphen.

G-string. Capital *G* and hyphen.

(gryphon). Spell it *griffin.*

(guage). Misspelling of *gage.*

guano, guanos.

guarantee, guaranty. The common spelling is *guarantee.*

guarantor ends in *-or.*

guard. Don't leave out the *u.*

guardhouse. One word.

guardian. Don't leave out the *u.*

guardrail, guardroom. One word.

guck. Listed in dictionaries as slang.

guerrilla, gorilla. A *guerrilla* (two *r*'s) is an underground fighter, a *gorilla* (one *r*) is an ape.

guess, in the sense of think, believe, suppose, is standard usage.

guesstimate is listed as standard usage in the Oxford English Dictionary.

guesswork. One word.

guesthouse, guestroom. One word.

guidance ends in *-ance.*

guidebook, guideline, guidepost. One word.

guide rail. Two words.

guild, gild. *Guild* with *u* means a *u*nion, *gild* means cover with gold.

guilder is spelled with *ui.*

guile, guileless, guilelessness.

guillotine. Two *l*'s, one *t.*

guilt, gilt. *Guilt* means culpability, *gilt* means gold covering.

guinea, guinea fowl, guinea hen, guinea pig. The spelling is *-inea.*

guise. Spelled with *ui* and *s.*

guitar ends in *-ar.*

gulf, gulfs.

gullible ends in *-ible.*

gumchewer, gumdrop. One word.

gumption is listed in Webster's as standard usage.

gumshoe in the sense of detective is listed in Webster's as standard usage.

gun-. Almost all compounds are spelled as one word.

gunfight, gunfire. One word.

gung ho. Listed in Webster's as standard usage.

gunk. Listed in Webster's as standard usage.

gunman. One word.

gun moll is slang. Two words.

(gunnel). The common spelling is *gunwale.*

gunplay, gunpoint, gunpowder, gunrunner, gunrunning, gunshot. One word.

gun-shy. Hyphened.

gunslinger, gunslinging, gunsmith. One word.

gunwale. So spelled, though pronounced *gunnel.*

guru, gurus. Now standard usage in the sense of intellectual leader or guide.

gussy up is listed in Webster's as standard usage.

gusto, gustoes.

guts in the sense of courage is listed in Webster's as standard usage.

guttapercha. One word.

guttural. Watch the second *u.*

guy in the sense of man or fellow is listed in Webster's as standard usage.

gym, short form of *gymnasium,* is standard usage.

gymnasium, gymnasiums.

gymno-. Spell compounds as one word, e.g. *gymnosperm.*

gyneco-. Spell compounds as one word.

gynecologist, gynecology. *E* after the *n.*

gyp, meaning cheat, is listed in Webster's as standard usage.

gypsy, gypsies. Common spelling.

gyrate, gyration start with *gy.*

gyro-. Spell compounds as one word.

gyrocompass, gyroscope. One word.

gyve, meaning fetter or shackle, is spelled with *gy.*

H

h-. If you can't find the word you're looking for under *h-,* try *wh-.*

habeas corpus. Two words, no hyphen. *Habeas* ends in *-eas.*

habitué. Accent on the *e.*

(Habsburg). Usually spelled *Hapsburg.*

hackneyed ends in *-eyed.*

had better, in the sense of *ought to,* is a common idiom. The word *had* is often shortened to *'d,* e.g. *You'd better do it,* or left out altogether, e.g. *We better leave.* There's a trend toward leaving it out.

hadn't. Common contraction of *had not.*

had rather is a common idiom, often shortened to *'d rather,* as in *I'd rather be there.*

(haemo-). The modern spelling is *hemo-.*

hail, hale. You *hail* a cab, but you *hale* someone before a judge.

hail-fellow-well-met. Three hyphens.

hailstone, hailstorm. One word.

hair-. Most compounds are spelled as one word.

hairband. One word.

(hairbrained). Misspelling of *harebrained.*

hairbreadth, hairbrush, haircloth, haircut. One word.

hairdo, hairdos. One word, no *e* in plural.

hairdresser, hairdressing. One word.

-haired. Spell compounds with a hyphen, e.g. *long-haired.*

hairline. One word.

hair net. Two words.

hairpiece, hairpin. One word.

hair-raiser, hair-raising. Hyphened.

hair ribbon. Two words.

hairsbreadth. Spell without a hyphen.

hair shirt. Two words.

hairsplitter, hairsplitting, hairspring, hairstyle, hairstyling, hairstylist. One word.

hair tonic. Two words.

hairtrigger. One word.

hairy in the sense of risky is listed in Webster's as standard usage.

halberd. Commonly spelled with *d.*

halcyon days means calm days. Spelled with *y.*

hale, hail. You *hale* someone before a judge, but you *hail* a cab.

half, halves.

half-. Compounds are hyphened, one word, or two words.

half-afraid, half-and-half. Hyphened.

halfback. One word.

half-baked, half-breed, half-brother, half-caste, half-clad, half-cocked. Hyphened.

half dollar. Two words.

half-done, half-dozen, half-full. Hyphened.

halfhearted, halfheartedness. One word.

half-holiday. Hyphened.

half hour. Two words.

half-jokingly, half-life, half-light, half-mast, half-moon. Hyphened.

half pay. Two words.

halfpenny. One word.

half-pint. Hyphened. In the sense of unimportant person listed in Webster's as standard usage.

half-sister, half-slip, half-sole, half-staff. Hyphened.

halftime, halftone. One word.

half-truth. Hyphened.

halfway, halfwit. One word.

halitosis. *I* after *l.*

hallboy. One word.

hallelujah. First two *l*'s, then one. Ends in *-jah.*

(halliard). Spell it *halyard.*

hallmark. One word.

(hallo). The common spelling is *hollo* for a general shout or cry, *hello* for the phone or an expression of surprise.

Halloween. Capital *H,* double *e.*

hallucinate, hallucination. Two *l*'s.

hallway. One word.

halo, halos.

halvah. Commonly spelled with *h* at the end.

halyard. Common spelling.

ham-fisted, ham-handed. Hyphened.

hammerlock, hammertoe. One word.

hamstring. The past tense is *hamstrung.*

hand. *To hand,* meaning *received,* is hopelessly old-fashioned.

hand-. Most compounds are spelled as one word.

handbag, handball, handbill, handbook, handbrake, handcart, handcuff. One word.

-handed. Compounds with a literal meaning are usually hyphened, e.g. *empty-handed, left-handed,* but compounds with a figurative meaning are usually spelled as one word, e.g. *evenhanded, highhanded.*

handful, handfuls.

handgrip, handgrenade, handgun, handhold. One word.

handicap, handicapped, handicapper, handicapping. Double *p* in all forms except *handicap.*

handicraft, handiwork. Spelled with *i.*

handkerchief, handkerchiefs. Follows the rule *"I before e except after c."* The plural ends in *-fs.*

hand-knit. Hyphened.

handmade, handmaiden. One word.

hand-me-down. Hyphened.

handout, handpick, handpicked, handrail. One word.

handset, handshake, handshaking. One word.

hands-off. Hyphened.

handsome, hansom. *Handsome,* with a *d* in the middle and an *e* at the end, means beautiful, *hansom* means a cab.

handspring, handstand. One word.

hand-to-hand, hand-to-mouth. Hyphened.

handwoven, handwriting, handwritten. One word.

handyman. One word, spelled with *y.*

hang. A criminal is *hanged,* a picture is *hung.*

hangar, hanger. An airplane shed ends in *-ar,* a coathanger in *-er.*

hangdog. One word.

hanger-on, hangers-on.

hang in, meaning persist or stick it out, is listed as standard usage in Webster's.

hangman. One word.

hangout (noun). One word. Listed as standard usage in Webster's.

hangover. One word.

hangup (noun). One word. Listed as standard usage in Webster's.

hankie, for *handkerchief,* is standard usage. The spelling with *-ie* is common.

hanky-panky. Hyphened.

Hanukkah, Chanukah. Both spellings are common.

haphazard, haphazardly.

hapless. Don't write *hapless* when *unfortunate* will do.

haply. Don't write *haply* when *perhaps* or *maybe* will do.

happening, meaning *event,* is standard usage.

happily, happiness. Spelled with *i.*

Hapsburg. Commonly spelled with *p.*

hara-kiri. The vowels run *a-a-i-i.* Hyphened.

harangue ends in *-gue.*

harass, harassment. One *r.* Remember *"harassed* as a hunted *hare."*

harbor ends in *-or.*

hard-. Some compounds are written as one word, some are hyphened.

hard-and-fast. Two hyphens.

hardback, hardball. One word.

hard-bitten, hard-boiled. Hyphened.

hardbound, hardcore, hardcover. One word.

hard-earned. Hyphened.

hardfisted, hardhanded, hardhat, hardheaded, hardhearted. One word.

hard-hitting. Hyphened.

hardihood, hardiness. Spelled with *i.*

hardline, hardliner, hardlining. One word.

hardly. Often idiomatically used to form a double negative. William H. Prescott wrote "The Indian monarch, stunned and bewildered, saw his faithful subjects falling round him, *without hardly* comprehending his situation."

hardly . . . than. Listed as standard usage in Webster's.

hardmouthed, hardnosed, hardpan. One word.

hard-shell. Hyphened.

hardtack, hardtop, hardware, hardwood. One word.

harebrained, harelip. One word.

harem. The vowels are *a* and *e.*

(hari-kari). The common spelling is *hara-kiri.*

harken. This spelling is more common than *hearken.*

harlequin. Spelled with *qu.*

harmonize ends in *-ize.*

harpsichord. Spelled with *ch*.

harried. Two *r*'s, even though *harass* has only one *r*.

hartebeest. Double *e*.

hart, heart. A *hart* is a stag, a *heart* pumps blood.

harum-scarum. Hyphen.

harvester ends in *-er*.

harvesttime. One word.

has-been. Hyphened.

hashish. Spell it with *i*.

hasn't. Common contraction of *has not*.

hassle is listed as standard usage in Webster's.

hasten is spelled with a silent *t*.

hatband, hatbox, hatbrim, hatbrush. One word.

hatchetman. One word.

hate in the sense of *dislike* ("I hate to bother you") is standard usage.

hatful, hatfuls.

hat in hand. No hyphens.

hatmaker, hatmaking, hatpin, hatrack, hatstand. One word.

hat tree. Two words.

haughty, haughtiness.

(hautbois, hautboy). The modern spelling is *oboe*.

haute couture, haute cuisine. Watch the *e* at the end of *haute*.

hauteur.

haut monde. No *e* at the end of *haut*.

have. Use the perfect tense with *have* for something that's still going on or has a lasting effect. In February write *we have had a very cold winter,* in July write *we had a very cold winter.*

Don't use two *have*'s where one will do. Instead of *I should have liked to have been there* write *I should have liked to be there.*

You can leave out the main verb in such sentences as *we asked people to tell us and a lot of them have*—even though what's left out is *told us* rather than *tell us*. It's common usage.

have got in the sense of *have* is standard usage.

have-not (noun, adjective). Hyphened.

haven't. Standard contraction of *have not*.

have reference to. Don't use *have reference to* when *mean* will do.

have the desire to. Don't use *have the desire to* when *want* will do.

have to. Standard usage for *must*.

havoc ends in *c*.

Hawaii, Hawaiian. Two *i*'s.

hay-. Most compounds are spelled as one word.

hay baler, hay fever. Two words.

hayfield, hayloft, haymaker, hayrack, hayrick, hayride, hayseed, haystack. One word.

hay wagon. Two words.

haywire. One word.

hazard, hazardous. One *z.*

hazelnut. One word.

haziness is spelled with *i.*

H-bomb. Capital *H* and hyphen.

he instead of *him,* as in *what with Jack and he being friends,* is listed as substandard in Webster's. But the idiom has been in use since 1560.

He with a capital *H,* referring to God, is getting rare.

he (name) looks awkward. Usually this device is unnecessary because the reference is clear without it. *Jim told Frank he had nothing to do with it* is clear—you don't need to write *he (Jim).* If there *is* a possibility of misreading, repeat the name without *he.*

head-. Almost all compounds are spelled as one word.

headache, headachy, headband, headboard, headcheese, headdress, headfirst, headgate, headgear, headhunter, headlight, headline, headliner, headlong, headman, headmaster, headmistress, headnote. One word.

head-on. Hyphened.

headphone, headpiece. One word.

headquarters. You can write either *the headquarters are in New York* or *the headquarters is in New York.*

headrest, headroom, headset, headstart, headstrong. One word.

head tax. Two words.

headwaiter, headway, headwind. One word.

healthful, healthy. Dictionaries now say you can use either word to mean either wholesome or well.

hear, here. You *hear* with your ears; what is *here* isn't there.

hearing aid. Two words.

(hearken). The spelling *harken* is more common.

hearse is spelled with *ea.*

heart-. Almost all compounds are spelled as one word.

heartache. One word.

heart attack. Two words.

heartbeat, heartbreak, heartbreaker, heartbreaking, heartbroken, heartburn. One word.

-hearted. Spell words ending in *-hearted* as one word, e.g. *half-hearted, lionhearted, softhearted.*

heartfelt. One word.

hearthrug, hearthstone. One word.

heartrending, heartsease, heartsick, heartsore, heartstrings, heartthrob, heartwarming. One word.

heathen, heathens.

heat rash. Two words.

heatstroke. One word.

heat wave. Two words.

heaved is more common than *hove* as the past tense of *heave.*

heaven-sent. Hyphen.

heavenward, heavenwards. Used with or without the ending *s.*

heavy-duty. Hyphened.

heavyhanded, heavyhearted. One word.

heavy-set. Hyphened.

heavyweight. One word.

hecatomb has a silent *b.*

hectic in the sense of exciting or confusing is standard usage.

hecto-. Compounds are spelled as one word, e.g. *hectogram.*

he'd. Common contraction of *he had* or *he would.*

hedge trimmer. Two words.

hedonism is spelled with *o.*

hegemony ends in *-ony.*

hegira. Spell it with *-gi-.*

heifer is spelled with *ei.*

heigh-ho is spelled with *ei.*

height ends in *t.*

heighten is spelled with *ei.*

(heighth). Common misspelling of *height.*

heinous is spelled with *ei.* It's pronounced with an *a* sound and follows the rule "Write *I* before *e* except after *c* or when sounded like *a* as in *neighbor* and *weigh.*"

heir is spelled with *ei.* Remember "The *heirs* took *theirs.*"

heir apparent, heir presumptive. An *heir apparent* is certain to inherit if he survives the ancestor, an *heir presumptive* may be cut out by the birth of a nearer relative.

heist is spelled with *ei.*

helicopter ends in *-er.*

helio-. Spell compounds as one word, e.g. *heliograph.*

helix, helices.

hell. Small *h.*

he'll. Common contraction of *he will* or *he shall.*

hellbent, hellcat. One word.

Hellenize ends in *-ize.*

hellhole, hellhound. One word.

hello, hellos.

helluva is standard usage, as in *he's a helluva nice guy.*

help. *Can't help but, cannot help but* is a long-established idiom. Stephen Vincent Benét wrote "And cannot help but see him, day after day."

helpmate is more common than *helpmeet.*

helter-skelter. Hyphen.

he-man. Hyphened.

hematoma, hematomas.

hemi-. Spell compounds as one word.

hemisphere.

hemo-. Common modern spelling (not *haemo-*). Spell compounds as one word.

hemoglobin, hemophilia, hemophiliac. Common modern spellings.

hemorrhage, hemorrhoids. Spelled with *-rrh-.*

hence. Don't write *hence* when *so* or *therefore* will do.

henceforth. Don't write *henceforth* when *from now on* will do.

henna, hennaed, hennaing.

henpecked. One word.

hep, hip, in the sense of informed, is listed in Webster's as standard usage.

hepatitis, hepatitides.

hepped up is listed in Webster's as standard usage.

her instead of the more formal *she* after *is* or *was* is idiomatic English. Dickens wrote "There was him and her asitting by the fire."

herald. Don't use *herald* when *announce* will do.

herbaceous ends in *-aceous.*

here. The phrase *this here* is listed as substandard in Webster's.

hereafter. Don't use *hereafter* when *from now on* or *later* will do.

hereby. Don't use *hereby* when *by this* will do or when no adverb is necessary.

hereditary ends in *-ary.*

herein. Don't use *herein* when *here* will do.

hereinabove. Don't use *hereinabove* when *earlier* will do.

hereinafter. Don't use *hereinafter* when *later* will do.

hereof. Don't use *hereof* when *of this* will do.

here's. Common contraction of *here is.*

heresy ends in *-sy.*

heretofore. Don't use *heretofore* when *earlier* or *until now* will do.

hereunto. Don't use *hereunto* when *to this* will do.

hereupon. Don't use *hereupon* when *on this* will do.

herewith. Don't use *herewith* when *with this* will do or when no adverb is necessary.

hero, heroes. But the plural *heros* is more common for submarine sandwiches.

heroic. It's *a heroic effort* (not *an*).

heroin, heroine. *Heroin* is a drug, a *heroine* is a female hero.

(her's). Misspelling of *hers.*

he's. Common contraction of *he is* or *he has.*

hesitancy, hesitant end in *-ancy, -ant.*

hetero-. Spell compounds as one word.

heterogeneity, heterogeneous end in *-eity, eous.*

het up is listed in Webster's as standard usage.

hew, hue. *Hew* means cut with heavy blows, *hue* means complexion or shade.

hexa-. Spell compounds as one word, e.g. *hexagram.*

hey. The exclamation is so spelled.

heyday is spelled with *ey* first, *ay* second.

hi. The greeting is so spelled.

hiatus, hiatuses.

hibachi ends in *i.*

hiccup, hiccuped, hiccuping are the common spellings.

hide, hid, hidden.

hide-and-seek. Hyphenated.

hideaway, hidebound. One word.

hideous ends in *-eous.*

hideout. One word.

hie, hied, hying (more common than *hieing*).

hierarchy is spelled with *ie.*

hieroglyphics is spelled with *ie.*

hifalutin, highfalutin. Both spellings are common. Standard usage.

hi-fi. This is the common spelling.

higgledy-piggledy. Hyphenated.

high-. Most compounds are spelled as one word.

highball, highbinder, highborn, highbrow. One word.
high chair. Two words.
high-class, high-colored. Hyphened.
higher-up, higher-ups. Hyphen.
highfalutin, hifalutin. Both spellings are common. Standard usage.
highflier, highflying. One word.
high-grade. Hyphened.
highhanded, highhandedness. One word.
high-hat. Hyphened.
high horse. Two words.
(highjinks). The spelling *hijinks* is more common.
highland, highlander, highlight. One word.
high-minded, high-muck-a-muck, high-power, high-pressure, high-priced. Hyphened.
high priest. Two words.
high-rise. Hyphened. Also spelled *hi-rise.*
highroad. One word.
high school. Never hyphened.
high-sounding, high-speed, high-spirited, high-strung. Hyphened.
hightail, highway, highwayman. One word.
hijack, hijacked, hijacking, hijacker. Commonly so spelled. Standard usage.
hijinks. Commonly so spelled.
hike in the sense of increase is standard usage.
hill-. Almost all compounds are spelled as one word.
hillbilly, hillcrest, hillside, hilltop. One word.
him instead of the more formal *he* after *is, was, be* or *than* is idiomatic English. Shakespeare (Macbeth, V, viii, 34) wrote "And damn'd be him that first cries 'Hold, enough!' " The idiom dates back to 1381.
hindrance ends in *-ance*. No *e* between *d* and *r*.
Hindu. Spell it with *u*.
hinge, hinged, hinging (no *e*).
hinterland.
hip, hep, in the sense of informed, is listed in Webster's as standard usage.
hippie ends in *-ie*. Standard usage.
hippo, hippos. Standard usage.
hippo-. Spell compounds as one word, e.g. *hippocampus.*
Hippocratic oath. Capital *H,* two *p*'s, ends in *-atic.*
hippopotamus, hippopotamuses.

hi-rise. Another spelling of *high-rise.*

histo-. Compounds are spelled as one word, e.g. *histogram.*

historian ends in *-ian.*

historic, historical. *Historic* means memorable, *historical* means dealing with past events. Write *a historic(al),* not *an.*

histrionics. No vowel between *t* and *r.*

hit-and-miss, hit-and-run (adjectives). Hyphens.

hitchhike, hitchhiker. One word.

hither is obsolete. Write *here.*

hitherto. Don't write *hitherto* when *up to now* will do.

hit-or-miss (adjective). Hyphens.

hoard, horde. A *hoard* is a hidden supply, a *horde* is a crowd.

hoarse, meaning harsh in sound, is spelled with *oa.*

hobbyhorse. One word.

hobnob, hobnobbed, hobnobbing.

hobo, hoboes.

hocus, hocused, hocusing.

hocus-pocus. Hyphened.

hod carrier. Two words.

hodgepodge. No hyphen.

hoe, hoed, hoeing.

hog, hogged, hogging, hoggish. Two *g*'s except in *hog.*

hogshead, hogtie, hogtied, hogtying. One word.

hog-wild. Hyphen. Listed in Webster's as standard usage.

ho-hum. Hyphen.

hoi polloi. *Hoi* is Greek for *the,* but *the hoi polloi* is common usage.

hoity-toity. Hyphen. Standard usage.

hokey, meaning corny, is listed in Webster's as standard usage. Ends in *-ey.*

hokum is listed in Webster's as standard usage.

-holder. Spell compounds as one word, e.g. *householder, policyholder, stockholder.*

holdout, holdover, holdup (nouns). One word.

hole, whole. A *hole* is an opening, *whole* means total.

holey, holy, wholly. *Holey* means having holes, *holy* means sacred, *wholly* means totally.

holiday has an *i* in the middle.

holiness is spelled with an *i.*

holler, meaning shout, ends in *-er.*

hollo is more common than *hallo, halloo,* or *halloa.*

holo-. Spell compounds as one word, e.g. *holograph.*

holy, holey, wholly. *Holy* means sacred, *holey* means having holes, *wholly* means entirely.

home-. Almost all compounds are spelled as one word.

homebound, homecoming, homegrown. One word.

homely, homey. *Homely* means familiar, plain, *homey* means homelike.

homeland, homemade, homemaker. One word.

homeo-. Spell compounds as one word.

homeopathy is spelled with *-eo-.*

homeowner, homeownership. One word.

home plate. Two words.

homeroom. One word.

home rule, home run. Two words.

homesick, homesite, homespun, homestead, homestretch, hometown. One word.

homeward, homewards. Both forms are common.

homework. One word.

homey. Ends in *-ey.*

homicidal, homicide. *I* after *m.*

homo-. Spell compounds as one word.

homogeneity, homogeneous end in *-eity, -eous.*

homogenize ends in *-ize.*

(homy). Spell it *homey.*

Hon. Abbreviation of *The Honorable.* Don't use *The* with *Hon.*

honeycomb. One word.

honeyed.

honkie, honky, honkies. Listed in Webster's as standard usage.

honor ends in *-or.*

honorable. As a title, write *The Honorable* or abbreviate *Hon.* (without *The*).

honorbound. One word.

honor guard, honor roll, honor system. Two words.

hooey is listed in Webster's as standard usage.

hoof, hooves.

hookah ends in *-ah.*

hookup. One word.

hooky. Spell it with *y.* Webster's lists it as standard usage.

hootenanny. First one *n,* then two.

hope chest. Two words.

hopefully in the sense of *it is hoped* is now standard usage. Harvard president Pusey wrote "Hopefully better coordinated and more effective programs may result."

hoping, hopping. *Hoping* means trusting, *hopping* means jumping.

Horatio Alger was the author, not the hero, of the rags-to-riches novels.

horde, hoard. A *horde* is a crowd, a *hoard* is a hidden supply.

horizon ends in *-on*.

horrible, horribly end in *-ible, -ibly*.

hors de combat. Three words.

hors d'oeuvre, hors d'oeuvres. Watch the spelling.

horse-. Almost all compounds are spelled as one word.

horseback, horsecar. One word.

horse chestnut. Two words.

horse-drawn, horse-faced. Hyphened.

horseflesh, horsehair, horsehide, horselaugh, horseman, horse-meat, horseplay, horseplayer, horsepower, horserace, horserac-ing, horsesense, horseshoe, horseshoer, horseshoeing, horse-thief. One word.

horse trade. Two words.

horsewhip, horsewhipped, horsewhipping, horsewoman. One word.

horsey. Spell it with *-ey*.

hosanna. Spelled with *sa* and double *n*.

hosiery is spelled with *ie*.

hospitable ends in *-able*.

hospitalize ends in *-ize*.

host (verb) in the sense of *emcee* is now standard usage.

hostel, hosteled, hosteling, hosteler. One *l* in all forms.

hostile ends in *-ile*.

hotbed. One word.

hot-blooded. Hyphen.

hotbox, hotcake. One word.

(hotchpotch). The common spelling is *hodgepodge*.

hotdog (verb) in the sense of showing off is listed in Webster's as standard usage. One word.

hot dog, meaning a showoff, is also listed as standard usage. Two words.

hotel. Write *a hotel* (not *an hotel*).

hotfoot, hothead, hotheaded, hothouse, hotline, hotrod, hotshot. One word.

houndstooth. One word.

hourglass. One word.

houri. Spelled with *ou.*

-house. Compounds are spelled as one word, e.g. *hothouse, ice-house, penthouse.*

house-. Almost all compounds are spelled as one word.

houseboat, housebound, houseboy, housebreaker, housebreaking, housebroken. One word.

house call. Two words.

houseclean, housecoat, housedress, housefront. One word.

houseful, housefuls.

houseguest, household, householder, housekeep, housekeeper, housekeeping, houselights, housemaid, houseman, house-mother. One word.

house organ, house painter, house party. Two words.

house-proud. Hyphen.

houseroom, housetop, housewarming, housewife, housewives, housework. One word.

(hove). *Heaved* is more common.

how in the sense of *that* is an old English idiom. Dickens wrote "Bob Cratchit told them how he had a situation in his eye for Master Peter."

(howbeit). Obsolete. Write *though* or *although.*

how come in the sense of *why* is standard usage.

howdah (on an elephant) ends in *-ah.*

however. Don't use *however* when *but* will do. If you do use *however* in the sense of *but,* put a semicolon or—better—a period before it, e.g. *I won't vote against the proposal; however, I won't vote for it either.* Or *I won't vote against the proposal. However, I won't vote for it either.*

   If you put *however* inside a sentence, put it after the word you want to emphasize, e.g. *This, however, was not what I meant.* You can leave out the commas. Thomas Jefferson wrote "It is however an evil for which there is no remedy."

   However in the sense of *how in the world* is spelled as one word, e.g. *However did you do it?*

howitzer is spelled with *tz.*

how's. Common contraction of *how is.*

howsoever. Don't write *howsoever* when *however* will do.

hoyden is spelled with *y.*

huarache. Spelled with *hua.*

hubbub. First two *b*'s, then one.

hue, hew. *Hue* means shade of color, *hew* means cut by blows.

huggable. Two *g*'s, ends in *-able.*

hugger-mugger. Hyphened.

Huguenot. Two *u*'s.

hullabaloo. First two *l*'s, then one.

(hullo). Spell it *hello* for the phone.

human (noun) in the sense of human being has been used since 1533. William James wrote "incomprehensible to us humans."

human, humane. *Human* means of man, *humane* means compassionate.

humanize ends in *-ize.*

humble. Write *a humble* (not *an humble*). *In my humble opinion* sounds phony.

humbug, humbugged, humbugging. Two *g*'s except in *humbug.*

humero-. Spell compounds as one word.

humerus, humeri. The upper arm bone.

humiliate is spelled with *-ili-.*

humor, humorous. Spelled with *-or.*

humpback, humpbacked. One word.

humpty-dumpty. Hyphened.

humus ends in *-us.*

hunch in the sense of premonition is listed as standard usage in Webster's.

hunchback, hunchbacked. One word.

hundred is sometimes carelessly misspelled.

hung, hanged. A picture is *hung,* but a criminal is *hanged.*

hungry. No *e.*

hung up, meaning anxiously nervous, is listed as standard usage in Webster's.

hunk is listed as standard usage in Webster's.

hunky-dory. Hyphened. Listed in Webster's as standard usage. Ends in *-y.*

hurly-burly. Hyphened.

hurrah ends in *-ah.*

hurry, hurried, hurrying.

hurt in the sense of suffer is listed in Webster's as standard usage.

hush-hush is listed in Webster's as standard usage.

hussar. Two *s*'s.

hustle has a silent *t.*

huzzah. Spell it with an *h* at the end.

hyacinth. First *y,* then *i.*

(hyaena). The common spelling is *hyena.*

hybrid is spelled with *y.*

hydrangea ends in *-ea.*

hydro-. Spell compounds as one word, e.g. *hydrofoil.*

hyena. Common spelling.

hymn is spelled with *mn.*

hype, hyped-up is slang.

hyper-. Compounds are spelled as one word.

hyperbola, hyperbole. A *hyperbola* is a geometrical figure, a *hyperbole* is an exaggeration.

hypercritical, hypocritical. *Hypercritical* means overcritical, *hypocritical* means pretending to virtue etc.

hyphen. The following rules are based on Webster's, the GPO Style Manual and common newspaper usage.

1. Use a hyphen to divide a word at the end of a line (see DIVISION OF WORDS).

2. Hyphen fractions and compound numerals between 21 and 99, e.g. *two-thirds, forty-seven.*

3. Hyphen measurements and adjectives with numbers referring to age, e.g. *1-inch ruler, 9-year-old boy.*

4. Except for words with the prefixes *co-, pre-, pro-* and *re-,* hyphen words to avoid doubling a vowel or tripling a consonant, e.g. *anti-inflation, micro-organism, shell-like, ultra-atomic.* But *coordinate, preempt, prooxidant, reenter.*

5. Hyphen the prefixes *ex-, self-* and *quasi-,* e.g. *ex-governor, self-conscious, quasi-judicial.*

6. Hyphen words to avoid ambiguity, e.g. *co-op, re-cover* (a sofa), *un-ionized.*

7. Put a hyphen between a prefix and a capital letter, e.g. *un-American, pro-Arab, pre-Renaissance.*

8. Hyphen the suffixes *-elect, -designate, -odd* and *-in,* e.g. *president-elect, ambassador-designate, twenty-odd, drive-in.*

9. Hyphen compounds consisting of three words, e.g. *do-it-yourself, editor-in-chief, good-for-nothing, hand-me-down, sister-in-law.*

10. Hyphen compounds whose first part is a single capital letter, e.g. *H-bomb, X-ray.* But there's no hyphen in *T square.*

11. Hyphen compounds of two capitalized words, e.g. *European-American.*

12. Hyphen a compound modifier used before a noun, except if the first part ends in *-ly,* e.g. *ivy-covered walls, long-term loan, lower-income group, much-admired painter, well-known lawyer.*

But *simply dressed woman, widely known expert.* If the word ending in *-ly* is not an adverb but an adjective, hyphen the compound modifier, e.g. *a scholarly-minded reviewer.*

13. Hyphen three-point compass directions, e.g. *north-northeast. south-southwest.*

14. Don't hyphen a Latin compound, e.g. *ad hoc committee, per capita basis.*

15. Don't hyphen words always spelled as two words, even if used as modifiers before a noun, e.g. *civil rights case, high school education, life insurance company, social security check, special delivery letter.*

Otherwise there are no hard-and-fast rules. The trend is toward writing compound words as one word, e.g. *antiaircraft, byproduct, ceasefire, lameduck, lifestyle, pigheaded, takeout, tipoff.*

hypnotize ends in *-ize.*

hypo-. Compounds are spelled as one word.

hypochondria, hypochondriac are spelled with *ch.*

hypocrisy ends in *-isy.* Remember "Hypocrisy is no good in a *crisis.*"

hypocritical, hypercritical. *Hypocritical* means pretending to virtue etc., *hypercritical* means overcritical.

hypotenuse. No *th.*

hypothecate, hypothesize. *Hypothecate* means mortgage, *hypothesize* means assume.

hypothesis, hypotheses.

hypothetically ends in *-ally.*

hysterically ends in *-ally.*

hystero-. Compounds are spelled as one word, e.g. *hysterotely.*

I

I in the sense of *me,* as in *between you and I,* though disapproved by conservative grammarians, has been a common idiom since 1596. Shakespeare (Sonnet lxxii) wrote "And hang more praise upon deceased I." See also ME.

It's pure superstition to think that *I* shouldn't be used at the beginning of a letter. *I'm pleased to send you this check* is a fine opening.

I am, I remain at the beginning of the last paragraph of a business letter is old-fashioned.

I-beam. Hyphened.

ibid. is an abbreviation of Latin *ibidem* (in the same place). It's used in footnotes to refer to the source given in the preceding footnote. Don't forget the period. No underlining (italics). Many modern writers don't use *ibid.* but simply repeat the author's last name, e.g. *Miller, p. 87.*

-ible, -able. There's no reliable rule to follow when you're in doubt whether a word ends in *-ible* or *-able.* The *-ible* words are rarer, so chances are if you spell it *-able,* you'll be right.

ice, iced, icing.

ice-. Most compounds are spelled as one word.

ice age, ice bag. Two words.

iceberg, iceboat, icebound, icebox, icebreaker, icecap. One word.

ice-cold. Hyphened.

ice cream. Two words.

iced tea. Don't leave out the *d.*

ice floe. Two words.

icehouse, iceman. One word.

ice milk, ice pack, ice show. Two words.

ice-skate (verb). Hyphened.

ice skate (noun), **ice skater, ice storm, ice water.** Two words.

ichthyo-. So spelled. Write compounds as one word.

ichthyology. Spelled with *-chthy-*.

-ics. With names of studies or activities use the singular verb, e.g. *Politics makes strange bedfellows.—Athletics wasn't his forte.* But with matters of behavior or operations use the plural verb, e.g. *His tactics were poor.—Her hysterics were ridiculous.—The underlying mechanics are obscure.*

icy. No *e*.

I'd. Common contraction of *I would, I should* or *I had.*

ID card. No periods necessary.

ideally ends in *-ally.*

(idealogy). Misspelling of *ideology.*

identical. Write *identical with* or *to.* Don't use *identical* when *same* will do.

identified with. Don't use *is identified with* when *works for* will do.

ideo-. Spell compounds as one word.

ideology ends in *-ology.*

idiosyncrasy, idiosyncrasies end in *-asy, -asies.*

idle, idol, idyll. *Idle* means not working, an *idol* is an image, an *idyll* is a peaceful, rustic scene or episode.

idolater ends in *-er.*

idolatrous, idolatry. No *e*.

I don't think, as in *I don't think it's going to rain,* is good idiomatic English.

idyll. Commonly spelled with two *l*'s. Means a peaceful, rustic scene or episode.

idyllic. Two *l*'s.

i.e., e.g. *I.e.* means *that is, e.g.* means *for example.* Don't use *i.e.* when *that is* will do just as well.

-ie-, -ei-. The basic rule is:

> Write *i* before *e*
>
> Except after *c*
>
> Or when sounded like *ay*
>
> As in *neighbor* and *weigh.*

But there are a few exceptions like *either, height, leisure, neither, seize, seizure, sleight, stein* and *weird.*

if, though. Don't use *if* when *though* will be clearer.

if, whether. There's nothing wrong in using *if* instead of *whether.* The King James Bible says "He sent forth a dove from him, to see if the waters were abated." (Genesis 8:8)

if and when. Don't use *if and when* when either *if* or *when* alone will do.

if . . . was, if . . . were. The idiom *was* in such expressions as *if I was President* (condition contrary to fact) goes back to 1684. John Bunyan in Pilgrim's Progress wrote "as if I was awake." The subjunctive form *were* is more formal. It is always used in the fixed phrase *if I were you*.

-ify. There are many verbs ending in *-ify*, but three exceptions ending in *-efy—liquefy, rarefy, stupefy*.

igneous ends in *-eous*.

ignominious ends in *-ious*.

ignorance, ignorant end in *-ance, -ant*.

ileo-. Compounds are spelled as one word.

ilex, ilexes.

ilk in the sense of kind, sort is standard usage.

ill, sick. Interchangeable in the US, but *ill* is slightly more formal. Don't use *ill* when *sick* will do.

I'll. Common contraction of *I will, I shall*.

ill-. Compounds are hyphened.

ill-advised, ill-defined, ill-disposed. Hyphened.

illegal, illegible, illegitimate. All starting with *ill-*.

ill-fated, ill-gotten, ill-humored. Hyphened.

illiberal, illicit. Start with *ill-*.

illimitable ends in *-able*.

illiteracy, illiterate. *E* between *t* and *r*.

ill-mannered, ill-natured. Hyphened.

illogical starts with *ill-*.

ill-omened, ill-starred, ill-tempered, ill-timed, ill-treat, ill-treated. Hyphened.

(illume). The modern word is *illuminate*.

ill-usage, ill-use. Hyphened.

illusion, delusion. An *illusion* comes from a deceptive appearance, a *delusion* from a state of mind.

illustrator ends in *-or*.

ill will. Two words.

ill-wisher. Hyphened.

(illy). Use *ill-* with a hyphen.

im-. If you can't find the word you're looking for, try *imm-*.

I'm. Common contraction of *I am*.

imaginable ends in *-able*. Means "that can be imagined."

imaginary, imaginative. *Imaginary* means not real, *imaginative* means having imagination.

imbecile ends in *-ile*.

(imbed). The common form is *embed*.

imbibe. Don't use *imbibe* when *drink* will do.

imbroglio, imbroglios. Watch the silent *g*.

imitable ends in *-able*.

imitate, imitation. One *m*.

imitator ends in *-or*.

immaculate. Two *m*'s.

immalleable. Two *m*'s, two *l*'s, ends in *-eable*.

immanent, imminent. *Immanent* means being within, *imminent* means threatening.

immaterial. Two *m*'s. Means unimportant.

immature. Two *m*'s.

immeasurable. Two *m*'s.

immediately. Two *m*'s.

immense, immensely. Two *m*'s.

immigrant, emigrant. An *immigrant* enters a country to settle there, an *emigrant* leaves a country to settle elsewhere.

imminent, immanent. *Imminent* means threatening, *immanent* means being inside. "*Imminent* is what can happen any *minute*."

immobile, immobilize, immoderate, immodest, immolate, immolation. Two *m*'s.

immoral, amoral. *Immoral* means wicked, *amoral* means indifferent to moral standards.

immortal. Two *m*'s.

immortalize ends in *-ize*.

immovable ends in *-able*. No *e* after *v*.

immune. When *immune* means exempt, it's used with *from,* e.g. *immune from taxation.* When it means protected, it's used with *from* or *against,* e.g. *immune from interruptions, immune against criticism.* When *immune* means not susceptible, it's used with *to,* e.g. *immune to a virus.*

immuno-. Compounds are spelled as one word, e.g. *immunotherapy.*

immutable ends in *-able*. Two *m*'s.

impair, impairment. Don't use *impair* or *impairment* when *harm, damage* etc. will do.

impalpable ends in *-able*.

impanel, impaneled, impaneling. One *l* in all forms. (Not *em-*.)

impassable, impassible. What's *impassable* can't be passed, he who's *impassible* can't feel.

impasse has an *e* at the end.

impassive means unfeeling. More common than *impassible*.

impeccable ends in *-able*. Two *c*'s.

impecunious. Don't write *impecunious* when *penniless* or *poor* will do.

impedance ends in *-ance*.

impede. Don't use *impede* when *hinder* will do.

impel, impelled, impelling. Two *l*'s except in *impel*.

impend. Don't use *impend* when *threaten* or *come up* will do.

impenetrable ends in *-able*.

impenitence, impenitent end in *-ence, -ent*.

imperceptible ends in *-ible*.

imperial, imperious. *Imperial* means of an emperor, *imperious* means overbearing.

imperil, imperiled, imperiling. One *l* in all forms.

imperishable ends in *-able*.

impermanence, impermanent end in *-ence, -ent*.

impertinence, impertinent end in *-ence, -ent*.

imperturbable ends in *-able*.

impetigo. *E* after *p*.

impetuous ends in *-uous*.

impetus, impetuses.

implacable ends in *-able*.

implausible ends in *-ible*.

implement. Don't use *implement* when *fulfill* or *carry out* will do.

implicit, explicit. *Implicit* means unexpressed but implied, *explicit* means expressed.

imply, infer. *Imply* means hint, *infer* means guess. See also INFER.

import. Don't say *import* when *meaning* or *importance* will do.

importable ends in *-able*.

importance, important end in *-ance, -ant*.

impose. Don't use *impose* when *charge* will do.

impossible ends in *-ible*.

impost. Don't use *impost* when *tax* will do.

impostor ends in *-or*. Remember "An impost*or* must be a good act*or*."

impotence, impotent end in *-ence, -ent*.

impracticable, impractical. In the US there's no distinction in meaning and *impractical* is the common form.

impregnable ends in *-able*.

impresario, impresarios. One *s*.

impressible ends in *-ible*.

impressionable ends in *-able.*
imprimatur.
improbable ends in *-able.*
impromptu, impromptus.
improvable ends in *-able.* No *e* after *v.*
improvidence, improvident end in *-ence, -ent.*
improvise, improvisation. No *z.*
imprudence, imprudent end in *-ence, -ent.*
impudence, impudent end in *-ence, -ent.*
impugn has a silent *g.*
in in the sense of fashionable is listed in Webster's as standard
usage.
in, at. Use *in* with the name of a city, no matter how small—*in
New York, in Podunk.*
in, into. *In* in the sense of *into* is standard usage.
in-. If you can't find the word you're looking for, try *inn-.*
-in. Compounds ending in *-in* are hyphened, e.g. *sit-in, drive-in.*
in-, un-. There's no hard-and-fast rule when to use *in-* and when
un- to mean *not* with adjectives. *In-* is more common with
Latin-derived words and *un-* with old English words, but there
are lots of exceptions, e.g. *unessential, unnecessary, unresponsive.*
(inacceptable). The common form is *unacceptable.*
inaccessible ends in *-ible.*
inaccuracy, inaccurate. Double *c.*
in addition. Don't use *in addition* when *and* or *also* will do.
in addition to. Don't use *in addition to* when *besides* will do.
inadequacy, inadequate. *E* after *d.* Don't use *inadequate* when *not
enough* will do.
inadmissible ends in *-ible.*
inadvertence, inadvertency. Commonly *inadvertence* in the singular, *inadvertencies* in the plural.
inadvertent ends in *-ent.*
inadvisable. Not *un-.*
inalienable ends in *-able.*
(inalterable). *Unalterable* is more common.
inamorata. One *n.*
in an effort to. Don't use *in an effort to* when *to* will do.
inapplicable ends in *-able.*
(inapproachable). The common form is *unapproachable.*
inappropriate. First two *p*'s, then one.

inapt, inept, unapt. *Inapt* means inappropriate, e.g. *an inapt quotation*. *Inept* means awkward, e.g. *an inept handyman*. *Unapt* means unlikely, e.g. *unapt to agree*.

inasmuch as. Don't use *inasmuch as* when *since* will do.

in association with. Don't use *in association with* when *with* will do.

inaudible ends in *-ible*.

inaugurate, inauguration, inaugurator. *U* after *g*. Don't use *inaugurate* when *start* will do.

inauspicious ends in *-icious*.

in back of, meaning *behind,* is listed in Webster's as standard usage.

in behalf of, on behalf of. Both are standard usage.

inborn, inbound, inbred. One word.

Inc. Abbreviation of *Incorporated* following the name of a company without comma. Leave out *Inc.* when the name alone will do.

incalculable ends in *-able*.

incandescent ends in *-scent*.

incapable ends in *-able*.

(incase). The common form is *encase*.

incautious ends in *-tious*.

incense. First *c* then *s*.

inception. Don't use *inception* when *start* or *beginning* will do.

incentive. Spelled with *c*.

incessant, incessantly. One *c*, two *s*'s.

incestuous ends in *-uous*.

inchoate means just begun, still unorganized.

incidence, incident end in *-ence, -ent*. An *incident* is something minor. Don't use the word for major events.

incidentally ends in *-ally*. Remember, "It *all* happened incident-*ally.*"

incipience, incipient end in *-ence, -ent*.

incise, incision, incisive. First *c*, then *s*.

incisor ends in *-or*.

inclement weather. Don't use this phrase when *stormy weather* or *bad weather* will do.

inclined to think. Don't use *I am inclined to think* when *I think* will do.

(inclose). The common form is *enclose*.

(inclosure). The common form is *enclosure*.

includable, includible. Spell it *includable* with *a* (GPO Style Manual).

include. Don't use *include* when you give a complete list. Don't write *they had five pets, including four cats and a dog.* Write *they had five pets—four cats and a dog.*

(includible). Spell it *includable.*

incognito, incognitos.

incoherence, incoherent end in *-ence, -ent.*

income tax. Never hyphened.

incommensurate. Two *m*'s.

incommunicado. Two *m*'s.

(incommunicative). The common form is *uncommunicative.*

imcomparable. The common form.

imcompatible ends in *-ible.*

incompetence, incompetency. *Incompetence* is generally used in the sense of incapacity, *incompetency* is strictly a legal term.

imcomprehensible ends in *-ible.*

inconceivable ends in *-able.* Spelled with *ei.*

incongruence, incongruent end in *-ence, -ent.*

incongruous ends in *-uous.*

in connection with. Don't use *in connection with* when *about, in* or *on* will do.

in consequence of. Don't use this phrase when *because of* or *due to* will do.

inconsequential ends in *-tial.*

inconsiderable ends in *-able.*

inconsistency, inconsistent end in *-ency, -ent.*

inconsolable ends in *-able.*

inconspicuous ends in *-uous.*

inconstancy, inconstant end in *-ancy, -ant.*

incontestable ends in *-able.*

incontinence, incontinent end in *-ence, -ent.*

(incontrollable). The common form is *uncontrollable.*

incontrovertible ends in *-ible.*

inconvenience ends in *-ence.* An *inconvenience* is something minor. Don't use the word to downplay someone else's trouble or annoyance.

inconvenient ends in *-ent.*

incorporeal ends in *-eal.*

incorrigible ends in *-ible.* Two *r*'s.

incorruptible ends in *-ible.* Two *r*'s.

incredible, incredulous. *Incredible* means hard to believe, *incredulous* means skeptical.

incriminate. Three *i*'s.

incrust, incrustation. Common form (not *en-*).

incubator ends in *-or*.

incubus, incubuses.

inculcate. You inculcate something *in* (or *upon*) someone, e.g. *He inculcated a scientific attitude in his students*, or you inculcate someone *with* something, e.g. *He inculcated his students with a scientific attitude.*

incumbent. Instead of *the present incumbent* write *the incumbent.*

(incumber, incumbrance). The common forms are *encumber, encumbrance.*

incunabulum, incunabula.

incur, incurred, incurring. Two *r*'s except in *incur.*

incurable ends in *-able.*

incurious. Not *un-.*

indebted, indebtedness. Silent *b.* Don't use *indebtedness* when *debt* or *debts* will do.

indecipherable ends in *-able.*

indeed needs no commas before or after it.

indefatigable ends in *-able.* No *u.*

indefensible ends in *-ible.*

indefinable ends in *-able.*

indefinite, indefinitely. *I* before the *t.* Remember "That's definite-ly *it.*"

indelible ends in *-ible.*

indelicacy ends in *-acy.*

indelicate ends in *-ate.*

indemnify, indemnified, indemnifying.

indentation, indention. *Indentation* means a notch, *indention* means a blank space to the right or left of a written line. The first line of a paragraph in typewritten copy is usually indented from five to eight spaces.

independence, independent end in *-ence, -ent.* Independence Day, July 4, has four *e*'s.

in-depth. Hyphened when used before a noun.

indescribable ends in *-able.* Spelled with *des* (not *dis*).

indestructible ends in *-ible.* Spelled with *des* (not *dis*).

index, indexes. The plural *indices* is now used only in mathematics.

india rubber. Spell it with a small *i*.

indicate. Don't use *indicate* when *hint, suggest, mean, show, say* will do.

indicator ends in *-or*.

indicia. Use a plural verb.

indict, indite. *Indict* (pronounced like *indite*) means charge or accuse, *indite* means compose or write.

indifference, indifferent end in *-ence, -ent*.

indigence ends in *-ence*.

indigene ends in *e*.

indigenous. Don't use *indigenous* when *native* will do.

indigent ends in *-ent*.

(indigested). The common form is *undigested*.

indigestible ends in *-ible*.

indigo, indigos.

indiscernible ends in *-ible*. Spelled with *sc*.

(indisciplined). The common form is *undisciplined*.

indiscreet, indiscrete. *Indiscreet* means imprudent, *indiscrete* means not separate.

(indiscribable). Misspelling of *indescribable*.

indiscriminate ends in *-ate*.

(indiscriminating). The common form is *undiscriminating*.

indispensable ends in *-able*. Remember "Indispensable as sable."

indisputable ends in *-able*.

indissoluble ends in *-uble*. Double *s*.

indistinguishable ends in *-able*.

(indistructible). Misspelling of *indestructible*.

indite, indict. *Indite* means compose or write, *indict* (pronounced like *indite*) means charge or accuse.

individual. Don't use *individual* when *person, man* or *woman* will do.

individually. Don't use *individually* when *each* will do.

indivisible ends in *-ible*.

indolence, indolent end in *-ence, -ent*.

indomitable ends in *-able*.

indoor, indoors. *Indoor* is an adjective, e.g. *an indoor sport, indoors* is an adverb, e.g. *we stayed indoors*.

(indorse, indorsement). The common forms are *endorse, endorsement*.

indubitable ends in *-able*.

(indue). The common form is *endue*.

indulgence, indulgent end in *-ence, -ent.*

(indure). The common form is *endure.*

industrywide. One word.

inebriated. Don't use *inebriated* when *drunk* will do.

inedible, uneatable. *Inedible* means unfit to be eaten, *uneatable* means spoiled, unfit to be served.

(inedited). The common form is *unedited.*

ineffable ends in *-able.*

in effect. No commas before or after.

ineffective, ineffectual, inefficacious, inefficient. *Ineffective* means not performing well, *ineffectual* means futile, *inefficacious* is rare and means the same as *ineffective* and *inefficient* means wasteful of time or energy.

ineligible ends in *-ible.*

inept, inapt, unapt. *Inept* means awkward, *inapt* means inappropriate, *unapt* means unlikely.

inequitable ends in *-able.*

inequity, iniquity. *Inequity* means unfairness, *iniquity* means vice.

ineradicable ends in *-able.*

inescapable ends in *-able.* (Not *un-.*)

(inessential). The common form is *unessential.*

inestimable ends in *-able.*

inevitable ends in *-able.*

in excess of. Don't use *in excess of* when *more than* or *over* will do.

inexcusable ends in *-able.*

inexhaustible ends in *-ible.* Watch the silent *h.*

inexorable ends in *-able.*

inexpediency, inexpedient end in *-ency, -ent.* Don't use *inexpedient* when *unwise* will do.

inexperience, inexperienced end in *-ence, -enced.*

inexplicable ends in *-able.*

inexpressible ends in *-ible.*

inextinguishable ends in *-able.*

inextricable ends in *-able.*

infallible ends in *-ible.*

infant. Don't use *infant* when *baby* will do.

infarction, infraction. An *infarction* is diseased tissue in the body, an *infraction* is the violation of a rule.

in favor of. Don't use *in favor of* when *for* will do.

infer, inferred, inferring. Two *r*'s except in *infer.*

infer, imply. *Infer* means guess, *imply* means suggest or hint. But Webster's lists *infer* also in the sense of *imply* or *hint*. Milton wrote "Consider first that great or bright infers not excellence." The usage goes back to 1530.

inferable ends in *-able*. One *r*.

inference ends in *-ence*.

inferno, infernos.

infield, infielder. One word.

infighting. One word.

infiltrate. No *e* between *t* and *r*.

infinite ends in *-ite*. Three *i*'s.

infinitive. See SPLIT INFINITIVE.

infirmary ends in *-ary*.

inflammable. *Flammable* is now the more common form.

inflammatory ends in *-ory*.

inflatable ends in *-able*.

inflection is spelled with *ct*.

inflexible ends in *-ible*.

in-flight. Hyphened.

info, the abbreviated form of *information,* is listed as standard usage in Webster's.

(infold). The common form is *enfold*.

(inforce). The common form is *enforce*.

inform. Don't use *inform* when *tell* will do.

informant, informer. An *informant* is a neutral source of information, an *informer* informs against another.

infra. *Below* is more common.

infra-. Compounds are spelled as one word.

infraction, infarction. An *infraction* is the violation of a rule, an *infarction* is diseased tissue in the body.

infrahuman, infrared. One word.

infrequency, infrequent end in *-ency, -ent.*

infringe, infringed, infringing. Both *infringe something* and *infringe on* or *upon something* are standard usage.

infusible ends in *-ible*.

(in future). British idiom. The US idiom is *in the future*.

-ing. Watch out for so-called dangling participles, as in this classic example: "Mr. Zapruder, filming the Presidential motorcade recorded the exact instant the President was shot. Then, sobbing, his fingers slipped from the camera." This is bad writing since it says that Mr. Zapruder's fingers were sobbing. But many times the same kind of thing sounds all right. Lord Byron wrote "Awakening with a start, the waters heaved around me."

It is more common today to write *I'm surprised at Bob saying that* than *I'm surprised at Bob's saying that.* When in doubt, leave out the *'s.*

ingenious, ingenuous. *Ingenious* means clever, *ingenuous* means innocent, childlike.

ingenue needs no accent.

ingenuity, ingenuousness. *Ingenuity* means cleverness, *ingenuousness* means artlessness.

(ingraft). The common form is *engraft.*

ingrained starts with *in-.*

(ingrave). Commonly spelled *engrave.*

ingredient ends in *-ent.*

in-group. Hyphened.

(ingulf). The common form is *engulf.*

inhabitant ends in *-ant.*

inherent ends in *-ent.*

inheritance ends in *-ance.*

inheritor ends in *-or.*

inhibitor. Spell it with *-or.*

inhospitable ends in *-able.*

in-house. Hyphened.

inhuman, nonhuman, unhuman. *Inhuman* means cold, brutal, *nonhuman* means not a human being. *Unhuman* is almost never used.

inimical. First *n,* then *m.* Don't use *inimical* when *hostile* or *adverse* will do.

inimitable ends in *-able.*

iniquity, inequity. *Iniquity* means vice, *inequity* means unfairness.

initial. Don't use *initial* when *first* will do.

initial, initialed, initialing. One *l* in all forms.

initials. Leave out the middle initial in informal references, e.g. write *Charles Lindbergh* instead of *Charles A. Lindbergh.*

initiate. Don't use *initiate* when *start* or *begin* will do.

injudicious ends in *-cious.*

ink-. Almost all compounds are spelled as one word.

inkblot, inkhorn, inkstain, inkstand, inkwell. One word.

in-law. Hyphened.

-in-law. Compounds with *-in-law* take the plural *s* before the ending *-in-law,* e.g. *sons-in-law, daughters-in-law.*

in length. Often unnecessary, as in *this book is shorter (in length) than the earlier one.*

in lieu of. Don't use the formal phrase *in lieu of* when *instead of* will do.

in most cases, in most instances. Don't use these phrases when *mostly* will do.

inn-. If you can't find the word you're looking for, try under *in-.*

innate. Two *n*'s.

innerspring. One word.

innervate, enervate. To *innervate* means to give nerves to, to *enervate* (one *n*) means to weaken.

innkeeper. One word.

innocence, innocent end in *-ence, -ent.* The phrase *to plead innocent* is widely used although the exact legal term is *to plead not guilty.*

(innoculate). Misspelling of *inoculate.*

innocuous. Two *n*'s. Ends in *-uous.*

innovate, innovation, innovative, innovator. Two *n*'s.

innuendo, innuendos.

in number. Usually unnecessary.

innumerable. Two *n*'s.

inoculate, inoculation. One *n*. Think of an *inoculation* as a "one-shot affair."

inoperable ends in *-able.*

inopportune. Two *p*'s.

in order that. Don't write *in order that* when *so* or *so that* will do.

in order to. Don't write *in order to* when *to* will do.

in possession of. Don't use *in possession of* when *with* will do.

in question. Don't use *in question* when *this* will do or when it is unnecessary.

inquire, starting with *i,* is the common US form. Don't use *inquire* when *ask* will do.

inquiry, starting with *i,* is the common US form.

in rare cases. Don't use *in rare cases* when *rarely* will do.

in receipt of sounds old-fashioned. Instead of *we are in receipt of* write *we have.*

in regard to, in relation to. Don't use *in regard to, in relation to* when *about* or *on* will do.

(in respect of). The idiom is *with respect to.*

insanitary, unsanitary. The form *insanitary* is more common.

insatiable ends in *-able.*

inscrutable ends in *-able.*

insensible ends in *-ible.*

inseparable ends in *-able.*

in short. Put a comma after it.

inside of. The *of* is unnecessary.

insignia. Commonly used with a singular verb. *Insignias* is the common plural.

insignificance, insignificant end in *-ance, -ant.*

insistence, insistent end in *-ence, -ent.*

in size. Unnecessary in such expressions as *large in size.*

insofar as. Two words. Don't use *insofar as . . . is concerned,* when *as to* will do.

insolence, insolent end in *-ence, -ent.*

insoluble, unsolvable. *Insoluble* means incapable of being solved or dissolved, *unsolvable* means incapable of being solved but is rare.

insolvency, insolvent end in *-ency, -ent.*

insomuch as. Two words. Don't use *insomuch as* when *since* will do.

insouciance, insouciant end in *-ance, -ant.* Watch the *ou.*

inspector ends in *-or.*

inspissated. Double *s.*

inst. Old-fashioned business English. Write the name of the month.

install, installation, installed, installing, installment. Two *l*'s in all forms.

instance. Often unnecessary. Don't write *in this instance* when *here* will do.

instant ends in *-ant.*

instantaneously, instantly. Don't use *instantaneously* when *instantly* will do.

instead ends in *-ead.*

instigator ends in *-or.*

instill, instilled, instilling. Two *l*'s in all forms.

institute (verb). Don't use *institute* when *start* or *set up* will do.

instrumental. Don't use *was instrumental in* when *helped* will do.

insubstantial, unsubstantial. *Insubstantial* is the common form.

insufferable ends in *-able.*

insufficient. Don't use *insufficient* when *not enough* will do.

insular ends in *-ar.*

insuperable ends in *-able.*

insupportable ends in *-able.*

insure, ensure. *Insure* is the only form used in the sense of guarantee against loss, but both *insure* and *ensure* are used to mean make sure.

insurer ends in *-er.*

insurgency, insurgent end in *-ency, -ent.*

insurmountable ends in *-able.*

insurrection. Two *r*'s.

insusceptible ends in *-ible.* Watch the *sc.*

intaglio, intaglios. Silent *g.*

intangible ends in *-ible.*

intellectual, intelligent. *Intellectual* means guided by the intellect, *intelligent* means smart.

intelligence, intelligent end in *-ence, -ent.*

intelligentsia is spelled with *ts.*

intelligible ends in *-ible.*

intemperance, intemperant end in *-ance, -ant.*

intended. Don't use *intended* when *fiancé* or *fiancée* will do.

intense, intensive. *Intense* means to a very high degree, *intensive* means highly concentrated. Don't use *intensive* when *intense, strong, thorough* will do.

inter, interred, interring. Two *r*'s in all forms except *inter.*

inter-. Spell all compounds as one word except when *inter-* is followed by a capital letter, as in *inter-American.*

inter alia means among other things. When you mean among other persons, write *among others.*

interallied. One word.

intercede ends in *-cede.*

interceptor ends in *-or.*

intercession, intersession. *Intercession* means praying for someone, *intersession* means the time between two academic sessions.

interchangeable ends in *-eable.*

intercollegiate. One word.

intercom is listed as standard usage in Webster's.

interdependence, interdependent end in *-ence, -ent.*

interfere, interfered, interfering. One *r* in all forms.

interference ends in *-ence.*

intergovernmental, intergroup. One word.

interlocutor ends in *-or.*

interment, internment. *Interment* means burial, *internment* means confinement during a war.

intermezzo, intermezzos. Musicians often use the plural *intermezzi.*

interminable ends in *-able.*

intermingle. Don't use *intermingle* when *mingle* will do.

intermittent ends in *-ent.*

in terms of. Don't use *in terms of* when *at, in, for, by, with* will do.

intern. The common spelling has no *e* at the end.

internal-combustion engine. Hyphened.

international date line. No capitals.

internecine. So spelled. Commonly used in the sense of mutually destructive.

internment, interment. *Internment* means confinement during a war, *interment* means burial.

interoffice. One word.

interpellate, interpellation. Two *l*'s.

interplanetary. One word.

interpolate, interpolation. *O* after *p.*

interpretative, interpretive. The longer form is more common.

interracial. One word.

interregnum, interregnums.

interrogate. Don't use *interrogate* when *question* will do.

interrogation point. See QUESTION MARK.

interrogator ends in *-or.*

interrupt, interruption. Two *r*'s.

intersection. Don't write *at the intersection of* when *at* will do.

interstate, intrastate. *Interstate* means between states, *intrastate* means within a state.

intersession, intercession. *Intersession* means between academic sessions, *intercession* means praying for someone.

interstice, interstices. So spelled.

interstitial ends in *-tial.*

intervenor. Spell it with *-or.*

intervention ends in *-tion.*

intestacy ends in *-cy.*

in that. Don't use *in that* when *since* will do.

in the absence of. Don't use *in the absence of* when *without* will do.

in the altogether. No hyphens.

in the circumstances. The common idiom is *under the circumstances.*

in the course of. Don't use *in the course of* when *during* will do.

in the event that. Don't use *in the event that* when *if* will do.

in the matter of. Don't use *in the matter of* when *in* will do.

in the nature of. Don't use *in the nature of* when *like* will do.

in the near future. Don't use *in the near future* when *soon* will do.

in the neighborhood of. Don't use *in the neighborhood of* when *about* or *around* will do.

in the vicinity of. Don't use *in the vicinity of* when *about* or *around* will do.

in this connection. Often unnecessary.

intimacy ends in *-acy.*

intimate. Don't use *intimate* when *hint* will do.

into in the sense of involved with, as in *she's into astrology,* is listed in Webster's as standard usage.

intolerable ends in *-able.*

intolerance, intolerant end in *-ance, -ant.*

intoxicated. Don't write *intoxicated* when *drunk* will do.

intra-. Compounds are spelled as one word except for such words as *intra-abdominal, intra-atomic, intra-European.*

intractable ends in *-able.*

intramural. One word.

intransigence, intransigent end in *-ence, -ent.*

intrastate, interstate. *Intrastate* means within a state, *interstate* means between states.

intrauterine, intravenous. One word.

(intrench). The common form is *entrench.*

intricacy, intricate end in *-acy, -ate.*

intrigant. Spell it without *u.*

intrigue, intrigued, intriguing. Spelled with *u* after *g.* Standard usage in the sense of *interest, fascinate.*

intro-. Compounds are spelled as one word.

introduce, introduction. Spelled with *o.*

(intrust). The common form is *entrust.*

intumescent ends in *-ent.* Spelled with *sc.*

inundate. Don't use *inundate* when *flood* will do.

inure. Spell it with *i.* Don't use *inured to* when *used to* will do.

invaluable ends in *-uable.* Means priceless.

inveigh is spelled with *-eigh.*

inveigle is spelled with *ei.* Pronounced either *ay* or *ee.*

inventor ends in *-or.*

investigator ends in *-or.*

investor ends in *-or*.

in view of the fact that. Don't use *in view of the fact that* when *since* will do.

invincible ends in *-ible*.

inviolable ends in *-able*.

invisible ends in *-ible*.

invite, meaning invitation, is a dialect word. Avoid.

invocation. Spelled with *c*.

invoke. Spelled with *k*.

involuntary ends in *-ary*.

involve. Don't use *involve* when *mean* or *deal with* will do.

invulnerable ends in *-able*.

inward, inwards. As an adverb, use either form, e.g. *his thoughts turned inward* or *inwards*. As an adjective, use *inward,* e.g. *an inward look.*

(inwrap). The common form is *enwrap*.

iodine. Spell it with *e* at the end.

IOU. No periods. Standard usage.

ipecac is spelled with *e* in the middle.

IQ. No periods.

ir-. If you can't find the word you're looking for, try *irr-*.

Iraq, Iraqi. So spelled. No *u*.

irascible ends in *-ible*. Watch the *sc*.

I remain . . . at the end of a business letter is old-fashioned. The complimentary close, e.g. *Sincerely yours,* needs no transition.

iridescence, iridescent end in *-ence, -ent*. One *r* and *sc*.

iris, irises.

ironclad, ironfisted, ironhanded. One word.

irr-. If you can't find the word you're looking for, try *ir-*.

irradiate. Two *r*'s.

(irrascible). Misspelling of *irascible*.

(irrecognizable). The common form is *unrecognizable*.

irreconcilable ends in *-able*. Two *r*'s.

irredeemable ends in *-able*. Two *r*'s.

irreducible ends in *-ible*. Two *r*'s.

irrefutable ends in *-able*. Two *r*'s.

(irregardless). Listed as nonstandard in all dictionaries. Write *regardless*.

irregular, irregularity. Two *r*'s.

irrelevance, irrelevancy, irrelevant end in *-ance, -ancy, -ant*. The *l* comes before the *v*.

irreligious, nonreligious, unreligious. *Irreligious* means impious, *nonreligious* means secular. *Unreligious* is rare.

irremediable ends in *-iable.* Two *r*'s.

irremovable ends in *-able.* Two *r*'s.

irreparable, unrepairable. *Irreparable* means *irretrievable, unrepairable* means not capable of being repaired.

irreplaceable ends in *-eable.* Two *r*'s.

irrepressible ends in *-ible.* Two *r*'s.

irreproachable ends in *-able.* Two *r*'s.

irresistible ends in *-ible.* Two *r*'s.

irrespective of. (Not *irrespectively of.*)

irresponsible ends in *-ible.* Two *r*'s.

(irresponsive). The common form is *unresponsive.*

irretrievable ends in *-able.* Spelled with *ie.*

(irrevelance, irrevelancy, irrevelant). Misspellings of *irrelevance, irrelevancy, irrelevant.*

irreverence, irreverent end in *-ence, -ent.* Two *r*'s.

irreversible ends in *-ible.* Two *r*'s.

irrevocable ends in *-able.* Spelled with *c.*

(irridescence, irridescent). Misspellings of *iridescence, iridescent.*

irritable ends in *-able.* Two *r*'s.

irritant ends in *-ant.* Two *r*'s.

irritate, irritation. Two *r*'s.

irruption, eruption. *Irruption* means bursting in, *eruption* means bursting out.

IRS. Standard abbreviated form of Internal Revenue Service. No periods.

is, are. When there's a question whether to write *is* or *are,* go by the noun that comes first. Write *my only concern is the children,* but *the children are my only concern.* But in a question go by the real subject: *what kind of collateral are these shares?*

-ise, -ize. Most words ending in the sound *-ize* are spelled with *z,* but there are exceptions like *advertise, chastise, despise.* If in doubt, look for the specific word.

-ish. Words ending in *-ish* drop the silent *e,* e.g. *latish, fivish.*

isle, aisle. *Isle* in the sea, *aisle* in a theater.

ism in the sense of doctrine is standard usage.

isn't. Common contraction of *is not.*

iso-. Compounds are spelled as one word, e.g. *isogram.*

isosceles is spelled with *sc.*

issuable, issuance end in *-uable, -uance.*

isthmus, isthmuses. Spelled with *sth.*

is when, is where used in definitions. A common idiom. The US Weather Bureau wrote "A severe blizzard is where winds are 45 mph or more, temperatures 10 degrees above zero or lower, and great density of snow either falling or whipped from the ground."

it. Don't use *it* and the passive voice if you can help it. Instead of *it will be recalled . . .* write *you remember. . . .*

Such idioms as *I've had it, this is it* are listed in Webster's as standard usage.

italicize ends in *-ize.*

italics. Here are some simple rules for using italics (or underlining on the typewriter). They're based on Webster's, the GPO Style Manual and newspaper usage.

1. Italicize (underline) titles of books, magazines, plays, movies, works of art and music, ships and airplanes. But you can also follow newspaper style and simply capitalize such titles or put them in quotes. Examples: Shakespeare's *Hamlet* or Shakespeare's Hamlet or Shakespeare's "Hamlet." Beethoven's *Fidelio* or Beethoven's Fidelio or Beethoven's "Fidelio." Lindbergh's *Spirit of St. Louis* or Lindbergh's Spirit of St. Louis or Lindbergh's "Spirit of St. Louis."

2. Italicize (underline) words, letters and figures referred to as words, letters and figures, e.g. *it* is a pronoun, *a* is an article, *5* is a number.

3. Italicize (underline) foreign words and phrases not naturalized in English, e.g. "He followed the rule *fortiter in re, suaviter in modo.*" But don't use italics or underlining for foreign words and phrases naturalized in English, e.g. "She was full of joie de vivre."

4. Italicize (underline) words, phrases and sentences for emphasis, if you'd stress them by raising your voice in speaking. E.g.: "This does *not* mean I'm satisfied."—"After all, it wasn't *his* money."—"He then had a friendly chat with the waiter. *In fluent Italian.*"

it'd. Common contraction of *it had, it would.*

itemize ends in *-ize.*

itemized paragraphs. See PARAGRAPHS.

it is. Don't start sentences with *it is* and the passive voice if you can help it.

it'll. Common contraction of *it will, it shall.*

its, it's. *Its* means belonging to it, *it's* means *it is.*

it's me, it's her, it's him, it's us, it's them. Standard usage since 1500. Keats wrote "If it was me, I did it in a dream." William Faulkner wrote "It is us, we simple men and women, who must decide."

-ive. Don't write *it is productive of* when *it produces* will do or *it is supportive of* when *it supports* will do.

I've. Common contraction of *I have.*

-ix. The trend is toward replacing feminine forms ending in *-ix* by forms ending in *-or* with no distinction in gender, e.g. *aviator* instead of *aviatrix, executor* instead of *executrix, testator* instead of *testatrix.*

-ization. Words ending in *-ization* are spelled with *z.*

-ize is the common ending. Some exceptions, ending in *-ise,* are *advise, chastise, despise, devise, exercise, supervise, surprise.* Don't use *-ize* words if you can help it, e.g. don't use *martyrize* instead of *martyr* or *utilize* instead of *use.*

J

j-. If you can't find the word you're looking for, try under *g-*.

jabot. Silent *t*.

jackal ends in *-al*.

jack-in-the-box. Three hyphens.

jackknife. One word.

jack-of-all-trades. Three hyphens.

jack-o'-lantern. Two hyphens, one apostrophe.

jackpot, jackrabbit. One word.

jack up, in the sense of raise, is listed as standard usage in Webster's.

Jacquard is spelled with *cqu*. Capital J.

jai alai starts with *j*.

jail, jailer. US spelling.

jailbird, jailbreak, jailkeeper. One word.

jail-like. Hyphened.

jailmate. One word.

jalopy, jalopies. So spelled. Listed as standard usage in Webster's.

jam, jamb. *Jam* means squeeze, crush, preserve, *jamb* means the sidepiece of a door or window.

jampacked. One word.

janitor ends in *-or*.

japan, japanned, japanning. Two *n*'s in all forms except *japan*.

jar, jarred, jarring. Two *r*'s in all forms except *jar*.

jardiniere. No accent.

jawbone, jawbreaker, jawline. One word.

jaybird, jaywalk, jaywalker, jaywalking. One word.

jazz in the sense of humbug, stuff is listed as standard usage in Webster's.

jazz up, meaning make lively or speed up, is listed as standard usage in Webster's.

jealous, jealousy are spelled with *ea.*
jellyfish. One word.
jelly roll. Two words.
jeopardize, jeopardy. Watch the *eo.* Don't use these words when *risk* will do.
jerk, in the sense of stupid person, is listed as standard usage in Webster's.
jerrican. Spell it as one word.
jerry-built. Hyphen.
jersey, meaning a sweater or fabric, is spelled with a small *j.*
jet, jetted, jetting. Standard usage.
jetliner, jetport. One word.
jetsam. Flotsam and jetsam aren't the same. *Flotsam* means floating debris, *jetsam* means what is thrown overboard and found floating or washed ashore.
jet set. Two words.
jet-setter. Hyphened.
jet stream. Two words.
jewel, jeweled, jeweler, jeweling, jewelry. One *l* in all forms.
Jewess is now considered offensive.
Jew's harp. Two words. Apostrophe before *s.*
jibe, gibe. To *jibe* means to match, to *gibe* means to taunt.
jiffy. No *e.*
jimjams is listed as standard usage in Webster's.
jinx, jinxed. Listed as standard usage in Webster's.
jitters. Standard usage.
(jiujitsu). Spell it *jujitsu.*
jobholder. One word.
job-hopping. Hyphened.
jobless. One word.
job lot. Two words.
jobseeker, jobsite. One word.
jockey, jockeys, jockeyed, jockeying.
jocular ends in *-ar.*
jocund ends in *-und.*
jodhpurs is spelled with *dh.*
Johnny, Johnnies.
johnnycake. One word.
Johnny-come-lately, Johnny-come-latelies.
joie de vivre. No italics or underlining.
joint in the sense of place or marijuana cigarette is listed in Webster's as standard usage.

join together. Established usage.

jostle. Silent *t.*

journey, journeys.

joyride. One word.

Jr. Put no comma before *Jr.* in names, e.g. *Joseph E. Blow Jr.*

jubilance, jubilant end in *-ance, -ant.*

Judea. Spell it with *-ea.*

Judeo-Christian. Spell it with *eo.*

judge advocate, judge advocates. No hyphen.

judgment. No *e* after *g.*

judicial, judicious. *Judicial* means related to judges, *judicious* means with good judgment.

jugful, jugfuls. One word.

juggler, jugular. A *juggler* is someone who juggles, the *jugular* is a vein in the neck.

jujitsu. The common spelling.

jukebox. One word.

julep ends in *-ep.*

jumpoff, jumpsuit. One word.

juncture. Don't write *at this juncture* when *now* will do.

junkie, junkies. Listed in Webster's as standard usage.

junkyard. One word.

junta, junto. A *junta* is a ruling group, a *junto* is a secret group or cabal. The plural of *junto* is *juntos.*

jurisprudence ends in *-ence.*

jurist. Don't use *jurist* when *judge* or *lawyer* will do.

juror ends in *-or.*

jury box, jury room. Two words.

justifiable ends in *-iable.*

K

k-. If you can't find the word you're looking for, try under *c-, ch-,* or *qu-.*

(kabob). Spell it *kebab.*

kaffeeklatsch.

(kahki). Misspelling of *khaki.*

kaleidoscope, kaleidoscopic. Spelled with *ei.*

kamikaze.

kangaroo. *A* after *g.*

kapellmeister. One *p,* two *l*'s.

kapok begins and ends with *k.*

karakul, caracul. *Karakul* is the lamb, *caracul* is the fur.

karat, carat, caret. A *karat* is a unit of fineness for gold, a *carat* is a unit of weight for diamonds, a *caret* is a proofreader's mark.

kayak. So spelled.

kayo. Spell the plural *kayos,* the verb forms *kayoes, kayoed, kayoing.* Variant of *KO, KO's, KO'd, KO'ing.* Listed as standard usage in Webster's.

kebab. The common spelling is with *e* and *a.*

keen-edged. Hyphened.

keenness. Two *n*'s.

keen-sighted, keen-witted. Hyphened.

-keeper, -keeping. Compounds are spelled as one word, e.g. *bookkeeper, housekeeping.*

(Kelt, Keltic). The common forms are *Celt, Celtic.*

kennel, kenneled, kenneling. One *l* in all forms.

(kerb). The common US spelling is *curb.*

kerchief, kerchiefs.

kernel, kerneled, kerneling. One *l* in all forms.

kerosene. Spell it with *-ene.*

ketchup. The most common spelling.

kettledrum, kettledrummer. One word.

key, quay. A *key* fits a lock, a *quay* is a wharf.

key-. Compounds are spelled as one word.

keyboard, keyhole, keynote, keypunch, keyring, keystone, keystroke. One word.

key word. Two words.

khaki starts with *kh.*

kibbutz, kibbutzim.

kibitz, kibitzer. One *b.*

kibosh. So spelled.

kickback, kickoff. One word.

kid in the sense of child, young person is listed as standard usage in Webster's.

kidnap, kidnapped, kidnapper, kidnapping. The common spelling is with double *p* in all forms except *kidnap.* Remember "The kidnapper was caught napping."

kidney, kidneys.

kid stuff. Two words.

kilo-. Compounds are spelled as one word.

kilogram, kilowatt. One word.

kimono, kimonos.

kindergarten, kindergartner. Watch the *t.*

(kindlily). Use *kindly.*

kindly. Don't use *kindly* when *please* will do.

kind of, in the sense of rather, is a common idiom. The idiom *these kind of* has been common since 1380. Shakespeare (King Lear, II, ii, 107) wrote "These kind of knaves I know."

kingmaker, kingpin. One word.

king-size. Hyphened.

kiosk. So spelled.

kitchenette ends in *-ette.*

kitty-corner. So spelled. (No *-ed.*)

Kleenex. Capital *K.*

klieg lights. Spelled with *lie.* Think of "all the lies spoken under klieg lights."

klutz, klutzy is slang.

kn-. If you can't find the word you're looking for, try under *n-.*

knack, knapsack, knave, knead. Silent *k.*

knee-. Some compounds are spelled as one word, some hyphened.

knee breeches. Two words.

kneecap. One word.

-kneed. Hyphened, e.g. *bare-kneed, weak-kneed.*

knee-deep, knee-high. Hyphened.

kneehole. One word.

knee jerk. Two words.

kneel, knelt, kneeling. *Knelt* is more common than *kneeled.*

kneepad, kneepan. One word.

knell, knickerbockers, knickknack. Silent *k.*

knife, knives, knifed, knifing.

knight-errant, knights-errant.

knit, knit or **knitted, knitting.** *Knit* is more common than *knitted* in figurative uses, e.g. *a closely-knit family, knitted* in literal uses, e.g. *she knitted him a sweater.*

knob, knock. Silent *k.*

knockabout (noun, adj.), **knockdown** (noun, adj.), **knockoff** (noun, adj.), **knockout** (noun, adj.). One word.

knock up, in the sense of make pregnant, is listed as standard usage in Webster's.

knockwurst. Common spelling.

knoll. Silent *k.*

knot is a measure of speed, not distance, and means 1 nautical mile per hour. But the loose meaning of 1 nautical mile is common.

knothole. One word.

knout. Silent *k.*

knowable ends in *-able.*

know-how. Hyphened. Standard usage.

knowledge. So spelled. Contains the words *know* and *ledge.*

knowledgeable ends in *-eable.*

knuckle. Silent *k.*

knucklebone. One word.

knuckle-duster. Hyphened.

knucklehead. One word.

KO, KOs, KO'd, KO'ing. Spell it so. No periods, no apostrophe before *s.*

Kodak. Capital *K.*

kohlrabi, kohlrabies. The plural ends in *-ies.*

kook, kooky. Listed in Webster's as standard usage.

kopeck. Spell it with *-ck.*

Koran. Capital *K.*

kosher.

koumiss is spelled with *ou.*

kowtow. Two *ow*'s.

KP. No periods.
kraal. Double *a*.
K ration. No hyphen.
kraut is spelled with *au*.
kudos is not a plural. Use it with a singular verb.
Ku Klux Klan. Three capital *K*'s.
kulak.
kumquat.
kvetch is slang.

L

-l-, -ll-. An *l* at the end of a word is doubled before the suffixes *-ed, -er, -ing, -ant, -ent,* if there's only one vowel before the *l* and the accent is on the last syllable. Examples: *rebel, rebelled; propel, propeller; control, controlling; excel, excellent.*

In US usage the *l* is *not* doubled before *-ed, -er, -ing* if the accent is not on the last syllable, e.g. *canceled, jeweler, modeling.*

La. Names starting with *La* are usually spelled with a capital *L,* either as one word, e.g. *Marquis de Lafayette,* or, more commonly, as two words, e.g. *Fiorello La Guardia, Robert La Follette, Jean de La Fontaine.*

lab for *laboratory* is standard usage.

label, labeled, labeling. One *l* in all forms.

labor ends in *-or.* But the British Labour Party is spelled with *ou.*

labor a point. The standard idiom is *belabor a point.*

laboratory is spelled with *o* between *b* and *r.*

laborsaving. One word.

(labour). The standard US spelling is *labor.*

labyrinth, labyrinthine. First *y,* then *i.*

lacerations. Don't use *lacerations* when *cuts* will do.

lachrymose. Spell it so. Don't use *lachrymose* when *tearful* will do.

lackadaisical is spelled with *ai.*

lackey, lackeys. Spelled with *ey.*

lacquer is spelled with *cqu.*

(lacrimose). The spelling *lachrymose* is more common.

lacuna, lacunae. Don't use *lacuna* when *gap* will do.

Ladies. Used as salutation in a letter to an organization consisting of women only.

ladies' aid, ladies' auxiliary. Apostrophe after *s.*

Ladies and Gentlemen. Used as salutation in a letter to an organization consisting of men and women.

lady, woman. *Lady* is the courteous word, used in salutations or in the presence of the person referred to, as in *Ladies and Gentlemen* or *the lady was here first.* *Woman* is the regular word, as in *a woman in the audience spoke up* or *the room was empty except for a young woman sitting at a table in the back.*

lady-in-waiting, ladies-in-waiting.

ladykiller, ladykilling. One word.

ladylike, ladyship. Spelled with *y*.

lagniappe is spelled with *gni*.

laid. Past tense of *lay*. See LAY, LIE.

lain. Past tense of *lie*. See LAY, LIE.

laissez-faire. Hyphened.

lakefront, lakeshore. One word.

lama, llama. A *lama* is a Tibetan monk, a *llama* is a South American animal.

lamasery ends in *-ery*.

lambaste. Spell it with an *e* at the end.

lameduck (adj.). One word.

lamentable ends in *-able*.

lampblack, lamplight, lamppost, lampshade. One word.

lance corporal. Two words.

land-. Most compounds are spelled as one word.

landfall, landfill. One word.

land-grant. Hyphened.

landholder, landlady, landlocked, landlord, landlubber, landmark. One word.

land-office. Hyphened.

landowner, landowning. One word.

land-poor. Hyphened.

landslide, landsman. One word.

landward. Spell it without *s*.

languor, languorous. *U* after *g*.

lapboard, lapdog. One word.

lapel, lapelled. One *l* at end of *lapel,* double *l* in *lapelled.*

lapis lazuli. So spelled.

lap robe. Two words.

largehearted. One word.

large-minded. Hyphened.

largemouthed. One word.

large number. Don't say *a large number of* when *much* will do.

large portion. Don't say *a large portion of* when *many* will do.

largess. The common spelling is without final *e*.

larghetto, larghettos.

largo, largos.

larva, larvae.

larynx, larynges.

lascivious is spelled with *sc.*

lager ends in *-er.*

lasso, lassos, (he) lassoes, lassoed, lassoing, lassoer.

last, latest, past. Often used interchangeably.

last-ditch. Hyphened.

(lastly). Use *last.*

latchkey, latchstring. One word.

latecomer. One word.

latest, last, past. Often used interchangeably.

lath, lathe. A *lath* is a strip of wood, a *lathe* is a machine.

Latin plurals. If in doubt, follow the trend and use an English rather than a Latin plural, e.g. *formulas, indexes, gladioluses.*

Latin words. Don't use a Latin word when an English one will do, e.g. don't use *in toto* when *altogether* will do.

latish. No *e.*

latter. Don't use *the former* and *the latter* since they force the reader to go back to see which is which. It is better to repeat the noun or nouns. Boswell wrote of Dr. Samuel Johnson "He never used the phrases the former and the latter, having observed that they often occasioned obscurity; he therefore contrived to construct his sentences so as not to have occasion for them, and would even rather repeat the same words, in order to avoid them."

latterly. Don't use *latterly* when *lately* or *recently* will do.

laudable, laudatory. *Laudable* means praiseworthy, *laudatory* means expressing praise.

laughable ends in *-able.*

laughingstock. One word.

laundry. No *e.*

laurel, laureled, laureling. No double *l.*

lavaliere. No double *l,* no accent.

lavender ends in *-er.*

law-. Most compounds are spelled as one word.

law-abiding. Hyphened.

lawbook, lawbreaker, lawbreaking, lawgiver, lawgiving, lawmaker, lawmaking. One word.

lawn mower. Two words.

lawsuit. One word.

laxative. *A* after *x*.

lay, lie. Conservative grammarians distinguish between *lay, laid, laid,* meaning put or place, and *lie, lay, lain,* meaning recline. But *lay, laid, laid* is commonly used in both senses even though Webster's marks it as nonstandard. The usage goes back to 1300. Lord Byron wrote "Thou dashest him again to earth— there let him lay."

lay-. Almost all compounds are spelled as one word.

layabout, layaway (noun)**, layman, layoff** (noun)**, layout** (noun)**, layover** (noun)**.** One word.

laziness is spelled with *i.*

lazybones. One word.

lazy Susan. Small *l,* capital *S.*

le. In names, the French article *le* is usually capitalized, e.g. *John Le Carré, Le Corbusier, Eva Le Gallienne.*

lead, led. *Lead* (pronounced *led*) is the heavy metal, *led* means guided.

lead-in (noun)**.** Hyphened.

leaf, leaves.

leak, leek. To *leak* means to escape or let get out, a *leek* is a vegetable.

lean, lien. To *lean* means to incline, a *lien* is a legal right.

lean-to. Hyphened.

leapfrog, leapfrogged, leapfrogging. Two *g*'s in all forms except *leapfrog.*

(leary). Misspelling of *leery.*

leaseback, leasehold, leaseholder, leaseholding. One word.

Leatherette. Capital *L.*

leave, let. The use of *leave* instead of *let,* as in *leave us go,* is not standard usage. But *leave alone,* meaning *let alone,* is a common idiom.

leaven, leavened, leavening. Pronounced *leven,* but spelled with *ea.*

leave-taking. Hyphened.

lecher, lecherous, lechery. No *t.*

lectern ends in *-ern.*

led, lead. *Led* means guided, *lead* (pronounced *led*) means the heavy metal.

ledger is spelled with *dg.*

leek, leak. A *leek* is a vegetable, to *leak* means to escape or let get out.

leery. Double *e*.

leeward.

leeway is standard usage.

left-. Some compounds are hyphened, some spelled as one word.

left field, left fielder. Two words.

left-hand, left-handed, left-hander. Hyphened.

leftover. One word.

leftward, leftwards. Both forms are common.

leftwing, leftwinger. One word.

legalize ends in *-ize*.

legerdemain.

legible ends in *-ible*.

legionnaire. Two *n*'s.

legislation, legislature. *Legislation* is the act of legislating, *legislature* is the body that does it.

legislator (lawmaker) ends in *-or*.

legit for legitimate is slang.

legitimate, legitimatize, legitimize. Don't use *legitimatize* or *legitimize* instead of the simple word *legitimate*.

legpull, legpulling, legroom, legwork. One word.

leisure, leisurely are spelled with *ei*.

leitmotif. Spell it with *f* at the end.

lend, lent, lending.

lend, loan. The use of the verb *loan* instead of *lend* has been standard usage for many centuries.

length. Watch the *g*.

lengthening. *E* after *th*.

lengthwise. Watch the *g*.

lengthy means not just long, but overlong and tedious. Don't use it when *long* will do.

leniency, lenient end in *-ency, -ent*.

lens, lenses. No final *e* in the singular.

lent. Past tense of *lend*. *Loaned* is more common.

leopard. Silent *o*.

leprechaun is spelled with *ch*.

leprosy. *O* after *r*.

leprous. No *e* after *p*.

lese majesty. Commonly spelled as two words with no accents and *y* at the end.

less, fewer. *Less* instead of the more formal *fewer* in referring to numbers has been common usage since 888. H. L. Mencken wrote "Less family ties than a wild thing in the woods."

-less. Words ending in *-less* are spelled as one word, e.g. *useless,* except when there are three *l*'s, e.g. *bell-less.*

less-. Compounds are hyphened before a noun but spelled as two words after a noun, e.g. *a less-known instance,* but *this side of his character was less known.*

lessee, lessor. The *lessee* leases property from the *lessor* who owns it.

lessen, lesson. To *lessen* means to decrease, a *lesson* is a piece of instruction.

lesser-. Compounds are hyphened before a noun, but spelled as two words otherwise, e.g. *a lesser-known figure,* but *his brother was lesser known.*

lest. Don't use *lest* when *so, so that, or that* will do.

let. The use of *I* instead of *me* is common in such phrases as *let Dick and I help you* or *let's you and I go out to dinner.* The idiom has been traced back to 1634.

let, leave. The use of *leave* instead of *let,* as in *leave us go,* is *not* standard usage. But *leave alone,* meaning *let alone,* is a common idiom.

letdown. One word.

let's. Common contraction of *let us.* See also LET.

letter-. Most compounds are spelled as one word.

letterbox. One word.

letter carrier. Two words.

letter forms. See ADDRESS, COMPLIMENTARY CLOSE.

letterhead. One word.

letter-perfect. Hyphened.

letter writer. Two words.

letup. One word. Standard usage.

leucocyte is spelled with *eu.*

leukemia is spelled with *eu.*

levee, levy. *Levee* means embankment or reception, *levy* means tax.

level. Don't use *level* when it is unnecessary, e.g. instead of *sales at the retail level* write *retail sales.*

level, leveled, leveling. One *l* in all forms. Don't use *level* when *bring* or *make* will do.

levelheaded. One word.

levy. Don't use *levy* when *tax* will do.

levy, levee. *Levy* means tax, *levee* means embankment, reception.

lewd is spelled with *ew.*

lexicon, lexica.

liable in the sense of likely is standard usage.

liaison is spelled with *iai.*

liar, lyre. A *liar* is telling falsehoods, a *lyre* is a musical instrument.

libation. Don't use *libation* when *drink* or *beverage* will do.

libel, libeled, libeling, libelant, libelee, libelor, libelous. One *l* in all forms.

libel, slander. If a defamation is published or broadcast, it's *libel,* if it's spoken or done by gesture, it's *slander.*

liberalize ends in *-ize.*

liberal-minded. Hyphened.

librarian, library. *R* after *b.*

libretto, librettos. Musicians often use the plural *libretti.*

Libya. First *i,* then *y.*

license. Spell it with *-se.*

licentiate, licentious are spelled with *ti.*

(lichee). Spell it *litchi.*

lichen is spelled with *ch.*

(lich-gate). The common spelling is *lych-gate.*

lickety-split. Hyphened. Listed in Webster's as standard usage.

licorice.

lie, lay. See LAY, LIE.

lie, lied, lying.

Liederkranz cheese. Spelled with *ie.*

lien, in the sense of security interest, is spelled with *ie.*

lieu. Don't use *in lieu of* when *instead of* will do.

lieutenancy ends in *-ancy.*

lieutenant ends in *-ant.*

lieutenant colonel, lieutenant commander, lieutenant general, lieutenant governor. No hyphen.

life, lives.

life-. Most compounds are spelled as one word.

life belt. Two words.

lifeblood, lifeboat. One word.

life buoy. Two words.

life-giving. Hyphened.

lifeguard. One word.

life insurance. Never hyphened.

lifejacket, lifelike, lifeline, lifelong. One word.

life preserver. Two words.

lifer. Listed in Webster's as standard usage.

lifesaver, lifesaving. One word.

life-size. Hyphened.

lifestyle, lifetime, lifework. One word.

liftoff. One word.

light, lighted, lighting. The past tense *lighted* is more common than *lit*.

-light. Compounds are spelled as one word, e.g. *lamplight, skylight, sunlight.*

light-. Compounds are spelled as one word or hyphened.

lightening, lightning. *Lightening* means making lighter, *lightning* (without *e*) means the electric flash of light.

lightface. One word.

lightheaded, lighthearted, lighthouse. One word.

lightning, lightening. *Lightning* means the electric flash of light, *lightening* means making lighter.

lightship, lightweight. One word.

light-year. Hyphened.

likable. No *e* after *k*.

like, as, as if. Webster's lists the use of *like* as a conjunction in the sense of *as* or *as if* as standard usage. The idiom has been traced back to 1530. Darwin wrote "Unfortunately few have observed like you have done." Norman Mailer wrote "Middle-aged men who looked like they might be out for their one night of the year." A New York Times editorial said "The G.O.P. may be nearing a sudden collapse and extinction like the Whigs suffered."

-like. Compounds are spelled as one word, except if the first part ends in *l*. Examples: *birdlike, childlike, ladylike* but *girl-like, bell-like, cell-like.*

likelihood is spelled with *i* in the middle.

likely in the sense of probably is standard usage.

like-minded, like-natured. Hyphened.

likewise. Don't write *likewise* when *so* or *also* will do.

Lilliput, Lilliputian. First one *l*, then two.

lily, lilies. No double *l*.

-lily. Adverbs ending in *-lily* are commonly avoided. (Don't use *lonelily, wilily,* etc.)

lily-white. Hyphened.

limb, limn. *Limb* with a silent *b* means arm, leg or branch, *limn* with a silent *n* means to draw or outline.

limbo, limbos.

limeade is spelled with *ea.*

lime juice. Two words.

limelight. One word.

limey, limeys. Slang.

limitation. Don't write *limitation* when *limit* will do.

limn. Silent *n.* Don't write *limn* when *describe* will do.

limousine is spelled with *ou.*

linage, lineage. Spell it *linage* when you mean number of lines, *lineage* when you mean descent.

linchpin. One word.

-line. Compounds are spelled as one word, e.g. *airline, deadline, skyline, waistline.*

line-. Most compounds are spelled as one word.

lineage, linage. Spell it *lineage* for descent, *linage* for number of lines.

lineament, liniment. *Lineament* means outline, *liniment* means ointment.

linen. One *n* in the middle.

linesman, lineup. One word.

lingerie. Spelled with *in,* ends in *-ie.*

lingo, lingoes.

liniment, lineament. *Liniment* means ointment, *lineament* means outline.

linkup. One word.

linoleum ends in *-eum.*

lionhearted. One word.

lionize ends in *-ize.*

lipread, lipreader, lipreading. One word.

lip service. Two words.

liquefy, liquefaction are spelled with *e* after *qu.*

liqueur, liquor. A *liqueur* is flavored and sweetened, *liquor* means any kind of distilled beverage.

(liquorice). Spell it *licorice.*

lira, lire. Italian currency.

lissome. Spell it with *e* at the end.

listener-in, listeners-in. Hyphened.

lit, lighted. Both forms are standard usage, but *lighted* is more common.

litany is spelled with *a* in the middle.

litchi, litchis. Spell it with *tch*.

liter. The common US spelling ends in *-er*.

literacy ends in *-acy*.

literally, in the sense of *virtually,* is listed as standard usage in Webster's.

literati ends in *i*.

literature. *E* after *t*.

(lithesome). The common form is *lissome*.

litho-. Spell compounds as one word, e.g. *lithophane*.

litigant ends in *-ant*.

litigious ends in *-ious*.

litmus ends in *-us*.

(litre). The common US spelling is *liter*.

litterateur. No accent. Double *t*.

litterbug. Standard usage.

little-. Compounds are hyphened before a noun, but spelled as two words otherwise, e.g. *a little-known resort,* but *the resort was little known.*

littoral, meaning coast. Spelled with double *t* and *o*.

livable. No *e* after *v*.

livelihood is spelled with *i* in the middle.

livelong, lifelong. *The livelong day* means the whole day, but *lifelong* means lasting through life.

liverwurst.

live wire. Two words. Listed in Webster's as standard usage for an alert, active person.

livid may mean black-and-blue, ashen, pallid, reddish or enraged. Webster's lists all these meanings as standard usage.

living room. Never hyphened.

-ll-. See -L-, -LL-.

llama, lama. A *llama* is a South American animal, a *lama* is a Tibetan monk.

llano, llanos.

load, lode. *Load* means burden, *lode* means vein of metal ore.

(loadstar). Spell it *lodestar*.

loadstone. Spell it so.

loaf, loaves.

loan, lend. The use of the verb *loan* instead of *lend* has been standard usage for many centuries.

loan shark. Two words.

loansharking. One word.

loath, loathe. *Loath* means unwilling, to *loathe* means to hate.
loathsome. No *e* in the middle.
locale is spelled with *e* at the end when it means scene.
locality, location. Don't use either word when *place* will do.
localize ends in *-ize.*
locate. Don't use *locate* when *find* or *settle* will do.
location. Don't use *location* when *place* will do.
lock-. Compounds are spelled as one word.
lockbox, lockjaw, lockout, locksmith, locksmithing, lockstep, lockstitch, lockup (noun). One word.
locus, loci.
lode, loan. *Lode* means vein of metal ore, *load* means burden.
lodestar. Spell it so.
(lodestone). Spell it *loadstone.*
lodginghouse. One word.
lodgment. No *e* after *g.*
logarithm, logarithmically.
loggia. Two *g*'s.
logically ends in *-ally.*
logjam. One word.
logo-. Compounds are spelled as one word, e.g. *logogram.*
logroll, logroller, logrolling. One word.
logy. One *g.*
loid is slang. It means a piece of celluloid used by a burglar to open locks.
loincloth. One word.
lollipop. Spell it with *i* in the middle.
loneliness is spelled with *i* in the middle.
lonely, lonesome are spelled with *e* in the middle.
long-. Some compounds are hyphened, some are spelled as one word.
long-awaited. Hyphened.
longboat, longbow. One word.
long-distance, long-drawn-out, long-eared. Hyphened.
longevity. Spelled with *ge.*
longfelt. One word.
longhair. Listed as standard usage in Webster's.
long-haired. Hyphened. In literal sense.
longhand, longhorn, longplaying. One word.
long-range. Hyphened.
longshoreman. One word.

long shot. Two words.

long-sought. Hyphened.

longspun, longstanding. One word.

long-suffering, long-term. Hyphened.

longtime. One word.

longueur is spelled with *ueu.*

long-winded. Hyphened.

look-alike. Hyphened.

looker-on, lookers-on. Hyphened.

look-in (noun). Hyphened.

lookout (noun). One word.

look-see. Hyphened.

loony, loony bin. No *e.* Listed in Webster's as standard usage.

loophole. One word.

loose, lose. To *loose* means to let or make loose, to *lose* means to suffer a loss. Remember "a moose let loose."

loose, loosen. Commonly *loose* is used when you mean undo or let free, *loosen* when you mean make loose.

loose-jointed. Hyphened.

looseleaf, loosemouthed. One word.

loot, in the sense of money, is listed as standard usage in Webster's.

lopsided. One word.

loquacious ends in *-cious.*

lorgnette ends in *-ette.*

lose, loose. To *lose* means to suffer a loss, to *loose* means to let or make loose.

losing. No *e.*

lot, lots. *A lot of* or *lots of* in the sense of much or many is listed as standard usage in Webster's. So is *a lot* and *lots* used as an adverb, as in *I feel a lot* (or *lots) better.*

(loth). Spell it *loath.*

lotus, lotuses.

loudmouth, loudmouthed, loudspeaker. One word.

(lour). Spell it *lower.*

louse, lice.

louse up is listed in Webster's as standard usage.

lousy in the sense of contemptible is listed in Webster's as standard usage. It goes back to 1386. R. L. Stevenson wrote "The lousiest, lowest story to hand down to your namesakes in the future."

louver ends in *-er.*

lovable. No *e* after *v.*

love affair. Two words.

lovebird. One word.

love-crossed. Hyphened.

lovelily. Awkward form. Avoid.

loveliness is spelled with an *i* in the middle.

lovelorn, lovemaking. One word.

love seat. Two words.

lovesick. One word.

lovers' lane. Apostrophe after *s.*

low-. Some compounds are spelled as one word, some are hyphened.

lowborn, lowbred, lowbrow. One word.

lowdown. One word. Listed as standard usage in Webster's.

lower in the sense of frown is commonly so spelled in the US.

lowercase. One word.

low-grade. Hyphened.

lowland, lowlands. One word.

lowlily. Awkward form. Avoid.

low-necked, low-pressure, low-spirited. Hyphened.

lox. The plural is *lox* too.

loyally ends in *-ally.*

lu-. If you can'd find the word you're looking for, try *leu-* or *lieu-.*

luau.

lubricious ends in *-icious.*

lucre ends in *-re.*

luggage is spelled with double *g.*

lumbar, lumber. *Lumbar* refers to the loins, *lumber* means timber.

lumberjack, lumberyard. One word.

luminary ends in *-ary.*

lummox is listed in Webster's as standard usage.

lunacy ends in *-acy.*

lunar ends in *-ar.*

lunchbox. One word.

luncheon. Don't say *luncheon* when *lunch* will do.

luncheonette ends in *-ette.*

lunchroom, lunchtime. One word.

lunging. No *e.*

lupine is spelled with *e* at the end.

luscious ends in *-scious.*

lush for drunkard is slang.

luster ends in *-er.*

lustrous. No *e* after *t*.

luxe. Spell *deluxe* as one word.

luxuriance, luxuriant end in *-ance, -ant*.

luxuriant, luxurious. *Luxuriant* means growing abundantly, like hair, *luxurious* means voluptuous, in luxury.

-ly. Avoid unusual, odd-sounding adverbs like *firstly, muchly, thusly, unreservedly, whitely*. Don't hyphen such phrases as *neatly furnished, poorly disguised, quickly absorbed*.

(Lybia). Misspelling of *Libya*.

lych-gate. Commonly so spelled.

lye, lie. A *lye* is a chemical solution, a *lie* is an untruth.

lying is spelled with *y*.

lying-in (noun, adj.). Hyphened.

lynch is spelled with *y*.

lynx is spelled with *y*.

lyonnaise. Two *n*'s.

lyrically ends in *-ally*.

M

-m-, -mm-. An *m* at the end of a word is doubled before the suffixes *-ed, -er, -ing, -ly* if there's only one vowel immediately before the *m* and the accent is on the last syllable. Examples: *cram, crammed; drum, drummer; trim, trimming; ham, hammy; flimflam, flimflammed.*

ma'am. Standard usage.

Mac, Mc. Watch the spelling of proper names. General MacArthur spelled his name with an *a*, General McClellan without.

macabre ends in *-re.*

macadamize ends in *-ize.*

macaroni. One *c.*

macaroon. One *c.*

machete.

Machiavelli, Machiavellian. Capital *M, ch,* double *l.*

machine gun, machine shop, machine tool. Two words.

Mach number. Capital *M.*

mackerel.

mackintosh. Spell it with *ck.*

macro-. Compounds are spelled as one word, e.g. *macrocosm.*

mad in the sense of angry has been standard usage since 1300. The Bible (Psalm 102:8) says "They that are mad against me are sworn against me."

mad-. Compounds are spelled as one word.

madam, without *e* at the end, is either the word for a woman in charge of a brothel or a polite form of address, e.g. *Madam Chairman.* The plural of the word in this sense is *Mesdames.*

Madame with an *e* at the end is the title used for married women of non-English-speaking nations, e.g. *Madame* (or *Mme.*) *de Gaulle, Madame* (or *Mme.*) *Franco.*

madcap. One word.

Mademoiselle is the title used for unmarried women of non-English-speaking nations, e.g. *Mademoiselle* (or *Mlle.*) *Dayan.* The plural is usually *Mademoiselles.*

made-over (adj.), **made-up** (adj.). Hyphened.

madhouse, madman. One word.

madrilene. No accent.

madwoman. One word.

maelstrom is spelled with *ae.*

maestro, maestros.

Mafia. Capital *M,* one *f.*

Mafioso, Mafiosi. One *f.*

magdalen. Spell it without *e* at the end.

maggot, maggoty. Double *g.*

magically ends in *-ally.*

magician ends in *-ician.*

magisterial. Don't use *magisterial* when *masterly* will do.

Magna Charta. The common spelling is with *Ch.*

magnanimity, magnanimous. The sequence is *m, n, n, m.*

magnate, magnet. A *magnate* is a person of rank and power, a *magnet* attracts iron.

magnetism, magnetize. *E* before *t.*

magneto, magnetos.

magnificence, magnificent end in *-ence, -ent.*

magnifico, magnificos.

magniloquence, magniloquent end in *-ence, -ent.*

magnitude. Don't use *magnitude* when *size* will do. Don't use *of the first magnitude* when *top* etc. will do.

maharaja, maharani. The common spellings.

mah-jongg. Lower case and double *g.*

mahogany. The vowels are *a—o—a.*

(Mahomet). The common spelling is *Muhammad.*

maid of honor. No hyphens.

maidservant. One word.

mail-. Most compounds are spelled as one word.

mailbag, mailbox, mailboat, mailman. One word.

mail-order. Hyphened.

mainline, that is, to inject into a vein, is listed as standard usage in Webster's.

maintain. Don't use *maintain* when *say* or *keep up* will do.

maintenance is spelled with *e* after *t.* Think of "maintenance for tenants." Don't use *maintenance* when *upkeep* will do.

maitre d', maitre d's.

maize, maze. *Maize* means corn, a *maze* is a labyrinth.

major. Don't use *major* when *great* or *greater* will do.

majordomo, majordomos. One word.

major general. Two words.

majority. Don't use *a majority of* when *most* will do.

major portion of. Don't use *a major portion of* when *most* will do.

make in the sense of earn has been standard usage since 1315.

make-. Most compounds are spelled as one word.

make-believe. Hyphened.

-maker, -making. Compounds are spelled as one word, e.g. *shoe-maker, policymaking.*

makeshift, makeup (noun), **makeweight.** One word.

mal-. Compounds are spelled as one word.

malapropos. One word, no accent.

malarkey ends in *-ey.* Listed in Webster's as standard usage.

male. Don't say *males* when you mean *men.*

malefactor ends in *-or.*

malevolence, malevolent end in *-ence, -ent.*

malfeasance ends in *-ance.*

malicious ends in *-icious.*

malign, malignant, malignancy. *Malignant* and *malignancy* are used in medical contexts, *malign* in other senses, e.g. *a malign influence.*

malleable. Double *l.* Ends in *-eable.*

mama, mamma. Both spellings are common.

mammalogy ends in *-alogy.*

man, manned, manning, mannish. Two *n*'s in all forms but *man.*

man, gentleman. *Gentleman* is the courteous word, used in salutations or in the presence of the person referred to, as in *Gentlemen* or *the gentleman was here first. Man* is the regular word, as in *a man in the audience spoke up* or *the room was empty except for a young man sitting at a table in the back.*

-man. Compounds are spelled as one word, e.g. *fisherman, woodsman.*

manageable ends in *-eable.*

managing. No *e.*

man-child. Hyphened.

mandamus, mandamuses.

mandatory ends in *-ory.*

man-day, man-eater, man-eating. Hyphened.

manege. No accent.

maneuver. No *o*.

mango, mangoes.

mangy. No *e*.

manhandle, manhole. One word.

man-hour. Hyphened.

manhunt. One word.

mania, phobia. A *mania* is a craze *for* something, a *phobia* is a crazy *fear of* something.

manicure. *I* in the middle.

manifesto, manifestos.

manifold in the sense of various is spelled with *i* in the middle. *(Manyfold* means *by many times.)*

manikin. Spell it with one *n* in the middle. For a model, *mannequin* is more common.

manila. One *l*.

man-made. Hyphened.

mannequin. So spelled. More common than *manikin*.

manner. Don't use *in a . . . manner* when a simple adverb will do.

(manoeuvre). Spell it *maneuver*.

man-of-war, men-of-war. Hyphened.

manor ends in *-or*.

manpower. One word.

manqué. Spell it with the accent.

manservant, menservants. One word.

manslaughter. One word. Means killing without malice aforethought.

mantel, mantle. A *mantel* is a shelf, a *mantle* is a cloak. Remember "There's a *tel*ephone on the *mantel.*"

mantelpiece. One word.

manual ends in *-ual*.

manufacture, manufacturer end in *-ure, -urer*. Don't use *manufacture* when *make* will do.

many-colored. Hyphened.

manyfold. One word. Means *by many times*.

many-hued, many-sided. Hyphened.

mapmaker, mapmaking. One word.

marabou ends in *ou*.

maraschino is spelled with *sch*.

marbleize. *E* before *-ize*.

marchese. Italian marquess.

marchioness is spelled with *ion.*

mare's nest, mare's nests. Apostrophe and *s,* no hyphen.

margarine. The common spelling has *e* at the end.

marginalia is followed by a plural verb.

marijuana. Spell it with *j,* not *h.*

mariner ends in *-er.*

marionette ends in *-ette.*

marital, martial. *Marital* has to do with marriage, *martial* with war.

mark. Write the West German currency *deutsche mark* (singular and plural). Abbreviate it *DM.*

markdown (noun). One word.

marketplace. One word.

markoff (noun), **markup** (noun). One word.

marmalade. Three *a*'s.

marquee, marquis. A *marquee* is a canopy over a theater entrance, a *marquis* (or *marquess*) is a nobleman.

marquess. More common spelling than *marquis.*

marquise. The more common English term is *marchioness.*

marriageable ends in *-eable.*

marry, marrying, married.

Marseillaise. First *ei,* then *ai.*

marshal, marshaled, marshaling. One *l* in all forms.

marshland, marshmallow. One word.

marten, martin. A *marten* is a furry animal, a *martin* is a swallow.

martial, marital. *Martial* has to do with war, *marital* with marriage.

martinet ends in *-et.*

martini, martinis.

martyr ends in *-yr.*

martyrize ends in *-ize.* Don't use *martyrize* when *martyr* will do.

marvel, marveled, marveling, marvelous. One *l* in all forms.

Mary. The plural is *Marys.*

marzipan. Spelled with *z.*

mask, masque. A *mask* covers the face, a *masque* is a kind of entertainment.

masochism. Spelled with *ch.*

mason jar. Small *m.*

masque. An entertainment. Otherwise spell it *mask.*

masquerade is spelled with *qu.*

Massachusetts. First double *s,* then one *s,* then double *t.*

massacre ends in -re.

massacre, massacred, massacring.

massage, massaged, massaging.

masseur, masseuse. Spelled with *eu*.

mass-produce. Hyphened.

-master. Compounds are spelled as one word, e.g. *chessmaster, ringmaster.*

master-at-arms. Two hyphens.

master bedroom. Two words.

masterful, masterly. *Masterful* means domineering, *masterly* means highly skilled.

master key. Two words.

mastermind, masterpiece. One word.

master plan, master race, master sergeant. Two words.

masterstroke, masterwork. One word.

mat. Spell it so when you mean not glossy.

matador. *A* in the middle.

matchboard, matchbook, matchbox, matchmaker, matchmaking. One word.

-mate. Compounds are spelled as one word, e.g. *cellmate, roommate.*

material, materiel. *Material* means matter in general, *materiel* means supplies and equipment in contrast to personnel.

materialize. Don't use *materialize* when *happen, work out, show up* will do.

materiel. Spell it without accent.

matey ends in -*ey*.

math, meaning mathematics, is listed in Webster's as standard usage.

mathematics is commonly used with a singular verb. Watch the *e* after *th*.

matinee. No accent.

matins. One *t*. Use with a singular verb.

matriarch ends in -*ch*.

matrix. The common plural is *matrices.*

matron of honor. No hyphens.

matt. Spell it *mat.*

matter-of-fact, matter-of-factly, matter-of-factness. Two hyphens.

mattress. Two *t*'s, two *s*'s.

matutinal. Don't use *matutinal* when *morning* will do.

matzo, matzos. The common spellings.

matzo ball. Two words.

maudlin.

(maulstick). Spell it *mahlstick.*

maunder, meander. *Maunder* means grumble, *meander* means follow a winding course.

mausoleum, mausoleums.

mauve is spelled with *au.*

maven, meaning expert, is standard usage. Spell it with *e.*

mawkish is spelled with *aw.*

maximize ends in *-ize.*

maximum. The plural is either *maximums* or *maxima.*

may, can. The idea that you should use *can* only for (physical) ability and *may* for (legal) permission has long been discredited. *Can* for permission has been in use since 1542. The Bible (I Cor. 10:21) says "Ye cannot drink the cup of the Lord, and the cup of devils."

maybe, may be. *Maybe* is standard usage for perhaps, *may be* is a verb form, e.g. *I may be mistaken.*

mayn't. Common contraction of *may not.*

mayonnaise. Double *n.*

mayoral, mayoralty.

maypole. One word.

mazy. No *e.*

Mc in names. Make sure whether the name is spelled *Mc* or *Mac.*

MC. Abbreviation of *Master of Ceremonies.* Capital *M,* capital *C,* no periods. The form *emcee* is listed in Webster's as standard usage.

me instead of *I* in such expressions as *it's me* is listed in Webster's as standard usage. It dates back to 1500. Keats wrote "If it was me, I did it in a dream."

meager. Spell it with *er.*

mealtime. One word.

mealymouthed. One word.

mean, median. Both are averages. The (arithmetic) *mean* is the sum of several quantities divided by their number, the *median* is that quantity in a series that has an equal number above and below it.

mean, mien. *Mien* is the spelling of air or bearing showing mood or character. In all other senses the word is spelled *mean.*

meander, maunder. *Meander* means follow a winding course, *maunder* means grumble.

meanness. Double *n.*

mean-souled, mean-spirited. Hyphened.

meant is spelled with *ea.*

meantime, meanwhile. It is common to say *in the meantime,* but *meanwhile* (without *in the*).

measly, in the sense of contemptibly small, is listed as standard usage in Webster's.

measurements. Use figures, e.g. *2 by 4, 5 feet 10, a 26-foot boat.*

meatball, meatcutter, meatpacker, meatpacking. One word.

mechanically ends in *-ally.*

medal, meddle. A *medal* is a metal disk, to *meddle* is to interfere.

medaled, medaling. One *l.*

medalist. One *l.*

medallion. Double *l.*

Medal of Honor. The adjective *Congressional* is not necessary.

meddle, medal. *Meddle* means interfere, *medal* means a metal disk.

media is the plural of *medium,* but is commonly used with a singular verb.

median, mean. Both are averages. The *median* is that quantity in a series that has an equal number above and below it, the (arithmetic) *mean* is the sum of several quantities divided by their number.

medic, medico are listed in Webster's as standard usage.

Medicaid, Medicare. Capital *M.*

medicine. *I* after *d.*

medico-. Spell compounds as one word, e.g. *medicolegal.*

medieval. The common spelling.

medio-. Spell compounds as one word.

mediocre ends in *-re.*

Mediterranean. Double *r,* ends in *-ean.*

medium, media. The plural *media* is commonly used with a singular verb. Use the plural *mediums* when you mean psychics.

medium-brown, medium-size, medium-sized. Hyphened.

mediumweight. One word.

medley, medleys.

meerschaum.

meetinghouse, meetingplace. One word.

megalo-. Spell compounds as one word, e.g. *megalomaniac.*

melancholia, melancholic, melancholy. Spelled with *ch.*

mélange has an accent on the *e.*

melba toast. Small *m.*

melee. No accents.

mellifluence, mellifluent end in *-ence, -ent.*

mellifluous ends in *-uous.*

melodrama. One *l.*

melon. One *l.*

memento, mementos. Starts with *me-.*

memo, memos. Standard usage.

memorable ends in *-able.*

memorandum, memorandums.

memorialize ends in *-ize.*

memorize ends in *-ize.*

menace ends in *-ace.*

ménage. Spell with the accent.

ménage à trois. Spelled with accents.

mendacious ends in *-acious.*

mendacity, mendicity. *Mendacity* means habitual lying, *mendicity*
  begging.

menial (noun). Don't use this derogatory word.

menopause. *O* in the middle.

menorah. *H* at the end.

mensch. Slang for decent human being.

menstruate, menstruation. *U* after *r.*

mentality. Don't write *mentality* when *mind* will do.

(mental telepathy). *Mental* is unnecessary. Say *telepathy.*

mentor ends in *-or.*

menu, menus.

meow. Spelled with one *e* and *ow.*

(merangue). Misspelling of *meringue.*

mercenary ends in *-ary.*

mercerize ends in *-ize.*

merchandise, merchandiser, merchandising. The common spelling
  is with *s.*

merciful, mercifully, merciless, mercilessly. *I* in the middle.

mercurial ends in *-ial.*

merely. Spelled with *ere.*

meretricious ends in *-icious.*

meridian ends in *-ian.*

meringue. Spelled with *i.*

merino, merinos.

merit, merited, meriting, meritorious. One *t* in all forms.

merrily, merriment. *I* in the middle.

merry-go-round. Two hyphens.

merrymaker, merrymaking. One word.

mesalliance. No accent. The English form *misalliance* is more common.

Mesdames. Plural of *Madam.* Used in salutations.

(Mesdemoiselles). As the plural of *Mademoiselle, Mademoiselles* is more common.

mesmerize ends in *-ize.*

meso-. Compounds are spelled as one word, e.g. *mesomorph.*

message (verb). Listed as standard usage in Webster's.

Messeigneurs. Plural of *Monseigneur.*

Messieurs. Plural of *Monsieur.*

Messrs. Plural of *Mr.,* used in salutations. But *Dear Mr. Smith and Mr. Jones* is more common than *Dear Messrs. Smith and Jones.* In addresses (with first names) use *Mr. John Smith and Mr. Robert Jones.*

mestizo, mestizos.

meta-. Compounds are spelled as one word.

metal, mettle. *Metal* means a substance, *mettle* means stamina.

metal, metaled, metaling. One *l* in all forms.

metallic, metallurgical, metallurgy. Double *l.*

metalware, metalwork, metalworker, metalworking. One word.

metamorphosis, metamorphoses.

metaphor ends in *-or.* See also MIXED METAPHORS.

metaphysics is used with a singular verb.

meteorology, metrology. *Meteorology* deals with the weather, *metrology* with weights and measures.

meter ends in *-er.*

meter man, meter maid. Two words.

methodology. Don't use *methodology* when *method* will do.

meticulous in the sense of painstaking is standard usage.

métier. Spelled with accent.

metro-. Compounds are spelled as one word.

mettle, metal. *Mettle* means stamina, *metal* means a substance.

mews is used with a singular verb.

mezzanine. Double *z,* two single *n*'s.

mezzo-soprano. Hyphened.

mezzotint. One word.

(miaow). The common spelling is *meow.*

miasma, miasmas.

micro-. Spell compounds as one word.

microorganism. No hyphen.

mid-. Compounds are spelled as one word except if the second part starts with a capital, e.g. *mid-Atlantic.*

midair, midbrain, midcourse, midday. One word.

middle-. Compounds are mostly hyphened.

middle-aged. Hyphened.

Middle Ages. No hyphen.

middle-class. Hyphened.

middleman. One word.

middle-of-the-road, middle-of-the-roader. Hyphened.

middle-sized. Hyphened.

middleweight. One word.

midpoint, midriff, midsection, midship, midstream, midsummer, midterm, midtown, midway, midweek. One word.

Midwest. Capital *M.*

midwife, midwifery, midwives.

midwinter, midyear. One word.

mien, mean. *Mien* is an air or bearing showing mood or character. In all other senses spell it *mean.*

miffed is standard usage.

mighty as an adverb is listed as standard usage in Webster's, e.g. *a mighty fine day.*

mignonette ends in *-ette.*

migraine is spelled with *ai.*

migratory ends in *-ory.*

mike, for *microphone,* is listed as standard usage in Webster's.

mil, mill. A *mil* is 1/1000 inch, a *mill* is 1/1000 dollar.

milch cows. Spelled with *ch.*

mileage ends in *-eage.*

milieu, milieus.

militate, mitigate. To *militate* against is to have an effect against, to *mitigate* is to soften.

militiaman, militiamen. One word.

milk-. Most compounds are spelled as one word.

milkmaid, milkman, milkshake, milkshed, milksop, milkweed, milkwhite. One word.

-mill. Compounds are spelled as one word, e.g. *gristmill, sawmill, windmill.*

mill-. Most compounds are spelled as one word.

millboard, milldam. One word.

millenary, millinery. *Millenary* has to do with 1000, *millinery* with hats.

millennium, millennia. Spelled with two *l*'s and two *n*'s. Think of a "*L*ong-*l*ost *n*ever-*n*ever land."

milliner, millinery. Two *i*'s when you mean women's hats.

million. Spell out the word million instead of using six zeros. Instead of *$4,000,000* write *$4 million*. Don't use a hyphen between the figure and the word *million*.

millionaire has one *n*. Think of a millionaire *on a* yacht.

millowner, millpond, millrace, millstream, millstone, millwork, millworker, millwright. One word.

mimic, mimicked, mimicking, mimicker, mimicry.

minable. No *e* after *m*.

minaret ends in *-et*.

minatory. Don't use *minatory* when *threatening* will do.

mind-blowing is listed in Webster's as standard usage.

-minded. Compounds are hyphened, e.g. *broad-minded, open-minded*.

mindreader, mindreading. One word.

minefield, minelayer. One word.

miner, minor. A *miner* works in a mine, a *minor* is underage.

mineralogy. *A* after *r*.

minesweeper, minesweeping. One word.

mini-. Spell compounds as one word.

miniature has *ia* in the middle.

minibike, minibus, minicar, minicomputer. One word.

minimal. Don't use *minimal* when *very small* will do.

minimize ends in *-ize*. *Minimize* in the sense of belittle or play down is standard usage.

minimum, minimums.

(miniscule). Misspelling of *minuscule*.

miniskirt, ministate. One word.

minister. See REVEREND.

minstrel, minstrelsy end in *-el, -elsy*.

minuet ends in *-uet*.

minuscule is spelled with *u* in the middle. Remember, the word starts with *minus*.

minute is so spelled in all meanings, including *very small* and the record of a meeting.

minuteman. One word.

minutia, minutiae.

miracle. *A* after *r*.

mirror ends in *-or*.

mis-. Spell compounds as one word. Spell them *mis-*, not *miss-*, unless the second part starts with *s*, like *misstatement*.

misalliance ends in *-ance*. (More common than *mésalliance*.)

misanthrope, misanthropic.

misapply, misapprehension, misappropriate. One *s*.

miscegenation is spelled with *sc*.

miscellaneous. *Sc*, double *l*, ends in *-eous*.

miscellany. *Sc*, double *l*.

mischief, mischiefs. Spelled with *ie*.

mischievous. Spelled with *ie*. No *i* after *v*.

miscible is spelled with *sc*, ends in *-ible*.

miscreant ends in *-eant*.

misdemeanor ends in *-or*.

misdoubt is standard usage.

misguidance. One *s, ui*, ends in *-ance*.

mishmash. Standard usage.

mislaid ends in *-aid*.

mislead, misled. *Mislead* is the present, *misled* the past tense.

misogynist is spelled with *y* after *g*.

(mispell). Misspelling of *misspell*.

misplace. One *s*.

misprision ends in *-sion*. Its main meaning is concealment of a felony by a nonparticipant.

mispronounce, mispronunciation. *Mispronounce* is spelled with *ou*, but *mispronunciation* with *u*.

misquotations are so common that the exact form often seems pedantic and fussy. If you write *to paint the lily* instead of to *gild the lily* or *an ill-favored thing, sir, but mine own* instead of *a poor thing but my own,* you'll be right but it won't necessarily improve your style.

miss-. If you can't find the word you're looking for, try *mis-*.

Miss, Misses. It is customary to use *Miss* in addresses if the marital status of the addressee is unknown or if she is known to prefer *Miss* to *Mrs.*

Miss is also commonly used in the second reference to an unmarried woman whose first and last names have been given. But when her unmarried status is not known or even when it is known, the trend is toward using the last name alone. E.g. *Elizabeth Cartwright was born . . . Cartwright later entered business. . . .*

The plural *The Misses Smith* for unmarried sisters now sounds old-fashioned. Write *Miss Mary Smith and Miss Anne Smith* or, if the first names are unknown, *The Miss Smiths.*

See also MS.

Never use *Miss* in referring to yourself.

missal, missile. A *missal* is a book of prayers, a *missile* is a weapon.

missend, missent.

misshapen. Two *s*'s.

missile, missive. *Missile* (weapon) ends in *-ile.* A *missive* is a letter.

missilery. The more common spelling is with *e.*

Mississippi. Two double *s*'s, one double *p.*

missive. Don't use *missive* when *letter* will do.

misspeak. Two *s*'s.

misspell. Two *s*'s. Remember 'She never *miss*pelled *Miss*issippi."

misspend, misspent. Two *s*'s.

misstate, misstatement. Two *s*'s.

misstep. Two *s*'s.

missus for wife is listed in Webster's as standard usage. Spelled with *u.*

mistakable ends in *-able.*

mistakenness. Two *n*'s.

mistletoe. Silent *t.*

-mistress. Spell compounds as one word, e.g. *headmistress, post-mistress.*

miter. The US spelling ends in *-er.*

mitigate, militate. To *mitigate* is to soften, to *militate* against is to have an effect against.

mitrailleuse. Spelled with *aill* and *eu.*

mix for mixture is standard English.

mixable ends in *-able.*

mixed metaphors. Don't use combinations of metaphors that don't match, like *the fox has risen to the bait* or *the view was echoed by many experts.*

mixed-up. Hyphened.

mixup. One word.

mizzen. Double *z.*

-mm-. See -M-, -MM-.

mnemonic starts with a silent *m.*

moat, mote. A *moat* is a ditch, a *mote* is a speck.

mob, mobbed, mobbing.

mobilize ends in *-ize.*

moccasin has two *c*'s and one *s.* Remember "Moccasins were worn by *C*herokees, *C*omanches and *S*ioux."

mocha is spelled with *ch.*

mockingbird. One word.

mock turtle. Two words.

mockup. One word.

mode. Don't use *mode* when *mood, style, way, method* will do.

model, modeled, modeler, modeling. One *l* in all forms.

moderator ends in *-or.*

modernization, modernize are spelled with *z.*

modernness. Two *n*'s.

modicum. Don't use *a modicum of* when *some* will do.

modify. Don't use *modify* when *change* will do.

modus operandi. Don't use *modus operandi* when *method* will do.

modus vivendi in the sense of way of life is standard usage.

Mogul. Spell it so. Small *m* in *movie mogul* etc.

(Mohammed). The common form is *Muhammad.*

(Mohammedan). The common word is *Muslim.*

Mohave, Mojave. The common spelling for the Indian tribe is *Mohave,* but it's *Mojave Desert.*

moiety. Don't use *moiety* when *half* will do.

moire. No accent necessary.

moisturize. Don't use *moisturize* when *moisten* will do.

Mojave Desert. But the common spelling for the Indians is *Mohave.*

molar ends in *-ar.*

mold, molder, molding, moldy. Spell without *u.*

molecule. Spelled with *e* between *l* and *c.*

moll. Listed in Webster's as standard usage.

mollusk. Spell it with *k.*

mollycoddle is spelled with *y.*

Molotov cocktail. Capital *M.*

molt. No *u.*

momentarily, momently. Now used interchangeably. *Momently* is getting rare.

(momento). Misspelling of *memento.*

momentous ends in *-ous.*

momentum, momenta.

monarch ends in *-ch.* Don't use *monarch* when *king, queen* or some other common word will do.

monarchical. The common form.

monarchy ends in *-archy.*

monastery. *E* after *t.*

monaural is spelled with *au.*

monetary ends in *-ary.*

money. The plural *moneys* is more common than *monies.*

money-. Spell most compounds as one word.

moneybags. One word.

moneyed ends in *-eyed.*

moneylender, moneylending, moneymaker, moneymaking. One word.

money order. Two words.

moneysaver, moneysaving. One word.

-monger. Compounds are spelled as one word, e.g. *fishmonger, warmonger.*

mongoose, mongooses.

(monies). Spell it *moneys.*

monitor ends in *-or.*

monkey, monkeyed, monkeying. The verb is listed as standard usage in Webster's.

monkeyshines. Listed as standard usage in Webster's.

monkey wrench. Two words.

mono-. Compounds are spelled as one word.

monogram, monogrammatic, monogrammed, monogramming. Two *m*'s in all forms except *monogram.*

monologue is more common than *monolog.*

monopolize ends in *-ize.*

monotonous. *O* after *t.*

Monseigneur, Messeigneurs. French titles.

Monsieur, Messieurs. French titles.

Monsignor, Monsignors. Roman Catholic titles.

monstrous. No *e* after *t.*

months. In dates use the following forms: *Jan. 1, Feb. 2, March 3, Apr. 4, May 5, June 6, July 7, Aug. 8, Sept. 9, Oct. 10, Nov. 11, Dec. 12.*

moo, mooed, mooing.

moonbeam, mooncalf, moonface, moonfaced. One word.

moonlight, moonlighted, moonlighter, moonlighting. Listed in Webster's as standard usage for working on a second job.

moonlit. Common form in the sense of lighted by the moon.

moonrise, moonscape, moonstruck. One word.

moose. The plural is also *moose.*

mop-up. Hyphened.

mopping-up (adj.). Hyphened.

moraine (of a glacier) is spelled with one *r.*

moral, morale. *Moral* means the lesson of a story, *morale* means a mental state.

moralize ends in *-ize.*

morass. One *r,* two *s*'s.

moratorium, moratoriums.

mordancy, mordant end in *-ancy, -ant.*

more, most. Don't use forms with *more* and *most* when forms with *-er* and *-est* are in use, e.g. say *sillier* rather than *more silly, commonest* rather than *most common.*

more importantly, most importantly are common forms.

moreover. Don't use *moreover* when *also* will do or when no connective is needed.

(more preferable, more preferably). Says the same thing twice. Say *preferable, preferably.*

mores. Don't use *mores* when *customs* or *manners* will do.

more than one is used with the singular verb, e.g. *more than one family was distressed.*

morgue ends in *-gue.*

morocco. Three *o*'s, two *c*'s.

mortarboard. One word.

mortgage, mortgageable, mortgagee, mortgagor. All these words have a *t* between the *r* and the *g. Mortgageable* ends in *-eable.* The *mortgagee* is the lender (the bank), the *mortgagor* (no *e* before *-or*) is the debtor (homeowner). To remember the silent *t* think of "a *t*en thousand dollar mortgage."

mortgageholder. One word.

mortician ends in *-ician.* Don't use *mortician* when *undertaker* or *funeral director* will do.

mortise. Spell it with *s.*

mosey around is listed in Webster's as standard usage.

(Moslem). The common form is *Muslim.*

mosquito, mosquitoes.

most in the sense of almost is listed as standard usage in Webster's. The usage has been traced back to 1584. Thackeray wrote "Most everybody's here."

-most. Compounds are spelled as one word, e.g. *northernmost.*

most-favored-nation (adjective). Hyphens.

most importantly. Common usage.

mostly. Don't use *mostly* when *most* will do.

mote, moat. A *mote* is a speck, a *moat* is a ditch.

motet ends in *-et*.

mothball, mothballed, mothballing. One word.

moth-eaten. Hyphened.

mother country. Two words.

mother-in-law, mothers-in-law.

motherland. One word.

mother-of-pearl. Hyphens.

mother tongue. Two words.

motif, motive. A *motif* is a central theme in a work of art, a *motive* is a cause of action.

motivate. Don't use *motivate* when *cause* will do.

motivation. Don't use *motivation* when *reason* will do.

motley ends in *-ey*.

motorbike, motorboat, motorcar, motorcycle, motorman, motor-truck. One word.

motto, mottoes.

(moujik). The most common spelling is *muzhik*.

(mould, moulder, mouldy). The common US spellings are *mold, molder, moldy*.

(moult). The common US spelling is *molt*.

mountaineer, mountaineering, mountainous. All spelled with *ai*.

mourn, mournful. Spelled with *ou*.

mousetrap. One word.

moussaka.

mousse.

(moustache). The common US spelling is *mustache*.

mousy. No *e*.

-mouthed. Most compounds are spelled as one word, e.g. *close-mouthed, foulmouthed, loudmouthed, openmouthed*.

mouthful, mouthfuls.

mouthpiece, mouthwash. One word.

movable. No *e* after *v*.

movie, movies. Listed in Webster's as standard usage.

moviegoer, moviemaker, moviemaking. One word.

mowed, mown. Use either form for the verb, but only *mown* for the adjective, e.g. *new-mown hay*.

Mr. is not necessary in the second reference to a man whose first and last names have been given. E.g. *Moses Cartwright was born . . . Cartwright later entered business. . . .*

Don't use *Mr.* in referring to your husband. Say "my husband" or use his first name. Never use *Mr.* in referring to yourself.

Mrs. is commonly used in the second reference to a married woman whose first and last names have been given. But when her married status is not known or even when it is known, the trend is toward using the last name alone. E.g. *Elizabeth Cartwright was born . . . Cartwright later entered business. . . .*

Don't use *Mrs.* in referring to your wife. Say "my wife" or use her first name. Never use *Mrs.* in referring to yourself.

Ms. Used instead of *Miss* or *Mrs.* Listed in Webster's and the GPO Style Manual as standard usage.

much-. Hyphen compound modifiers with *much,* e.g. write *the much-admired painter.* But don't use a hyphen when the word *much* is modified, e.g. write *a very much admired painter.* Don't use a hyphen either when *much* comes after the noun, e.g. *the painter was much admired.*

(muchly). Unidiomatic. Say *much.*

mucilage. Don't say *mucilage* when *gum* or *glue* will do.

muckrake, muckraker, muckraking. One word.

mucous, mucus. The adjective ends in *-ous,* the noun ends in *-us.*

muddleheaded. One word.

mudslinger, mudslinging. One word.

mufti ends in *i.*

mugwump. Two *u*'s.

Muhammad, Muhammadan. The common spelling.

(mujik). The common spelling is *muzhik.*

mulatto, mulattoes.

muleteer. First one *e,* then two.

mulish. No *e.*

mulligatawny.

multi-. Compounds are spelled as one word.

multicolored, multifold, multiform, multilateral, multilayered, multimillionaire, multinational. One word.

multiple-choice. Hyphened.

multipliable ends in *-iable.*

multiply, multiplied, multiplier, multiplying.

multiprocessing, multiprogramming, multipurpose. One word.

multitudinous. Don't use *multitudinous* when *many* will do.

mum is listed in Webster's as standard usage for *silent, chrysanthemum* and *mom* (British usage).

mumbo jumbo. Two words.

mumps. Use a singular verb.

munificence, munificent end in *-ence, -ent.* Don't use *munificent* when *lavish* will do.

murderee is listed in Webster's as standard usage.

murderous. *E* after *d.*

murmur, murmured, murmuring. Two *u*'s.

muscle is spelled with *sc.*

musclebound. One word.

muscular ends in *-ar.*

museum, museums.

musical, musicale. A *musical* is a musical comedy, a *musicale* is a social entertainment with music.

music-conscious. Hyphened.

musiclover, musicroom. One word.

muskmelon. One word.

Muslim. The common word. (*Moslem* and *Mohammedan* are old-fashioned.)

mussel ends in *-el.*

must in the sense of essential is listed in Webster's as standard usage, as both a verb and an adjective, e.g. *the bill was a must, must legislation.*

mustache. The common US spelling.

mustachio, mustachios, mustachioed.

mustn't. Common contraction of *must not.*

muttonchops. One word.

mutual in the sense of "shared in common" (rather than reciprocal) is listed in Webster's as a standard usage. The usage goes back to 1591, when Shakespeare wrote (Two Gentlemen of Verona, V, iv, 172–173) "That done, our day of marriage shall be yours; One feast, one house, one mutual happiness."

(mutual cooperation). Leave out *mutual.*

(mutual satisfaction). Don't use *mutual* when the satisfaction is one-sided.

My dear, in salutations, is more formal than plain *Dear.* Don't use *My dear* except in letters to government officials etc.

myna. Spell it without *h.*

myopic may mean literally nearsighted or figuratively short-sighted.

myriad means a very large number, not necessarily ten thousand (literal sense).

myrmidon. Small *m*. Someone who carries out orders.

myrrh ends in *-rrh*.

myself. Don't use *myself* when *I* or *me* will do.

mysterious, mystic, mystical. *Mysterious* means puzzling, *mystic* or *mystical* means occult, spiritual etc.

mystify, mystified, mystifying.

mystique ends in *-que*.

mythmaker, mythmaking. One word.

mythopoeia. Spelled with *oeia*.

N

n-. If you can't find the word you're looking for, try *gn-, kn-, mn-, pn-*.

-n-, -nn-. An *n* at the end of a word is doubled before the suffixes *-ed, -er, -ing, -ish, -y* if there's a single vowel immediately before the *n* and the accent is on the last syllable. Examples: *thin, thinned; man, mannish; japan, japanning; sun, sunny; span, spanner.*

nacre ends in *-re.*

nacreous ends in *-eous.*

nadir. Don't use *nadir* when *low point* will do.

(naif). The common spelling is *naive.*

naive, naivete. Spell them so. No accent.

namable. No *e* after *m.*

namby-pamby. Hyphened.

namely. Don't use *namely* when *that is* will do. Don't put a comma after *namely.*

name of. Don't say *by the name of* when *called* or *named* will do.

nameplate. One word.

names. Be sure people's names are spelled right. If the spelling is odd or unusual, check your source to make doubly sure.

Use people's actual names unless the context is derogatory. If so, or if you write about people in an example or illustration, use fictitious names. Don't use *Smith, Jones* or *Robinson,* but use realistic names, e.g. picked at random from the phone book. Introduce fictitious names naturally, e.g. *a woman I'll call Anne Brooks* or *Sydney Vernon (not his real name).*

nanny. Spell it with *y.*

naphtha is spelled with *phth.*

narc or **nark** is listed in Webster's as slang.

narcissism, narcissist. The common spellings.

narcissus. The common plural is *narcissus,* same as the singular.

narrate. Don't use *narrate* when *tell* will do.

narrative. Don't use *narrative* when *tale* or *story* will do.

narrowminded. One word.

nary is listed in dictionaries as dialect. Don't use it in writing.

nascent is spelled with *sc.*

nasturtium, nasturtiums.

natal day. Don't use *natal day* when *birthday* will do.

natatorium. Don't use *natatorium* when *swimming pool* will do.

nation. Lower case *n.*

nationalization, nationalize end in *-ization, -ize.*

nationwide. One word.

native. Don't use *native* when the word may be offensive.

native-born. Hyphened.

naturalization, naturalize end in *-ization, -ize.*

naturally ends in *-ally.*

nature. Don't use *nature* when it is unnecessary, e.g. *of a dangerous nature* instead of *dangerous.*

naught, nought. The spelling *naught* is more common. Don't use *naught* when *nothing* or *zero* will do.

nauseated, nauseous. Webster's lists *nauseous* as standard usage in the sense of *nauseated.*

nautilus, nautiluses. Ends in *-us.*

Navaho, Navahos. Commonly spelled with *h.*

naval, navel. *Naval* has to do with the navy, the *navel* is the umbilicus. It's *navel orange.*

navigable ends in *-able.*

navigator ends in *-or.*

navy blue. Small *n.* Two words.

nay. Don't use *nay* when *no* will do.

Nazi, Nazism. Capital *N.*

NB. No periods. Abbreviation for Latin *nota bene* (note well). It is more common to write *note.*

neap tide. Two words. Spelled with *ea.*

nearby. One word.

near future. Don't write *in the near future* when *soon* will do.

nearsighted. One word.

nebula, nebulas.

necessarily, necessary. One *c,* two *s*'s.

necessitate. Don't use *necessitate* when *call for* will do.

neckerchief, neckerchiefs.

necklace, neckline, necktie, neckwear. One word.

necro-. Compounds are spelled as one word.

necropolis, necropolises.

nectar ends in *-ar.*

nee. No accent. Don't write *nee* when *born* will do.

needn't. Common contraction of *need not.*

needs. Don't use *needs* when *necessarily* will do.

ne'er. Poetic. Use *never* in prose.

ne'er-do-well. One apostrophe, two hyphens.

nefarious. Don't use *nefarious* when *vicious, evil, wicked* will do.

negate. Don't use *negate* when *say no, deny, rule out* will do.

negative, in the negative. Don't use *negative* or *in the negative* when *no* will do.

negative, double. See DOUBLE NEGATIVE.

negatives are tricky. Watch out for such naturally canceling negatives as *it was want of imagination that failed them* or *not even a blizzard prevented his friends from missing the party.*

negligee ends in *ee.* No accent.

negligence, negligent end in *-ence, -ent.*

negligible ends in *-ible.*

negotiable ends in *-able.*

negotiate in the sense of tackle a difficulty is standard usage.

Negress is offensive. Don't use.

Negro, Negroes. Capital *N.* Now being displaced by *black* (with small *b*).

neigh, neighing. The horse's cry is spelled with *eigh.*

neighbor ends in *-or.*

neighborhood. Don't write *in the neighborhood of* when *about* will do.

neighborliness. *I* in the middle.

neither. The plural verb has long been used with *neither* alone or *neither . . . nor.* Dr. Samuel Johnson wrote "Neither of them were in."

nelson. Small *n* for the wrestling hold.

nemesis, nemeses.

(nemonic). Misspelling of *mnemonic.*

neo-. Compounds are spelled as one word, except for such words as *neo-Darwinism, neo-Freudian.*

Neoclassicism. Capital *N,* one word.

Neo-Impressionism. Capital *N,* hyphen, capital *I.*

Neo-Nazi. Capital *N,* hyphen, capital *N.*

neophyte. Don't use *neophyte* when *novice* or *beginner* will do.

nerve-racking. No *w*.

nervous ends in *-ous*.

nervy in the sense of brash is listed in Webster's as standard usage.

nescience, nescient end in *-ence, -ent*. Spelled with *sci*.

-ness. Don't use words ending in *-ness* when more familiar words will do. Don't use *anxiousness* instead of *anxiety, pompousness* instead of *pomposity, vulnerableness* instead of *vulnerability*.

nestle is spelled with a silent *t*.

net is spelled with one *t* in all senses.

network. One word.

neu-. If you can't find the word you're looking for, try *pneu-*.

neural, neuralgia, neurasthenia, neuritis. Spelled with *eu*.

neuro-. Compounds are spelled as one word.

neurosis, neuroses.

neurotic, neuter, neutral. Spelled with *eu*.

neutralize ends in *-ize*.

never-ending, never-failing, never-never. Hyphened.

nevertheless doesn't need a comma before or after it. Example: "They decided nevertheless to stay home." Don't use *nevertheless* when *but* will do.

newborn, newcomer, newfangled, newfound, newlywed. One word.

new-mown. Hyphened.

new record. Don't write *new record* when *record* will do.

news takes a singular verb.

newsletter, newsmagazine, newsman, newspaperman, newspaperwoman, newsprint, newsroom, newsstand. One word.

new words. Whenever you're tempted to form a new word, don't. Try to use familiar words instead of such words as *apocalypticizing* or *demythification*.

nexus, nexuses.

niacin. No *e*.

Niagara. *A* after *g*.

nice in the sense of pleasing, agreeable has been standard usage since the late 18th century. Jane Austen wrote ". . . the nice long letter which I have received from you."

nickel ends in *-el*. Remember "It cost a nickel to ride the old el."

nickelodeon.

nicotine.

niece is spelled with *ie*, following the rule "*i* before *e* except after *c*."

Nietzsche. Spelled with *tzsch.*

nifty is listed in Webster's as standard usage.

nigh. Don't use *nigh* when *near* will do.

night-. Most compounds are spelled as one word.

night blindness. Two words.

nightcap, nightclothes, nightclub, nightdress, nightfall, nightgown. One word.

nightie. Spell it with *ie.* Standard usage.

night letter. Two words.

nightlife. One word.

night light. Two words.

nightmare, nightmarish. One word.

night owl. Two words.

night school. Two words.

nightshirt, nightside, nightstand, nightstick. One word.

night table. Two words.

nighttime, nightwalker. One word.

night watch, night watchman. Two words.

(nighty). Spell it *nightie.*

Nigger is offensive. Don't use.

nihilism, nihilist. Three *i*'s.

nil. One *l.*

nimble-fingered. Hyphened.

nimblefooted. One word.

nimbus, nimbi.

nincompoop.

ninefold, ninepins. One word.

nines. No apostrophe.

nineteen. Watch for the *e* between *n* and *t.*

19th century. Don't spell it out. It means the 1800s.

nineties or **90s.** No apostrophe.

ninety. Watch the *e* between *n* and *t.*

ninety-one etc. Hyphened.

ninish. No *e.*

ninth. No *e.*

Nip for Japanese is offensive. Don't use.

nip and tuck. No hyphens.

nirvana. Spell it with a small *n.*

Nisei. The common plural is *Nisei,* like the singular.

nisi, as in *decree nisi,* is so spelled.

(nite). Not commonly accepted as a reformed spelling of *night.* Don't use.

niter ends in *-er.*

nitpicker, nitpicking. One word.

nitro-. Compounds are spelled as one word, e.g. *nitroglycerin.*

nitty-gritty is listed in Webster's as standard usage.

nix is listed in Webster's as standard usage.

-nn-. See -N-, -NN-.

no, noes. Don't use quotation marks or capitals. Write *he said no.*

No. Abbreviation of *number.* Capital *N, o,* period.

no-. Most compounds are hyphened.

no-account. Hyphened.

nobody followed by *they, their* or *them* has been used since 1548. Leslie Stephen wrote "Nobody ever put so much of themselves into their work."

no-fault, no-good. Hyphened.

nohow, in the sense of *anyhow,* is a dialect word. Don't use.

noisemaker, noisemaking. One word.

noisome means disgusting and has nothing to do with noise.

no-load. Hyphened.

nol-pros, nol-prossed, nol-prossing. Two *s*'s except in *nol-pros.*

no-man's-land. Two hyphens, one apostrophe.

nom de guerre, noms de guerre.

nom de plume, noms de plume.

nominate. Don't use *nominate* when *name* will do.

non-. Compounds are spelled as one word. Don't use a word with *non-* when a familiar synonym will do, e.g. *non-success* instead of *failure* or *non-sick* instead of *healthy.*

nonalcoholic, nonaligned, nonalignment, nonbelligerency, nonbelligerent, noncandidate. One word.

nonchalance, nonchalant end in *-ance, -ant.*

noncombatant, noncommissioned, noncommittal, noncommunicable, noncompliance, nonconformist, nonconformity, noncooperation, noncooperative, noncredit, nondeductible, nondescript. One word.

none with the plural verb has been standard usage since 888.

nonenforceable ends in *-eable.*

nonentity. One word.

nonesuch. Spell it with *e* in the middle.

nonetheless. Don't use *nonetheless* when *but* will do.

nonexistence, nonexistent end in *-ence, -ent.*

nonfattening, nonfiction, nonfictional, nonfulfillment. One word.

non-Jew. Hyphen, capital *J.*

non-native. Hyphened.

nonnegotiable. One word.

no-no. Slang.

no-nonsense. Hyphened.

nonpareil ends in *-eil.*

nonpartisan, nonperson. One word.

nonplus, nonplused, nonplusing. One *s* in all forms.

nonprofit, nonproliferation. One word.

nonpros, nonprossed, nonprossing. One word, two *s*'s in all forms except *nonpros.*

nonrecognition, nonrefundable, nonreligious, nonrenewable, non-resident, nonreturnable, nonscheduled, nonsectarian. One word.

non sequitur. Two words.

nonsked. Listed in Webster's as standard usage.

nonskid, nonsmoker, nonstarter, nonstop. One word.

(nonsuch). Spell it *nonesuch.*

nonsupport, nontenure, nonunion, nonuser, nonviolence, non-white. One word.

no one. Two words, no hyphen. *They, their* and *them* referring to *no one* is common usage, e.g. *No one was hurt, were they?*

no place. Two words. Listed as standard usage in Webster's.

nor. You can use either *or* or *nor* after a negative. This has been standard usage since 1400. Edmund Spenser wrote "She could not hear nor speak nor understand."

normalcy is standard usage.

north. Small *n* if you mean a compass direction, capital *N* if you mean a region.

north-. Most compounds are spelled as one word.

northbound, northeast. One word.

northerly means coming from the north.

north-northeast, north-northwest. One hyphen.

northward, northwards. The adverb may be spelled with *s* or without.

northwest. One word.

nose-. Most compounds are spelled as one word.

nosedive, nosegay, nosepiece. One word.

no-show is listed as standard usage in Webster's.

nostrum, nostrums.

nosy. No *e*.

notable ends in *-able*.

notarization, notarize. Spelled with *z*.

notary public, notaries public.

notation. Don't use *notation* when *note* will do.

not hardly. The double negative is common usage.

noticeable ends in *-eable*.

notification. Don't use *notification* when *notice* will do.

notify. Don't use *notify* when *let know* will do.

not in a position to. Don't write *not in a position to* when *can't* will do.

notorious, notoriety. Not just famous or fame, but for unfavorable reasons.

not scarcely. The double negative is common usage.

not too distant future. Don't write *in the not too distant future* when *soon* will do.

not to exceed. Don't write *not to exceed* when *up to, no more than* or *not over* will do.

not un-. Don't use *not un-* when a direct statement will do, e.g. instead of *the unique and not unambitious object* write *the unique and ambitious object.*

notwithstanding. So spelled. Don't write *notwithstanding* when *in spite of* or *despite* will do.

nought, naught. The spelling *naught* is more common. Don't use *naught* when *nothing* or *zero* will do.

nouveau riche, nouveaux riches.

novelette ends in *-ette*.

Novocaine. Capital *N, e* at the end.

now-. Hyphen compound modifiers with *now*, e.g. *the now-established usage.*

nowadays. No hyphen.

noway, noways. Standard usage. One word.

nowhere near. Standard usage.

nowheres with *s* is dialect. Don't use.

nowise. Standard usage.

nth, as in *to the nth degree.* No vowel.

nu-. If you can't find the word you're looking for, try under *neu-* or *pneu-*.

nuance.

nuclear. No vowel between *c* and *l*.

nucleo-. Compounds are spelled as one word.

nucleus, nuclei.

nuisance is spelled with *ui* and ends in *-ance.*

null and void. Leave out *null and.*

nullify, nullified, nullifying.

numb, numbly, numbness.

numbers. Follow the newspaper style "rule of nine" and spell out numbers from one through nine. Use figures from 10 up.

There are the following exceptions and special rules:

1. When there are two or more numbers within a sentence or short section, be consistent. Either spell out all numbers or use figures throughout. e.g. *There were some eight or ten people present.—The population dropped from 23 to 9.*

2. Use figures for specific measurements, ages, times of day, money, addresses, statistics, percentages, page numbers, years, e.g. *5 ft. 6 in., age 4, 3%, page 2, 8 B.C.*

3. Spell out round numbers, e.g. *about a hundred, half a million people.*

4. Write out the words *million* and *billion,* e.g. *26 million, $5 billion.*

5. Use full inclusive numbers, e.g. *21–29, 110–135.*

6. Don't use commas in four-digit numbers unless they appear together with five-digit numbers, e.g. *4215, 8643* but *the deductions were $12,678, $6,985 and $42,356.*

7. Use figures for dates, e.g. *August 1914.*

8. Use figures for four-digit decades, e.g. *the 1960s.* Two-digit decades are commonly either spelled out or written as figures, e.g. *the sixties, the 60s.* (No apostrophes.)

9. It is still common usage to spell out numbers at the beginning of a sentence inside a paragraph, but the trend is toward using figures except for numbers up to nine. Anyway, try to avoid spelling out higher numbers. Don't use artificial devices like *Exactly* or *A total of,* but rearrange the sentence if possible. Or start a new paragraph. It *is* common usage to use figures (for numbers from 10 up) at the beginning of a paragraph.

numerator ends in *-or.* Above the line.

numerous. Don't use *numerous* when *many* will do.

numskull. Spell it without a *b.*

nuncio, nuncios.

nuptials. Don't use *nuptials* when *marriage* or *wedding* will do.

nursemaid. One word.

nursery school. Two words.

nut in the sense of eccentric person is listed in Webster's as standard usage.

nutcracker. One word.

nutrition, nutritious end in *-ition, -itious.*

nutritive. *I* after *r.*

nuts in the sense of crazy or enthusiastic is listed in Webster's as standard usage.

nuts-and-bolts (adj.). Two hyphens.

nutshell. One word.

nympho, short for *nymphomaniac,* is listed in Webster's as standard usage.

O

O is commonly capitalized and spelled without an *h* before the name in direct address, e.g. *Hear, O Israel.* The exclamation is usually spelled *oh.*

-o. The plural of nouns ending in *-o* ends in *-os* or *-oes.* There's no hard-and-fast rule and most common nouns ending in *-o* are listed in this book with their plurals. A rough guide to follow is this:

1. Very common, long-established nouns have plurals in *-oes,* e.g. *echoes, heroes, mottoes, Negroes, noes, potatoes, tomatoes, vetoes.*

2. All words with a vowel immediately before the *o* have plurals in *-os,* e.g. *duos, curios, embryos, folios, patios, radios, rodeos, studios.*

3. Most other words have plurals ending in *-os,* particularly words derived from the Spanish or Italian and musical terms, e.g. *altos, autos, banjos, bassos, burros, concertos, Eskimos, kimonos, pianos, sombreros, virtuosos.*

Verbs ending in *-o* form *-oed, -oes, -oing,* e.g. *echoed, echoes, echoing.*

oaf, oafs.

oak-leaf (adjective). Hyphened.

oarlock. One word.

oasis, oases.

oatmeal. One word.

obbligato, obbligatos. Two *b*'s.

obdurate. *U* after *d.*

obedience, obedient end in *-ence, -ent.*

obeisance, obeisant end in *-ance, -ant.* Spelled with *ei.*

obelisk ends in *-sk.*

obiter dictum, obiter dicta.

obituary ends in *-uary*.

objective. Don't use *objective* when *object* or *aim* will do.

objector ends in *-or*.

objet d'art, objets d'art. No *c*.

obligated, obliged. *Obligated* means fully bound legally or morally, *obliged* means bound by circumstances, gratitude etc., e.g. *He was obligated to fulfill his contract,* but *We are much obliged to you.*

(obligato). Spell it *obbligato*.

obligatory ends in *-ory*.

obliqueness, obliquity. *Obliquity* is more common in all senses.

obliterate. Don't use *obliterate* when *wipe out* will do.

oblivious in the sense of unaware has been standard usage since 1852, when H. T. Buckle wrote "He was so little given to observation as to be frequently oblivious to what was passing around him." The preposition *to* is used commonly.

obloquy, obloquies.

oboe, oboes, oboist.

obscene, obscenity. Spelled with *sc*.

observance, observation. *Observance* means keeping a custom, *observation* means taking notice.

observer ends in *-er*.

obsess, obsession. First one *s*, then two.

obsolescence, obsolescent end in *-ence, -ent*. Spelled with *sc*.

obsolete.

obstetrician ends in *-ician*.

obstreperous. *E* after *p*.

obtain. Don't use *obtain* when *get* will do.

obtrusive, obtrusively. No *s* after *b*.

ocarina. One *c*.

occasion, occasional are spelled with two *c*'s and one *s*. Think of "*c*offee with *c*ream and *s*ugar."

occasion (verb). Don't use the verb *occasion* when *cause* will do.

Occident, Occidental. Capital *O* when referring to Europe and America, lowercase *o* in the sense of *west, western*.

occupation. Don't use *occupation* when *job* will do.

occur, occurred, occurring. Two *r*'s in all forms except *occur*. Don't use *occur* when *happen* will do.

occurrence ends in *-ence*.

oceanborne, oceanfront, oceangoing. One word.

ocher. Spell it with *er*.

o'clock. Always spelled with the apostrophe.

octavo, octavos.

octet ends in *-et.*

octupus, octopuses.

octoroon. *O* after *t.*

oculist, ophthalmologist, optician, optometrist. An *oculist* is an eye doctor. So is an *ophthalmologist.* An *optician* makes and deals in eyeglasses. An *optometrist* examines eyes and prescribes glasses.

odd-. Compounds are hyphened, e.g. *odd-looking, odd-shaped.*

-odd. Always hyphened. Use only with round figures, e.g. *40-odd.*

odd-job man. Hyphened.

odd lot. Two words.

odor ends in *-or.* Don't use *odor* when *smell* will do.

odyssey, odysseys. One *d,* ends in *-ey.*

oe. Almost all words formerly spelled with *oe* are now spelled with *e,* such as *ameba, fetus.*

Oedipus. Spelled with *Oe.*

o'er. Poetic contraction of *over.*

-oes, -os. See -o.

(oesophagus). Spell it *esophagus.*

of. Don't write *of* when you mean *have* or *'ve.* Instead of *I should of known* write *I should have known* or *I should've known.*

Forms like *he's the worst liar of anyone I know, a child of ten years old, that long nose of his* have been idioms since the 14th century.

of course. Beware of the snobbish use of *of course,* as in "The most famous [chess] game of Fischer's youth, perhaps of his career so far, is of course that against Donald Byrne in the Lessing J. Rosenwald Tournament of 1956."

-off. Spell compounds as one word, e.g. *layoff, liftoff, takeoff.*

off-. Most compounds are spelled as one word.

offbeat. One word.

off-chance, off-color. Hyphened.

offhand, offhandedly. One word.

off-hour. Hyphened.

office boy. Two words.

officeholder, officeseeker, officeworker. One word.

official, officious. *Official* means of the office, *officious* means meddlesome.

off of. Don't use *off of* when *off* will do.

offprint, offscreen. One word.

off-season. Hyphened.

offshoot, offshore, offside. One word.

offspring. The plural is also *offspring*.

offstage. One word.

off-white. Hyphened.

off year. Two words.

of late. Don't use *of late* when *lately* or *recently* will do.

(oft). The modern word is *often*.

often-. Hyphened in compound modifiers, e.g. *often-heard*.

oftentimes, ofttimes. Don't use *oftentimes* or *ofttimes* when *often* will do.

ogre, ogreish, ogress. All forms spelled with *re*.

oh, O. *Oh* is the general exclamation, spelled with a small *o* except at the beginning of a sentence. *O* is used in invocations as in *O Lord*.

oh well. No comma between *oh* and *well*.

oil-. Most compounds are spelled as one word.

oil burner. Two words.

oilcan, oilcloth, oilfield, oilman. One word.

oil painting. Two words.

oilpaper, oilseed. One word.

oil shale. Two words.

oilskin. One word.

oil slick. Two words.

oilspill, oilstone, oilstove. One word.

oil well. Two words.

oily, oilier, oiliest.

OK, OKs, he OK's, OK'd, OK'ing. Spell them so. No periods, no apostrophe before plural *s*. Listed in Webster's as standard usage.

okay, okays, okayed, okaying. Variants of *OK, OKs, OK's OK'd, OK'ing*. Listed in Webster's as standard usage.

-old. Always hyphened in such forms as *14-year-old*.

old-. Compounds are spelled as one word or hyphened.

older, oldest, elder, eldest. *Older, oldest* are now more common in all contexts.

old-fashioned. Hyphened.

old fogy. No *e*.

old-fogyish. Hyphened.

old-line, old-maidish, old-school (adjective). Hyphened.

oldster is offensive. Don't use.

oldtime. One word.

old-timer, old-world. Hyphened.

oleo-. Compounds are spelled as one word, e.g. *oleomargarine.*

oligarchy ends in *-archy.*

-ology. Don't use words ending in *-ology* when simpler words will do, e.g. *method* instead of *methodology, symptoms* instead of *symptomatology.*

Olympian, Olympic. *Olympian* refers to Greek gods, *Olympic* to games.

ombudsman, ombudsmen.

omelet. Spell it with *et.*

ominous ends in *-ous.*

omission. One *m.*

omit, omitted, omitting. Two *t*'s in all forms except *omit.*

omnibus, omnibuses.

omnipotence, omnipotent end in *-ence, -ent.*

omniscience, omniscient end in *-ence, -ent.* Spelled with *sci.*

omnivorous. *O* after *v.*

on, upon. Don't use *upon* when *on* will do.

-on. Compounds are hyphened, e.g. *hanger-on, run-on.*

on-. Compounds are spelled as one word, e.g. *ongoing.*

on account of. Don't say *on account of* when *because, because of* or *since* will do.

on behalf, in behalf. Both forms are standard usage.

once-. Compound modifiers are hyphened, e.g. *once-famous.*

once-over. Hyphened. Listed in Webster's as standard usage.

one. Don't use *one* when *I* or *you* will do. Don't use *a (an)* . . . *one* unnecessarily. E.g. instead of *The task won't be an easy one* write *The task won't be easy.*

Use of the indefinite pronoun *one* followed by *his* or *he* is standard US usage, e.g. *One must watch his step.* (Better: *You must watch your step.*)

-one. Write *anyone, everyone, someone,* but *no one.*

one-. Most compounds are hyphened.

one another, each other. Both forms are used for two or more than two.

one in three, four etc. Commonly used with the plural verb.

one of the, one of those. Commonly used with the singular verb, e.g. *one of those who understands.*

one-man. Hyphened.

one out of three, four etc. Commonly used with the plural verb.

one-piece. Hyphened.

onerous.

ones. No apostrophe for the plural of the number, whether spelled out or not—*ones, 1s.*

oneself. Spell it so, not *one's self.*

one-shot. Hyphened. Listed as standard usage in Webster's.

one-sided, one-sidedness. Hyphened.

onetime. One word.

one-to-one. Two hyphens.

one-two, one-way. Hyphened.

ongoing. One word.

onionskin. One word.

onlooker, onlooking. One word.

only is usually put before the word it modifies, but exceptions are common. Hemingway wrote "They only opened one bag and took the passports in and looked at them."

The use of *only* as a conjunction has been standard usage since 1382. Shakespeare wrote (Merry Wives of Windsor, II, ii, 242), "Spend all I have! Only give me so much of your time in exchange of it as to lay an amiable siege to the honesty of this Ford's wife."

onomatopoeia ends in *-oeia* (4 vowels).

on or about. Don't use the legal phrase *on or about* when *on* will do.

onshore, onsite, onslaught, onstage. One word.

on the basis of. Don't use *on the basis of* when *by, for, on* etc. will do.

on the grounds of. Don't use *on the grounds of* when *because of* will do.

on the part of. Don't use *on the part of* when *by* will do.

onto, on to. One word in such phrases as *got onto the horse, put me onto your methods.* Two words in such phrases as *he went on to tell me all about it.*

onward, onwards. Use *onward* as an adjective, e.g. *the onward movement,* either form as an adverb, e.g. *he went onward* or *onwards.*

onyx is spelled with *y.*

oodles is listed as standard usage in Webster's.

oozy. No *e.*

opalescense, opalescent end in *-ence, -ent.* Spelled with *sc.*

opaqueness. *Opacity* is more common.

op. cit. Latin abbreviation meaning *in the work cited.* Two periods, no underlining or italics. Many modern writers don't use *op. cit.* but simply repeat the author's last name, e.g. *Miller, p. 87.*

open-. Compounds are spelled as one word, two words or hyphened.

open-air. Hyphened.

open door. Two words.

open-end, open-eyed. Hyphened.

openhanded, openhearted. One word.

open house. Two words.

open-minded. Hyphened.

openmouthed. One word.

openness. Two *n*'s.

open shop. Two words.

openwork. One word.

opéra bouffe, opéra comique. Spell with the accent.

operagoer, operagoing. One word.

ophthalmologist. Spelled with *phth.* An eye doctor. See also OPTICIAN.

opine. Don't use *opine* when *think, suppose, say* will do.

(opinionative). *Opinionated* is the common form.

opinionmaker. One word.

opponent, opportune, opportunism, opportunistic, opportunity. Double *p.*

oppressible, oppression, oppressive, oppressor. Double *p,* double *s.*

opprobrious. Double *p.*

opprobrium. Don't use *opprobrium* when *reproach* or *blame* will do.

opt for. Don't use *opt for* when *pick* or *choose* will do.

optician, optometrist, oculist, ophthalmologist. An *optician* is a maker of and dealer in eyeglasses. An *optometrist* examines eyes and prescribes glasses. An *oculist* or *opthalmologist* is an eye doctor.

optimal. Don't use *optimal* when *best* will do.

optimism, optimistic. Don't use *optimism, optimistic* when *hope, hopeful* will do.

optimum. Don't use *optimum* when *best* will do.

optometrist. See OPTICIAN.

opulence, opulent end in *-ence, -ent.*

opus, opera.

or, nor. You can use either *or* or *nor* after a negative. This has been standard usage since 1400. Edmund Spenser wrote "She could not hear nor speak nor understand."

You can use *Or* at the beginning of a sentence. Don't put a comma after it.

-or, -our. The ending is *-or* in the US, *-our* in Britain and Canada. But *glamour* is spelled with *-our* in the US.

oral, aural. *Oral* means by mouth, *aural* means by ear.

oral, verbal. It is standard usage to use the two words interchangeably in the sense of spoken. *Verbal* is more common, e.g. *a verbal agreement.*

orally. Two *l*'s.

orangeblossom, orangepeel. One word.

orangutan. The most common spelling. One word.

orate refers to pompous speechmaking. Be sure that's what you mean.

orator ends in *-or.*

oratorio, oratorios.

orb. Don't use *orb* when *eye* will do.

orbit, orbited, orbiting. One *t* in all forms.

orchestra, orchestrate, orchestration. Spelled with *ch.*

order. Don't say *in order to* when *to* will do. Don't say *on the order of* when *about* will do.

ordinance, ordnance, ordonnance. An *ordinance* is a local or municipal regulation, *ordnance* is military hardware, *ordonnance* means the arrangement of a literary, architectural or artistic composition.

organdy. Spell it with *y.*

organ grinder. Two words.

organization, organize, organizer. Spelled with *z.*

orientate. Don't use *orientate* instead of the simple word *orient.* The two words mean the same.

ornamentally ends in *-ally.*

orphan, orphaned, orphaning. One *n* in all forms.

ortho-. Spell compounds as one word.

orthopedia, orthopedic. Spelled with *e.*

-os, -oes. See -O.

oscillate, osculate. *Oscillate* means swing, *osculate* means kiss. Don't use *osculate* when *kiss* will do.

ossify. *I* after double *s.*

ostensible ends in *-ible.*

ostentatious ends in *-atious.*

ostracize ends in *-ize.*

other than. Don't use *other than* when *except* will do.

otherworldliness, otherworldly. One word.

otiose. Don't use *otiose* when *idle, vain, futile* will do.

oto-. Spell compounds as one word, e.g. *otolaryngologist.*

-our, -or. Words spelled with *-our* in Britain are spelled with *-or* in the US. Exception: *glamour.*

ours. Never spelled with an apostrophe.

ourself. Don't use *ourself* instead of *ourselves* when you refer to the editorial *we.* Better still, don't use the editorial *we.* Say *I.*

oust. Don't use *oust* when *drive out* or *expel* will do.

-out. Compounds are spelled as one word, e.g. *cookout, dropout.*

out-. Compounds are spelled as one word, except when there are two hyphens, e.g. *out-of-date,* or a proper noun, e.g. *out-Machiavelli.*

out-and-out. Hyphens.

outbid, outboard, outbound, outbreak, outclimb, outcome, outdated, outdistance, outdo, outdoor, outdoors, outdoorsman, outdraw, outface, outfield. One word.

outfit, outfitted, outfitter, outfitting. Double *t* in all forms except *outfit.*

outgeneral, outgeneraled, outgeneraling. One *l* in all forms.

outgroup, outlaid, outlay. One word.

out loud. Two words. Listed in Webster's as standard usage.

out-of-date, out-of-doors, out-of-pocket, out-of-print, out-of-state, out-of-the-way. Hyphened.

outpatient. One word.

outrageous ends in *-eous.*

outré. Spell with the accent.

outrigger, outscore, outshine. One word.

outside of. Listed in Webster's as standard variant of the preposition *outside.*

outspoken. One word.

outspokenness. Two *n*'s.

outtake, outtalk, outthink, outvote. One word.

outward, outwards. Use *outward* as the adjective, e.g. *outward appearances,* and *outward* or *outwards* as an adverb, e.g. *outward bound* or *the city stretches outwards.*

outwit, outwitted, outwitting. Two *t*'s in all forms except *outwit.*

ouzo. The Greek liqueur is spelled with *ou* and *z.*

ovenbaked. One word.

over in the sense of *more than* has been standard usage since 1330.

-over. Compounds are spelled as one word, e.g. *takeover, pullover.*

over-. Compounds are spelled as one word.

overabundant, overage. One word.

overall. One word in all senses.

overanxious, overconfident, overemphasis, overemphasize, over-enthusiastic, overestimate, overexcitable, overexpand, overextend, overindulgence, overindulgent. One word.

overly. Don't use *overly* when *over-* will do, e.g. don't use *overly zealous* instead of *overzealous.*

overproduction, overprompt, overrated, overreact, overreaction, override, overrun. One word.

overseas. Spell it with *s* at the end.

overseer, oversensitive, oversexed, oversimplification, overspecialization. One word.

over-the-counter. Hyphens.

overwrought. One word. Spelled with *rwr.*

ovum, ova.

owing to. Don't use *owing to* instead of the preposition *due to. Due to* is listed in Webster's as standard usage.

owing to the fact that. Don't use this phrase when *because* will do.

owllike. One word.

own. Don't use *own* when *confess* or *admit* will do.

-owner. Spell compounds as one word, e.g. *homeowner.*

owner-operator. Hyphen.

ox, oxen.

oxblood, oxbow. One word.

oxford (shoe). Lower case.

oxidize ends in *-ize.*

oxtail. One word.

ox team. Two words.

oyez, oyesses. So listed in Webster's.

oyster bed, oyster cracker. Two words.

oysterman. One word.

P

-p, -pp-. A *p* at the end of a one-syllable word is doubled before the suffixes *-able, -ed, -er, -est, -ie, -ing, -ish, -y* etc. if there's only one vowel and no *r* before the *p*. Examples, *stop, unstoppable; rip, ripped; slip, slipper; flip, flippest; nap, nappie; drop, dropping; up, uppish; scrap, scrappy*. The same rule applies to two-syllable words ending in *p* and accented on the second syllable e.g. *equip, equipping; reship, reshipped*. In words of more than one syllable ending in *p*, the *p* is not doubled before suffixes if the last syllable isn't accented, e.g. *gallop, galloping; develop, developed; wallop, walloped*. But the *p* is doubled in *handicapped* and *kidnapping* and such two-part words as *horsewhipping, sideslipped* and *backslapper*.

pablum, pabulum. Both forms are common.

pacemaker, pacemaking, pacesetter. One word.

pachyderm. Don't use *pachyderm* when *elephant* will do.

pachysandra is spelled with *chy*.

packhorse, packinghouse, packthread. One word.

pack rat. Two words.

packup (noun). One word.

pact. Don't use *pact* when *agreement, contract, treaty* will do.

paean, peon. *Paean* with *aea* means a song of praise, *peon* means a laborer or foot soldier.

pageant, pageantry. Spelled with *ea*.

page boy, pageboy. Two words meaning a boy, one word meaning a hairstyle.

page proof. Two words.

paid, payed. The past tense of *pay* is spelled *paid* except in the sense of *payed out a rope*.

pail, pale. *Pail* means a container, *pale* means colorless.

pailful, pailfuls.

pain, pane. *Pain* means suffering, *pane* means a sheet of glass.

painkiller, painkilling, painstaking. One word.

paintbrush. One word.

pair, pare, pear. A *pair* means two, to *pare* means to cut, a *pear* is a fruit.

paisley ends in *-ey.*

pajamas, pyjamas. The US spelling starts with *pa.*

palatable ends in *-able.*

palate, palette, pallet. The *palate* is a part of the mouth, a *palette* is a paintboard, a *pallet* is a bed.

paleo-. Spell it with *eo.* Spell compounds as one word.

palette, pallet. One *l,* double *t, e* for the paintboard; two *l*'s, one *t,* no *e* at the end for the bed.

pallbearer. One word.

palliative. Two *l*'s.

pall-mall. Hyphened.

palm leaf. Two words.

palpable ends in *-able.* Don't use *palpable* when *plain* or *obvious* will do.

palsy. No *e.*

pamphlet.

pan-. Compounds are spelled as one word, except for compounds with proper nouns, e.g. *pan-American.*

panacea ends in *-ea.* Means a cure for all ills.

panache.

Panama. Capital *P* for the hat.

pancreas ends in *-eas.*

pandemonium, pandemoniums.

pander ends in *-er.*

pane, pain. A *pane* is a sheet of glass, *pain* means suffering.

panegyric. Don't use *panegyric* when *praise* will do.

panel, paneled, paneling. One *l* in all forms.

panic, panicked, panicking, panicky. *Ck* in all forms except *panic.*

panic-stricken. Hyphened.

pannier. Spell it with two *n*'s.

(pantie). The common spelling is *panty.*

pants. Standard usage for trousers.

pantsuit. One word.

panty hose. Two words.

pantywaist. One word.

-paper. Some compounds are spelled as one word, like *curlpaper, flypaper, newspaper, sandpaper, wallpaper.* Some are spelled as two words, like *carbon paper, wax paper.*

paper-. Compounds are spelled as one word or two or hyphened.

paperback, paperbound, paperboy. One word.

paper chase. Two words.

paper-covered. Hyphened.

paper cutter. Two words.

paperhanger, paperhanging, papermaking, papermill. One word.

paper-thin. Hyphened.

paperweight, paperwork. One word.

papier-mâché. Two accents.

papist. Small *p.*

para-. Compounds are spelled as one word.

parachute is spelled with *ch.*

paradigm. Don't use *paradigm* when *model* will do.

paraffin. One *r,* two *f*'s.

(paragoric). Misspelling of *paregoric.*

paragraphs. Keep paragraphs short. One-sentence paragraphs are common in modern newspaper style.

Itemized paragraphs are common for listing. The simplest style is to set them off by dashes.

parakeet.

parallel, paralleled, paralleling, parallelism. First two *l*'s, then one. Remember *"All el* tracks are parallel."

parallelepiped. So spelled.

parallelogram. So spelled.

paralysis, paralyses.

paralyze ends in *-yze.*

paramedic. One word.

parameter, perimeter. *Parameter* means characteristic, *perimeter* means circumference.

paramount. Don't use *paramount* when *supreme* or *top* will do.

paranoia ends in *-oia.*

parapet ends in *-et.*

paraphernalia. So spelled. Takes a plural verb, but the singular is also standard usage.

paraplegia, paraplegic.

paraprofessional. One word.

parcel, parceled, parceling. One *l* in all forms.

parcel post. Two words.

pare, pair, pear. To *pare* means to cut, a *pair* means two, a *pear* is a fruit.

paregoric. *E* after the first *r*.

parenthesis, parentheses.

parentheses. Use parentheses to enclose explanations, comments or asides in a sentence or to set off part of a sentence that would be confusing if you just used commas.

When a clause in parentheses comes at the end of a sentence, put the period outside the parenthesis mark, e.g. *He decided to stay for dinner (spaghetti with meatballs).* But if a whole sentence is put between parentheses, the period comes *before* the second parenthesis mark, e.g. *After the first act he walked out. (He'd paid $12 for his ticket.)*

A comma, when needed, should always go outside a parenthesis mark, e.g. *Considering his age (86), he was in surprisingly good shape.*

See also BRACKETS.

parentheses to explain pronouns look awkward. Usually this device is unnecessary because in the context the reference is clear without it. *Jim told Frank he had nothing to do with it* is clear —you don't need to write *he (Jim).* If there *is* a possibility of misreading, repeat the name without *he.*

parenthetic, parenthetical. *Parenthetic* is more common.

parenthetically ends in *-ally.*

par excellence. No italics or underlining.

pariah ends in *-ah.*

parimutuel. The GPO Style Manual spells it without a hyphen.

parlay, parley. To *parlay* means to transform into something of much greater value, a *parley* is a conference.

parliament, parliamentary. Spelled with *ia.* Remember "*I am* in parliament."

parlor ends in *-or.*

parlor game. Two words.

parlormaid. One word.

parlous. Don't use *parlous* when *risky* or *dangerous* will do.

parol, parole. *Parol* (without *e*) means by word of mouth, *parole* means conditional release.

parole, paroled, paroling. One *l* in all forms.

paroxysm ends in *-ysm.*

parquet, parqueted, parqueting. One *t* in all forms.

(parrafin). Misspelling of *paraffin.*

(**parrakeet**). Spell it *parakeet.*

parricide is spelled with double *r.*

Parsi, Parsee. *Parsi* is more common.

part. Don't use *on the part of* when *by* will do.

partake. Don't use *partake* when *share* or *use* will do.

parti-. Most compounds are hyphened.

partially, partly. Don't use *partially* when *partly* will do.

participant ends in *-ant.*

participate. Don't use *participate* when *share* or *take part* will do.

participles. Don't use a compound participle to start a sentence, e.g. *Mississippi-born and Illinois-raised, he went to college in Kentucky.* See also -ING.

parti-colored. Hyphened.

particular. Don't use *particular* when it could be just as well left out, e.g. instead of *the particular person I had in mind* write *the person I had in mind.*

particularize ends in *-ize.*

particularly in the sense of *very* is standard usage.

partisan. Spell it with *s.*

partition ends in *-ition.*

part owner. Two words.

parttime. One word.

partway. One word.

party. Don't use *party* when *person* will do.

party line. Two words.

pass, passed, passed.

pass-. Compounds are spelled as one word.

passable, passible. *Passable* means good enough, *passible* means able to feel.

passageway. One word.

pass away has been used as a euphemism for *die* since 1375.

passbook. One word.

passé. Spell with accent.

passenger mile, passenger pigeon. Two words.

passerby, passersby. One word.

passible, passable. *Passible* means able to feel, *passable* means good enough or able to be passed.

passim, used in footnotes, means mentioned repeatedly in a book. Don't italicize or underline.

passive voice. It's a basic rule of good style that the active voice is better than the passive voice. Example: the verb *love* in *John* *loves Mary* is in the active voice, in *Mary is loved by John* it's in the passive voice. Don't use the passive voice unless it's essential, as in *he was murdered.*

Avoid double passives like *illumination is required to be extinguished.*

passkey. One word.

pass out in the sense of faint is listed in Webster's as standard usage.

passport, password. One word.

(passtime). Misspelling of *pastime.*

(past). The verb forms are spelled *passed.*

pastel ends in *-el.*

pasteup (noun) is spelled as one word in the GPO Style Manual.

pasteurize is spelled with *eu* and *z.*

pastiche.

pastille ends in *-ille.*

pastime. Spelled with one *s.*

past master. Two words.

pastrami ends in *-ami.*

patchouli. Spell it with *i.*

patch test. Two words.

patchwork. One word.

pâté (food). Spell with two accents.

patent. Don't use *patent* when *plain* or *obvious* will do.

paterfamilias, paterfamiliases. One word.

pathfinder. One word.

patio, patios.

patois, patois.

patriarch ends in *-ch.*

patrician ends in *-ician.*

patriot, patriotism. *O* after *i.*

patrol, patrolled, patrolling. Two *l*'s in all forms except *patrol.*

patrolman. One word.

patrol wagon. Two words.

patronize ends in *-ize.*

patsy, patsies. Standard usage in the sense of dupe or victim.

pattycake. One word.

patty shell. Two words.

paucity. Don't use *paucity* when *little* or *few* will do.

pavilion. One *l.*

pawnbroker, pawnshop. One word.

pawn ticket. Two words.

pay, paid, paid. But in the sense of *let out rope,* it's spelled *pay, payed, payed.*

pay-as-you-go. Three hyphens.

payback (noun), **paycheck, payday, paydirt.** One word.

(payed). Misspelling of *paid* in the sense of *gave money.*

payer. The common spelling ends in *-er.*

payload, paymaster, payoff (noun). One word.

payola. Listed in Webster's as standard usage.

(payor). Spell it *payer.*

payout (noun), **payroll.** One word.

peace, piece. *Peace* means no war, *piece* means portion or unit.

peaceable ends in *-eable.*

peacekeeping, peacemaker, peacemaking, peacetime. One word.

peacock. One word.

pea green. Two words.

peahen. One word.

pea jacket. Two words.

peak load. Two words.

peal, peel. It's the *peal* of bells, but *peeling* an onion.

(pean). Spell it *paean.*

pear, pair, pare. A *pear* is a fruit, a *pair* means two, to *pare* means to cut.

pearlfisher, pearlfishing. One word.

pear-shaped. Hyphened.

peasant, peasantry. Spelled with *ea.*

peashooter. One word.

pea soup. Two words.

(peavish). Misspelling of *peevish.*

peccadillo, peccadilloes. Two *c*'s, two *l*'s. Plural ends in *-oes.*

peculiar, peculiarity, peculiarly. Watch the *iar.*

pecuniary. Don't use *pecuniary* when *money* will do.

pedagogue. The common spelling.

pedal, peddle. To *pedal* means to use a foot pedal, to *peddle* means to sell.

pedal, pedaled, pedaling. One *l* in all forms.

peddler. The common spelling.

pedestal ends in *-al.*

pediatrician ends in *-ician.*

pediatrics is used with the singular verb.

(pedlar). Spell it *peddler.*

peel, peal. You *peel* an onion, but it's the *peal* of bells.

peen (of a hammer). Spelled with double *e.*

peephole. One word.

peep show. Two words.

peer, pier. A *peer* means an equal, a *pier* means a landing place.

peer group. Don't use *peer group* when *friends* will do.

peeve (verb and noun) is standard usage.

peevish is spelled with double *e.*

peewee in the sense of small person is listed as standard usage in Webster's.

peignoir.

pejorative. Don't use *pejorative* when *disparaging* will do.

Pekingese. Commonly spelled with capital *P* and *g,* in both senses of inhabitant of Peking and small dog.

pelf is almost obsolete.

pellagra. Two *l*'s.

pell-mell. Hyphened.

pellucid. Don't use *pellucid* when *clear* will do.

pen (verb). Don't use *pen* when *write* will do.

pen-. Almost all compounds are spelled as one word.

penalty. *A* after *n.*

penchant ends in *-ant.*

pencil, penciled, penciling. One *l* in all forms.

pendant, pendent. A *pendant* is a hanging ornament, *pendent* means suspended. Remember "My *aunt* wore a *pendant.*"

pending. Don't use *pending* when *during* or *until* will do.

pendulum, pendulums.

penetrable ends in *-able.*

penicillin. Two *l*'s. Remember there's i*ll* in it.

penitence, penitent end in *-ence, -ent.*

penknife, penman, penmanship. One word.

pen name. Two words.

pennant. Double *n,* ends in *-ant.*

penniless is spelled with *i* in the middle.

penny ante, penny arcade, penny dreadful. Two words.

penny-pinching. Hyphened.

pennyweight. One word.

penny-wise. Hyphened.

pennyworth. One word.

pen pal. Two words.

penthouse. One word.

pent-up. Hyphened.

penultimate. Don't use *penultimate* when *next to the last* will do.

penumbra. Don't use *penumbra* when *fringe* will do.

penurious. Don't use *penurious* when *stingy* will do.

penury. Don't use *penury* when *poverty* will do.

penwiper. One word.

peon, paean. *Peon* mean a laborer or foot soldier, *paean* means a song of praise.

people, persons. The idea that the word *persons* rather than *people* has to be used with specific numbers is a superstition. *Six people* is more common than *six persons.*

pep in the sense of energy is listed as standard usage in Webster's.

pepperbox, peppermill. One word.

peppy is listed in Webster's as standard usage.

pep talk. Two words.

per. Don't use *per* when *a* will do.

peradventure is archaic. Don't use.

per annum. Don't use *per annum* when *a year* will do.

per capita. Commonly used. Two words.

(percaution). Misspelling of *precaution.*

perceive. *E* before *i.*

percent. One word, no period. Don't hesitate to use the symbol % with figures. *Percent* in the sense of *percentage* is standard usage.

percentage doesn't mean a small part. Don't say *a large percentage* when you mean *many* or *a small percentage* when you mean *few.*

perceptible ends in *-ible.*

perception starts with *per-.*

perchance. Don't use *perchance* when *perhaps* or *maybe* will do.

percipience, percipient end in *-ence, -ent.*

(perclude). Misspelling of *preclude.*

percolator ends in *-or.*

per contra. Don't use *per contra* when *on the other hand* or *on the contrary* will do.

per diem. Don't use *per diem* when *a day* will do.

(perdominant). Misspelling of *predominant.*

père. Spelled with the accent. *Senior* will usually do.

peregrinate, peregrination. Don't use these words when *travel* will do.

peremptory, preemptory. *Peremptory* means decisive, *preemptory* refers to privilege.

perennial means enduring, not necessarily year after year.

perfect doesn't necessarily mean absolutely perfect. "In order to form a more perfect union" (in the Declaration of Independence) is not wrong.

perfectible ends in *-ible.*

perfect infinitive. See HAVE.

perfect tense. See HAVE.

(perfessor). Misspelling of *professor.*

perhaps starts with *per-.*

peri-. Compounds are spelled as one word, e.g. *perihelion.*

peril. Don't use *peril* when *risk* or *danger* will do.

peril, periled, periling. One *l* in all forms.

perilous. Don't use *perilous* when *hazardous* or *dangerous* will do.

perimeter, parameter. *Perimeter* means circumference, *parameter* means characteristic.

period. Use periods after sentences or sentence fragments that are neither questions nor exclamations, e.g. *Rare taste. Either you have it. Or you don't. A & B has it. And always will.* Even questions and exclamations can often be followed by periods, e.g. *What's the use. What a bore.*

In typing, put two spaces between a period and the beginning of the next sentence.

Abbreviations are often followed by a period, e.g. *Blvd., Dr.* When an abbreviation period ends a sentence, don't put another period after it, e.g. *He lived in Scarsdale, N.Y.*

An ellipsis (words left out) is marked by three periods within a sentence and four periods at the end of a sentence, e.g. *No corporation engaged in commerce . . . shall acquire . . . the assets of another corporation also in commerce. . . .*

See also PARENTHESES, QUOTATION MARKS.

period of is usually unnecessary. Instead of *a period of six years* write *six years.*

period of time. Don't use *period of time* when *period* or *time* will do.

perishable ends in *-able.*

perjurer ends in *-er.*

(perliminary). Misspelling of *preliminary.*

permanence, permanent end in *-ence, -ent.*

permissible ends in *-ible.*

permit, permitted, permitting. Two *t*'s in all forms except *permit.*

permitholder. One word.

permit of. Strike out *of.*

permittee. Two *t*'s, two *e*'s.

pernicious ends in *-icious.*

pernickety, persnickety. Both spellings are common.

(perogative). Misspelling of *prerogative.*

perpetrate, perpetuate. *Perpetrate* means do or commit, *perpetuate* means make lasting or enduring.

perpetrator ends in *-or.* Don't use *perpetrator* when *criminal* etc. will do.

perpetuate, perpetrate. *Perpetuate* means make lasting, *perpetrate* means commit or do.

perquisite, prerequisite. A *perquisite* is a fringe benefit, a *prerequisite* is something necessary for the purpose.

per se. Don't use *per se* when *as such* will do.

persecute, prosecute. To *persecute* means to harass, to *prosecute* means to take legal action.

perseverance ends in *-ance.*

persevere. No *r* before *v.*

persistence, persistency. Used interchangeably.

persistence, persistent end in *-ence, -ent.*

persnickety, pernickety. Both forms are used.

persona, personae.

personable ends in *-able.*

personage means a person of importance. The terms *VIP* and *personality* are now more common.

personal is often unnecessary, as in *a personal friend.*

personality is commonly used in such expressions as *a TV personality.*

personalize ends in *-ize.*

personally is often unnecessary, as in *I (personally) think so.*

personalty, meaning personal property, has no *i* after *l.*

persona non grata. Listed in Webster's (1973) as an adjective with no plural.

personnel as a plural, meaning *persons,* is listed in Webster's as standard usage.

persons, people. The idea that the word *persons* rather than *people* has to be used with specific numbers is a superstition. *Six people* is more common than *six persons.*

perspective, prospective. *Perspective* means view, *prospective* means expected.

perspicacious, perspicuous. *Perspicacious* means shrewd, *perspicuous* means clear.

perspicacity, perspicuity. *Perspicacity* means shrewdness, *perspicuity* means clarity.

perspiration, perspire start with *per-*.

persuadable is more common than *persuasible*.

persuasion in the sense of religious belief is old-fashioned.

(persuit). Misspelling of *pursuit*.

pertain. Don't use *pertain* when *belong* or *refer to* will do.

(pertend). Misspelling of *pretend*.

pertinacious ends in *-acious.*

pertinence, pertinent end in *-ence, -ent.*

perturbation. Don't use *perturbation* when *wrong* will do.

perusal, peruse. Don't use *perusal* or *peruse* when *reading* or *read* will do.

(pervail, pervaricate). Misspellings of *prevail, prevaricate.*

(pervent, pervention). Misspellings of *prevent, prevention.*

perverse starts with *per-*.

peseta, pesetas. Spanish currency.

peso, pesos. Mexican currency.

pessimism, pessimistic. *I* after double *s.*

pesthole, pesthouse. One word.

pestilence, pestilent end in *-ence, -ent.*

pestkiller. One word.

pestle. Silent *t.*

petaled. One *l.*

petit four, petits fours.

(petit jury, petit larceny). Spell them *petty jury, petty larceny.*

petit point. Two words.

petrel, petrol. A *petrel* is a bird, *petrol* is gasoline.

petri dish. Small *p.*

petroleum ends in *-eum.*

pettifog, pettifogged, pettifogging, pettifogger, pettifoggery, petty jury, petty larceny. The common forms.

petulance, petulant end in *-ance, -ant.*

pewholder. One word.

peyote.

phaeton is spelled with *ae.*

phalanx, phalanxes.

phallus, phalli.

(phantasy). Spell it *fantasy.*

Pharaoh. Capital *P,* ends in *-aoh.*

pharisaic, pharisaical (adjective).

Pharisee (noun).

pharmaceutical is spelled with *eu.*

pharmacist, pharmacy spelled with *c.*

pharmacopoeia. The common spelling ends in *-oeia.*

pharynx, pharynges.

phase, faze. *Phase* means aspect, *faze* means disturb.

phase-in. Hyphened.

phaseout (noun). One word.

pheasant is spelled with *ea.*

(phenix). The common spelling is *phoenix.*

phenomenal. *E* after *m.*

phenomenon. The common plural is *phenomena.* Don't use *phenomenon* when *thing* or *fact* will do.

(phial). The form *vial* is more common.

phil-. Spell compounds as one word.

philatelist, philately. Don't use *philatelist, philately* when *stamp collector, stamp collecting* will do.

-phile. The suffix *-phile* means lover. A *bibliophile* is a booklover.

philharmonic. Don't forget the second *h.*

philippic. One *l,* two *p*'s.

Philippines. One *l,* double *p.* Think of a *l*ush *P*acific *p*aradise. The people born there are *Filipinos* with one *p.*

philistine.

philodendron, philodendrons.

philosophize ends in *-ize.*

philosophy. Don't use *philosophy* when *idea* or *view* will do.

philter, filter. Spell both words with *-er.* A *philter* is a magic love potion, a *filter* is a porous substance to remove impurities.

phlebitis starts with *ph.*

phlegm. Silent *g.*

phlox starts with *ph.* The common plural is *phlox* too.

-phobe. The suffix *-phobe* means hater. An *Anglophobe* hates the English.

phobia, mania. A *phobia* is a crazy *fear of* something, a *mania* is a craze *for* something.

Phoebe, Phebe. *Phoebe* is the more common spelling.

Phoenicia, Phoenician. Commonly spelled with *oe.*

phoenix. Commonly spelled with *oe.*

phone (verb and noun) in the sense of *telephone* is listed in Webster's as standard usage. No apostrophe. Dates back to 1884.

phony. Spell it without *e.* Listed in Webster's as standard usage. Hendrik Willem Van Loon wrote "He who writes and composes without the true inner fire will always be a phony."

phosphorescence, phosphorescent end in *-ence, -ent.* Watch the *sc.*

phosphorous, phosphorus. *Phosphorous* (with *-ous*) is the adjective, meaning containing phosphorus, *phosphorus* (with *-us*) is the noun, meaning the chemical element.

photo, photos. Listed in Webster's as standard usage. Dates back to 1870.

photo-. Compounds are spelled as one word.

photocopy, photoengraving. One word.

photo finish. Two words.

photojournalism, photomontage. One word.

photo-offset. Hyphened.

photoplay. One word.

photostat. Small *p.* Don't use *photostat* when *copy* will do.

phrasemaker, phrasemaking. One word.

phraseology. Spelled with *eo.*

(phrenetic). The common spelling is *frenetic.*

phthisic, phthisis. Spelling bee words meaning *tuberculous, tuberculosis* or *TB.*

phylum, phyla. Spelled with *y.*

physic, physicked, physicking.

physic, physique. *Physic* means remedy, *physique* means body.

physically ends in *-ally.*

physician. So spelled. Don't use *physician* when *doctor* will do.

physiognomy. Don't use *physiognomy* when *features* will do.

physique, physic. *Physique* means body, *physic* means remedy.

pi. The common US spelling for a mess of type has no *e.*

pianissimo, pianissimos. Musicians often prefer the plural *pianissimi.*

piano, pianos.

piano player. Two words.

piaster. Spell it with *-er.* Currency of Egypt, Lebanon, Sudan and Syria. (1/100 of a pound.)

piazza. Two *z*'s.

picaresque. A picaresque novel deals with the adventures of a rogue or vagabond.

picayune, in the sense of trivial, is standard usage.

piccalilli. Two *c*'s, one *l,* then two *l*'s.

piccolo, piccolos.

pick, in the sense of choice, is standard usage.

pick-. Most compounds are spelled as one word.

(pickaback). Spell it *piggyback.*

pickaninny. First one *n,* then two. Offensive.

pickax. Spell it without *e.* One word.

picket, picketed, picketing. One *t* in all forms.

picket line. Two words.

pickle ends in *-le.*

picklock. One word.

pick-me-up. Two hyphens.

pickoff (noun), **pickpocket, pickproof, pickup** (noun). One word.

picnic, picnicked, picnicking, picnicker. Spelled with *ck* in all
forms except *picnic.*

picture book. Two words.

picturegoer. One word.

picturesque ends in *-esque.*

pidgin, pigeon. The common spelling of the language is *pidgin.*

pie-. Most compounds are spelled as one word.

piece, peace. *Piece* means portion or unit, *peace* means no war.
Remember "a *piece* of *pie.*"

-piece. Spell compounds as one word, e.g. *earpiece, mouthpiece.*

pièce de résistance, pièces de résistance. One accent on *pièce,* one
on *résistance.*

piecemeal, piecework, pieceworker. One word.

piecrust. One word.

pied-à-terre. Accent on the *à.*

pie-eyed, pie-faced. Hyphened.

pier, dock. Now interchangeable in standard usage.

pierce is spelled with *ie.*

pierceable ends in *-eable.*

pigeon in the sense of dupe or object of special concern is listed
as standard usage in Webster's. There's no *d* in *pigeon.*

pigeonhole, pigeonholed, pigeonholing. One word.

pigeon-toed. Hyphened.

piggyback. One word.

piggy bank. Two words.

pigheaded, pigheadedness. One word.

pig iron, pig Latin. Two words.

(pigmy). The common spelling is *pygmy.*

pigpen, pigskin, pigsty, pigtail, pigtailed, pigweed. One word.
pilaf. Spell it with one *l.* (Not *pilaff* or *pilau.*)
pile driver, pile driving. Two words.
pileup. One word.
pillar, meaning post, ends in *-ar.*
pillbox, pillowcase, pillpusher. One word.
pilot, piloted, piloting. One *t* in all forms.
Pilsner. Spell it without *e* between *s* and *n.*
pin-. Almost all compounds are spelled as one word.
pinball machine. Two words.
pince-nez.
pinch-hit. Hyphened.
pinch hitter. Two words.
pin curl. Two words.
pincushion. One word.
pinewood, pinewoods. One word.
pinfeather. One word.
ping-pong. Small *p*'s, hyphen.
pinhead, in the sense of fool, is listed as standard usage in Webster's.
pinhole. One word.
pinion, pinioned. One *n* in the middle.
pinkeye. One word.
pinkie. The common spelling ends in *-ie.*
pinko, pinkos. Listed in Webster's as standard usage.
pinnacle, pinochle. A *pinnacle* is a peak, *pinochle* is a card game.
pinpoint, pinprick. One word.
pinto, pintos.
pinup (noun, adj.). One word. Listed in Webster's as standard usage.
piny. Spell it without *e.*
pipage. The common spelling.
pipe cleaner. Two words.
pipe down is listed in Webster's as standard usage.
pipe dream. Two words.
pipefitter, pipefitting. One word.
pipeful, pipefuls. One word.
pipeline, pipelined, pipelining. One word.
pipe organ. Two words.
pipestem. One word.
pipette. The common spelling ends in *-ette.*

pip-squeak. Hyphened.

piquancy, piquant end in *-ancy, -ant.*

pique, piqued.

piqué, piquet. *Piqué* (with accent) is the fabric, *piquet* is the card game.

piranha is spelled with *nh.*

pirouette ends in *-ette.*

pistachio, pistachios.

pistil, pistol. A *pistil* is part of a flower, a *pistol* is a gun.

piston rod. Two words.

pit-a-pat. Two hyphens.

pitch-black. Hyphened.

piteous, pitiable, pitiful. If you mean lamentable, use *piteous* or *pitiable.* If you mean contemptible, use *pitiable* or *pitiful.*

pithecanthropus. Two *th*'s.

pittance ends in *-ance.*

pitter-patter. Hyphened.

Pittsburgh, Pa. has an *h* at the end.

pity, pitied, pitying.

pixie, pixieish. Common spellings.

pizza. Two *z*'s.

pizzazz. The common spelling has four *z*'s. Listed in Webster's as standard usage.

pizzeria. Two *z*'s.

pizzicato, pizzicati.

place (verb). Don't say *place* when *put* will do.

placebo, placebos.

placekick. One word.

place mat. Two words.

place-name. Hyphened.

place setting. Two words.

plagiarism, plagiarize are spelled with *gia.*

plague, plagued, plaguing. *U* after *g.*

plaguey. Spell it with *e.*

plaice, the fish, is spelled with *ai.*

plaid is spelled with *ai,* although pronounced with a short *a.*

plain, plane. Don't confuse *plain* (treeless country) with *plane* (level).

plainclothesman, plainclothesmen. One word.

plainness. Double *n.*

plainspoken. One word.

plaintiff, plaintive. A *plaintiff* is someone who starts a lawsuit, *plaintive* means melancholy.

plait, plate. *Plait* means braid, *plate* means dish.

plan, planned, planning, planner. Double *n* in all forms except *plan.*

planeload. One word.

planning. Don't use *advance planning* when *planning* will do.

plantain ends in *-ain.*

plaster of Paris. Capitalize the *P* in Paris.

plateau, plateaus.

plateful, platefuls.

plate glass. Two words.

platonic, in the sense of nonsexual, is standard usage. Small *p.*

platypus, platypuses.

plausible ends in *-ible.*

play-. Compounds are spelled as one word.

playact, playacting, playback (noun), **playbill, playbook, playboy, playfellow, playfield, playgirl, playgoer, playgoing, playground, playhouse, playoff** (noun), **playpen, playroom, plaything, playtime, playwear.** One word.

playwright. Spelled with silent *w* and *igh.*

plead innocent. There's no such plea in a criminal trial. The proper form is *plead not guilty.* But *plead innocent* is common.

pleasant, pleasantry. Spelled with *ea.*

please be advised that sounds stiff and old-fashioned. Leave out.

please find. Old-fashioned business jargon. *Here is* or *here's* will usually do.

pleasurable ends in *-able.*

pleasure. Say *I have the pleasure* or *it is a pleasure,* but don't use *it is my pleasure*—that's a phrase reserved for kings and rulers.

plebeian is spelled with *ei.*

plebiscite. Watch the *sc.*

(pled). *Pleaded* is more common.

pledger, pledgor. The first is the usual spelling, the second is only used by lawyers. It ends in *-or,* although it's pronounced like *pledger.*

pleiad. No *e* at the end.

pleistocene. Spell it with *ei.*

plenary ends in *-ary.*

plenipotentiary ends in *-iary.*

plenitude. Don't use *plenitude* when *plenty* or *abundance* will do.

plenteous ends in *-eous.* Don't use *plenteous* when *plentiful* will do.

plentiful has an *i* in the middle.

plenty. *Plenty* instead of *plenty of* is listed in Webster's as standard usage, e.g. *There is plenty work to be done.* So is *plenty* as an adverb, e.g. *plenty large enough.* The idiom goes back to 1842.

plethora. Don't use *a plethora of* when *plenty* or *plenty of* will do.

pleurisy is spelled with *eu* and ends in *-isy.*

pliable ends in *-able.*

pliancy, pliant end in *-ancy, -ant.*

pliers is spelled with *i.*

(plough). The common US spelling is *plow.*

plowboy, plowman, plowshare. One word.

plug-in (adj.), **plug-ugly.** Hyphened.

plumb has a silent *b.* Commonly used as an adverb, as in *she was plumb crazy.*

plumb, plumbed, plumbing, plumber.

plumb line, plumb rule. Two words.

plum pudding. Two words.

plunderous. *E* after *d.*

plunk down is listed in Webster's as standard usage.

plurality, majority. In a contest between more than two candidates, a *plurality* may be under 50%, but a *majority* is always over 50%.

plurals. Don't use plurals when the singular will do, e.g. *ceremonies, learnings, skills, strengths, values.*

(plurisy). Misspelling of *pleurisy.*

plus, pluses.

p.m. Use lowercase letters with periods.

pneumatic, pneumococcus, pneumonia, pneumothorax. Spelled with silent *p* and *eu.*

pocketbook. One word.

pocketful, pocketfuls.

pocketknife. One word.

pocket money. Two words.

pocket-size, pocket-sized. Hyphened.

pocket veto. Two words.

pockmark, pockmarked. One word.

podium, podiums. A *podium* is a platform, a *lectern* is a reading desk.

poem. So spelled.

poetess is now considered offensive. Say *poet*.

poet laureate, poets laureate. No hyphen.

poi. The plural is *poi* too.

poignancy, poignant. Silent *g*.

poinsettia. Double *t*. Ends in *-ia*.

point-blank. Hyphened.

point in time. Don't say *at this point in time* when *now* will do. Don't say *at that point in time* when *then* will do.

pointillism, pointillistic. Double *l*.

poky. No *e*.

polar bear. Two words.

polarization, polarize. Spelled with *z*.

pole, poll. A *pole* is a staff or one of two opposites, a *poll* is a vote or straw vote.

poleax, poleaxed. One word.

(policlinic). Misspelling of *polyclinic*.

policy, polity. *Policy* means a plan or course of action, *polity* is a rare word meaning a politically organized unit.

policyholder, policymaker, policymaking. One word.

polio (abbreviation of *poliomyelitis*) is standard usage.

poliovirus. One word.

politburo. One word, ends in *-o*.

politically ends in *-ally*.

politicize ends in *-ize*.

politicked, politicking. Spelled with *ck*.

politico, politicos.

politics is commonly used with the singular verb, as in *politics makes strange bedfellows*.

polity, policy. *Polity* means a politically organized unit, *policy* means plan or course of action. Don't use *polity* when you mean *policy*.

poll, pole. A *pole* is a vote or straw vote, a *pole* is a staff or one of two opposites.

pollack (fish). Common US spelling.

pollen. Double *l*, ends in *-en*.

pollinate, pollination. Spelled with *i* in the middle.

polliwog. Common US spelling.

pollster. Standard usage.

poll tax. Two words.

pollute, pollution. Double *l*.

polo coat, polo shirt. Two words.

poltergeist is spelled with *ei*.

poly-. Compounds are spelled as one word.

polyandry, polyclinic, polyester, polygamous, polygamy, polyglot, polygon, polygraph, polyhistor, polymer. One word, spelled with *y*.

Polynesian. Capital *P*.

polysyllabic, polyunsaturated. One word, spelled with *y*.

pomegranate. *E* between *m* and *g*.

(pommel, pommeled, pommeling). The spelling *pummel* is more common.

pompano, pompanos.

Pompeii (city). Double *i*. But the adjective is commonly spelled *Pompeian*.

Pompey (Roman general). Spelled with *ey*.

poncho, ponchos.

pongee ends in *-ee*.

poniard. No *g*.

pontiff. Don't say *pontiff* when *pope* will do.

pontoon. Spell it with double *o*.

pony, ponies.

ponytail. One word.

pony up. Standard usage.

Pooh Bah. Capital *P* and *B*.

pooh-pooh. Standard usage. Hyphened.

poolroom. One word.

pool table. Two words.

poor farm. Two words.

poorhouse. One word.

poor-mouth. Hyphened.

pop, as in *pop art, pop music,* is listed in Webster's as standard usage.

pope. Small *p,* as in the *pope in Rome,* but capital *P* before a name, as in *Pope Paul.*

popeyed. One word.

pop-off (noun). Hyphened.

popover. One word.

poppy seed. Two words.

Popsicle. Capital *P*.

populace, populous. *Populace* means population, *populous* means crowded.

popular ends in *-ar*.

pop-up (adjective). Hyphened.

porcelain ends in *-ain.* Don't use *porcelain* when *china* will do.

pore, pour. You *pore* over a book, but you *pour* tea.

pork barrel, pork chop. Two words.

porkpie. One word.

porous ends in *-ous.*

porridge ends in *-idge.*

port is the left side of a ship. Remember, both *port* and *left* have four letters.

portable ends in *-able.*

porte cochere. No accent. Two words.

porte-monnaie. Hyphened. Ends in *-aie.*

portend. Don't use *portend* when *foreshadow* will do.

portent. Don't use *portent* when *omen* will do.

portentous ends in *-tous.* No *i.*

porterhouse. One word.

portfolio, portfolios.

portico, porticoes.

portiere. No accent.

portion. Don't use *portion* when *part* will do.

portland cement. Small *p.*

portmanteau, portmanteaus.

(portmonnaie). Misspelling of *porte-monnaie.*

Portuguese has two *u*'s.

poseur ends in *-eur.*

position. Don't use *position* when *job* will do.

position (verb). Don't use *position* when *place* will do.

posse ends in *-e.*

possess, possession. Four *s*'s.

possessives. See APOSTROPHE.

possessor. Four *s*'s, ends in *-or.*

possible ends in *-ible.*

post-. Compounds with the prefix *post-* are spelled as one word, except when there's a capital letter after *post-,* which calls for a hyphen as in *post-Freudian.* Compounds with the noun *post* are usually spelled as two words, e.g. *post office.*

postage meter, postage stamp. Two words.

postbellum, postcard, postdate. One word.

posterior to. Don't use *posterior to* when *behind* or *after* will do.

postgraduate, posthaste. One word.

posthumous. Silent *h* after the *t.*

posthypnotic. One word.

postilion. Spell it with one *l*.

postmark, postmaster. One word.

postmaster general, postmasters general.

postmistress, postmortem, postnasal, postnuptial. One word.

post-obit. Hyphened.

post office. Never hyphened.

postoperative, postpaid. One word.

postpone. Don't forget the *t*.

postprandial. Don't use *postprandial* when *after-dinner* will do.

post road. Two words.

postulate. Don't say *postulate* when *assume* will do.

postwar. One word.

posy. No *e*. The plural is *posies.*

pot in the sense of marijuana is listed in Webster's as standard usage.

potable ends in *-able.*

potato, potatoes.

pot-au-feu. Two hyphens.

potbellied, potbelly, potboiler. One word.

pot cheese. Two words.

potency, potent end in *-ency, -ent.*

potful, potfuls.

pothead is listed in Webster's as common usage.

pother. The word *bother* is more common.

pot holder. Two words.

pothole, pothook. One word.

potlatch ends in *-atch.*

potluck, potpie. One word.

potpourri. One word, so spelled.

pot roast. Two words.

potshot. One word.

poultice is spelled with *ou.*

poultry is spelled with *ou.*

pound cake. Two words.

pound-foolish. Hyphened.

pour, pore. You *pour* tea, but you *pore* over a book.

pourboire. Don't use *pourboire* when *tip* will do.

pourparler ends in *-er.*

pousse-café. Hyphen and accent on the *é.*

poverty-stricken. Hyphened.

powderbox. One word.

powder keg. Two words.

powder puff (noun). Two words.

powder-puff (adj.). Hyphened.

powder room. Two words.

-power. Compounds are spelled as one word, e.g. *horsepower, manpower.*

powerboat, powerhouse. One word.

power mower, power play, power saw, power steering, power structure. Two words.

powwow. Double *w.*

pox. The common plural is *pox* too.

poxvirus. One word.

-pp-. See -P-, -PP-.

practicable, practical. *Practicable* means possible, *practical* means useful.

practically in the sense of almost has been standard usage since 1748.

practice (noun and verb). The common US spelling ends in *-ice.*

practitioner ends in *-er.*

prairie is spelled with *air* in it.

praline ends in *-ine.*

pray, prey. You *pray* to God, but *prey* on an innocent victim.

prayer. Always so spelled.

prayer beads, prayer book. Two words.

pre-. Compounds are spelled as one word, except if the main part starts with a capital, e.g. *pre-Christian.*

preadolescence, preadolescent end in *-ence, -ent.*

prearrange, prearrangement, preassigned. One word.

precaution, precautious end in *-tion, -tious.*

precede, proceed. *Precede* means to be earlier or in front of, *proceed* means to go on. *Precede* ends in *-ede, proceed* in *-eed.*

precedence, precedents. *Precedence* means priority, *precedents* are earlier instances.

preceding. Don't use *preceding* when *earlier* or *former* will do.

precinct. *C* before *t.*

precipice ends in *-ice.*

precipitate, precipitous. The two words are often used interchangeably. Don't use either when *rash, hasty, headlong, sudden* will do.

precipitation. Don't use *precipitation* when *rain* or *snow* will do.

précis. Use the accent. The plural is *précis* too.

preciseness. The word *precision* is more common.

precisian, precision. A *precisian* is an exact person, *precision* means exactness.

precocious ends in *-cious.*

preconceive. *E* before *i.*

precursor ends in *-or.*

predaceous. Spell it with *-eous.*

predecease. Don't use *predecease* when *die first* will do.

predecessor. First *c,* then double *s.* Ends in *-or.*

predicate, predict. *Predicate on* means base on, *predict* means foretell. Don't use *predicated on* when *based on* will do.

predictable ends in *-able.*

predilection. Don't use *predilection* when *liking* will do.

predominant, predominantly; predominate, predominately. The forms ending in *-ant* and *-antly* are more common, but don't use any of these words when *chief, main, prevailing, chiefly, mainly* will do.

preelection, preemergence, preemergent. No hyphen.

preemie. Listed in Webster's as standard usage.

preeminence, preeminent, preemployment, preempt, preemption, preemptive, preengineered, preexist, preexistence. No hyphen.

prefab. Standard usage.

preface. More common than *foreword.*

prefer, preferred, preferring. Double *r* except in *prefer.*

prefer ... than. *Prefer ... to* and *prefer ... above* are the more common idioms.

preferable ends in *-able.* One *r* before *-able.* Don't say *more preferable—preferable* alone is enough.

preference ends in *-ence.*

preferential ends in *-tial.*

prefigure, preflight. One word.

pregnancy, pregnant end in *-ancy, -ant.*

preheat, prehistory, preignition, preinduction, preindustrial, prejudge. No hyphen.

prejudgment. No *e* after *g.*

prejudice. No *d* before *j.*

prejudicial. Don't use *prejudicial* when *harmful* will do.

prelacy, prelate end in *-acy, -ate.*

preliminary. Don't use *preliminary to* when *before* will do.

premarital. One word.

premed. Listed in Webster's as standard usage.

(premie). The common spelling is *preemie.*

premier. Don't use *premier* when *foremost* or *principal* will do.

premiere. No accent.

premise. Common US spelling.

premises. Don't use *premises* when *building* or *property* will do.

premium, premiums.

premix. One word.

preoccupy, preoccupied, preoccupying.

preoperative, preordain. One word.

prep. Listed as standard usage in Webster's.

prepackage. One word.

preparation is spelled with *par* in it.

preparatory. Don't use *preparatory to* when *before* will do.

prepared to. Don't use *prepared to* when *willing to* will do. Or leave it out.

prepay. One word.

preponderance, preponderant, preponderantly end in *-ance, -ant, -antly.* Don't use *preponderance, preponderant, preponderantly* when *most, many, mostly, largely, chiefly* will do.

preposition at end. The preposition at the end (after the verb) has been an English idiom for over 600 years. Shakespeare wrote "We are such stuff as dreams are made on" (Tempest, IV, i, 156). And the Bible (Genesis, 28:15) has "I will not leave thee, until I have done that which I have spoken to thee of." Francis Bacon wrote "Houses are built to live in, and not to look on." Defoe wrote "Going no oftener into the shore than we were obliged to for fresh water."

prepossessing. Two double *s*'s.

preposterous. *E* between *t* and *r.*

preprint, prepublication. One word.

Pre-Raphaelite. Capital *P,* hyphen, capital *R.*

prerequisite, prerogative. One word.

presage. Don't use *presage* when *foreshadow* will do.

Presbyterian has the word *by* in it.

prescience, prescient end in *-ence, -ent.* Watch the *sc.*

prescribe, proscribe. *Prescribe* means order, dictate; *proscribe* means forbid.

prescription, proscription. *Prescription* means direction, *proscription* means ban.

presence, presents. *Presence* means being here, *presents* means gifts or a legal document.

presentable ends in *-able*.

presentiment, presentment. A *presentiment* is a premonition, a *presentment* is a statement by a jury or a legal document.

presently may mean soon or now, but don't use *presently* when *soon* or *now* will do.

present writer. Don't write *the present writer* when *I* will do.

preserve. Don't use *preserve* when *jam* will do.

presidency. Small *p*.

president. Capital *P* when you refer to the President of the US or when the word is used as a title, e.g. *President John Smith*. Otherwise small *p*.

presidential. Small *p*.

(prespiration, prespire). Misspellings of *perspiration, perspire*.

press agent. Two words.

press-gang. Hyphened.

press release. Two words.

pressroom, pressrun, presstime. One word.

prestidigitator. A famous spelling-bee word. It has *digit* in it.

prestigious ends in *-ious*.

presumable ends in *-able*.

presume, assume. If you *presume* something, you think it's so, e.g. "Dr. Livingstone, I presume?" But you can freely *assume* whatever you feel like, e.g. *let's assume your annual income is $1 million*.

presumption has a *p* before the *t*.

presumptuous ends in *-uous*.

pretense. The common US spelling ends in *-se*.

pretension ends in *-sion*.

pretentious ends in *-tious*.

pretty in the sense of moderately is standard usage. The idiom goes back to 1565.

pretzel.

prevail. Don't use *prevail* when *be* or some other simple word will do.

prevalence, prevalent end in *-ence, -ent*. A before *l*.

prevaricate, prevaricator. Don't use when *lie* or *liar* will do.

preventable. The common form ends in *-able*.

preventive. Shorter and more common than *preventative*.

prevention ends in *-ion*.

previous, previously. Don't use when *earlier* will do.

previous to. Don't use when *before* will do.

prewar. One word.

prey, pray. You *prey* on an innocent victim, but you *pray* to God.

price, prize. A *price* is what you pay, but a *prize* is what you win.

price list, price tag. Two words.

prickle ends in *-le*.

prie-dieu, prie-dieux.

priest. A *priest* can be an Episcopalian clergyman. He doesn't have to be Roman Catholic.

priggish. Double *g*.

prima donna, prima donnas.

prima facie. Never hyphenated.

primeval. Spell it with *e*.

primitive. Three *i*'s.

prince regent. Two words.

principal, principle. Spell it with *le* at the end only when you mean a *rule* (remember the *le* in *rule*). Otherwise spell it *principal*. Think of the high school *principal* who wants to be a *pal* to the students.

principal (adj.). Don't use *principal* when *chief* or *main* will do.

principally ends in *-ally*.

printable ends in *-able*.

printmaker, printmaking, printout, printshop. One word.

prior to. Don't say *prior to* when *before* will do.

(prise). The common US spelling of the verb meaning to capture or move with a lever is *prize*.

prisoner ends in *-er*.

privacy ends in *-cy*.

privilege. The vowels go *i--i--e*. Remember that a *privilege* gives you a *leg* up.

prize. Common spelling of award, move with a lever and capture.

prizefight, prizefighter, prizefighting, prizewinner, prizewinning. One word.

pro, meaning a professional, is listed in Webster's as standard usage. The plural is *pros*. (No apostrophe.)

pro-. Compounds are spelled as one word except when the main part starts with a capital, e.g. *proslavery,* but *pro-Arab*.

pro and con, pros and cons.

probably ends in *-ably*.

proboscis, proboscises. Don't use *proboscis* when *nose* will do.

procedure. One *e* after *c*.

proceed, proceeding. Double *e*. Don't use *proceed* when *go, go ahead* or *go on* will do.

procès-verbal, procès-verbaux. Spelled with accent.

proclivity. Don't use *proclivity* when *bent* will do.

proconsul. One word.

proctor ends in *-or.*

procurable ends in *-able.*

procure. Don't use *procure* when *get* will do.

producible ends in *-ible.*

productive of. Don't write *it is productive of* when *it produces* will do.

prof for *professor* is slang.

profession, professional, professionalize, professor. One *f.*

proffer. Don't use *proffer* when *offer* will do.

proficient ends in *-cient.*

profitable ends in *-able.*

profitmaker, profitmaking. One word.

profit-sharing (adj.). Hyphened.

prognosis, prognoses.

prognosticate, prognosticator.

program, programmed, programmer, programming. Double *m* in all forms except *program.*

programmatic. Two *m*'s.

prohibit. Don't use *prohibit* when *ban* or *forbid* will do.

prohibition. Watch the *h.*

proletariat ends in *-iat.*

prologue. The common spelling.

prominence, prominent end in *-ence, -ent.*

promiscuous ends in *-uous.*

promissory. One *m,* two *s*'s.

promontory ends in *-ory.* Three *o*'s.

promote to. Common idiom, e.g. *he was promoted to captain.*

promoter ends in *-er.*

prompt. *P* after *m.*

promptbook. One word.

promulgate. Don't use *promulgate* when *announce, publish* or *declare* will do.

prone, supine. *Prone* means lying face downwards, *supine* face upwards. *Prone to* means inclined to, apt to.

pronounceable ends in *-eable.*

pronouns. Don't shy away from pronouns. Instead of *the testator's will named the testator's son as his heir* write *the testator's will named his son as his heir.*

pronunciamento, pronunciamentos.

pronunciation. There's a *nun* in this word.

proof, proofs.

-proof. Compounds are spelled as one word, e.g. *fireproof.*

proofread, proofreader, proofreading. One word.

propaganda. *A* after the second *p.*

propagator ends in *-or.*

propel, propelled, propelling. Double *l* in all forms except *propel.*

propellant ends in *-ant.*

propeller ends in *-er.*

property, propertied.

prophecy, prophesy. A *prophecy* with a *c* is a noun that means prediction, *prophesy, prophesied, prophesying* with an *s* is a verb that means foretell.

prophetess isn't as offensive as some other *-ess* words.

prophetically ends in *-ally.*

prophylactic spelled with *phy.*

propitiate, propitiation, propitiator, propitiatory, propitious. All spelled with *ti.*

propjet. One word.

proportion. Don't use *proportion* or *proportions* when simpler words will do. Instead of *in greater proportion* write *more.*

proprietary ends in *-ary.*

proprietor ends in *-or.*

proprietress isn't as offensive as some other *-ess* words.

pro rata. Always two words.

prorogation. No *u* after *g.*

prorogue, prorogued, proroguing. *U* after *g.*

pros and cons. No apostrophes.

proscenium is spelled with *sc.*

prosciutto, prosciuttos. Spelled with *sciu.*

proscribe, prescribe. *Proscribe* means forbid, *prescribe* means order, dictate, direct.

prosecute, persecute. To *prosecute* means to take legal action, to *persecute* means to harass.

prosecutor ends in *-or.*

proselyte, proselytize. The shorter verb is standard US usage.

prospect in the sense of potential customer or candidate is standard usage.

prospectus, prospectuses.

prostate, prostrate. *Prostate* means the male sexual gland, *prostrate* means lying down.

prosthesis, prostheses. Spelled with *sth.*

prosy. No *e.*

protagonist in the sense of spokesman, leader, champion is standard usage.

protean, protein. *Protean* means variable, *protein* means an organic compound.

protector ends in *-or.*

protégé, protégée. Two accents each for the male and female forms.

protein is spelled with *ei.*

pro tem, pro tempore. Never hyphenated.

protester. The common spelling ends in *-er.*

protocol. Three *o*'s.

protractor ends in *-or.*

protuberance, protuberant end in *-ance, -ant.*

proudhearted. One word.

provable. No *e* after *v.*

proven is standard usage.

provide. Don't use *provide* when *give, say, have, offer* will do.

provided, providing. Don't use *provided* or *providing* when *if* will do.

providence, provident end in *-ence, -ent.*

provider ends in *-er.*

providing, provided. Don't use *providing* or *provided* when *if* will do. *Providing* is as commonly used as *provided.*

provision. Don't use *provision* when *clause* will do.

proviso, provisos.

provocation, provocative are spelled with *c* although *provoke* is spelled with *k.* Don't use *was provocative of* when *provoked* will do.

provost marshal, provosts marshal.

prox. Old-fashioned business jargon. Avoid.

proximity. Don't use *in close proximity* to when *close to* will do.

proximo. Old-fashioned business jargon. Avoid.

prudence, prudent end in -ence, -ent.

prudential. Don't use *prudential* when *prudent* will do.

prurience ends in *-ence.*

(pruriency). The common form is *prurience.*

prurient ends in *-ent.*

Prussian blue. Capital *P.*

prussic acid. Small *p.*

pry, pried, prying.

pryer. US spelling of someone who pries.

PS. Abbreviation of *postscript* or *public school.* No periods.

psalm, psalmbook, psalmist. Silent *p.*

p's and q's. Spelled with apostrophes.

psephologist. A student of elections. So spelled.

pseudo-. Compounds are spelled as one word except when the second part starts with a capital or an *o,* e.g. *pseudo-Messiah, pseudo-official.*

pseudonym, pseudonymous. Silent *p,* and *y.*

pshaw. Silent *p.*

psittacosis. Silent *p.*

psoriasis. Silent *p.*

psychiatric, psychiatrist, psychiatry.

(psychical). The shorter form *psychic* is the US common form.

psycho, psychos. Listed in Webster's as standard usage.

psycho-. Compounds are spelled as one word except when the second part starts with *o,* e.g. *psycho-organic.*

psychoanalysis, psychoanalyses.

psychoanalyst is spelled with *y.*

psychoanalyze ends in *-yze.*

psychological, psychologist, psychology. Watch the *ch.*

psychoneurosis, psychoneuroses. Spelled with silent *p,* and *eu.*

psychoneurotic. Spelled with silent *p,* and *eu.*

psychopath. Watch the *ch.*

psychosis, psychoses.

psych out, psych up are both listed as standard usage in Webster's.

ptarmigan. Silent *p.*

pterodactyl. Silent *p.*

ptomaine has *e* at the end.

pubescence, pubescent end in *-ence, -ent.* Watch the *sc.*

publicist means a press agent or an expert in public affairs.

publicly is so spelled. (Not *-ally.*)

public-spirited. Hyphened.

pueblo, pueblos.

puerile is spelled with *ue.*

puffback (noun). One word.

pug-nosed. Hyphened.

puissance, puissant end in *-ance, -ant.*

pukka is spelled with double *k*.

pulchritude, pulchritudinous are spelled with *ch*. Don't use these words when *beauty* and *beautiful* will do.

pull in the sense of influence is listed as standard usage in Webster's.

pullback, pulldown. One word.

pulley, pulleys. Spelled with *e*.

Pullman car. Capital *P*.

pullout, pullover, pullthrough, pullup (nouns). One word.

pulmonary ends in *-ary*.

pulmotor. One *l*.

pulp mill. Two words.

pulpwood. One word.

pulverize ends in *-ize*.

pumice ends in *-ice*.

pummel, pummeled, pummeling. One *l* in all forms.

pumpernickel ends in *-el*.

pumpkin. Two *p*'s.

pumpkinseed. One word.

pump room. Two words.

punchball, punchboard. One word.

punch bowl, punch card. Two words.

punch-drunk. Hyphenated.

punctilio, punctilios.

punctuation. See APOSTROPHE, COLON, COMMA, DASH, EXCLAMATION POINT, HYPHEN, PARAGRAPHS, PARENTHESES, PERIOD, QUESTION MARK, QUOTATION MARKS, SEMICOLON.

pundit in the sense of expert or authority is standard usage.

punishable ends in *-able*.

puns are plays on words. They are commonly used by serious newspapers and magazines. One example from the New York Times: "Acting on a knotty issue that has made some men hot under the collar, a federal arbitrator has ruled that the local Social Security employees cannot be required to wear neckties."

pupa, pupae. The Latin plural with *ae* is common.

pupilage. One *l*.

pupillary. Two *l*'s.

pup tent. Two words.

purchasable. No *e* before *-able*.

purchase. Don't use *purchase* when *buy* will do.

pureblood. One word.

pure-blooded. Hyphened.

purebred. One word.

puree. No accent.

purely. *E* before *-ly*.

purify, purified, purifying. *I* in the middle.

purlieu. Don't use *purlieu* when *neighborhood* will do.

purloin. Don't use *purloin* when *steal* will do.

purport (noun). Don't use *purport* when *meaning* or *gist* will do.

purport (verb). Don't use *purport* when *claim* or *be supposed to* will do. Don't use *purport* in the passive voice, as in *purported, purportedly.*

purpose. Don't use *for the purpose of* when *for* or *to* will do.

purr, purred, purring. Double *r*.

pursuant to. Don't use *pursuant to* when *under* or *by* will do.

pursuit starts with *pur-*.

purveyor ends in *-or*.

purview. Don't use *purview* when *reach, scope, range* will do.

pushball, pushbutton, pushcart, pushdown, pushover, pushup. One word.

pusillanimous. Two *l*'s. Don't use *pusillanimous* when *timid* or *cowardly* will do.

pussycat, pussyfoot, pussyfooted, pussyfooting. One word.

put across is listed in Webster's as standard usage.

put-down (noun). Hyphened. Standard usage.

put-on (noun). Hyphened. Standard usage.

putout (noun). One word.

put over. Listed in Webster's as standard usage.

putrefaction, putrefy. *E* in the middle.

putrescence, putrescent end in *-ence, -ent.* Watch the *sc*.

putsch is spelled with *sch*.

putt, putted is the spelling of the word used in golf.

putty knife. Two words.

put-up (adj.) Hyphened. Listed as standard usage in Webster's.

put-upon (adj.). Hyphened.

puzzleheaded. One word.

pygmy, pygmies. The common spelling.

(pyjamas). The common US spelling is *pajamas.*

pyorrhea is spelled with *rrh*.

pyromania, pyromaniac.

Pyrrhic victory. Capital *P* and *rrh*.

pyx, the vessel for the Host in a Roman Catholic service, is spelled with *y*.

Q

qua. Don't use *qua* when *as* will do.

quadrennial, quadrennium. Double *n*.

quadrille ends in *-ille*.

quadruped. *U* in the middle.

quadruplet. *U* in the middle.

quagmire.

(quai). The common form is *quay*.

qualify, qualified, qualifying.

quandary. There's an *a* after the *d*.

quantitative. The long form with three *t*'s is standard.

quantum, quanta. Use the Latin plural with *a*.

quarantine ends in *-ine*.

quarrel, quarreled, quarreling. One *l* in all forms.

quarryman, quarrystone. One word.

quarter-. Some compounds are hyphened, some spelled as one word, some as two.

quarterback, quarterdeck. One word.

quarter horse, quarter hour. Two words.

quartermaster, quartersaw, quarterstaff, quarterstretch. One word.

quartet. The common spelling ends in *-et*.

quarto, quartos.

quasi. Compound nouns with *quasi* are spelled as two words, e.g. *a quasi patriot*. Compound adjectives with *quasi-* are hyphened, e.g. *a quasi-scientific approach*.

quaternary.

quatrain ends in *-ain*.

quattrocento. The 15th century.

quay, key. A *quay* is a wharf, a *key* opens a lock.

quayside. One word.

queasy. The common spelling is with *s*.

queen consort, queen mother, queen regent. No hyphen.

queer in the sense of homosexual is listed as standard usage in Webster's.

querulous. *U* after *r.*

query. Don't use *query* when *question* or *doubt* will do.

quest. Don't use *quest* when *search* will do.

question. Don't use the phrase *in question* when *this* will do or when it is unnecessary.

question as to whether. Leave out *as to.*

question mark. A question mark is used after a direct question, e.g. *Who was on the phone?* Don't put a question mark after an indirect question, e.g. *He asked who was on the phone.* Don't put a question mark after a request, e.g. *Will you please answer the phone.*

Don't use a comma after a question mark, e.g. *"Who was on the phone?" he asked.*

questionnaire is spelled with double *n.* Think of a *questionnaire* o*n* *n*ational issues.

question of whether. Leave out *of.*

quetzal. Currency of Guatemala.

queue, cue. Spell it *cue* in all senses except braid. In England people *queue up,* but in America they *stand in* or *on line.* The verb forms are *queue, queued, queuing* and *cue, cued, cuing.*

quick-. Most compounds are hyphened or spelled as one word.

quick-acting, quick-fire, quick-freeze, quick-freezing. Hyphened.

quickie is listed as standard usage in Webster's.

quicklime, quicksand, quicksilver, quickstep. One word.

quick-tempered, quick-witted. Hyphened.

quid pro quo. No hyphens.

quiescence, quiescent end in *-ence, -ent.* Watch the *sc.* Don't use *quiescence* or *quiescent* when *stillness* or *still* will do.

quiet, quite. *Quiet* means still, *quite* means entirely.

(quieten). The common form of the verb is *quiet.*

quietude. Don't use *quietude* when *quiet* will do.

quint for *quintuplet* is listed in Webster's as standard usage.

quintessence. Double *s.* There's no *sc.*

quintet. The common spelling ends in *-et.*

quire, choir. A *quire* is 24 sheets of paper, a *choir* is a group of singers. The pronunciation of the two words is the same.

quisling. Small *q.*

quit, quitter, quitting. Double *t* in all forms except *quit.*

quitclaim, quitclaimed, quitclaiming. One word.

quite in the sense of *rather* is standard usage. So is *quite a* as in *quite a few.*

quittance ends in *-ance.*

quiver. One *v.*

quixotic.

quiz, quizzed, quizzes, quizzical, quizzing. Double *z* in all forms except *quiz.*

quondam. Don't use *quondam* when *former* or *once* will do.

quorum, quorums.

quotation marks. The following rules are based on Webster's and common newspaper usage.

1. Use quotation marks to enclose direct quotations, e.g. *She said "Have a nice day."—"However," he said, "I'm not fully satisfied."—The policy was based on "plausible denial."*

2. Use quotation marks to enclose titles of short poems, short stories, articles, lectures, chapters of books, songs, short musical compositions and radio and TV programs.

3. If you use newspaper style, you can use quotation marks to enclose titles of books, magazines, plays, movies, works of art and music, and names of ships and airplanes. Or you can simply capitalize such titles and names. (In a more formal style, such titles or names are italicized or underlined.)

4. Use quotation marks to enclose words or phrases used ironically, e.g. *The President went on a "nonpolitical" trip.*

5. Don't use quotation marks to apologize for words you consider informal or slang. For instance, if you want to use the word *hassle* in the sentence *There's no hassle,* use it without quotation marks. If you feel the word *hassle* is too novel or daring, use another word.

6. Put periods and commas inside quotation marks, but colons and semicolons outside. Put question marks and exclamation points before or after quotation marks depending on the sense.

7. Use single quotation marks for a quotation inside a quotation, e.g. *He said "The best movie ever made is 'Brief Encounter.' "*

8. There's a trend toward omitting the comma before a quotation, e.g. *She said "Have a nice day."*

quote, short for *quotation,* is standard usage.

(quoth) is archaic. Avoid.

quotient ends in *-ient.*

q.v. Don't use *q.v.* when *which see* will do.

R

r-. If you can't find the word you're looking for, try under *rh-* or *wr-*.

-r, -rr-. An *r* at the end of a one-syllable word is doubled before the suffixes *-ed, -er, -ing, -y* etc. if there's only one vowel before the *r*. The same is true if the word has more than one syllable and the accent falls on the last syllable. Examples: *bar, barred; stir, stirrer; jar, jarring; star, starry; concur, concurred; demur, demurrer; inter, interring; occur, occurrence.*

rabbet, rabbit. A *rabbet* is a groove, a *rabbit* is a hare.

rabies ends in *-ies.*

raccoon. Double *c,* double *o.*

race-. Compounds are spelled as one word.

raceabout, racecourse, racegoer, racegoing, racehorse, racemate, racetrack, racetracker, raceway. One word.

rack, wrack. It's spelled *rack* in *clothes rack, hayrack, rack one's brains,* but *wrack* in *wrack and ruin.*

racket. Spell it so in all meanings. Standard usage in the sense of illegal business.

raconteur ends in *-eur.*

(racquet). The common US spelling is *racket.*

racy. No *e.*

radarscope. One word.

radiance, radiant end in *-ance, -ant.*

radiator ends in *-or.*

radio, radios (noun); **radio, radioes, radioed, radioing** (verb).

radio-. Compounds are spelled as one word.

radioactive, radioactivity, radiogram, radioisotope, radioman, radiopaque, radiophone, radiotelegraph, radiotherapy. One word.

radish. One *d.*

radius, radii. The plural *radiuses* is less common.

ragamuffin. One *g*.

ragout ends in *-out*.

ragpicker, ragtag, ragtime. One word.

rah-rah. Two *h*'s and hyphen.

rail-. Compounds are spelled as one word.

railhead, railroad, raliroading, railsplitter, railway. One word.

raiment. Don't say *raiment* when *clothing* or *garments* will do.

rain, reign, rein. *Rain* falls from the sky, to *reign* means to rule, to *rein* means to check or control.

rain-. Most compounds are spelled as one word.

rainbow. One word.

rain check. Two words.

raincoat, raindrop, rainfall, rainmaker, rainmaking, rainproof, rainstorm, rainwash, rainwater, rainwear. One word.

raise, rear. Both words are used in the sense of bringing up a child. *Rear* is more formal. Don't use *rear* when *raise* will do.

raise, rise. The common US word for an increase in pay is *raise*.

raison d'être. Spelled with apostrophe and accent on *ê*. Don't use *raison d'être* when *reason* will do.

rajah. The spelling with *h* at the end is more common.

rake-off. Hyphened. Listed as standard usage in Webster's.

rakish. No *e*.

rally, rallied, rallying.

rambunctious. Standard usage.

ramekin. Common spelling.

ramify, ramified, ramifying. *I* in the middle.

ramjet. One word.

rampant ends in *-ant*.

ramshackle. Standard usage.

ramshorn. One word.

ranch hand, ranch house. Two words.

rancor ends in *-or*.

rand. Currency of South Africa.

ranee. The wife of a rajah. This spelling is more common than *rani*.

rang. Past tense of *ring*.

rangefinder, rangerider. One word.

rangy. No *e*.

(rani). Spell it *ranee*.

rank and file. Three words.

ransack.

rap, wrap. To *rap* means to hit, to *wrap* means to cover. To *rap* in the sense of talk is listed in Webster's as standard usage.

rapid-fire. Hyphened.

rapid transit. Two words.

rapier ends in *-ier.*

rapport. Silent *t* at the end.

rapporteur ends in *-eur.*

rapprochement. Don't underline or italicize.

rapscallion has two *l*'s and ends in *-ion.*

(rapsody). Misspelling of *rhapsody.*

rapt, wrapped. *Rapt* means enraptured, *wrapped* means bundled up.

rara avis. Don't use *rara avis* when *rarity* will do.

(rarebit). The common form is *Welsh rabbit.*

rarefaction, rarefy, rarefied. *E* in the middle.

rarely ever. Standard usage since 1694.

rarity. *I* in the middle.

(rase). The common spelling is *raze.*

raspberry has a silent *p.*

ratable. No *e* after *t.*

rat-a-tat. Two hyphens.

rat-bite. Hyphened.

ratcatcher. One word.

(-rate). Compounds are spelled as two words, e.g. *birth rate, interest rate, tax rate.*

ratepayer, ratepaying. One word.

ratfink. One word. Listed in Webster's as standard usage.

rather. Don't use *rather* when it is unnecessary or affected, e.g. *Her taste was rather atrocious.*

rathole. One word.

rathskeller. Silent *h.*

ratify, ratified, ratifying. *I* in the middle.

ratio, ratios.

ratiocinate, ratiocination. Don't use these words when *think, thinking* will do.

rationale. Don't use *rationale* when *reason, plan, basis* will do.

rationalize ends in *-ize.*

rat race. Two words.

rattan. Double *t.*

rattlebrain, rattlebrained, rattlesnake, rattletrap. One word.

rattrap. One word.

raucous ends in *-ous.*

ravage, ravish. To *ravage* means to devastate, to *ravish* means to rape.

ravel, raveled, raveling. One *l* in all forms. The commonly used word is *unravel.*

rawboned, rawhide. One word.

raze is spelled with *z.*

razorback. One word.

razor blade. Two words.

razzle-dazzle. Hyphened.

razzmatazz. One word. Listed in Webster's as standard usage.

re. A legal term, meaning *in the matter of.* Avoid in sentences. Commonly used in business letter captions.

-re, -er. Words spelled with *-re* in Britain are spelled with *-er* in the US, e.g. *center, theater.* Exceptions: *massacre, ogre* etc.

re-. Compounds are spelled as one word, even when the main part starts with *e,* e.g. *reenact, reemerge, reelection.* But hyphen words to distinguish different meanings, e.g. *re-cover* (cover again) as against *recover* (get well).

reaction. Don't use *reaction* when *opinion, feeling* etc. will do.

readable ends in *-able.* Use *readable* when you mean understandable, *legible* when you mean decipherable.

readdress. Double *d.*

readiness. *I* in the middle.

reading chair, reading desk, reading room. Two words.

readout. One word.

ready, readied, readying.

ready-. Most compounds are hyphened.

ready-built, ready-made, ready-to-wear, ready-witted. Hyphened.

real. *Real* as an adverb meaning *very* is listed in Webster's as standard usage. The idiom has been used since 1658. The English historian J. A. Froude wrote "Last Friday was a real fine day."

real estate. Never hyphened.

realign, realignment. Spelled with the *gn.*

reality, realty. *Reality* means being real, *realty* means real estate.

realize, realization. Spelled with *z.*

really ends in *-ally.*

realm is spelled with *ea.*

realtor. The GPO Style Manual uses a small *r.*

reappearance ends in *-ance.*

reappoint, reappointment. No hyphen.

reapportion, reapportionment. Watch the *nm* in *reapportionment.*

reappraise, reappraisal. No hyphen.

rear, raise. Both words are used in the sense of bringing up a child. *Rear* is more formal. Don't use *rear* when *raise* will do.

rear end. Two words. Standard usage.

rearguard. One word.

reargue. One word.

rearview. One word.

rearward, rearwards. The adjective has no *s.* The adverb can be either form.

reason. Don't write *for the reason that* when *because* or *since* will do. Don't write *by reason of* when *because of* will do.

reason is because. Conservative grammarians oppose the construction *the reason is because,* but good writers have used it since 1656. George Eliot wrote "The reason Adam was walking along the lanes at this time was because his work for the rest of the day lay at a country house about three miles off."

reasonable ends in *-able.*

reason why. Standard usage.

reassess, reassessment. Two double *s*'s.

reassurance ends in *-ance.*

rebel, rebelled, rebelling, rebellious. Double *l* in all forms except *rebel.*

rebound, redound. *Rebound* means to spring back, *redound* means to lead to a result.

rebus, rebuses.

rebut, rebutted, rebutting, rebuttal. Double *t* in all forms except *rebut.*

recalcitrance, recalcitrant end in *-ance, -ant.*

recap in the sense of *recapitulate* and *recapitulation* is standard usage.

recede. Spelled so. No double *e.*

receipt is spelled with *ei* and a silent *p.* Remember "The *recep*-tionist gave me a *receipt.* "

receivable ends in *-able.* No *e* after *v.*

receive. Spelled with *ei,* following the rule "*I* before *e* except after *c.* " Don't use *receive* when *get* or *have* will do.

receptacle ends in *-acle.*

réchauffé. Two accents.

recherché. Accent on the last *é*.

rechristen. One word.

recidivist. Three *i*'s.

recipe, receipt. Use *recipe* for cooking directions, *receipt* for a written acknowledgment.

reciprocate, reciprocal, reciprocity. *O* after *pr*.

(recision). Obsolete variant spelling of *rescission*.

reckon in the sense of suppose or think is dialect, not standard usage.

reclaim, re-claim. *Reclaim* means reform, *re-claim* means to claim again.

reclamation. No *i* before *m*.

recognition ends in *-ition*.

recognizance is spelled with *z,* ends in *-ance*.

recognize is spelled with *g* before *n*. There's a *cog* in the word.

recollect, re-collect. *Recollect* means recall or remember, *re-collect* means rally or collect again. Don't use *recollect* when *recall* or *remember* will do.

recommend, recommendation. One *c,* double *m*.

reconcilable. No *e* before *-able*.

reconnaissance. Double *n, ai,* ends in *-ance*.

reconnoiter. One *c,* double *n*.

recordkeeping. One word.

record player. Two words.

recoup is spelled with *ou*.

recover, re-cover. *Recover* means regain, get well, *re-cover* means cover again.

recreate. One word in all senses.

recreation, re-creation. *Recreation* means refreshment, *re-creation* means renewed creation.

re-cross-examination. Two hyphens.

recrudescence, recrudescent end in *-ence, -ent*. Watch the *sc*.

recruit is spelled with *ui*.

recrystallize. One word.

rectify, rectified, rectifying, rectifiable.

recto-. Compounds are spelled as one word.

rector ends in *-or*.

recur, recurred, recurring. Double *r* in all forms except *recur*.

recurrence, recurrent end in *-ence, -ent*. Double *r*.

recyclable. No *e* before *-able*.

red, redder, reddest, reddish. Double *d* in all forms except *red*.

redbait, redbaiter, redbaiting. One word.

red-blooded. Hyphened.

redbreast, redbrick, redcap. One word.

red-carpet (adj). Hyphened.

redcoat. One word.

reddish-. Compounds are hyphened, e.g. *reddish-brown.*

redemption is spelled with *p.*

redescribe, redesign, redetermine, redevelop. One word.

red-handed. Hyphened.

redhead. One word.

red-hot. Hyphened.

redirect, rediscount, redistribute, redistrict. One word.

red-letter day. Hyphened.

redneck. One word.

redo. One word.

redolence, redolent end in *-ence, -ent.*

redoubt, redoubtable. Silent *b.*

redound, rebound. *Redound* means to lead to a result, *rebound* means to spring back.

redskin. One word.

red tape. Never hyphened.

reduce, reduction. Don't use these words when *cut* will do.

reducible ends in *-ible.*

reecho, reeducate. One word.

reef, reefs.

reelect, reelection, reemploy, reemployment, reenact, reenactment. One word.

(reenforce). The common spelling is *reinforce.*

reenlist, reenlistment, reenter, reentrance, reentry. One word.

(reevaluate, reevaluation). The common forms are *revaluate, revaluation.*

reexamine, reexamination. One word.

refer, referred, referring, referral. Double *r* except in *refer.*

referable. One *r* before *-able.*

referee. One *f,* one *r* before *ee.*

reference. Don't write *with reference to* or *in reference to* when *on* or *about* will do. Don't write *have reference to* when *mean* will do.

referendum, referendums.

referral. Double *r.*

refill, refillable, refinish, refit. One word.

reflect. Don't use *reflect* when *show* will do.

reflection. The US spelling is with *ct*.

reflective. Don't use *be reflective of* when *reflect* or *show* will do.

reflector ends in *-or*.

reflow, refocus, reforest, reforestation. One word.

reform, re-form. *Reform* means correct, *re-form* means form again.

reformatory. *A* after *m*.

refrain. Don't use *refrain from* when *do not* will do.

refrigerator ends in *-or*.

refuel. One word.

refuse, re-fuse. *Refuse* means say no, *re-fuse* means fuse again.

refute means disprove. It means more than just deny.

regalia takes a plural verb.

regard. Don't use *with regard to, in regard to, regarding, as regards* when *on* or *about* will do.

regardless. *Regardless* by itself, in the sense of *despite everything,* is standard usage.

regicide.

regime. No accent necessary.

regionwide. One word.

registrar ends in *-rar*.

regret, regretted, regretting. Double *t* except in *regret*. Don't use *regret* when *be sorry* will do.

regretful, regrettable. *Regretful* means feeling regret, *regrettable* means deserving regret.

regrow. One word.

regular ends in *-ar*.

rehabilitate. You can *rehabilitate* people and things.

rehash. Standard usage.

reign, rein. To *reign* means to rule, to *rein* means to check or control.

reimburse, reimbursement, reincarnate, reincarnation. One word.

reindeer. Spelled with *ei*.

reinforce. Common spelling.

reinforceable ends in *-eable*.

reinsert, reinstate, reinstatement, reinsure, reinsurance, reintegrate, reintegration, reinterpret, reinterpretation, reinvent, reinvest, reinvestigate, reinvestigation, reinvestment, reinvigorate, reissue. No hyphen.

reiterate, reiteration. Don't use these words when *repeat* or *repetition* will do.

relaid, relayed. *Relaid* means laid again, *relayed* means sent on.

relate. Don't use *relate* when *tell* or *say* will do.

related to, relating to, relative to, in relation to. Don't use these phrases when *on* or *about* will do.

relater ends in -*er.* The legal term *relator* ends in -*or.*

relation, relative in the sense of related person are interchangeable.

relationship. Don't use *relationship* when *relation* will do.

relatively. Often unnecessary.

relative pronouns. See THAT, WHICH, WHO, WHOM.

releasable. No *e* before -*able.*

release, re-lease. *Release* means free or publish, *re-lease* means lease again.

relevance, relevant end in -*ance,* -*ant.* The *l* comes before the *v.* Webster's lists *relevance* in the sense of social importance as standard usage.

reliable ends in -*iable.*

reliance, reliant end in -*ance,* -*ant.*

relict. Don't use *relict* when *widow* will do.

relief is spelled with *ie,* following the rule "*I* before *e* except after *c.*"

relieve. Also spelled with *ie.*

religio-. Compounds are spelled as one word.

relocate, relocation. Don't use these words when *move* or *transfer* will do.

reluctance, reluctant end in -*ance,* -*ant.*

remain. The phrase *I remain* or *We remain* at the end of business letters is old-fashioned. Put the complimentary close of your letter, e.g. *Sincerely yours,* or *Cordially yours,* on a separate line after the last sentence.

remainderman. One word.

remake, remanufacture, remap. One word.

remark. Don't use *remark* when *say* will do.

remarkable ends in -*able.*

rematch. One word.

remediable, remedial. *Remediable* means capable of being remedied, *remedial* means as a remedy.

remedy. *E* after *m.*

remembrance ends in -*ance.*

reminisce is standard usage.

reminiscence, reminiscent end in *-ence, -ent.* Watch the *sc.*

remit, remitted, remitting. Double *t* in all forms except *remit.* Don't use *remit* when *send* or *pay* will do.

remittance ends in *-ance.* Don't use *remittance* when *money, cash, payment* will do.

remodel, remodeled, remodeling. One *l* in all forms.

remonstrance ends in *-ance.*

removable. No *e* before *-able.*

remove. Don't use *remove* when *take away, get rid of* will do.

remunerate, remuneration. Don't use these words when *pay* will do.

renaissance, renascence. *Renaissance* is commonly used for the artistic revival that began in the 14th century in Italy, *renascence* is used to mean rebirth.

(rencounter). The form *encounter* is more common.

render. Don't use *render* when *make* or *sing* will do.

rendezvous, rendezvoused, rendezvousing.

rendition. Don't use *rendition* when *making, singing* or another simple word will do.

renege, reneged, reneging. Standard usage in the sense of *go back on a promise.*

renounceable. *E* before *-able.*

renowned is spelled with *ow.*

rent-a-car. Two hyphens.

renunciation has *nun* in it.

(reoccur). The common form is *recur.*

reoffer, reopen, reorder, reorganization, reorganize. One word.

rep, short for *representative* or *repertory.* Listed as standard usage in Webster's.

rep in the sense of reputation is slang.

rep, repp. The spelling with one *p* is more common for the fabric.

repackage. One word.

repairable, reparable. *Repairable* is more common in the sense of a material object that can be repaired, *reparable* is more often used for immaterial damage, e.g. a mistake.

repairman. One word.

repair shop. Two words.

repast. Don't use *repast* when *meal* will do.

repatriate. One word.

repay. Don't use *repay* when *pay* will do.

repeat again. You don't need *again.* Say *repeat.*

repel, repelled, repelling. Double *l* in all forms except *repel.*

repel, repulse. Used interchangeably.

repellent. The common spelling ends in *-ent.*

repellent, repulsive. *Repulsive* is the stronger word. A raincoat may be *water-repellent,* but anything *repulsive* is disgusting.

repentance, repentant end in *-ance, -ant.*

repertoire, repertory. *Repertoire* is more often used for a list or supply, *repertory* for a stock company theater.

repetition, repetitious. *E* after *p.*

repetition of words. Repetition of words is often bad, e.g. "Any move for a *sweeping* inquiry is likely to be *swept* under the rug." But it's far worse to go out of your way to avoid repetition, e.g. "This varies from the Administration's tax *cut* proposal, which would *trim* corporate rates to 48 percent and *slash* personal taxes by $8.5 billion." (The sentence would be much better if *trim* was changed to *cut* and *slash* left out.) See also SYNONYMS.

replace can be used with *with* or *by.*

replaceable ends in *-eable.*

replete. Don't use *replete* when *full* or *filled* will do.

reply. Don't use *reply* when *answer* will do.

reportedly is standard usage.

repository ends in *-ory.*

repossess, repossession. Two double *s*'s.

(repp). Commonly spelled *rep* with one *p.*

reprehensible ends in *-ible.*

represent. Don't use *represent* when *be, say, claim* will do.

representative. *A* between the two *t*'s.

repressible ends in *-ible.*

reprieve is spelled with *ie,* following the rule "*I* before *e* except after *c.*"

repro, repros.

reprocess. One word.

reproducible ends in *-ible.*

reprogram, reprogrammed, reprogramming. One word.

reproof, reproofs.

republish. One word.

repugnance, repugnant end in *-ance, -ant.*

repulse, repel. Used interchangeably.

repulsive, repellent. *Repulsive* is the stronger word. A raincoat may be *water-repellent,* but anything *repulsive* is disgusting.

request. Don't use *request* when *ask* will do.

require. Don't use *require* when *want, need,* or *call for* will do.

requirement. Don't use *requirement* when *need* will do.

requisite. Don't use *requisite* when *needed* will do.

reread, rerun. One word.

resalable. No *e* before *-able.*

rescind is spelled with *sc.* Don't use *rescind* when *repeal* or *cancel* will do.

rescission. *Sc* and double *s.*

reservoir ends in *-oir.*

reshape. One word.

reship, reshipped, reshipping. One word. Double *p* in all forms except *reship.*

reshipment. One word.

reside. Don't use *reside* when *live* will do.

residence. Don't use *residence* when *house, home, apartment* or *address* will do.

residuum, residua.

resign. Don't use *resign* when *quit* or *give up* will do.

(resiliency). The form *resilience* is more common.

resin, rosin. *Resin* is the natural organic substance, *rosin* is the distilled solid.

resistance, resistant end in *-ance, -ant.*

resister, resistor. A *resister* is a person, a *resistor* is an electrical device.

resistible. Spell it with *-ible.*

resonance, resonant end in *-ance, -ant.*

resort, resource, recourse. *To resort to* means the same as *to have recourse to,* that is, turn to when needed. The thing you turn to is a *resource.*

respect. Don't use *with respect to, in respect to* or *respecting* when *on* or *about* will do.

respectable ends in *-able.*

respectfully yours. Ending for letters to high officials.

respective, respectively. These words mean *separate, separately* or *in the order given.* They're almost always unnecessary. Leave them out whenever possible.

resplendence, resplendent end in *-ence, -ent.*

respond. Don't use *respond* when *answer* will do.

respondent ends in *-ent.*

response. Don't use *response* when *answer* will do.

responsible ends in *-ible.* It is US standard usage to use the word *responsible* in referring to things, e.g. *The weather was responsible for the cancellation.*

restage, restart, restate, restatement. One word.

restaurant. Spelled with *au.* Ends in *-ant.*

restaurateur. There's no *n* in this word.

rest cure. Two words.

rest home, rest house. Two words.

restive, restless. The two words don't mean quite the same. *Restive* means balky, contrary, *restless* means fidgety, uneasy.

restrictive and nonrestrictive clauses. See COMMA; WHICH, THAT.

rest room. Two words.

restructure, restudy. One word.

result. Don't use *as a result of* when *because of* will do. Don't use *with the result that* when *so that* will do.

résumé. The spelling with both accents is the most common.

resumption is spelled with *p.*

resupply, resurface, resurge. One word.

resurgence, resurgent end in *-ence, -ent.*

resurrect, resurrection. Double *r.*

resuscitate, resuscitation are spelled with *sc.*

retain. Don't use *retain* when *keep* will do.

retake, retell. One word.

retention ends in *-tion.*

retest, rethink. One word.

reticence, reticent end in *-ence, -ent.*

retina, retinas.

retire. Don't use *retire* when *go to bed* will do.

retort. Don't use *retort* when *answer* will do.

retraceable ends in *-eable.*

retrain, retranslate, retrial. One word.

retrievable, retrieval, retrieve, retriever. Spelled with *ie,* following the rule "*I* before *e* except after *c.*"

retro-. Compounds are spelled as one word, e.g. *retroactive.*

retry. One word.

return back. Leave out *back.*

reunify, reunion, reunite, reuse. One word.

reusable. No *e* before *-able.*

Rev. See REVEREND.

rev, revved, revving. Double *v* in all forms except *rev.*

revaluate, revaluation. More common forms than *reevaluate, reevaluation.*

reveal. Don't use *reveal* when *show* will do.

reveille ends in *-eille.*

revel, reveled, reveler, reveling. One *l* in all forms.

(revelance, revelant). Misspellings of *relevance, relevant.*

revelry.

revenge, avenge. You *revenge* yourself to even up a score, but you *avenge* a wrong done to someone else.

reverence, reverent end in *-ence, -ent.*

reverend. Never use the title *Reverend* or the abbreviation *Rev.* in addresses or references without the first name or at least initials or *Mr.* Write *Reverend James T. Brown, Rev. J. T. Black, Rev. Mr. Green.* It is common to leave out the word *the* before *Reverend* or *Rev.* The noun *reverend,* meaning clergyman, is listed in Webster's as standard usage.

reverential. Don't use *reverential* when *reverent* will do.

reverie. The common spelling ends in *-ie.*

revers, meaning lapel, has no *e* at the end.

reversible ends in *-ible.*

review, revue. Spell the show *revue.* Don't use *review* when *look* or *study* will do.

reviser. The common ending is *-er.*

revivify, revivification. *I* before *f.*

revocable, revocation. Spelled with *c.*

revoke. Spelled with *k.*

revolutionary ends in *-ary.*

revolutionize ends in *-ize.*

revue. The show is spelled with *-ue.*

reward, award. A *reward* is a compensation, an *award* is a prize.

rewind, reword, rework, rewrite, rezone. One word.

rhapsody is spelled with *rh.*

rhesus, rhetoric, rhetorical. Spelled with *rh.*

rheumatic, rheumatism. Spelled with *rh* and *eu.*

Rh factor. Capital *R,* small *h.* No period.

Rhine, Rhineland. Spelled with *Rh.*

rhinestone. One word.

Rhine wine. Two words.

rhinitis. Spelled with *rh.*

rhino, short for *rhinoceros,* is standard usage.

rhinoceros, rhinoceroses.

Rh-negative. Hyphened.
Rhode Island. Spelled with *Rh.*
Rhodesia, Rhodes scholar. Spelled with *Rh.*
rhododendron. Spelled with *rh.*
(rhodomontade). The common spelling is *rodomontade.*
rhombus, rhombuses.
rhubarb is spelled with *rh.*
(rhumba). Spell it *rumba.*
rhyme, rhymed, rhyming, rhymester. Common spellings.
rhythm, rhythmic, rhythmical, rhythmically.
rialto, rialtos.
(riband). The common form is *ribbon.*
rib roast. Two words.
ricefield, ricegrower, ricegrowing. One word.
riches is a plural noun.
rickets. One *t.*
rickettsia. *Ck* and double *t.*
rickrack. One word.
ricksha. Spell it without *w* at the end.
ricochet, ricocheted, ricocheting. One *t* in all forms.
ridable. No *e* before *-able.*
riddance ends in *-ance.*
ride, rode, ridden.
ridgepole. One word.
ridicule. *I* after *d.*
ridiculous starts with *ridi-.*
riffraff. One word.
right away is standard usage.
righteous ends in *-eous.*
right-hand (adjective), **right-handed.** Hyphened.
rightly, right. Use *rightly* before the verb when you mean *properly,*
    e.g. *He rightly apologized.* Otherwise use *right,* e.g. *He answered
    right.*
right-minded. Hyphened.
right off. Standard usage.
right-of-way, rights-of-way. Hyphened.
right on. Listed in Webster's as standard usage.
right wing (noun). Two words.
rightwing (adj.), **rightwinger.** One word.
rigmarole. No *a* after *g.*
rigor, rigorous. Spelled with *or.*

rile in the sense of irritate is standard usage.

(rime, rimed, riming, rimester). Spell these words *rhyme, rhymed, rhyming, rhymester.*

ring, rang, rung.

ring binder, ring finger. Two words.

ringleader, ringmaster, ringside. One word.

riot, rioted, rioting. One *t* in all forms.

rip cord. Two words.

ripoff (noun). One word. Listed in Webster's as standard usage.

rip off (verb). Two words. Listed in Webster's as standard usage.

rip-roaring. Hyphened.

ripsaw, ripsnorter, riptide. One word.

rise, rose, risen. Don't use *rise* when *get up* will do. Don't use *give rise to* when *raise* will do.

(rise). *Raise* for pay increase is more common in the US.

risibility. Don't use *risibilities* when *laughter* will do.

risible. Don't use *risible* when *ridiculous* will do.

risqué. Accent on the *é.*

ritzy. Listed in Webster's as standard usage.

rival, rivaled, rivaling. One *l* in all forms.

river. Capitalize only when part of a name, e.g. *Mississippi River.*

riverbank, riverbed, riverboat, riverfront, riverside. One word.

rivet, riveted, riveting, riveter. One *t* in all forms.

rivulet has a *u* in the middle.

road. Capitalize only when part of a name, e.g. *Post Road.*

-road. Some compounds are spelled as two words, e.g. *back road,* some are spelled as one word, e.g. *byroad, crossroad, highroad, railroad.*

road-. Most compounds are written as one word.

roadbed, roadblock, roadbuilder, roadbuilding, roadhouse, roadmap. One word.

road show. Two words.

roadside, roadway, roadwork. One word.

roast beef, roast lamb. No hyphen.

rob, robbed, robbing, robber. Double *b* in all forms except *rob.*

(rock and roll). The common spelling is *rock 'n' roll.*

rock-bottom. Hyphened.

rocking horse. Two words.

rock 'n' roll. The common spelling. No hyphens.

rococo. Three *o*'s, two *c*'s.

rodeo, rodeos.

rodomontade. No *h*.

roentgen, roentgenize, roentgenology. Watch the *oe*.

rogue ends in *-ue*.

roguish. Spelled with *u*.

role, roll. You play a *role* (no accent), but a *roll* is something rolled up.

rockback (noun). One word.

roll call. Two words.

roller coaster, roller skate, roller skating. Two words.

rollicking. Spelled with *ck*.

rollmop. No *s*.

roll-off (noun, adj.), **roll-on** (noun, adj.). Hyphened.

rollout (noun, adj.), **rollover** (noun, adj.), **rolltop.** One word.

roly-poly. Hyphened.

roman. It's *roman* letters and types, but *Roman* numerals.

Romania, Romanian. So spelled by the GPO Style Manual and the Associated Press Stylebook.

Roman Catholic. The word *Roman* is usually unnecessary.

Roman numerals. $I = 1$, $V = 5$, $X = 10$, $L = 50$, $C = 100$, $D = 500$, M = 1000. A bar over a letter multiplies it by 1000, e.g. $\overline{M} = 1$ million. $IV = 4$, $LV = 55$. Don't use Roman numerals except when absolutely necessary, as in *Louis XIV* (family members with the same first name). In footnote references to plays, use capital Roman numerals when referring to acts, lowercase Roman numerals *(i, v, x)* when referring to scenes.

rondeau, rondeaux.

rondo, rondos.

roof, roofs.

roof garden. Two words.

roofline, rooftop, rooftree. One word.

rookie, rookies. Ends in *-ie*.

-room. It's *bedroom, bathroom, playroom, workroom,* but *dining room, living room.*

room clerk. Two words.

roomette ends in *-ette*.

roomful, roomfuls.

rooming house. Two words.

roommate. One word.

root beer. Two words.

ropedancer, ropedancing. One word.

ropewalk, ropewalker. One word.

Roquefort. Capital *R*.

Rorschach test.

rosary ends in *-ary*.

rosebud, rosebush. One word.

rosette ends in *-ette*.

rose water. Two words.

Rosh Hashanah. Spell it with *h* at the end.

rosin, resin. *Rosin* is the distilled solid, *resin* is the natural organic substance.

rostrum, rostrums.

rotisserie. No accent.

rottenness. Double *n*.

(rouble). Spell it *ruble*.

roué. Accent on the *é*.

rouge, rouged, rouging.

rough-and-ready, rough-and-tumble. Hyphened.

roughcast, roughhouse, roughhousing, roughneck, roughrider, roughshod. One word.

rouleau, rouleaux.

roulette ends in *-ette*.

(Roumania, Roumanian). The GPO Style Manual and the Associated Press Stylebook spell the words *Romania, Romanian*.

round. Phrases like *all year round* need no apostrophe.

round-. Most compounds are spelled as one word.

roundabout. One word.

round-bottomed. Hyphened.

roundhouse. One word.

round robin, round steak. Two words.

roundtable (adj.). One word.

round trip. Two words.

roundup (noun). One word.

rouse, arouse. Use *rouse* literally, e.g. *We were roused at 6 a.m.,* and *arouse* figuratively, e.g. *This aroused suspicion*.

rout, route. *Rout* means defeat, *route* means line of travel.

routine is spelled with *ou*.

routing. No *e*.

rowboat. One word.

rowdy, rowdies, rowdyism.

row house. Two words.

royally ends in *-ally*.

-rr-. See -R-, -RR-.

rubber band. Two words.

rubberneck, rubbernecking. One word.

rubber-stamp in the sense of routine approval is hyphened.

rubdown (noun). One word.

ruble. Spell it so.

rucksack. Two *ck*'s.

rudiment is spelled with one *d* and *i*.

(rue). Old-fashioned. Use *regret.*

ruleless.

rulemaker, rulemaking. One word.

rule of thumb. No hyphen.

ruler. Don't use *ruler* when *king* or *emperor* will do.

(Rumania, Rumanian). The GPO Style Manual and the Associated Press Stylebook spell them *Romania, Romanian.*

rumba. No *h.*

ruminant ends in *-ant.*

rumor ends in *-or.*

rumormonger. One word.

rumpus room. Two words.

rumrunner. One word.

run, ran, run. Standard usage in the sense of manage, operate.

runabout, runaround, runaway, runback, rundown. One word.

run-in. Hyphened. Listed as standard usage in Webster's in the sense of quarrel.

runner-up, runners-up. Hyphened.

runoff (noun). One word.

run-of-the-mill, run-of-the mine. Hyphens.

run-on sentences. See COMMA 5.

runover (noun). One word.

run-through. Hyphened.

runway. One word.

rupee. Currency of India, Pakistan, Sri Lanka etc.

rupiah. Currency of Indonesia.

rush hour. Two words.

rustproof, rustproofing. One word.

rutabaga. Three *a*'s.

rye, wry. *Rye* is a grain, *wry* means twisted.

rye bread. Two words.

S

s. If you can't find the word you're looking for under *s,* look under *c, ps, sc* or *sch.*

's, s', -s. See APOSTROPHE.

-s-, -ss-. An *s* at the end of a one-syllable word is *not* doubled before *-ed, -es, -ing,* regardless of how many vowels there are before the *s.* The same is true of two-syllable words ending in *s.* Examples: *bus, bused, busing; gas, gases; bias, biased; focus, focusing; surplus, surpluses; bonus, bonuses; trellis, trellised.* (But it's *nol-prossed* and *nonprossed.*)

Sabbath. Capital *S,* two *b*'s. Sunday for Christians, Saturday for Jews and Seventh-day Adventists, Friday for Muslims.

sabbatical. Double *b.* Small *s.*

saber ends in *-er.*

sabertooth. One word.

saber-toothed. Hyphened.

saboteur ends in *-eur.*

sac, sack. *Sac* without *k* is a bag with fluid in an animal or plant, a *sack* with *ck* is a bag in general.

saccharin, saccharine. The noun, meaning the chemical, is spelled without an *e* at the end, the adjective, meaning sweet, is spelled with an *e.*

sack, meaning dismiss or fire, is standard usage in Britain.

sackcloth. One word.

sacrifice. *I* after *r.*

sacrilege. No *d.*

sacrilegious. Don't spell it like *religious.* The *i* comes before the *e.*

sacro-. Compounds are spelled as one word.

sacroiliac.

saddleback, saddlebag. One word.

saddle horse. Two words.
saddler. Double *d*.
saddle shoe. Two words.
saddle-stitched. Hyphened.
safe (noun), **safes.**
safe-. Most compounds are spelled as one word.
safeblower, safeblowing, safebreaker, safebreaking. One word.
safe-conduct. Hyphened.
safecracker, safecracking. One word.
safe-deposit. Hyphened.
safeguard, safeguarded, safeguarding, safekeeping. One word.
safety pin. Two words.
sagacious ends in *-cious*.
said. Don't use the adjective *said* when *the, that, he, she, it* will do, even in legal documents. Don't use words like *affirmed, asserted, declared, stated, contended, argued, interposed, smiled, frowned, grumped, allowed, shrugged, avowed, averred, claimed* etc. when *said* will do.
said he. Use normal, idiomatic word order. Write *he said*.
sailboat, sailcloth, sailfish, sailmaker, sailmaking. One word.
sailor ends in *-or*.
sake. Write *for God's sake, for Jones's sake, for Alex's sake,* but *for goodness' sake, for conscience' sake, for appearance' sake, for peace' sake.*
sake. The common spelling of the Japanese rice wine ends in *e*.
salaam is spelled with a double *a*.
salable, salability. No *e* after the *l*.
salacious ends in *-cious*.
salami.
salary. Don't use *salary* when *wages* or *pay* will do.
salesclerk, salesgirl, saleslady, salesman, salespeople, salesroom. One word.
sales slip, sales tax. Two words.
saleswoman. One word.
salicylic acid.
salient. Don't use *salient* when *important, striking* will do.
Salisbury steak. Capital *S*.
(salm). Misspelling of *psalm*.
salmon. Silent *l*.
salon, saloon. A *salon* is a drawing room, a *saloon* is a bar.
saloonkeeper. One word.

saltbox, saltcellar. One word.

saltpeter ends in *-er.*

saltshaker, saltwater. One word.

salubrious, salutary. *Salubrious* refers to air, climate etc., *salutary* means wholesome in general. (Ends in *-ary.*)

salutation. See ADDRESS.

salvageable. *E* before *-able.*

salve. Silent *l.*

salvo, salvos.

same, the same. Don't use *same* or *the same* when *it, he, him, she, her, they, them* will do.

sample case, sample room. Two words.

sanatorium, sanitarium. The form *sanitarium* is more common. Its plural is *sanitariums.*

sanctuary ends in *-uary.*

sand-. Almost all compounds are spelled as one word.

sandaled, sandaling. One *l.*

sandbag, sandbank, sandblast, sandblasted, sandblasting, sandbox, sandhog, sandlot, sandlotter, sandman, sandpaper, sandwich. One word.

sandwich board, sandwich man. Two words.

sang. Past tense of *sing.*

sangfroid. One word.

sanguine. Don't use *sanguine* when *hopeful* or *confident* will do.

sanitarium, sanitariums. More common than *sanatorium.*

sanitary. *I* in the middle, ends in *-ary.*

sanitation. *I* in the middle.

sanitation man, sanitation men. There's a trend toward spelling these words as one word, *sanitationman, sanitationmen.*

sank. Past tense of *sink.*

sans. Don't use *sans* when *without* will do.

sans serif. Two words.

sapient. Don't use *sapient* when *wise* will do.

Sapphic is spelled with *pph.* Capital *S.*

sapphire is spelled with *pph.*

Sappho is spelled with *pph.*

sarcastically ends in *-ally.*

sarcophagus, sarcophagi.

sarge, short for *sergeant,* is listed as standard usage in Webster's.

(sargent). Misspelling of *sergeant.*

sari. Spell it so.

sarsaparilla. Double *l.*

sartorial. Don't use *sartorial* when a simple word will do or when it can be left out.

sashay is listed in Webster's as standard usage.

sash weight. Two words.

sassy is listed in Webster's as standard usage.

sated. Don't use *sated* when *satisfied* or *full* will do.

satellite. Double *l,* ends in *-ite.*

satiety ends in *-iety.*

satin ends in *-in.*

satinet ends in *-et.*

satiric, satyric. *Satiric* means sarcastic, *satyric* has to do with woodland gods in Greek mythology.

satirize ends in *-ize.*

satisfied. Don't use *satisfied* when *sure* or *convinced* will do.

satyr. The lecherous Greek gods are spelled with *y.*

saucepan. One word.

saucer.

sauerbraten is spelled with *auer.*

sauerkraut is spelled with *auer.*

sauna is spelled with *au,* ends in *a.*

sauté, sautéed, sautéing. Accent, two *e*'s in the past tense.

sauterne ends in *-e.*

savable. No *e* after *v.*

savanna. Spell it without *h* at the end.

savant. Don't use *savant* when *scientist, expert* etc. will do.

save. Don't use *save* when *but* or *except* will do.

savior. The common US spelling ends in *-or.* Capital *S* when referring to Christ.

savor ends in *-or.*

savory ends in *-ory.*

savvy. Double *v.*

saw, sawed, sawed.

saw-. Most compounds are spelled as one word.

sawbones, sawbuck, sawdust, sawhorse, sawlog, sawmill, sawtooth. One word.

say. Don't strain for synonyms for *said.* Use *said. Say* in the sense of *about, for instance* is standard usage.

says.

say-so (noun). Hyphened. Standard usage.

scab, scabbed, scabbing. Double *b* in all forms except *scab.*

scalable ends in -*able,* not -*eable.*

scalawag. One *l.*

scallop, scalloped, scalloping. One *p* in all forms.

scallopini. Double *l,* one *p.*

scaly. No *e.*

scampi. The plural is *scampi* too.

scan in the sense of skim is now standard usage.

scandalize ends in -*ize.*

scandalmonger, scandalmongering. One word.

scant. Don't use *scant* when *little, barely, only* will do.

scarcely, like *hardly,* is often idiomatically used to form a double negative.

scarcely . . . than. Listed as standard usage in Webster's.

scare up is listed as standard usage in Webster's.

scarf, scarfs.

scar-face, scar-faced. Hyphened.

scarfpin. One word.

scary. No *e.*

scatterbrain, scatterbrained, scattershot, scattersite. One word.

scenario, scenarios. Spelled with *sc.*

scene, scenery. Spelled with *sc.*

sceneshifter. One word.

scenic. Spelled with *sc.*

scepter ends in -*er.*

(sceptic, sceptical, scepticism). The common US spellings are *skeptic, skeptical, skepticism.*

schedule starts with *sch.*

scheme, schemed, scheming.

schism starts with *sch.*

schist starts with *sch.*

schizo-. Compounds are spelled as one word.

schizophrenia, schizophrenic.

schlemiel. Spell it so. Listed as standard usage in Webster's.

schlepp. Double *p.* Slang.

schlock. Listed as standard usage in Webster's.

schmaltz, schmaltzy are spelled with *tz.* Listed as standard usage in Webster's.

schmear. Slang.

schmo, schmoes. Slang.

schmooze. Spell it with *z.* Slang.

schmuck. Slang.

schnapps. Double *p*.

schnauzer.

schnitzel ends in *-el*.

schnook. Slang.

schnorrer is listed in Webster's as standard usage.

scholar, scholarly, scholarship are spelled with *ar*.

scholastically ends in *-ally*.

school-. Almost all compounds are spelled as one word.

schoolbag. One word.

school board. Two words.

schoolbook, schoolboy. One word.

school bus. Two words.

schoolchild, schoolchildren, schoolgirl, schoolhouse. One word.

schoolmarm. More common than *schoolma'am*.

schoolmaster, schoolmate, schoolmistress, schoolroom, school-teacher, schoolteaching, schooltime, schoolwork, schoolyard. One word.

school year. Two words.

schooner starts with *sch*.

(schtick). Spell it *shtick*. Listed in Webster's as standard usage.

schuss is spelled with *sch*.

sciatica starts with *sc*.

sci-fi is listed in Webster's as standard usage. Hyphened.

scimitar start with *sc* and ends in *-ar*.

scintilla, scintillas. *Sc* and double *l*.

scintillate, scintillating. *Sc* and double *l*.

scion, cion. The spelling varies. In the sense of a shoot or twig, the common spelling is *cion*, but for a descendant or child it's always *scion*.

scissors. Spelled with *sc* and double *s*. Use the plural verb. For the singular, say *a pair of scissors*.

sclerosis, scleroses.

scofflaw. One word.

scoreboard, scorecard, scorekeeper. One word.

Scotch, Scotchman, Scotchwoman. These are the common US forms. In England and Scotland *Scot, Scots* and *Scottish* are also used.

scot-free. Hyphened.

scotch plaid. Small *s*.

Scotch tape. Capital *S*.

scoundrel ends in *-el*.

scour is spelled with *our.*

scourge is spelled with *our.*

scram is listed in Webster's as standard usage.

scrapbook. One word.

scrap heap, scrap iron, scrap paper. Two words.

scratch board, scratch pad, scratch paper. Two words.

screenplay, screenwriter. One word.

screwball, screwdriver. One word.

screw up is listed in Webster's as standard usage.

screwy is listed in Webster's as standard usage.

scrip, script. *Scrip* means certificate, paper money etc., a *script* is a piece of writing.

Scripture. Capital *S.*

scrollwork. One word.

scrumptious is listed in Webster's as standard usage.

scrupulous. *U* after *p.*

scrutinize ends in *-ize.*

(sculduggery). Spell it *skulduggery.*

scull, skull. A *scull* is an oar, a *skull* is the skeleton of a head.

sculpt. Standard usage.

sculptor ends in *-or.*

sculptress. Not considered objectionable.

sculpture.

scurrilous. Double *r,* followed by *i.*

(scutcheon). The common form is *escutcheon.*

Scylla. The phrase is *between Scylla and Charybdis.*

scythe is spelled with *y* and ends in *-the.*

sea-. Most compounds are spelled as one word.

seabed, seabird, seaboard, seaborne, seacoast, seafare, seafarer, seafaring, seafood, seafront, seagirt, seagoing. One word.

sea green, sea gull, sea horse, sea level. Two words.

Sealyham terrier. Capital *S.*

seaman, seamanlike, seamanship. One word.

seamstress.

séance. Accent.

seaplane, seaport. One word.

searchlight, searchplane. One word.

seascape, seashell, seashore, seasick, seasickness, seaside. One word.

seasonable, seasonal. Frost in winter is *seasonable,* Christmas card sales are *seasonal.*

seasons. Don't capitalize *spring, summer, autumn, fall, winter.*

seat belt, seat cover. Two words.

seawall, seaweed, seaworthy. One word.

sebaceous ends in *-ceous.*

secede ends in *-ede.*

secession. One *c,* double *s.*

second. Follow Webster's and the New York Times and write *2d,* not *2nd.*

second-best, second-class, second-degree, second-guess. Hyphened.

secondhand. One word.

second in command. Three words.

(secondly). The common form of the adverb is *second.*

second mate. Two words.

second-rate. Hyphened.

second sight. Two words.

second-string (adjective). Hyphened.

secrecy ends in *-cy.*

secretariat ends in *-iat.*

secretary ends in *-ary.*

secure. Don't use *secure* when *get* will do.

security blanket. Standard usage.

securityholder. One word.

-sede. Only *supersede* ends in *-sede.*

sedentary ends in *-ary.*

sedition, seditious end in *-ion, -ious.*

seduce starts with *se-.*

seducible ends in *-ible.*

see, meaning seat of a bishop, is so spelled.

seeable ends in *-able.*

seedbed, seedcake. One word.

seed money, seed plant. Two words.

seedpod. One word.

seeing that, seeing as. Listed in Webster's as standard usage.

seek. Don't use *seek* when *try* or *look for* will do.

-seeker. Compounds are spelled as one word, e.g. *truthseeker.*

seem. *Can't seem to, cannot seem to* is a common idiom, listed as standard usage in Webster's, e.g. *I can't seem to solve this problem.*

seer. Two *e*'s.

seesaw. One word.

see where, as in *I see where the Mets won the series,* is a common idiom.

(seige). Misspelling of *siege.*

seine is spelled with *ei.*

seisin. The common spelling of this legal term ends in *-sin.*

seismic, seismograph, seismology. Spelled with *ei.*

seize, seizure. Spelled with *eiz.*

seldom-. Compounds are hyphened, e.g. *seldom-seen, seldom-heard.*

select. Don't use *select* when *pick* or *choose* will do.

selection. Don't use *selection* when *choice* will do.

selectman. One word.

self, selves.

self-. Compounds are hyphened except for *selfhood, selfless, selfsame.*

self-abasement, self-absorbed, self-addressed, self-advancement, self-appointed, self-centered. Hyphened.

(self-confessed). Write *confessed.*

self-confidence, self-conscious. Hyphened.

self-controlled. Double *l.*

self-defense ends in *-se.*

self-destruct. Standard usage.

self-discipline is spelled with *sc.*

self-employed, self-employment. Hyphened.

self-fulfillment. First one *l,* then two.

selfhood, selfless. One word.

self-made. Hyphened.

selfness. One word.

self-possessed, self-possession. Two double *s*'s.

self-reliance, self-reliant end in *-ance, -ant.*

self-respect. Hyphened.

self-righteous ends in *-eous.*

selfsame. One word.

self-service. Hyphened.

self-starter, referring to a person, is listed as standard usage in Webster's.

(self-surrender). Write *surrender.*

selloff, sellout. One word.

selvage, salvage. *Selvage* is an edging, *salvage* means save.

semi-. Compounds are spelled as one word, except when the main part starts with *i* or a capital, e.g. *semi-invalid, semi-Christian. Semi-* means half.

semiannual, semicircle. One word.

semicolon. Semicolons are no longer common. Try to avoid them. Don't use a semicolon when a comma or period will do.

Semicolons are still sometimes used before such adverbs as *however,* e.g. *Semicolons are now rare; however, they're not yet extinct.* But it's more common today to use a period and write *Semicolons are now rare. However, they're not yet extinct.*

Another use of the semicolon is in long sentences with clauses or phrases that contain commas, e.g. *The elected officers are John Smith, president; Alexander Truman, vice president; Anna Newman, treasurer; and Benjamin Forster, secretary.* But it's more common today to use commas and write *The elected officers are John Smith, president, Alexander Truman, vice president, Anna Newman, treasurer, and Benjamin Forster, secretary.*

Finally, there's the balanced sentence, e.g. *The schnitzel was delicious; the wine was just right; and the apple strudel was superb.* But it's more common today to use commas and write *The schnitzel was delicious, the wine was just right and the apple strudel was superb.* (No comma before the *and.*)

semidarkness, semidetached, semifinal, semiformal. One word.

semi-independent, semi-invalid. Hyphened.

semiliterate. One word.

semimonthly means twice a month.

semiofficial, semiprecious, semiprivate, semiprofessional, semi-retired, semiskilled, semisoft, semisweet. One word.

semiweekly means twice a week.

(sempstress). Write *seamstress.*

senator ends in *-or.* Small *s* except before a name.

senatorial. Small *s.*

sendoff. One word.

senescence, senescent end in *-ence, -ent.* Watch the *sc.*

seneschal is spelled with *sch.*

senior citizen is listed as standard usage in the Random House dictionary.

senor, senora, senorita. The spelling without a tilde over the *n* is common.

sense in the meaning of grasp, perceive is standard usage.

sensibility does not mean sensibleness, but sensitivity or awareness.

sensible, sensitive, susceptible. The common meaning of *sensible* is reasonable, that of *sensitive* easily affected, that of *susceptible* liable to be influenced.

sensitize ends in *-ize*.

sensual, sensuous. *Sensual* means carnal, gross, worldly, *sensuous* means refined, sensitive. *Sensual* is used in a bad sense, *sensuous* in a good sense.

sentence fragments are common in good, idiomatic English. E.g. *Not that I know of. Of course. One more thing. No interruptions. Even more so. Ah well. Not to speak of the expense. Onwards and upwards.*

sentence length. Good newspaper and magazine writers' sentences average between 15 and 17 words. If your sentences are longer, break them up. Or try to write a very short sentence now and then. Or a sentence fragment. Like this one.

sententious ends in *-tious.*

sentience, sentient end in *-ience, -ient.*

separable ends in *-able.* It has *par* in it.

separate has *par* in it.

separation has *par* in it.

separator has *par* in it. Ends in *-or.*

(seperate). Misspelling of *separate.*

sepsis, sepses.

septet ends in *-et.*

septicemia.

septuagenarian. Watch the *ua.*

sepulcher is spelled with *ch* and ends in *-er.*

sepulchral is spelled with *ch.*

sequela, sequelae.

sequence ends in *-ence.*

sequence of tenses. The tense of the subordinate clause is normally the same as that of the main clause, e.g. *He admitted he was wrong.* If what happened in the subordinate clause happened before the event told in the main clause, you have to go one step further into the past, e.g. *He admitted he had been wrong.* If the subordinate clause deals with something timeless, use the present tense, e.g. *He admitted it is better to tell the truth.* See also HAVE, WOULD HAVE.

sequential ends in *-tial.*

sequined. One *n.*

seraglio, seraglios. Silent *g.*

serendipitous, serendipity. So spelled. Means the gift of making agreeable discoveries by accident.

serf, surf. A *serf* lives in bondage, *surf* is the swell of the sea.

serge, surge. *Serge* is a fabric, *surge* means swell.

sergeant is spelled with *er* even though pronounced with *ar*. Ends in *-ant*.

sergeant at arms. No hyphens.

sergeant major, sergeants major.

serial, cereal. A *serial* is a story in installments, a *cereal* is a breakfast food.

seriatim ends in *-im*.

series. The plural is also *series.*

    Follow newspaper usage and don't put a comma before the last item in a series, e.g. *tall, dark and handsome.*

serif.

serio-. Spell compounds as one word, e.g. *seriocomic.*

(serjeant). The US spelling is *sergeant.*

serum, serums.

serviceable ends in *-eable.*

serviceman, servicewoman. One word.

serviette ends in *-ette.* Don't use *serviette* instead of *napkin.*

servo-. Compounds are spelled as one word.

sesame. Two single *s*'s, *e* at the end.

sesqui-. Compounds are spelled as one word.

sesquicentennial, sesquipedalian.

session, cession. *Session* means meeting, *cession* means yielding.

sestet ends in *-et.* In music, use *sextet.*

set-. Most compounds are spelled as one word.

setaceous ends in *-eous.*

setback. One word.

set forth. Don't use *set forth* when *write* will do.

set-in. Hyphened.

setoff, setout (nouns). One word.

set piece. Two words.

settee. Double *t,* double *e.*

settler, settlor. The ordinary spelling is *settler,* the legal term is spelled *settlor.*

set-to. Hyphened.

setup (noun). One word.

sevenfold. One word.

sevens. No apostrophe. Or write *7s.*

17th century. Don't spell it out. It means the 1600s.

seventies. No apostrophe. Or write *70s*.

seventy-one etc. Hyphened.

sever, severed, severing.

severance ends in *-ance*.

severely, severity.

sew, sow. *Sew, sewed, sewn* means using needle and thread, *sow, sowed, sown* means plant or scatter.

sewage, sewerage. *Sewage* means waste matter, *sewerage* means a drainage system but is often used in the sense of sewage.

sex in the sense of sex act is standard usage.

sexpot is listed in Webster's as standard usage.

sextet ends in *-et*.

sexy is listed in Webster's as standard usage.

sforzando. So spelled.

shack up is listed in Webster's as standard usage.

shade, shadow. You can cast a *shadow*, but not a *shade*.

shadowbox, shadowboxing. One word.

shady in the sense of disreputable is listed in Webster's as standard usage.

shaft (verb) in the sense of treating someone unfairly or harshly is listed in Webster's as slang. But *shaft* (noun) in the sense of harsh or unfair treatment is listed as standard usage.

shagreen, chagrin. *Shagreen* is the leather, *chagrin* is a feeling of disappointment.

shakable. No *e* after *k*.

shakedown (noun, adj.). One word. Standard usage in the sense of extortion.

shakeout (noun). One word.

Shakespeare, Shakespearean. These are the standard spellings.

shakeup (noun). One word.

shako, shakos.

shaky. No *e*.

shall, will. In common US usage, *will* rather than *shall* is used to express the simple future, e.g. *I will be there at 10 o'clock.—You will see.*

　　Shall is used in first-person questions, e.g. *Shall we go?* and to express command or determination, e.g. *Jack shall go.—They shall not pass.*

shambles, with the singular verb, meaning a state of disorder, is standard usage.

shamefaced. One word.

shammy is a common variant spelling of *chamois.*

shampoo, shampooed, shampooing.

shanghai, shanghaied, shangaiing. Yes, *shanghaiing* is spelled with double *i.*

Shangri-la. So spelled. Capital *S.*

shan't. Common contraction of *shall not.*

shanty, chantey. *Shanty* is the spelling for the hut, *chantey* for the sailor's song.

shantytown. One word.

shapable. No *e* before *-able.*

-shaped. Compounds are hyphened, e.g. *bell-shaped.*

shapeup (noun). One word.

sharable. No *e* before *-able.*

sharecrop, sharecropper, shareholder, shareout. One word.

sharp (adverb) is standard usage, e.g. *eight o'clock sharp.*

sharpie, sharpies. Standard usage. Ends in *-ie.*

sharpshooter, sharpshooting. One word.

shashlik.

shave, shaved, shaved or **shaven.**

she. It is no longer common to use *she* in referring to nations, ships or cities. Write *it,* e.g. *Finland has paid its debts.—The Bolero begins its cruise on November 15.* On the other hand, *she* in referring to a car, machine etc. is standard usage.

   She instead of *her* is listed as substandard in Webster's. But Shakespeare wrote "You have seen Cassio and she together" (Othello, IV, ii, 3).

she (name) looks awkward. Usually this device is unnecessary because in context the reference is clear without it. *Susan told Emma she had nothing to do with it* is clear; you don't need to write *she (Susan).* If there *is* a possibility of misreading, repeat the name without *she.*

sheaf, sheaves.

shear, sheer. *Shear* means cut off hair, *sheer* means bright, pure.

sheared, shorn. The normal past participle is *sheared.* In figurative senses use *shorn,* e.g. *shorn lamb.*

shears, meaning scissors, is spelled with *ea.*

shebang is listed as standard usage in Webster's.

she'd. Common contraction of *she had* or *she would.*

sheep-. Almost all compounds are spelled as one word.

sheep-dip. Hyphened.

sheepdog, sheepherder, sheepherding, sheeplike, sheepshear, sheepshearer, sheepshearing, sheepskin. One word.

sheet metal. Two words.

sheetrock. One word.

sheik, chic. A *sheik* is an Arab chief, *chic* means stylish. The common spelling is *sheik* with no *h* at the end.

shelf, shelves.

shelf-ful, shelf-fuls.

shelf life, shelf list. Two words.

she'll. Common contraction of *she will, she shall.*

shellac, shellacked, shellacking. *Ck* in all forms but *shellac.*

shellback, shellfire, shellfish. One word.

shell game. Two words.

shell-like. Hyphened.

shell out is listed as standard usage in Webster's.

shell shock. Two words.

shell-shocked. Hyphened.

shenanigan. So spelled. Standard usage.

shepherd. Silent *h.*

sherbet ends in *-et.*

sheriff. One *r,* two *f*'s.

she's. Common contraction of *she is, she has.*

shibboleth in the sense of catchword or slogan is standard usage.

shield is spelled with *ie.*

shier, shiest. Common spellings of the comparative and superlative forms of *shy.*

shill is listed as standard usage in Webster's.

shillelagh. The common spelling ends in *-agh.*

shilly-shally, shilly-shallied, shilly-shallying. Hyphened.

(shily). The common spelling is *shyly.*

shimmy, shimmied, shimmying.

shindig is listed as standard usage in Webster's.

shine, shone or **shined, shining.** The sun *shone,* but he *shined* his shoes.

shinplaster. One word.

shiny. No *e.*

ship, boat. Webster's says it's standard usage to use the word *boat* in referring to a large ship. The word has been so used since 1572.

ship-. Compounds are spelled as one word.

shipboard, shipborne, shipbuilder, shipbuilding, shipfitter, ship-load, shipmaster, shipmate, shipowner, shipowning. One word.

shipping clerk. Two words.

shipshape, shipside, shipway, shipwreck, shipwrecked, shipyard. One word.

shirtfront, shirtmaker. One word.

shirt-sleeve. Hyphened.

shirttail, shirtwaist. One word.

shish kebab.

shiv is slang.

(shlemiehl). Spell it *schlemiel.* Listed as standard usage in Webster's.

(shlock). Spell it *schlock.* Listed as standard usage in Webster's.

shock absorber, shock therapy, shock troops, shock wave. Two words.

shoe, shod, shoeing.

shoe-. Compounds are spelled as one word.

shoeblack, shoehorn, shoelace, shoemaker, shoemaking, shoe-shine, shoestring. One word.

shoo, shooed, shooing.

shoo-in is listed in Webster's as standard usage.

shook up. Two words. Listed in Webster's as standard usage in the sense of agitated.

shootout (noun). One word. Listed in Webster's as standard usage.

-shop. Compounds are spelled as one word, e.g. *bakeshop, workshop.*

shop-. Almost all compounds are spelled as one word.

shopkeeper, shoplifter, shoplifting, shopowner. One word.

shop steward. Two words.

shoptalk, shopwindow, shopworn. One word.

shorefront. One word.

shore leave. Two words.

shoreline, shoreside. One word.

shoreward, shorewards. Both forms are common.

short-. Some compounds are spelled as one word, some as two, some are hyphened.

shortbread, shortcake, shortchange, shortchanger. One word.

short circuit (noun). Two words.

short-circuit (verb). Hyphened.

shortcoming, shortcut. One word.

shortened words. Many shortened words are now standard usage, e.g. *ad, bra, exam, gas, gym, lab, phone, pro, rhino, vet.* Use them without quotes or apostrophes.

shortfall, shorthand, shorthanded, shorthorn. One word.

short-lived. Hyphened.

short-order (adj.). Hyphened.

shortsighted, shortstop. One word.

short story. Never hyphened.

short supply. Don't use *in short supply* when *scarce* will do.

short-tempered, short-term. Hyphened.

shorttime. One word.

shortwave. One word.

short-winded. Hyphened.

shorty, shorties. Listed as standard usage in Webster's.

shotgun, shotproof, shotput, shotputting. One word.

should, would. In common US usage *should* is used in the sense of *ought to,* e.g. *You should have been there.* Otherwise it is common to say *would* rather than *should,* e.g. *I would say so* rather than *I should say so.* There are also some other standard idiomatic uses, e.g. *if this should happen.*

shoulder is spelled with *ou.*

shoulder bag, shoulder blade, shoulder strap. Two words.

should have. See WOULD HAVE.

shouldn't. Common contraction of *should not.*

should've. There's a trend toward contracting *should have* to *should've.*

shovel, shoveled, shoveler, shoveling. One *l* in all forms.

shovelful, shovelfuls.

show, showed, shown.

show-. Compounds are spelled as one word.

show biz. Two words. Listed as standard usage in Webster's.

showboat, showcase, showdown, showman, showoff (noun), **showpiece, showplace, showroom, showstopper.** One word.

show up. Listed as standard usage in Webster's.

show window. Two words.

shrewd is spelled with *ew.*

shriek is spelled with *ie.*

shrink, shrank, shrunk. The adjective is *shrunken.*

shrink in the sense of psychiatrist is listed as standard usage in Webster's.

shrive, shrived, shriven. The common forms.

shrivel, shriveled, shriveling. One *l* in all forms.

shtetl. One *e*.

shtick. Spelled with *sh*. Listed in Webster's as standard usage.

shutaway, shutdown (noun). One word.

shut-eye, shut-in (noun). Hyphened.

shutoff (noun), **shutout** (noun). One word.

shut up in the sense of stop talking is listed in Webster's as standard usage.

shy, shier, shiest, shied, shying, shyly, shyness. Common US spellings.

shyster. Listed in Webster's as standard usage.

sibilant ends in *-ant*.

sibling. Don't use *sibling* if *brother* or *sister* will do. Don't use *siblings* if *brothers and (or) sisters* will do.

sibyl is spelled with *by* in it. But the girl's name is spelled either *Sibyl* or *Sybil*.

sic. A Latin word meaning *so,* used in parentheses to show that a word was misspelled or misused in the quoted original, e.g. "This book is a set of clever miniature soliloquys *(sic)* and bi-liloquys *(sic)*."

sic, sicked, sicking. Set to attack.

sick, ill. Interchangeable in the US, but *ill* is slightly more formal. Don't use *ill* when *sick* will do. *Sick* in the sense of disgusted or morbid is standard usage.

sickbed. One word.

sick call. Two words.

sickle ends in *-le*.

sick leave. Two words.

sicklist, sickroom. One word.

side-. Most compounds are spelled as one word.

sidearm (baseball). One word.

side-arm (weapon). Two words.

sideboard, sideburns, sidecar, sidehead, sidekick, sidelight, sideline. One word.

side road. Two words.

sidesaddle, sideslip, sidestep, sidestroke, sideswipe, sidetrack, sidewalk. One word.

sideward, sidewards. Both forms are common.

sideways, sidewise. One word.

sidle, sidled, sidling.

siege is spelled with *ie*. Remember "the *sie*ge of *Si*ngapore."

Siena, the city, is spelled with a capital *S* and one *n*.

sienna, the color, is spelled with a small *s* and two *n*'s.

sieve is spelled with *ie*. Has *Eve* in it.

(sieze). Misspelling of *seize*.

sightread, sightreader, sightreading, sightsee, sightseeing, sightseer. One word.

signal, signaled, signaling. One *l* in all forms.

signalize. Don't use *signalize* when *signal* will do.

signatory ends in *-ory*.

signify, signified, signifying.

signoff (noun). One word.

sign painter. Two words.

signpost. One word.

sign up is standard usage.

silhouette ends in *-ette*.

silico-. Compounds are spelled as one word.

silk screen. Two words.

silkworm. One word.

silliness has an *i* in the middle.

silo, silos.

(silvan). The common spelling is *sylvan*.

silver fox. Two words.

silverware. One word.

silver wedding. Two words.

simian. Don't use *simian* when *ape* or *monkey* will do.

similar ends in *-ar*. There are only two *i*'s. Don't use *similar* when you mean *the same*.

similar to. Don't use *similar to* when *like* will do.

simile ends in *e*.

simon-pure. Hyphened.

simpatico. Standard usage.

simpleminded, simplemindedness. One word.

simulcast. One word, *u* after *m*.

simultaneous, simultaneously. Spelled with *eous*.

sin, sinned, sinning. Double *n* in all forms except *sin*.

since. Don't use *ago* before *since*. Just write *since*, e.g. *It's six years since my father died.*

sincerely ends in *-ely*. Remember, it contains the word *rely*. *Sincerely* and *Sincerely yours* are less formal than *Yours truly* and *Very truly yours* and are getting more common at the end of business letters.

sinecure is spelled with *e* in the middle.

sine die. Two words. Don't underline (italicize).

sine qua non. Three words. Don't use *sine qua non* when *essential* will do.

sing, sang, sung.

singing, singeing. *Singing* means vocalizing, *singeing* means burning.

singlehanded, singleminded, singlemindedness. Follow the trend and spell these words as one word.

singsong. One word.

sink, sank, sunk.

sinkhole. One word.

sinuous ends in *-uous.*

sinus, sinuses.

sinusitis. Spelled with *us* in the middle.

-sion. Don't use words ending in *-sion* when other words will do.

Sioux is spelled like this. The plural is *Sioux* too.

siphon. This is the common spelling.

sir. In referring to English knights and baronets, it is right to say *Sir William* or *Sir William Brown,* but wrong to say *Sir Brown.* In a second mention, write simply *Brown.*

siren.

sirocco, siroccos. One *r,* two *c*'s.

(sirup, sirupy). The spellings *syrup, syrupy* are more common.

(sirynge). Misspelling of *syringe.*

sister-in-law, sisters-in-law. Two hyphens.

Sisyphus. First *i,* then *y.*

sitcom. One word.

sitdown (noun, adj.). Spelled as one word in the New York Times and the GPO Style Manual.

site, cite. *Site* means place, *cite* means quote.

sit-in (adj.). Hyphened.

sitting room. Two words.

situate, situated. *Situate* is overformal for *situated.* But don't even use *situated* when you can leave it out.

situs, situses.

sitz bath. Two words.

sitzfleisch, sitzkrieg.

sixes. No apostrophe in *sixes* or *6s.*

six-shooter. Hyphened.

16th century. Don't spell it out. It means the 1500s.

sixties. No apostrophe in *the sixties* or *the 60s.*

sixty-one etc. Hyphened.

sizable. No *e* after *z*.

size, sized. *Size* as part of a compound adjective is standard usage, e.g. *a medium-size shirt.* The *d* at the end is commonly left out.

size. Don't use *in size* when it isn't necessary, e.g. write *the room was large* (not *large in size*).

size up is listed in Webster's as standard usage.

skedaddle. Standard usage.

skein is spelled with *ei*.

skeleton, skeletons.

skeptic, skeptical, skeptically. The common US spelling is with *sk*.

sketchbook. One word.

ski, skied, skiing, skier.

skidproof. One word.

ski jump, ski lift. Two words.

skillful. First two *l*'s, then one.

skim milk. Two words.

skindeep, skindive, skindiver, skindiving. One word.

skin flick. Two words. Listed in Webster's as standard usage.

skintight. One word.

skiwear. One word.

skulduggery. Spell it with one *l*.

skull, scull. A *skull* is the skeleton of a head, a *scull* is an oar.

skullcap. One word.

sky, skies.

sky-blue. Hyphened.

skyborne, skycap, skydiving. One word.

skyey is spelled with *e*.

skyhook, skyjack, skyjacker, skyjacking, skylark, skylight, skyline, skyrocket, skyscraper, skywrite, skywriter, skywriting. One word.

slalom ends in *-om*.

slam-bang. Hyphened.

slander, libel. If a defamation is spoken or done by gesture, it's *slander,* if it's published or broadcast, it's *libel.*

slanderous. *E* between *d* and *r*.

slang means very informal usage. Slang expressions are often quickly accepted as standard usage, e.g. *corny, gimmick, hangup, hunky-dory, pep, slob, snow job, spiffy.* Don't hesitate to use such words when they fit the context.

slapdash, slaphappy, slapstick. One word.

slaveholder, slaveholding. One word.

slave market. Two words.

slaveowner. One word.

slavey is spelled with *e*.

slay, slew, slain. Don't use *slay* when *kill* or *murder* will do.

sleazy is spelled with *ea*.

sledgehammer. One word.

sleeper in the sense of unexpected success is listed as standard usage in Webster's.

sleepwalk, sleepwalker, sleepwalking. One word.

sleigh is spelled with *eigh*.

sleight of hand. Three words. Spelled with *eigh*.

slenderize is standard usage.

sleuth is listed in Webster's as standard usage for *detective*. But don't use *sleuth* when *detective* will do.

sliceable ends in *-eable*.

slide rule. Two words.

slier, sliest. The common spellings.

(slily). The common spelling is *slyly*.

slimy. No *e*.

slimsy, slimpsy. Both spellings are listed in Webster's as standard usage.

sling, slung, slung.

slingshot. One word.

slink, slunk, slunk.

slipcase, slipcover, slipknot. One word.

slip-on (noun). Hyphened.

slipup (noun). One word. Listed in Webster's as standard usage.

slob. Listed in Webster's as standard usage.

slot machine. Two words.

slough, slew. The common spelling for the inlet or backwater is *slough*.

slow, slowly. Both forms of the adverb are common. *Slow*, as in *go slow*, has been used since 1500. Shakespeare wrote in Midsummer Night's Dream (I, i, 3): "But, O, methinks, how slow This old moon wanes!"

slowdown (noun), **slowpoke, slowup** (noun). One word.

sluggard. Double *g*.

sluggish. Double *g*.

sluice is spelled with *ui*.

slumber. Don't use *slumber* when *sleep* will do.

slumberous. Commonly spelled with *e.*

slumdweller, slumlord. One word.

slur, slurred, slurring.

sly, slier, sliest, slyly, slyness. These are the most common spellings for the various forms.

small businessman. The common spelling. No hyphen.

small-claims court. One hyphen.

(small in size). Say *small.*

smallpox, smalltalk. One word.

small-scale. Hyphenated.

smalltime, smalltown (adj.). One word.

smarmy. Listed in Webster's as standard usage.

smarty. Spell it with *y.* Listed in Webster's as standard usage.

smashup (noun). One word.

smell, smelled.

smidgen. Commonly so spelled.

-smith. Compounds are spelled as one word, e.g. *goldsmith, silver-smith.*

smithereens.

smog. Standard usage.

smokable. No *e.*

smoke-filled. Hyphenated.

smokehouse, smokeproof, smokescreen. One word.

smoky. No *e.* Makes *smokier, smokiest, smokiness, smokily.*

smolder. Commonly spelled without *u.*

smooth (verb). No *e* at the end.

smoothy. Spell it with *y.* Listed in Webster's as standard usage.

smorgasbord. No diacritical marks.

snack bar. Two words.

snafu. Standard usage.

snail-like. Hyphenated.

snakebite, snakepit, snakeskin. One word.

snaky. No *e.*

snapback. One word.

snap-brim. Hyphenated.

snapshot. One word.

sneak, sneaked, sneaking. The past tense *snuck* is listed in Webster's as a standard variant form.

snicker. More common than *snigger.*

snivel, sniveled, sniveling. One *l* in all forms.

(snobbism). The common word is *snobbery.*

snorkel, snorkeled, snorkeling.

snow-. Most compounds are spelled as one word.

snowball, snowbank. One word.

snow-blind. Hyphened.

snowbound, snowcapped, snowdrift, snowdrop, snowfall, snow-flake. One word.

snow job. Listed in Webster's as standard usage.

snowman, snowmobile, snowplow, snowshoe, snowstorm, snow-suit. One word.

snow-white. Hyphened.

snub-nosed. Hyphened.

so in the sense of *very* is standard usage, e.g. *I'm so tired.*
   Don't put a comma after *So* at the start of a sentence, e.g. *So the battle started.*

soapbox. One word.

soap bubble. Two words.

soap opera is listed as standard usage in Webster's.

soapsuds. One word.

soar, sore. *Soar* means rise high, *sore* means painful.

so as to. Don't write *so as to* when *to* will do.

sob sister, sob story. Two words.

sobersided, sobersides. One word.

so-called. Don't use *so-called* and quotes. Use quotes only.

soccer is spelled with double *c.*

socialism, socialist. Small *s* except in titles, e.g. *Socialist Party.*

socialite. Standard usage.

social security. Capitalize only when you mean the federal agency, otherwise use small *s*'s. This is the usage given in the GPO Style Manual.

socio-. Compounds are spelled as one word.

socioeconomic. One word.

sock away. Listed in Webster's as standard usage.

soda jerk, soda pop, soda water. Two words.

soddenness. Double *d,* double *n.*

(sodder). Misspelling of *solder.*

sofa bed. Two words.

so far as . . . is concerned. Don't use this phrase when a shorter, straightforward sentence will do. E.g. instead of *So far as women are concerned, discrimination is common* write *Discrimination against women is common.*

soft-boiled. Hyphened.

softbound, softheaded, softhearted. One word.

soft-pedal, soft-pedaled, soft-pedaling. Hyphened, one *l* in all forms.

soft-shoe, soft-soap, soft-spoken. Hyphened.

softy. The common spelling ends in *-y*. Listed as standard usage in Webster's.

soi-disant. No underlining (italics).

soigné, soignée. Spelled with accent. One extra *e* for feminine form.

soilless. Double *l.*

soiree. Commonly spelled without accent.

sojourn. Spelled with *ou.*

solarium, solariums.

solder is spelled with a silent *l.*

soldierlike. One word.

soldier-statesman. Hyphened.

solely. *E* between two *l*'s.

solemn. Silent *n* at the end.

solemnness. Double *n.*

solemnize ends in *-ize.*

solicitor ends in *-or.*

soliloquize ends in *-ize.* Two single *l*'s.

soliloquy, soliloquies.

solo, solos; soloed, (he) soloes, soloing.

solon. Don't use *solon* when *Congressman, senator, representative* etc. will do.

so long as. Standard usage in the senses of *as long as, if* and *since.*

soluble, solvable. *Solvable* is used only for problems, but *soluble* is used for problems and substances.

somato-. Compounds are spelled as one word, e.g. *somatogenic.*

somber ends in *-er.*

sombrero, sombreros.

someday, someone. One word.

someplace (one word) is listed in Webster's as standard usage.

somersault. Common spelling.

sometime, sometimes. One word.

someway, someways. Standard usage.

somewhere, somewheres. Webster's lists the form *somewheres* as a standard variant.

somnolence, somnolent end in *-ence, -ent.*

songwriter, songwriting. One word.

son-in-law, sons-in-law. Two hyphens.

soot. Spelled with double *o.*

soothsayer, soothsaying. One word.

sophisticated, sophistication.

sophomore. Three *o*'s.

soprano, sopranos.

sorcerer ends in *-er.*

sore, soar. *Sore* means painful, *soar* means rise high.

sorghum. Silent *h.*

sorry is standard usage. Don't use *regret* when *be sorry* will do.

sort of, in the sense of *rather,* is a common idiom.

SOS. No periods.

so-so is standard usage.

so that. Don't write *so that* when *so* will do.

so to speak. Don't use the apologetic phrase *so to speak.* If you feel an apology is needed for using an unusual expression, change it to something else. Otherwise use it without saying *so to speak.*

soubrette ends in *-ette.*

soufflé. Spell it with the accent.

soulless. Double *l.*

soulmate. One word.

sound out. Common idiom.

soundtrack, soundtruck. One word.

soup bone. Two words.

soupçon. Spelled with cedilla.

soup plate. Two words.

soupspoon. One word.

(sourbraten). Misspelling of *sauerbraten.*

sourcebook. One word.

(sourkrout). Misspelling of *sauerkraut.*

South, south. Capital *S* for a region, small *s* for the compass direction.

southbound. One word.

southerly, southern. Spelled with *ou.*

southward, southwards. As an adverb, use either form. As an adjective, use *southward,* e.g. *a southward direction.*

souvenir. Spelled with *ou.*

sovereign, sovereignty are spelled with *eign.*

Soviet, Soviets are now used interchangeably with *Russian, Russians.*

sow, sowed, sowed or **sown, sowing.**

so what is standard usage.

sox is standard usage.

soybean. One word.

spa, spas.

spacecraft, spaceflight, spaceman, spaceport, spaceship, spacesuit, spacewalk. One word.

(spacial). Misspelling of *spatial.*

spacious, specious. *Spacious* means roomy, *specious* means deceptive.

spadeful, spadefuls.

spadework. One word.

spaghetti. Silent *h.*

spaniel ends in *-iel.*

spareribs. One word.

spark plug, sparkplug. Two words when used literally, one word when used figuratively.

spate. Don't use *spate* when *flood* will do.

spatial ends in *-tial.*

speakeasy. One word.

special, especial; specially, especially. There used to be a fine distinction between *special, specially,* meaning for a particular purpose, and *especial, especially,* meaning to an exceptional degree. But *special* and *specially* are now commonly used in both senses.

(speciality). The common US word is *specialty.*

specialization, specialize are spelled with *z.*

specie, species. *Specie* means coin, *species* means class of plants or animals.

specified. Don't use *specified* when *named* will do.

specious, spacious. *Specious* means deceptive, *spacious* means roomy.

specs, meaning eyeglasses or specifications, is listed in Webster's as standard usage.

spectacle ends in *-acle.*

spectacular ends in *-ar.*

spectator ends in *-or.*

specter ends in *-er.*

spectro-. Compounds are spelled as one word, e.g. *spectroscope.*

spectrum, spectra.

speculator ends in *-or.*

(sped). The form *speeded* is now more common.

speechmaking, speechwriter, speechwriting. One word.

speed, speeded, speeding.

speed-. Compounds are spelled as one word.

speedboat, speedboating, speedtrap, speedup, speedway, speedwriting. One word.

speleology. Spelled with *eo*.

spellbind, spellbinder, spellbinding, spellbound, spelldown. One word.

spell out, meaning explain, is listed in Webster's as standard usage.

spendthrift. One word.

spermato-. Compounds are spelled as one word.

sphincter ends in *-er*.

sphinxlike. One word.

sphygmo-. Compounds are spelled as one word, e.g. *sphygmomanometer*.

spicebox, spicecake. One word.

spicy, spiciness. So spelled.

spiderweb. One word.

spiffy is listed in Webster's as standard usage.

spiky. No *e*.

spill, spilled, spilling.

spillover (noun), **spillway.** One word.

spin, spun, spun.

spindlelegs. One word.

spinet ends in *-et*.

spinney ends in *-ey*.

spinoff. One word.

spiny. No *e*.

spiral, spiraled, spiraling. One *l* in all forms.

(spiritism). The common word is *spiritualism*.

spiritual, spirituous. *Spiritual* refers to the soul, *spirituous* to liquor.

spirochete. Common US spelling.

(spirt). The common US spelling is *spurt*.

spit, spit or **spat, spitting.** The past tense *spit* is more common than *spat*.

spit and image. The right form (not *spitting image*).

spitball, spitfire. One word.

(spitting image). Write *spit and image*.

spittoon. Double *t*, double *o*.

splashboard, splashdown. One word.

splendiferous. Listed in Webster's as standard usage.

splendor ends in *-or.*

split in the sense of leave is listed in Webster's as standard usage.

split infinitive means an infinitive with one or more words between *to* and the verb form, e.g. *I refuse to even consider it.* Split infinitives are no longer considered taboo by modern grammarians.

split-level. Hyphened.

split second. Two words.

splitup (noun). One word.

splutter, sputter. The two words are almost interchangeable, but *splutter* is closer to *stammer* and *sputter* is closer to *spit.*

spoilsport. One word.

(spoilt). The common US spelling is *spoiled.*

spokesman, spokeswoman. One word. *Spokesperson* is rare.

spongecake. One word.

spongy. No *e.*

spontaneous ends in *-eous.*

(spontaneousness). *Spontaneity* is more common.

spoof. Standard usage.

spooky. No *e.*

spoonerism. Small *s.*

spoonful, spoonfuls.

sportfisherman, sportfishing. One word.

sports car. Two words. More common than *sport car.*

sportscast, sportswear, sportswriter, sportswriting. One word.

spot check (noun). Two words.

spot-check (verb). Hyphened.

spotlight, spotweld. One word.

spouse. Don't use *spouse* when *husband, wife* or *husband or wife* will do.

sprain, strain. *Sprain* means wrench, *strain* means stretch.

spray gun. Two words.

spread-eagle. Hyphened.

spring, sprang, sprung. The past tense *sprung* is less common.

spring, the season. Don't capitalize.

springboard. One word.

spring-cleaning. Hyphened.

spring fever. Two words.

springtide, springtime. One word.

(sprung). The common form of the past tense of *spring* is *sprang.*

spry, sprier, spriest, spryly, spryness. Common spellings.

spumoni. Spell it with *i*.

spurt. Common US spelling (not *spirt*).

splutter, splutter. The two words are almost interchangeable, but *sputter* is closer to *spit* and *splutter* is closer to *stammer*.

sputum, sputa.

spy, spies, spied, spying.

spyboat, spyglass, spyhole. One word.

squalor ends in *-or*.

square in the sense of conventional person is listed as standard usage in Webster's.

square dance. Two words.

squareshooter. One word. Listed in Webster's as standard usage.

squarish. No *e*.

squeeze play. Two words.

squirearchy. Spell it with *e* before *a*.

squirrel, squirreled, squirreling. One *l* in all forms.

Sr. Abbreviation of *Senior*. Capitalize and put no comma before it, e.g. *Edward White Sr.*

-ss-. See -s-, -ss-

stabilize ends in *-ize*.

stableboy, stableman, stablemate. One word.

staccato. Two *c*'s, one *t*.

stadium, stadiums.

staff, staffs.

staffer. Standard usage.

staff sergeant. Two words.

stagecoach, stagecraft. One word.

stage door, stage fright. Two words.

stagehand. One word.

stage-manage. Hyphened.

stage set. Two words.

stagestruck. One word.

stage whisper. Two words.

stagy. Commonly spelled without *e*.

staid, stayed. *Staid* means sober, *stayed* means remained.

staircase, stairway, stairwell. One word.

stakeholder, stakeout. One word.

stalactite, stalagmite. A *stalactite* is hanging down, a *stalagmite* is standing up.

stale makes *stalely*.

stalemate. One word.

stalking-horse. Hyphened.

stall, in the sense of play for time, is listed in Webster's as standard usage.

stalwart. One *l*.

stanch, staunch. Spell it *stanch* for the verb *(she stanched her tears)* and *staunch* for the adjective *(a staunch friend)*.

stand in the sense of tolerate is standard usage.

stand-. All compounds except *stand-in* are spelled as one word.

standard-bearer. Hyphened.

standardize ends in *-ize*.

standby (noun), **standfast.** One word.

stand-in (noun). Hyphened.

standoff, standoffish, standout (noun, adj.), **standpat, standpatter, standpoint, standstill, standup** (adj.). One word.

starboard. The right side of a ship or aircraft, looking forward.

stardom, stardust, stargaze, stargazer, stargazing. One word.

stark-naked, stark-raving. Hyphened.

starlight, starlit. One word.

starry. Double *r*.

starry-eyed. Hyphened.

star-spangled. Hyphened.

start-up (noun). Hyphened.

stash is listed in Webster's as standard usage.

state (verb). Don't use *state* when *say* will do.

state (noun). Don't capitalize except when part of a title.

statecraft, statehouse. One word.

state line. Two words.

stateroom. One word.

state's evidence. Two words.

states' rights. Two words.

statewide. One word.

stationary, stationery. *Stationary* means fixed, *stationery* means writing materials.

station house. Two words.

stationmaster. One word.

station wagon. Two words.

statistic in the singular is standard usage.

statistician ends in *-ician*.

statuary ends in *-uary*.

statue, stature, statute. A *statue* is a sculpture, *stature* means height, a *statute* is a law.

statuesque. Don't write *statuesque* when *tall* will do.

statuette ends in *-ette*.

status, statuses.

status quo. No hyphen.

statute. Don't say *statute* when *law* will do.

statute book. Two words.

statutory ends in *-ory*.

staunch, stanch. Spell it *staunch* for the adjective *(a staunch friend)* and *stanch* for the verb *(she stanched her tears)*.

stay-at-home (noun, adj.). Two hyphens.

stayed, staid. *Stayed* means remained, *staid* means sober.

stay-in (noun, adj.). Hyphened.

steadfast is spelled with *ea*.

steady, steadier, steadiest, steadily, steadiness.

stealthy, stealthily. Spelled with *ea*.

steam-. Most compounds are spelled as one word.

steamboat, steamboating. One word.

steam engine. Two words.

steamfitter, steamfitting. One word.

steam heating. Two words.

steamroll, steamroller, steamroom, steamship, steamtable. One word.

steelmaker, steelmaking, steelplate. One word.

steel-trap (adj.). Hyphened.

steel wool. Two words.

steelwork, steelworker, steelyard. One word.

steeplechase, steeplechaser, steeplejack. One word.

steering column, steering gear, steering wheel. Two words.

stein is spelled with *ei*.

stem. Don't use *stem* when *come* will do.

stem-winder, stem-winding. Hyphened.

stencil, stenciled, stenciler, stenciling. One *l* in all forms.

steno-. Compounds are spelled as one word.

step. Don't write *step this way, step in,* when *come this way, come in* will do.

step-. Most compounds are spelled as one word.

stepbrother, stepchild, stepdaughter. One word.

step-down (noun). Hyphened.

stepfather. One word.

step-in (noun). Hyphened.

stepladder, stepmother, stepparent. One word.

stepped-up (adj.). Hyphened.

steppingstone. One word.

stepsister, stepson. One word.

step-up (noun). Hyphened.

stereo-. Compounds are spelled as one word.

sterilize, sterilizer are spelled with *z*.

sternum, sternums.

stetho-. Compounds are spelled as one word.

stethoscope. Two *o*'s.

stevedore starts with *steve*.

sticking point. Two words.

stickle ends in *-le*.

stickpin. One word.

stick shift. Two words.

stick-to-itiveness. Two hyphens. Standard usage.

stickup (noun). One word.

stigma, stigmata.

stigmatize ends in *-ize*.

stile, style. *Stile* is a step over a fence, *style* is a mode of expression or dress.

stiletto, stilettos.

still and all. Standard usage.

stillbirth, stillborn. One word.

still life, still lifes. Two words.

stillness. Double *l.*

stillwater (adj.). One word.

stimulus, stimuli.

sting, stung, stung.

stingray. One word.

stingy, stingier, stingiest, stinginess. No *e* after *g*.

stink, stunk or **stank, stunk.** Webster's lists *stink* in the sense of being very bad as standard usage.

stink bomb. Two words.

stipend. Don't use *stipend* when *wage, fee, grant, salary* will do.

stir, stirred, stirrer, stirring. Double *r* in all forms except *stir.*

stirrup. Double *r.*

stock-. Almost all compounds are spelled as one word.

stockboy, stockbreeder, stockbreeding, stockbroker, stockbroker-age, stockbroking, stockcar, stockholder, stockholding. One word.

stock-in-trade. Two hyphens.

stockjobber, stockjobbing, stockkeeper, stocklist, stockman, stockowner, stockpile, stockpiled, stockpiling, stockroom. One word.

stock split. Two words.

stock-still. Hyphened.

stocktaker, stocktaking, stockyard. One word.

stogie, stogies. Spell it with *ie*.

stoic, stoical. The form *stoical* is more common.

stoically ends in *-ally*.

stomach in the sense of *belly* is standard usage.

stomachache. One word.

stomp (verb) is listed as standard usage in Webster's.

-stone. Compounds are spelled as one word, e.g. *hailstone, rhinestone.*

stone-. Most compounds are spelled as one word.

Stone Age. Capitals.

stone-blind, stone-broke, stone-cold. Hyphened.

stonecutter, stonecutting. One word.

stone-dead, stone-deaf. Hyphened.

stonemason, stonemasonry. One word.

stonewall, stonewalling in the sense of blocking is standard usage.

stoneware, stonework, stoneworker. One word.

stony. No *e*.

stonyhearted. One word.

stoolie is listed as standard usage in Webster's.

stoop, stoup. Spell it *stoup* when you mean a basin for holy water. Otherwise spell it *stoop*.

stop, stopped, stopper, stopping. Double *p* in all forms except *stop*.

stop, stay. *Stop* in the sense of stay has been used since 1800. Trollope wrote "But you'll stop and take a bit of dinner with us?"

stop-. Almost all compounds are spelled as one word.

stop-and-go. Two hyphens.

stopgap, stoplight, stopoff (noun), **stopover** (noun). One word.

stop payment, stop sign. Two words.

stopwatch. One word.

store, storing, storage.

-store. Compounds are spelled as one word, e.g. *bookstore, drugstore.*

store-. Most compounds are spelled as one word.

store-bought. Hyphened.

store cheese. Two words.

storefront, storehouse, storekeeper, storekeeping, storeroom, storewide. One word.

(storey). The common US spelling of the word meaning floor is *story.*

storied. Spell it with *ie.*

stormbound. One word.

storm cellar, storm door, storm sash, storm window. Two words.

storybook, storyteller, storytelling. One word.

stoup. Spelling of the basin for holy water.

stouthearted. One word.

stovepipe, stovewood. One word.

stowaway. One word.

straddle in the sense of being noncommittal is standard usage.

straight, strait. *Straight* means direct, *strait* means narrow.

straightaway, straightedge. One word.

straighten, straiten. *Straighten* means make straight, align, *straiten* means restrict.

straightforward. One word.

strain, sprain. *Strain* means stretch, *sprain* means wrench.

straiten, straighten. *Straiten* means restrict, *straighten* means make straight, align. Write *in straitened circumstances.*

straitjacket. So spelled. One word.

straitlaced. One word.

straits, meaning difficulties or narrows, is so spelled.

strange-looking. Hyphened.

stranglehold. One word.

straphanger. One word.

stratagem. The vowels are *a—a—e.*

strategic, strategically.

strategy, tactics. *Strategy* deals with planning, *tactics* deals with maneuvering.

strato-. Compounds are spelled as one word.

stratosphere.

stratum, strata. *Strata* is the plural of *stratum. Strata* with the singular verb is not standard usage.

straw boss. Two words. Listed in Webster's as standard usage.

strawhat. One word.

straw vote. Two words.

streamline, streamlined. One word.

street. Capitalize *Street* in addresses.

streetcar, streetlight, streetwalker, streetwalking, streetwise. One word.

strength. Don't forget the *g*.

strenuous ends in *-uous*.

strepto-. Compounds are spelled as one word.

streptococcus. First one *c*, then two. Ends in *-us*.

streptomycin.

stretcher-bearer. Hyphened.

strew, strewed, strewed or **strewn.**

stricken. Use *stricken* only in the sense of afflicted. Otherwise say *struck*.

strictly is spelled with *ct*.

stride, strode, stridden. The past participle *stridden* is rare.

strife, strifes.

strike, struck, struck or **stricken.** Use the past participle *stricken* only when you mean afflicted.

strikebound, strikebreaker, strikebreaking, strikeout (noun), **strikeover** (noun). One word.

string, strung, strung. But it's *stringed instruments.*

strip mine, strip mining. Two words.

striptease, stripteaser. One word.

strive, strove, striven. The form *strived* is now rare.

strong-arm. Hyphened.

strongbox, stronghold. One word.

strong man. Two words.

strong point, strong room, strong suit. Two words.

structure (verb). Don't use *structure* when *build* or *form* will do.

strychnine is spelled with *ych* and *e* at the end.

stubbornness. Double *n*.

stucco, stuccos, stuccoed, stuccoing.

stuck-up. Hyphened. Listed in Webster's as standard usage.

studbook, studhorse. One word.

studio, studios.

study, studied, studying.

stultify, stultified, stultifying. *I* after the second *t*.

stumblebum. One word.

stumbling block. Two words.

stump in the senses of baffle or make campaign speeches is listed in Webster's as standard usage.

stunt man. Two words.

stupefy, stupefied, stupefying. *E* after *p*. Think of a "stup*ef*ying *ef*fect."

stupor ends in *-or*.

sturgeon ends in *-eon*.

sty, sties. Spell it so in both senses—pimple on the eyelid or pigsty.

style, stile. *Style* is a mode of expression or dress, a *stile* is a step over a fence.

stylebook. One word.

stymie, stymied, stymieing. Standard usage.

suable. No *e* before *-able*.

suave.

sub. Standard usage in all senses.

sub-. Compounds are spelled as one word.

subarctic. *C* after *r*.

subaverage, subbasement, subcommittee, subconscious, subcutaneous, subdivision, subgroup. One word.

subject to. Don't write *subject to* when *open to, under* or *depends on* will do.

subjoin. Don't use *subjoin* when *enclose* or *attach* will do.

sub judice. Never hyphened.

subjunctive. See WAS, WERE.

submachine gun. Two words.

submerge, submerse. *Submerge* is more common.

submersible ends in *-ible*.

submission. Don't use *submission* when *filing* or *sending* will do.

submit, submitted, submitting. Don't use *submit* when *file* or *send* will do.

subnormal. One word.

suborn. Don't use *suborn* when *bribe* will do.

subpena, subpenaed, subpenaing. *Subpena,* rather than *subpoena,* is the spelling listed in the GPO Style Manual and used by many newspapers.

subplot, subprofessional. One word.

subsequent. Don't use *subsequent* when *later* will do.

subsequently. Don't use *subsequently* when *then* or *later* will do.

subsequent to. Don't use *subsequent to* when *after* will do.

subservience, subservient end in *-ence, ent.*

subsidize ends in *-ize*.

subsistence ends in *-ence*.

subspecies. One word.

substance ends in *-ance*.

substantial. Don't use *substantial* when *large, great* or *big* will do.

substantially. Don't use *substantially* when *largely, greatly* or *much* will do.

substantiate. Don't use *substantiate* when *prove* or *back up* will do.

substitute, replace. You *substitute* something in place of the real thing, but you *replace* the real thing by a *substitute.* Don't use *substitute* when you mean *replace.* Say *substitute for* and *replace by.* (Dictionaries list *substitute* in the sense of *replace,* but it's clearer not to use the word in that way.)

(substract, substraction). Misspellings of *subtract, subtraction.*

subterfuge.

subterranean. Double *r,* ends in *-ean.*

(subtile). The modern word is *subtle.*

subtle, subtler, subtlest, subtlety, subtly. Silent *b.*

subtopic, subtotal, subtropical, subzero. One word.

succeed. Double *c,* double *e.*

success. Double *c,* double *s.*

successfully. Double *c,* double *s,* double *l.*

succinct, succinctly. Double *c,* and *c* before *t.*

succor. Don't use *succor* when *relief* or *help* will do.

succotash. Spelled with double *c.*

succubus. Double *c,* ends in *-us.* The plural is *succubi.*

succulence, succulent end in *-ence, -ent.* Double *c.* Don't use *succulent* when *juicy* will do.

succumb. Double *c,* silent *b.* Don't use *succumb* when *yield* will do.

such. Don't use *such* when *any, all, one, it, they, them, this, that, those* will do.

such as. Don't use *such as* when *like* will do. No comma after *such as.*

such is the case, such is not the case. Don't write *such is the case* when *it is so* will do. Don't write *such is not the case* when *it isn't so* will do.

suchlike. Don't use *suchlike* when *similar* will do.

sucker in the sense of a person easily cheated is listed as standard usage in Webster's.

suddenness. Double *n.*

sue, sued, suing.

suede. Commonly spelled without accent.

sufferance ends in *-ance.*

suffice. Don't say *suffice* when *do* or *be enough* will do.

sufficiency. Don't say *a sufficiency* when *enough* will do.

sufficient, sufficiently. Don't say *sufficient* or *sufficiently* when *enough* will do.

suffragette ends in *-ette*.

sugarcane, sugarcoat, sugarcoating, sugarhouse, sugarloaf, sugar-plum, sugarspoon. One word.

suggest. Double *g*.

suggestible ends in *-ible*.

sui generis. No hyphen.

suing. No *e*.

suit, suite. It's a *suite* (pronounced *sweet*) of followers, rooms, furniture or music. Otherwise it's a *suit*.

suitable ends in *-able*.

suitcase. One word.

suitor ends in *-or*.

sukiyaki.

sulfa, sulfate, sulfide, sulfur, sulfuric, sulfurous. Spelled with *f*.

sullenness. Double *n*.

sumac. Commonly spelled without *h* at the end.

summarize ends in *-ize*.

summer. Don't capitalize.

summer day. Two words.

summerhouse. One word.

(summersault). Spell it *somersault*.

summer school. Two words.

summertime. One word.

summon. Don't use when *send for* will do.

summons (verb). Don't use *summons* when *send for* will do.

summons (noun), **summonses.**

sumptuous is spelled with *pt* and ends in *-uous*.

sums of money. Use the singular verb, e.g. *$7 million was paid*.

sun-. Almost all compounds are spelled as one word.

sunbaked, sunbath, sunbathe, sunbather, sunbeam, sunbonnet, sunburn, sunburned, sunburst. One word.

sundae ends in *-ae*.

sun deck. Two words.

sundial, sundown, sundress. One word.

(sung). *Sang* is more common as the past tense of *sing*.

sunglasses. One word.

(sunk). *Sank* is more common as the past tense of *sink*.

sunken (adj.). Standard usage.

sunlamp, sunlight, sunlit, sunrise, sunroom, sunroof, sunshade, sunspot, sunstroke, sunstruck, sunsuit, suntan, sunup. One word.

sunward, sunwards. *Sunwards* is more common.

super (adj.) is listed in Webster's as standard usage.

super-. Compounds are spelled as one word.

superabundant, superannuated, supercaution. One word.

(supercede). Misspelling of *supersede*.

supercilious ends in *-ious*.

superego, supereloquent. One word.

supererogation. Don't use *supererogation* when a simpler expression will do.

superfluous ends in *-uous*.

superhighway. One word.

superintendent ends in *-ent*.

superlatives of two. Expressions like the *smartest of the two* are common usage.

supernatural, supernumerary, superpower. One word.

supersede ends in *-sede*. Remember "When you're being super*sed*ed, take a *sed*ative."

superstition, superstitious end in *-ition, -itious*.

supertanker. One word.

supervise ends in *-ise*.

supervisor ends in *-or*.

supine, prone. *Supine* means lying face upward, *prone* face downward.

supplant. Double *p*.

supple, subtle. *Supple* means flexible, *subtle* means perceptive.

supportive of. Don't say *is supportive of* when *supports* will do.

suppose, supposed, supposing. So spelled.

supposed to. Don't forget the *d*.

supposition ends in *-ition*.

(supposititious). The form *supposititious* is more common.

supposititious. Don't use *supposititious* when *spurious* or *hypothetical* will do.

suppress. Double *p*.

suppressible ends in *-ible*.

(supprise). Misspelling of *surprise*.

supra. Don't use *supra* when *above* will do.

supra-. Compounds are spelled as one word, e.g. *suprarenal*.

supremacy ends in *-cy.*

surcease. Don't use *surcease* when *letup, respite, pause* or *end* will do.

sure. The adverb *sure* instead of *surely* is listed as standard usage in Webster's. It has been used since 1400. Daniel Defoe wrote "Sure it is a fine place."

sure enough. Listed in Webster's as standard usage.

surefire, surefooted, surefootedness. One word.

surely. Don't forget the *e.*

surety. Don't forget the *e.*

surfboard. One word.

surfeit is spelled with *ei.*

surgeon ends in *-eon.*

surgeon general, surgeons general.

surly. The adverb is *surlily.*

surmise ends in *-ise.* Don't say *surmise* when *think* or *guess* will do.

surmountable ends in *-able.*

surplusage.

surprise. *R* before *p* and *-ise* at the end. Think of "A *burp* gives *rise* to *surprise.*"

surreptitious. Double *r.*

surrogate. Double *r.*

surround, surrounded, surroundings. Double *r.*

surveillance is spelled with *ei,* double *l,* and *-ance.*

surveyor ends in *-or.*

survivor ends in *-or.*

susceptible ends in *-ible.* Spelled with *sc.*

suspense ends in *-se.*

suspension ends in *-sion.*

(suspicion). The verb *suspicion* is not standard usage. Say *suspect.*

sustain. Don't use *sustain* when *suffer* or *get* will do.

sustained. Don't use *sustained* when *steady* or *lasting* will do.

sustenance ends in *-ance.*

suzerain is spelled with *z* and ends in *-ain.*

svelte. *E* at the end.

swag in the sense of *loot* is listed in Webster's as standard usage.

swam. Past tense of *swim.*

swamp fever. Two words.

swampland. One word.

(swang). The past tense of *swing* is *swung.*

swank, swanky is listed in Webster's as standard usage.

swan song. Two words.

swap. Standard usage.

swath. Spell it without *e* at the end.

swayback, swaybacked. One word.

sweat shirt. Two words.

sweetbrier ends in *-er.*

sweetheart, sweetshop. One word.

sweet william. Small *w.*

swell, in the sense of stylish or excellent is listed in Webster's as standard usage.

swept-back (adj.). Hyphened.

swim, swam, swum.

swineherd. One word.

swing, swung, swung.

swinger is listed in Webster's as standard usage.

swing shift. Two words.

swinish. No *e.*

switchback (noun), **switchblade, switchboard.** One word.

swivel, swiveled, swiveling. One *l* in all forms.

swivel chair. Two words.

swivet. Listed in Webster's as standard usage.

(swop). The common form is *swap.*

sword. Silent *w.*

swordbearer, swordplay. One word.

(swum). The common form of the past tense of *swim* is *swam.* The past participle is *swum.*

swung. Past tense of *swing.*

(sy-). If you can't find the word you're looking for, try under *psy-.*

sybarite.

(sybil). Misspelling of *sibyl.* But the name is often spelled *Sybil.*

syllabication. See DIVISION OF WORDS.

syllable. *Y* and double *l.*

syllabus, syllabuses.

syllogism. Double *l,* followed by *o.*

sylphlike. One word.

sylvan. Common spelling.

symbol, cymbal. *Symbols* are signs, *cymbals* make a clashing sound.

symbolize ends in *-ize.*

symmetrical, symmetry. Double *m.*

sympathize ends in *-ize.*

sympathy. You're *in sympathy with* the poor, but you *have sympathy for* the poor.

symposium, symposia.

symptom, symptomatic. *P* before *t.* Don't use *symptom* when *sign* will do.

syn-. Compounds are spelled as one word.

synagogue. The common spelling.

sync. Standard usage. Spell it without *h* at the end.

synchronize ends in -ize. Spelled with *ch.*

syncopate. No *h.*

synonymous. Two *y*'s.

synonyms. Don't use a synonym just to avoid the repetition of a word. For example, *fork* would have been better than *utensil* in the following: "The fork suddenly dropped out of her hand. . . . She lowered her arm, placed her fingers on the utensil, and tried to pick it up. She could not lift it." And *there* would have been better than *in the French capital* in this: "He decided to go to Paris and within a few hours arrived in the French capital." See also REPETITION OF WORDS.

synopsis, synopses.

synthesis, syntheses.

synthesize ends in *-ize.*

(syphon). Commonly spelled *siphon.*

syringe. First *y,* then *i.*

syrup, syrupy. Spelled with *y.*

systematically ends in *-ally.*

systematize ends in *-ize.*

systemwide. One word.

syzygy. Famous spelling-bee word with three *y*'s.

T

t-. If you can't find the word you're looking for, try under *pt-*.

-t-, -tt-. A *t* at the end of a word is doubled before the suffixes *-ed, -er, -ing, -able, -ish, -y* if there's a single vowel immediately before the *t* and the accent is on the last syllable. Examples: *spot, spotted; set, setter; admit, admitting; regret, regrettable; fat, fattish; cat, catty.* If there's no accent on the last syllable, don't double the *t*. Write *riveted, benefiting, profitable* etc.

tableau, tableaus.

tablecloth. One word.

table d'hôte. Spell it with the accent.

table-hopper. Hyphened.

tableland. One word.

table linen. Two words.

tablemate, tablespoon. One word.

tablespoonful, tablespoonfuls.

tabletalk, tabletop, tableware. One word.

taboo, taboos, tabooed, tabooing. Spell with *oo*.

tabor ends in *-or*.

taboret. *O* after *b*.

tachy-. Compounds are spelled as one word, e.g. *tachycardia.*

tactician ends in *-ician*.

tactics, strategy. *Tactics* deal with maneuvering, *strategy* deals with planning.

taffeta. Double *f*.

tail in the sense of follow close behind is listed in Webster's as standard usage.

-tail. Compounds are spelled as one word, e.g. *oxtail, swallowtail.*

tail-. Compounds are usually spelled as one word.

tailboard, tailcoat. One word.

tail end, tail fin. Two words.

tailgate, taillight. One word.

tailor ends in *-or*.

tailor-made. Hyphened.

tailpiece, tailspin, tailwind. One word.

take, bring. You *take* something or someone *from* a place, but you *bring* something or someone *to* it.

takedown. One word.

take-home pay. One hyphen.

take issue. Don't write *take issue* when *disagree* will do.

takeoff, takeout, takeover. One word.

take place. Don't use *take place* when *happen* or *go on* will do.

takeup (noun). One word.

talc, talcum. Spelled with *c*.

talebearer, talebearing, talesman. One word.

talisman, talismans.

talking-to (noun). Hyphened.

talk show. Two words.

tallboy. One word.

tally sheet. Two words.

tamable. No *e* before *-able*.

tamale ends in *e*.

tambourine is spelled with *ou* and ends in *-e*.

tam-o'-shanter. Two hyphens, apostrophe.

tangible ends in *-ible*.

tango, tangos.

tantalize ends in *-ize*. Don't use *tantalizing* when *intriguing* will do.

tantamount. Don't use *is tantamount to* when *amounts to* or *means* will do.

tap-dance, tap-dancer, tap-dancing. Hyphened.

tape deck, tape measure, tape recorder. Two words.

tapeworm. One word.

taproom. One word.

tar, tarred, tarring. Double *r* in all forms except *tar*.

tarboosh. Spell it with *oo*.

tardy, tardily, tardiness.

tare, tear. *Tare* means vetch, weed or weight discount, *tear* means pull apart.

tariff. One *r*, double *f*.

(tarmigan). Misspelling of *ptarmigan*.

tar paper. Two words.

tarpaulin. Spelled with *au.*

tarry. Don't use *tarry* when *stay* will do.

tartar ends in *-ar.*

task force. Two words.

taskmaster, taskmistress. One word.

tassel, tasseled, tasseling. One *l* in all forms.

tasteful, tasty. *Tasteful* means with good taste, *tasty* means good-tasting.

tatterdemalion ends in *-ion.*

tattle, tattler. Double *t.*

tattletale. One word.

tattoo, tattooed, tattooing, tattooist. Double *t,* double *o.*

taught, taut. *Taught* is the past tense of *teach, taut* means tense.

taupe. The color is so spelled.

tawdry is spelled with *aw.*

tawny is spelled with *aw.* Means the color of well-tanned skin.

taxable ends in *-able.*

tax avoidance, tax evasion. *Tax avoidance* means saving taxes legally, *tax evasion* means deliberately not paying tax.

tax collector, tax dodger. One word.

tax-exempt, tax-free. Hyphened.

taxgatherer, taxgathering. One word.

taxi, taxis, taxied, taxiing.

taxicab, taxistand. One word.

taxpayer, taxpaying, taxpayment. One word.

tax rate, tax shelter. Two words.

tax-supported. Hyphened.

taxwise. One word.

TB for *tuberculosis* is standard usage. No periods.

T-bone steak. Capital *T,* hyphen, small *b.*

Tchaikovsky. The most common spelling.

tea-. Most compounds are spelled as one word.

tea bag. Two words.

teacup. One word.

teacupful, teacupfuls.

teahouse, teakettle. One word.

team, teem. A *team* is a group, to *teem* means to abound.

teammate, teamplay, teamwork. One word.

teapot. One word.

tearbomb, teardrop. One word.

tear gas. Two words.

tearjerker. One word.

tearoom. One word.

tear-out (adj.). Hyphened.

tearsheet, tearstain. One word.

tease, teased, teasing. Spelled with *s.*

teaspoonful, teaspoonfuls.

teatime. One word.

technic, technique. *Technique* is the common form.

technician ends in *-ician.*

(techy). There *is* a standard word meaning touchy, irritable, but it's commonly spelled *tetchy.*

teem, team. To *teem* means to abound, a *team* is a group.

teenage, teenager. One word. Write a *teenage boy* (not *teenaged*).

teens is standard usage for the years from 13 through 19.

teeny for *tiny* is a standard variant.

(teepee). The spelling *tepee* is more common.

(tee shirt). Spell it *T-shirt.*

teetotal, teetotaler, teetotalism. One *l* in all forms.

tele-. Compounds are spelled as one word.

telephonic. Don't use *telephonic* when *telephone* or *phone* will do.

televise ends in *-ise.*

telltale. One word.

temblor. No *r* after *t.*

temerity. Don't say *temerity* when *nerve, rashness, gall* will do.

temperament, temperamental has *ram* in it. *E* between *p* and *r.*

temperance ends in *-ance.*

temperate ends in *-ate* (not *-ant*).

temperature in the sense of fever is standard usage.

tempestuous ends in *-uous.*

Templar ends in *-ar.*

template. The common spelling ends in *-ate.*

tempo, tempi.

temporary, temporarily. *O* after *p.*

temporize ends in *-ize.*

tempt, tempter, temptress.

tempura. The Japanese dish is so spelled.

tenable ends in *-able.*

tenacious ends in *-acious.*

tenant, tenet. A *tenant* is a renter, a *tenet* is a principle.

tendency ends in *-ency.*

tendentious ends in *-tious.*

tender (verb). Don't write *tender* when *offer* will do.

tenderfoot, tenderhearted. One word.

tenement. Three *e*'s.

tenet, tenant. A *tenet* is a principle, a *tenant* is a renter.

tenfold. One word.

tenor ends in *-or.*

tens or **10s.** No apostrophe.

tension ends in *-sion.*

tentacle ends in *-acle.*

tentative ends in *-ative.*

tenterhooks. One word.

tentmaker, tentmaking. One word.

tenuous ends in *-uous.*

tepee. First one *e,* then two.

ter. Usually capitalized in names, as in *Gerard Ter Borch.*

tercentenary. Three *e*'s. Ends in *-ary.*

termagant ends in *-ant. A* in the middle.

terminable ends in *-able.*

terminate. Don't say *terminate* when *end, stop, drop, wind up, close, finish* will do.

terminus, termini.

terms. Don't say *in terms of* when *of, in, by, through, under* will do.

tern, turn. A *tern* is a sea bird, a *turn* is a change in direction.

(terodactyl). Misspelling of *pterodactyl.*

terpsichorean. Don't use *terpsichorean* when *dance* will do.

terra cotta. Two words.

terra firma. Two words.

terrain ends in *-ain.*

terra incognita, terrae incognitae.

terrarium, terrariums.

terrazzo. Double *r,* double *z.*

terrible ends in *-ible.*

terrier ends in *-ier.*

terrifically ends in *-ally.* One *f.*

territory ends in *-ory.*

terrorize ends in *-ize.*

terror-stricken, terror-struck. Hyphened.

tertiary ends in *-tiary.*

tessellate, tessellated, tessellation. Double *s,* double *l.*

testatrix, testatrices.

test case. Two words.
testify, testified, testifying.
test pilot, test tube. Two words.
tetanus ends in *-us.*
tetched, tetchy. Standard usage, so spelled.
tête-à-tête. Three accents and two hyphens.
tetra-. Compounds are spelled as one word.
tetralogy. *A* after *r.*
textbook. One word.
Thai, Thailand.
thalamus, thalami.
than, then. Don't confuse *than,* as in *more than one,* with *then,* as in *now and then.*
than him, than her, than them, than us. A common idiom since 1560. Sir Walter Scott wrote "I could not be expected to be wiser than her."
thankfully is sometimes used, as in *the book is thankfully free of jargon,* in the sense of *I am thankful.* The usage, like *hopefully* in the sense of *it is hoped,* is getting common.
thanking you in advance. Used in a letter, this phrase *assumes* the addressee will do what he's asked for—a poor way of asking anyone for anything. Avoid.
thanks, short for *thank you,* is standard usage.
thanks to, in the sense of *because of,* is standard usage.
than whom has been standard usage since 1548. But don't use *than whom* if you can say it more simply.
that. Don't write *that* when the sentence would be just as clear without it, e.g. instead of *he said that he would go* write *he said he would go.* And don't repeat *that* unnecessarily, e.g. *People think that if a product is advertised on TV (that) it is worth buying.*
that'll. Common contraction of *that will.*
that's. Common contraction of *that is.*
that, which; that, who. See WHICH, THAT; WHO, THAT.
thaumaturgist.
the. Don't capitalize *the* in such sentences as *I read it in the New York Times.*
theater ends in *-er.*
theatergoer. One word.
the author. Don't write *the author* when *I* will do.
(theif). Misspelling of *thief.*

their, there, they're. Don't confuse *their* (of them), *there* (not here) and *they're* (they are).

their in the sense of *his or her* is listed in Webster's as standard usage. W. H. Auden wrote "anyone in their senses."

theirs, there's. *Theirs* (no apostrophe) is what belongs to *them*. *There's* means *there is*.

(theirselves). Not standard usage. Write *themselves*.

them instead of *they* after *is, was, be* or *than* is idiomatic English. It dates back to the Bible (Proverbs 27:3): "A stone is heavy, and the sand weighty; but a fool's wrath is heavier than them both."

    Them in the sense of *him or her* is listed in Webster's as standard usage. In 1742 Samuel Richardson wrote "Little did I think to make a complaint against a person very dear to you, but don't let them be so proud as to make them not care how they affront everybody else."

then. Leave out *then* in an *if . . . then* sentence, e.g. *If we do it, (then) let's do it right away.*

then, than. Don't confuse *then* as in *now and then* with *than* as in *more than one.*

then-. No hyphen with a noun, e.g. *the then mayor.* Hyphen with an adjective, e.g. *the then-ruling dictator.*

thence. Don't use *thence* when *from this, from that, from there* will do.

thenceforth, thenceforward. Don't use *thenceforth, thenceforward* when *from then on* will do.

theo-. Compounds are spelled as one word, e.g. *theobromine.*

the present writer. Don't write *the present writer* when *I* will do.

therapeutic is spelled with *eu.*

there, their, they're. Don't confuse *there* (not here), *their* (of them) and *they're* (they are).

thereabouts is more common than *thereabout.* Don't use *thereabouts* when *so* will do.

thereafter. Don't use *thereafter* when *after that* or *then* will do.

there are. Don't start a sentence with *there are* if you can make it stronger by recasting it.

thereat. Don't use *thereat* when *at it* or *there* will do.

thereby. Don't use *thereby* when *by it* will do.

there'd. Common contraction of *there would.*

therefor, therefore. *Therefor* (without *e*) means *for it,* *therefore* (with *e*) means *because of it* or *so.* Don't use *therefor* when *for* *it* will do. Don't use *therefore* when *so* will do. Don't put a comma before or after *therefore.*

therefrom. Don't use *therefrom* when *from it* will do.

therein. Don't use *therein* when *in it* will do.

there is. Don't start a sentence with *there is* if you can make it stronger by recasting it.

there'll. Common contraction of *there will.*

thereof. Don't use *thereof* when *of it* will do.

thereon. Don't use *thereon* when *on it* will do.

there's. Common contraction of *there is, there has.*

thereto. Don't use *thereto* when *to it* will do

theretofore. Don't use *theretofore* when *up to then* will do.

thereunder. Don't use *thereunder* when *under it* will do.

thereunto. Don't use *thereunto* when *to it* will do.

thereupon. Don't use *thereupon* when *on it* or *then* will do.

there was. Don't start a sentence with *there was* if you can make it stronger by recasting it.

therewith. Don't use *therewith* when *with it* will do.

thermo-. Compounds are spelled as one word, e.g. *thermonuclear.*

thesaurus, thesauri.

these kind of. The idiom *these kind of* has been common since 1380. Shakespeare (King Lear, II, ii, 107) wrote "These kind of knaves I know."

thesis, theses.

thespian. Small *t.* Don't write *thespian* when *dramatic* or *actor* will do.

they in the sense of *he or she* is listed in Webster's as standard usage. Henry Fielding wrote in 1749 "Everybody fell alaughing, as how could they help it."

They in the sense of *people* is also standard usage, e.g. *They say it's going to be a hot summer.*

They, their, them often refer to a company or organization, e.g. "Con Edison has authorized us to accept payment of their bills."

they'd. Common contraction of *they would* or *they had.*

they'll. Common contraction of *they will.*

they're. Common contraction of *they are.*

they've. Common contraction of *they have.*

thiamine. *E* at the end.

thickset. One word.

thick-skinned, thick-witted. Hyphened.

thief, thieves. Spelled with *ie.*

thighbone. One word.

thimbleful, thimblefuls.

thimblerig, thimblerigged, thimblerigger, thimblerigging. Two *g*'s in all forms except *thimblerig.* No hyphen.

thingamabob, thingamajig. The common spellings.

think. *That* after *think* is commonly left out, e.g. *I think (that) we're in agreement.*

thinness. Double *n.*

thin-skinned. Hyphened.

third. Follow Webster's and the New York Times and write *3d,* not *3rd.*

thirdhand. One word.

(thirdly). The common form of the adverb is *third.*

third-rate. Hyphened.

thirties or **30s.** No apostrophe.

thirty-one etc. Hyphened.

this'll. Common contraction of *this will.*

thistle. Silent *t.*

this writer. Don't use *this writer* when *I* will do.

thither. Don't use *thither* when *there* will do.

tho is listed in Webster's as a standard variant of *though.*

Thomas is always spelled with *Th.*

thoro is listed in Webster's as a nonstandard variant of *thorough.*

thoroughbred, thoroughfare, thoroughgoing. One word.

those kind of. See THESE KIND OF.

though in the sense of *for all that, however,* is standard usage. It needs no comma before or after it. Shakespeare (Midsummer Night's Dream, III, ii, 343) wrote "Your hands than mine are quicker for a fray, My legs are longer though to run away."

thought-out, thought-provoking. Hyphened.

thousandfold. One word.

thousandth ends in *-dth.*

thralldom. Double *l.*

thrash, thresh. *Thrash* means flog, *thresh* means separate grain.

threadbare. One word.

three-decker, three-dimensional. Hyphened.

threefold. One word.

three-legged, three-piece, three-point, three-quarter, three-ring. Hyphened.

three R's. Apostrophe.

threes or **3s.** No apostrophe.

thresh, thrash. *Thresh* means separate grain, *thrash* means flog.

thrice. Don't use *thrice* when *three times* will do.

thrive, throve, thriven. Common forms.

thrombo-. Compounds are spelled as one word, e.g. *thromboplastic.*

through in the sense of finished is standard usage.

throughout. One word.

through road. Two words.

throw, threw, thrown.

throwaway, throwback, throwoff (nouns). One word.

throw rug. Two words.

thru is listed as a standard variant of *through* in Webster's.

thruway. Standard usage, so spelled.

thumbhole, thumbnail, thumbprint, thumbscrew, thumbtack. One word.

thunderbolt, thunderclap, thundercloud, thunderhead. One word.

thunderous. Spelled with *e.*

thundershower, thunderstorm, thunderstruck. One word.

thus. Don't write *thus* when *so* will do or when it can be left out.

(thusly). The word was formed as a joke in 1889. Now stale.

thwart. Don't use *thwart* when *frustrate* or *block* will do.

thyme. The herb is so spelled.

thyroid is spelled with *thy.*

tic, tick. A *tic* is a twitch, a *tick* is a rhythmic sound.

ticker-tape (adj.). Hyphened.

ticketholder. One word.

tickle ends in *-le.*

ticklish. No *e.*

ticktacktoe. One word.

ticktock. One word.

tidbit. First *id,* then *it.*

tideland, tidemark, tidewater. One word.

tie, tied, tying.

tieback (noun). One word.

tie breaker. Two words.

tie-in (noun, adj.). Hyphened.

tiepin. One word.

tie-up (noun). Hyphened.

tiff is standard usage.

-tight. Compounds are spelled as one word, e.g. *airtight, watertight.*

tightfisted, tightlipped, tightrope, tightwad. One word.

(tike). The common spelling is *tyke.*

till in the sense of *until* is spelled with double *l.* (*Til* and *'til* are misspellings.)

timber, timbre. *Timber* means wood, *timbre* means tone.

timberline, timberwork. One word.

-time. Compounds are spelled as one word, e.g. *summertime, dinnertime.*

time-consuming, time-honored. Hyphened.

timekeeper, timekeeping, timekiller, timekilling. One word.

time-out (noun). Hyphened.

timepiece, timepleaser, timesaving, timeserver, timeserving. One word.

time-sharing. Hyphened.

timetable. One word.

time-tested. Hyphened.

timework, timeworker, timeworn. One word.

timidity, temerity. *Timidity* means cowardice, *temerity* means rashness.

timothy grass. Small *t.*

timpani, timpanist. Common spelling.

tin can. Two words.

tinfoil. One word.

ting-a-ling. Two hyphens.

tinge, twinge. *Tinge* means shade, *twinge* means sudden pain.

tinker's damn. Commonly spelled with the final *n.*

tinman, tinplate. One word.

tinsel, tinseled, tinseling. One *l* in all forms.

tinsmith. One word.

tintinnabulation. First one *n,* then double *n.*

tintype, tinware, tinwork. One word.

tip-in (noun). Hyphened.

tipoff (noun) is listed in Webster's as standard usage. One word.

tipsy. Standard usage.

tiptoe, tiptoed, tiptoeing.

tiptop. One word.

tire. The US spelling.

(tiro). The US spelling is *tyro.*

'tis. Poetic contraction of *it is.* Avoid in prose.

(titbit). The common spelling is *tidbit.*

tithepayer, tithepaying. One word.

titian (color) ends in *-tian.* (Named after the painter Titian.)

titillate, titillation. Single *t,* double *l.* Means tickle or stimulate.

titivate means spruce up.

titleholder. One word.

title page. Two words.

titles. Italicize (underline) titles of books, magazines, plays, movies etc. But you can also follow newspaper style and simply capitalize such titles or put them in quotes. Examples: Shakespeare's *Hamlet* or Shakespeare's Hamlet or Shakespeare's "Hamlet"; Beethoven's *Fidelio* or Beethoven's Fidelio or Beethoven's "Fidelio."

Capitalize all words including parts of hyphened compounds except for these 15 words: *a, an, and, as, at, but, by, for, if, in, of, on, or, the, to.* But capitalize these words too if they are the first or last word of a title. Don't capitalize the second part of hyphened numbers and fractions. Examples: "Death of a Salesman." "As Time Goes By." "One-third of a Nation."

titles of persons. Capitalize common nouns used as titles preceding the names of persons, e.g. *Captain Robert Smith, Judge William Kennan.* But don't capitalize *"false"* titles, e.g. *trapeze artist Tony Cavalla, skillful negotiator Francis Klein.* They were originally invented by *Time* magazine and are now commonly used by the press.

titlist. No *e.*

(tittivate). Misspelling of *titivate.* Means spruce up.

tittle-tattle. Hyphened.

tizzy is listed as standard usage in Webster's.

to, too, two. Don't confuse the preposition *to, too* in the sense of *also* or *too much* and *two* meaning one plus one.

-to. Compounds are hyphened, e.g. *lean-to, set-to.*

toady, toadied, toadying.

to all intents and purposes. Don't use *to all intents and purposes* when *in effect* will do.

toastmaster, toastmistress. One word.

tobacco, tobaccos.

-to-be. Hyphened, e.g. *bride-to-be.*

toboggan, tobogganer, tobogganing.

toccata. Double *c.*

tocsin, toxin. *Tocsin* means warning bell, *toxin* means poison.

today. No hyphen.

to-do. Hyphened.

toe, toed, toeing.

toehold, toenail, toeprint. One word.

(toffee). The common US word is *taffy*.

togetherness. Standard usage.

(to hand). Old-fashioned business jargon. Avoid.

(toilette). Spell it *toilet* in all senses.

toilet training, toilet water. Two words.

toilworn. One word.

tolerable ends in *-able*.

tolerance, tolerant end in *-ance, -ant*.

tollbooth. One word.

toll bridge, toll call. Two words.

tollgate, tollhouse, tollkeeper. One word.

toll road. Two words.

tolltaker, tollway. One word.

(tomaine). Misspelling of *ptomaine*.

tomato, tomatoes.

tomb. Silent *b*.

tombstone. One word.

tomcat. One word.

tome. Don't use *tome* when *book* will do.

tomfoolery.

tommy gun. Two words.

tomorrow. No hyphen.

tom-tom. Hyphened.

tone-deaf. Hyphened.

tongue. Don't use *tongue* when *language* will do.

tongue-lashing, tongue-tied. Hyphened.

tongue twister. Two words.

tonight. No hyphen.

(tonite). Not standard.

tonneau, tonneaus.

tonsillitis, tonsillectomy. Double *l*.

tonsorial. Don't use *tonsorial* when *barber* will do.

too, to, two. Don't confuse *too*, meaning *also* or *too much*, with the preposition *to* or *two* meaning one plus one.

too in the sense of *also* doesn't need a comma before or after it. Oliver Goldsmith wrote "Take this book too." Sir Walter Scott wrote "I too have sometimes this dark melancholy."

toolbox. One word.

tool chest. Two words.

toolhouse, toolmaker, toolmaking, toolroom, toolshed. One word.

toothache, toothbrush, toothbrushing, toothpaste, toothpick. One word.

top-. Most compounds are spelled as one word.

topcoat. One word.

top-drawer. Hyphened.

topflight, topgallant. One word.

top hat. Two words.

top-heavy. Hyphened.

topknot. One word.

top-level. Hyphened.

toplofty, topmast, topmost, topnotch. One word.

topsail. One word.

top-secret. Hyphened.

top sergeant. Two words.

topside, topsoil. One word.

topsy-turvy. Hyphened.

toque ends in *-que.*

torchbearer, torchbearing, torchlight. One word.

torero, toreros.

tormentor. Commonly spelled with *-or.*

tornado, tornadoes.

torpedo, torpedoes, torpedoed, torpedoing.

torpor ends in *-or.*

torque ends in *-que.*

torrential ends in *-tial.*

torsion ends in *-sion.*

torso, torsos.

tortoise.

tortuous, torturous. *Tortuous* means twisting, *torturous* means causing torture.

tosspot, tossup. One word.

tot up, totted up, totting up. Double *t* in all forms except *tot up.*

total, totaled, totaling. One *l* in all forms. *Total a car* is listed as standard usage in Webster's.

totalizator is spelled with *z.*

to the extent that. Don't use *to the extent that* when *as far as* will do.

touch and go. Three words.

touchback (noun), **touchdown** (noun). One word.
touché. Spelled with accent.
touchhole, touchline, touchmark. One word.
touch-me-not. Two hyphens.
touchup (noun). One word.
toupee is spelled with *ou* and double *e*.
tour de force. Three words.
tournament, tourniquet. Spelled with *ou*.
tousle. Spelled with *ou*.
toward, towards. Both forms are common.
towboat. One word.
towel, toweled, toweling. One *l* in all forms.
to wit. Don't use *to wit* when *namely* or *that is* will do.
towpath, towrope. One word.
tow truck. Two words.
toxin, tocsin. *Toxin* means poison, *tocsin* means warning bell.
toymaker, toyshop. One word.
traceable ends in *-eable*.
trachea, tracheae.
tracheo-. Compounds are spelled as one word, e.g. *tracheobronchial.*
tracklayer, tracklaying. One word.
tractor ends in *-or.*
trade-in (noun, adj.). Hyphened.
trademark. One word.
tradeoff. One word.
traffic, trafficked, trafficking, trafficker. Spelled with *ck* in all forms except *traffic.*
tragedian ends in *-ian.*
tragedy, tragedies.
tragicomedy. One word.
trailblazer, trailblazing. One word.
train-mile. Hyphened.
traipse. Listed as standard usage in Webster's.
traitor ends in *-or.*
trammel, trammeled, trammeling. One *l* in all forms.
tranquilize, tranquilizer, tranquillity. In the US, *tranquilize* and *tranquilizer* are commonly spelled with one *l,* but *tranquillity* with two.
trans-. Compounds are spelled as one word, except for words like *trans-Canadian.* But it's *transatlantic* and *transpacific.*

transcend is spelled with *sc.*

transcendent, transcendental. *Transcendent* means surpassing, *transcendental* means supernatural, but the two words are often used interchangeably.

transfer, transferred, transferring. Double *r* except in *transfer.*

transferable, transferal, transferee. No double *r.*

transference. No double *r,* ends in *-ence.*

transferor. No double *r,* ends in *-or.*

transgressor ends in *-or.*

(tranship). The US spelling is *transship* with double *s.*

transistor ends in *-or.*

transitory ends in *-ory,*

translatable ends in *-able.*

translator ends in *-or.*

translucent, transparent. *Translucent* means letting some light pass through, like frosted glass. *Transparent* means letting all light pass through, like clear glass.

transmissible ends in *-ible.*

transmit, transmitted, transmitting. Double *t* in all forms except *transmit.* Don't use *transmit* when *send* will do.

transmittal. Double *t.*

(transmittance). *Transmission* is more common.

transonic. Commonly spelled with one *s.*

transpacific. One word.

transparency, transparent end in *-ency, -ent.*

transpire. Don't use *transpire* when *happen, go on* or *become known* will do.

(transposal). The common word is *transposition.*

transship, transshipment. Double *s.*

transubstantiation. One *s* before *u.*

trapdoor, trapshoot, trapshooter. One word.

trauma. The plural *traumas* is getting more common than *traumata.*

travail in the sense of toil ends in *-ail.*

travel, traveled, traveler, traveling. One *l* in all forms.

travelogue. The common spelling.

trayful, trayfuls.

treachery is spelled with *ea.*

tread, trod, trodden.

treasonable ends in *-able.*

treasure house, treasure hunt, treasure trove. Two words.

treatise ends in *-ise.*

treble, triple. *Triple* is the more common word except in music.

trecento. The 1300s.

treed. Two *e*'s. (Not three.)

treetop. One word.

trek, trekked, trekking. Double *k* in all forms except *trek.*

trellis, trellised. Spelled with one *s.*

(tremblor). Misspelling of *temblor.*

tremendous, tremendously. No *i.*

tremolo, tremolos.

tremor ends in *-or.*

trenchant ends in *-ant.*

trenchcoat. One word.

trepan, trepanned, trepanning. Double *n* except in *trepan.*

trespasser ends in *-er.*

trestle. Silent *t.*

tri-. Compounds are spelled as one word, e.g. *tricolor.*

tributary ends in *-ary.*

trickle ends in *-le.*

tricycle. First *i,* then *y.*

triennial. Double *n.*

trier. Spelled with *i.*

tries. So spelled, e.g. *he tries, two tries.*

trio, trios.

triple, treble. *Triple* is the more common word except in music.

triple-. Compounds are hyphened, e.g. *triple-spaced.*

triplicate ends in *-ate.*

triptych ends in *-ych.*

triumphal, triumphant. It's a *triumphal* arch, but a *triumphant* army.

troche, trochee. A *troche* is a lozenge, a *trochee* with two *e*'s is a metrical foot in poetry.

trod. Past tense of *tread.*

troglodyte means cavedweller. So spelled.

trolley, trolleys. Spelled with *ey.*

trolley car. Two words.

troop, (noun, verb), **troupe** (noun, verb). A *troop* of soldiers, but a *troupe* of actors.

trooper, trouper. *He swears like a trooper,* but *he's a real trouper.*

troubadour. Has two *ou*'s.

troublemaker, troublemaking, troubleshoot, troubleshooter, troubleshooting. One word.

troublous. Don't use *troublous* when *troublesome* will do.

troupe, troop. A *troupe* of actors, but a *troop* of soldiers.

trouper, trooper. *He's a real trouper,* but *he swears like a trooper.*

trousers is spelled with *ou.*

trousseau, trousseaux.

trout. The common plural is *trout.*

trowel, troweled, troweling. One *l* in all forms.

truant officer. Two words.

truckdriver. One word.

truculence, truculent end in *-ence, -ent.*

truly. No *e. Sincerely yours* or *Sincerely* is more common than *Yours truly* or *Very truly yours.*

truncated is spelled with *c.*

truncheon ends in *-eon.*

trunkful, trunkfuls.

trunnion. Double *n.*

trustee, trusty. The plural of *trustee* is *trustees,* the plural of *trusty* is *trusties. Trustee* is the general word. A *trusty* is a convict with special privileges.

truthseeker, truthteller, truthtelling. One word.

try and. The idom goes back to 1526. John Milton wrote "At least to try and teach the erring soul."

try-on (noun). Hyphenated.

tryout. One word.

tryst. Spelled with *y.* Don't use *tryst* when *date* or *assignation* will do.

(tsar). The common spelling is *czar.*

tsetse fly.

T-shirt. Capital *T* and hyphen.

T square. Capital *T,* no hyphen.

-tt-. See -T-, -TT-.

tube in the sense of TV is listed as standard usage in Webster's.

tubful, tubfuls.

tub thumper. Two words.

tularemia. *A* after *l.*

tulle is spelled with *lle.*

tumbrel. The common spelling is with *el.*

tummy is listed as standard usage in Webster's.

tumor ends in *-or.*

tumultuous ends in *-uous.*

tumulus, tumuli.

tunable. No *e* before *able.*

tunesmith. Listed as standard usage in Webster's.

tuneup (noun). One word.

tunnel, tunneled, tunneling. One *l* in all forms.

turban, turbine. A *turban* is a headdress, a *turbine* is a rotary engine.

turbid, turgid. *Turbid* means muddy, *turgid* means swollen.

turbulence, turbulent end in *-ence, -ent.*

tureen ends in *-een.*

turf, turfs.

turgid, turbid. *Turgid* means swollen, *turbid* means muddy.

Turkish bath, Turkish towel. Capital *T.*

turn-. Almost all compounds are spelled as one word.

turnabout, turnaround (nouns), **turncoat, turndown** (noun). One word.

turn-in (noun). Hyphened.

turnkey, turnoff (noun), **turnout** (noun), **turnover** (noun), **turnpike, turnstile, turntable, turnup** (noun, adj.). One word.

turpentine starts with *tur.*

turquoise. Ends in *e.*

turreted. One *t* before *-ed.*

turtleback, turtledove, turtleneck. One word.

turtle shell. Two words.

tutelage ends in *-age.*

tutor ends in *-or.*

tutti-frutti. Hyphen. Two double *t*'s.

tut-tut. Hyphened.

tutu.

TV. Standard usage. Capital *T,* capital *V,* no periods.

twaddle. Spelled with double *d.*

'twas, 'twere, 'twill. Don't use these words in prose for *it was, it were, it will.*

twelfth is spelled with *f.*

twenties or **20s.** No apostrophe.

20th century. Don't spell it out. Means the 1900s.

twenty-one, twenty-first etc. Hyphened.

twice-. Compounds are hyphened, e.g. *twice-born, twice-told.*

twinge, tinge. *Twinge* means sudden pain, *tinge* means shade.

two, to, too. Don't confuse *two* meaning one plus one, the preposition *to,* and *too* meaning *also* or *too much.*

two, twos.

two-. Almost all compounds are hyphened.

twofer. Standard usage.

twofold. One word.

two-way. Hyphened.

tycoon. Standard usage.

tying. Common spelling.

tyke. Common spelling.

(tympani). Commonly spelled *timpani.*

type in the sense of *type of,* as in *that type person,* is commonly used, but not listed as standard usage in 1975 dictionaries.

typecast, typeface, typescript, typeset, typesetter, typewriter, typewriting. One word.

typhoid.

typhoon. Spelled with *ph.*

typhus ends in *-us.*

typify. The vowels are *y-i-y.*

typo, typos. Listed in Webster's as standard usage.

tyrannical. One *r,* double *n.*

tyrannically ends in *-ally.*

tyrannize. One *r,* double *n,* ends in *-ize.*

tyrannous ends in *-ous.*

tyranny. One *r,* double *n.*

tyrant. One *r,* ends in *-ant.*

(tyre). The US spelling is *tire.*

tyro, tyros. Common US spelling.

Tyrol, Tyrolean. Common spellings.

(tzar). The common spelling is *czar.*

U

u-. If you can't find the word you're looking for, try under *-eu.*

U-boat. Capital *U,* hyphen, small *b.*

UFO, UFOs. No periods.

ugh. Spelled with *h* at the end.

uglify. Standard usage. Ends in *-ify.*

uglily looks odd but it's the proper adverb of *ugly.*

uh-huh is the spelling given in Webster's for the sound expressing "affirmation, agreement or gratification."

UK. Abbreviation of *United Kingdom.* No periods needed.

ukase. *E* at the end.

ukulele.

ult. is old-fashioned business jargon. Avoid.

ultimate. Don't use *ultimate* when *final* will do.

ultimately. Don't use *ultimately* when *in the end* or *finally* will do.

ultimatum, ultimatums.

ultimo. Old-fashioned business jargon. Avoid.

ultra-. Compounds are spelled as one word, except when the second part starts with *a* or a capital, e.g. *ultra-ambitious, ultra-Marxist.*

ultraconservative, ultrafashionable. One word.

ultrahigh frequency. Two words.

ultra vires. Two words.

ululate. Two single *l*'s

umbrageous ends in *-eous.*

umbrella. No *e* between *b* and *r.*

umpteen, umpteenth. Standard usage.

UN. Needs no periods.

un-. Compounds are spelled as one word except when the second part starts with a capital, e.g. *un-American.*

unabated. Don't use *unabated* when *in full force* will do.

unacceptable ends in *-able.*

unaccommodating. Double *c,* double *m.*

unaccompanied. Double *c.*

unaccomplished. Double *c.*

unaccountable. Double *c,* ends in *-able.*

unaccustomed. Double *c.*

(unalienable). Even though the Declaration of Independence speaks of "unalienable rights," the common word now is *in-*alienable.

unalterable ends in *-able.*

un-American. Hyphen and capital *A.*

unanimous. First *n,* then *n,* then *m.*

unappetizing. Spelled with *z.*

unapt, inapt, inept. Use *unapt* for not likely, *inapt* for inappropriate, *inept* for bungling.

(unartistic). The common word is *inartistic.*

unassailable ends in *-able.*

(unauspicious). The common word is *inauspicious.*

unavailable ends in *-able.*

unavoidable ends in *-able.*

unaware, unawares. In common usage *unaware* without *s* is the adjective, e.g. *I was unaware of what's going on; unawares* with *s* is the adverb, e.g. *He was taken unawares.*

unbearable ends in *-able.*

unbeknown, unbeknownst. Both forms are standard usage. *Unbeknownst* is more often used for the adverb, e.g. *All this happened unbeknownst to me.*

unbelief is spelled with *ie.*

unbelievable ends in *-able.*

unbeliever is spelled with *ie.*

unbending can be used in the sense of relaxing or in the opposite sense of unyielding.

unbiased. One *s.*

unbreakable ends in *-able.*

unbridgeable ends in *-eable.*

uncalled-for. Hyphened.

uncared-for. Hyphened.

unchallengeable, unchangeable end in *-eable.*

unchristian. One word.

uncircumcised ends in *-ised.*

unclad. Don't use *unclad* when *nude* will do.

unclassifiable ends in *-iable.*

uncollectible. Commonly spelled with *-ible.*

uncomfortable ends in *-able.*

uncommitted. Double *m,* double *t.*

uncommunicative. (Not *in-.*)

(uncomparable). The common word is *incomparable.*

unconquerable ends in *-able.*

unconscionable is spelled with *sci* and ends in *-able.* Don't use *unconscionable* when *unfair* or *excessive* will do.

unconscious is spelled with *sci.*

uncontrollable. The common form. Ends in *-able.*

uncooperative. No hyphen.

uncoordinated. No hyphen.

uncorrectable. Standard usage. Ends in *-able.*

uncorroborated. Three *o*'s.

uncouth is spelled with *ou.*

unctuous ends in *-uous.*

undeceive is spelled with *ei.*

undecipherable ends in *-able.*

undeniable ends in *-iable.*

undependable ends in *-able.*

under-. Compounds are spelled as one word.

underachiever is spelled with *ie.*

under advisement. Don't use *under advisement* when a simpler phrase will do.

underage. One word.

underestimate. Don't use *underestimate* when you mean *overestimate,* e.g. *The importance of this move cannot be underestimated.*

underfoot, undergraduate, underground, underhand, underhanded. One word.

underlay, underlie. *Underlay* has been used interchangeably with *underlie* since 1591. See also LAY, LIE.

underlining. See ITALICS.

underprivileged. No *d* before *g.* Don't use *underprivileged* when *poor* will do.

underrate, underripe. One word.

under secretary. Follow Webster's and the GPO Style Manual and spell it as two words. Capitalize when used as a title, e.g. *Under Secretary of State William Gibson.*

under separate cover. Don't write *under separate cover* when *separately* will do.

undersigned. Don't write *the undersigned* when *I* will do.

understrength. Don't forget the *g*. One word.

under the circumstances. Standard usage.

underway. The GPO Style Manual spells it as one word. Follow the trend.

(under weigh). Spell it *underway.*

underwrite, underwriter.

undesirable. No *e* before *able.*

undetectable ends in *-able.*

undies for *underwear* is standard usage.

undigested. (Not *in-.*)

(undigestible). The common word is *indigestible.*

undisciplined. (Not *in-.*)

undiscriminating. (Not *in-.*)

undissolved. Double *s.*

(undistinguishable). The common word is *indistinguishable.*

undistinguished. (Not *in-.*)

undoubtedly. Silent *b.*

undreamed-of. Hyphened.

undrinkable ends in *-able.*

undue, unduly. No *e* in *unduly.* Often used when it doesn't make sense (e.g. *They suffered no undue ill effects.—Don't be unduly alarmed.*). Avoid.

undulant ends in *-ant.*

uneatable, inedible. *Uneatable* means spoiled, unfit to be served, *inedible* means unfit to be eaten.

unembarrassed. Double *r,* double *s.*

unendurable ends in *-able.*

unenforceable ends in *-eable.*

un-English. Hyphen, capital *E.*

unequaled. One *l.*

(unequivocably). The word is *unequivocally.*

(unescapable). The common word is *inescapable.*

unessential. (Not *in-.*)

unevenness. Double *n.*

unexceptionable, unexceptional. *Unexceptionable* means unimpeachable, *unexceptional* means commonplace.

unfashionable ends in *-able.*

unfavorable ends in *-able.*

unfeigned is spelled with *eign.*

unfit, unfitted. Don't use *unfitted* when *unfit* will do.

unflappable. Listed in Webster's as standard usage.

unfold. Don't use *unfold* when *happen, come out, tell, explain* will do.

unforeseeable is spelled with *e* between *r* and *s.*

unforgettable ends in *-able.*

unforgivable. No *e* before *able.*

unfree, unfreer, unfreest. Two *e*'s in all forms.

(unfrequent). The common word is *infrequent.*

unfriendly is spelled with *ie.*

ungovernable ends in *-able.*

unguent ends in *-uent.*

unhand. Don't use *unhand* when *let go* will do.

unhealthful, unhealthy. Dictionaries say you can use either word to mean either unwholesome or unwell.

unheard-of. Hyphened.

unhoped-for. Hyphened.

(unhuman). *Inhuman* is commonly used in the sense of either pitiless or nonhuman.

unhygienic.

uni-. Compounds are spelled as one word.

unilateral. Don't use *unilateral* when *one-sided* will do.

unimaginable ends in *-able.*

uninformed. Don't leave out the second *n* and make it *uniformed.*

unintelligible ends in *-ible.*

uninterested, disinterested. Webster's and the Oxford English Dictionary list *disinterested* in the sense of *uninterested* as standard usage.

unionized, un-ionized. *Unionized* (one word) means organized into a union, *un-ionized* (hyphened) means without chemical ionization.

union shop. Two words.

unique. Webster's lists *more unique* and *most unique* as standard usage. Dorothy Canfield Fisher wrote "The story of his life is considerably more unique than most autobiographies." Arthur Miller wrote "She's the most unique person I ever met."

unisex. Standard usage.

United Kingdom means the United Kingdom of Great Britain and Northern Ireland. Abbreviated *UK* (no periods).

United Nations. Abbreviated *UN* (no periods).

United States. Abbreviated *US* (no periods).

universally ends in *-ally.*

unjustifiable ends in *-iable.*

unkempt is spelled with *p.*

unknowable. Silent *k.*

unknowledgeable ends in *-eable.*

unlabeled. Two single *l*'s.

unless and until. Don't use *unless and until* when either *unless* or *until* alone will do.

unlikable. No *e* before *-able.*

unlikelihood. *I* before *hood.*

unlooked-for. Hyphened.

unloose means loosen, even though it's illogical.

unlovable. No *e* before *-able.*

unmanageable ends in *-eable.*

unmerciful. *I* before *ful.*

unmistakable. No *e* before *-able.*

(unmoral). The common word for indifferent to moral standards is *amoral,* the common word for wicked is *immoral.*

unnamed. Double *n.*

unnatural. Double *n.*

unnavigable ends in *-able.*

unnecessary, unnecessarily. Double *n,* double *s.*

unneeded. Double *n,* double *e.*

unnegotiable. Double *n.*

unneighborly. Spelled with *eigh.*

unnerve, unnerved. Double *n.*

unnoted. Double *n.*

unnoticeable ends in *-eable.*

unnoticed, unnumbered. Double *n.*

unobtrusively. No *s* before *t.*

unparalleled. First double *l,* then single *l.*

unparliamentary is spelled with *lia.*

unperceived is spelled with *ei.*

unpleasantness, unpleasantry. *Unpleasantness* means an unpleasant experience, *unpleasantry* means an insult.

unplumbed. Silent *b.*

unpracticable, unpractical. *Unpracticable* means impossible, *unpractical* means not useful. But the form *impractical* is is more common.

unprecedented. Don't use *unprecedented* when *uncommon* or *unusual* will do. *Unprecedented* means without a single precedent.

unpredictable ends in *-able*.

unprepossessing. Two double *s*'s.

unpretentious ends in *-tious*.

unprincipled ends in *-pled*. No *a*.

unprivileged ends in *-eged*. No *d* before *g*.

unprofitable ends in *-able*.

unpronounceable ends in *-eable*.

unpropitious ends in *-itious*.

unproven. Standard usage.

unquenchable ends in *-able*.

unquote. *Quote . . . unquote* in speaking marks quotation marks in writing.

unravel, unraveled, unraveling. One *l* in all forms.

unreadable ends in *-able*.

unrealistic in the sense of not based on facts is standard usage.

unrecognizable is spelled with *z*.

unreliable ends in *-iable*.

unrelieved is spelled with *ie*.

unreligious in the sense of irreligious, sinful is standard usage.

unrepairable. Commonly used.

unrepentant ends in *-ant*.

unrighteous ends in *-eous*.

unrivaled. One *l*.

unsanitary. Means *not sanitary*. The form *insanitary* is more common.

unsavory ends in *-ory*.

unscented is spelled with *sc*.

unseasonable ends in *-able*.

unself-conscious. One hyphen.

unserviceable ends in *-eable*.

unshakable. No *e* before *-able*.

unshaven. Standard usage.

unskillful. First two *l*'s, then one.

unsociable ends in *-iable*.

unsocial, antisocial, asocial, nonsocial. *Unsocial* means withdrawn from society, *antisocial* means against society, *asocial* means self-centered, *nonsocial* means not social.

unsolvable, insoluble. *Unsolvable* refers to what can't be resolved, *insoluble* refers to either what can't be solved or what can't be dissolved.

unspeakable ends in *-able*.

(unsubstantial). *Insubstantial* is more common.

unsuitable ends in *-able*.

(unsupportable). *Insupportable* is more common.

unsusceptible ends in *-ible*. Spelled with *sc*.

unsymmetrical. Spelled with *y* and double *m*.

untamable. No *e* after *m*.

untenable ends in *-able*.

unthinkable. Standard usage since 1430.

unthought-of. Hyphened.

untie, untied, untying.

until, till. Used interchangeably. (Don't write *'til* or *til*. These forms are not standard usage.)

until and unless. Don't use *until and unless* when *until* or *unless* alone will do.

until such time as. Don't write *until such time as* when *until* will do.

unto. Don't write *unto* when *to* will do.

untraceable ends in *-eable*.

untrammeled. One *l*.

untranslatable ends in *-able*.

untrod, untrodden. Both forms are standard.

untutored is spelled with *or*.

unusable. No *e* before *-able*.

unusual, unusually. Three *u*'s.

unvarying. Spelled with *yi*.

unveil. Don't write *unveil* when *tell, reveal* will do.

unwieldy. No *l* before *y*.

unwonted. Don't use *unwonted* when *rare, unusual, unaccustomed* will do.

unworkable ends in *-able*.

up (verb) is listed as standard usage in Webster's, e.g. *He upped and went to New York.—They upped the prices.*

-up. Most compounds are spelled as one word, e.g. *closeup, grownup, holdup, makeup, setup, windup.*

up-. Compounds are spelled as one word.

up against, up against it are listed in Webster's as standard usage.

up-and-up. Hyphened. Listed in Webster's as standard usage.

upchuck. Listed in Webster's as standard usage.

upcoming. Standard usage.

upcountry. One word.

update. Standard usage as verb and noun.

upgrade. Standard usage as verb and noun.

upheaval ends in *-al.*

uphill. One word.

upon. Don't use *upon* when *on* will do.

up on in the sense of informed is listed as standard usage in Webster's.

upper crust. Two words.

uppish, uppity are listed as standard usage in Webster's.

uproarious ends in *-ious.*

upside-down (adj.) Hyphened.

uptake. Standard usage.

uptight. One word. Listed as standard usage in Webster's.

up to in the senses of *I wonder what he's up to, it's up to you, she's not up to the job* is listed as standard usage in Webster's.

up-to-date. Two hyphens.

uptrend. One word.

upward, upwards. The adjective has no *s,* e.g. *an upward movement.* The adverb can have either form.

upwards of. Standard usage.

urban, urbane. *Urban* means of a city, *urbane* means polished, suave.

uremia.

uro-. Compounds are spelled as one word, e.g. *urogenital.*

us instead of the more formal *we* in such expressions as *it's us* is listed in Webster's as standard usage. It dates back to 1489. Robert Louis Stevenson wrote "It's us must break the treaty when the times come."

-us. The plural of words with the Latin ending *-us* may end in *-uses* like *prospectuses, -i* like *alumni,* or *-era* like *opera.* Check the specific entry in this dictionary.

US. No periods.

usable. No *e* before *-able.*

usage. Don't write *usage* when *use* will do.

use. The phrase *it is no use* is standard English. Shelley wrote "Alas! It is no use to say 'I'm poor!' "

used to. Don't leave out the *d* in such sentences as *we used to go there.*

using. No *e*.
usually.
usurer ends in *-er*.
utensil ends in *-sil*.
utero-. Compounds are spelled as one word.
utilize ends in *-ize*. Don't write *utilize* when *use* will do.
utilization is spelled with *z*. Don't write *utilization* when *use* will do.
utopia, utopian. Small *u*. Write *a utopia* (not *an*).
utterance ends in *-ance*.
uttermost. Don't write *uttermost* when *utmost* will do.
uvula, uvulas.

V

vacation-bound. Hyphened.

vaccinate, inoculate. *Vaccinate* is commonly used to mean inoculate against smallpox. *Inoculate* commonly refers to immunization against other diseases.

vacillate, vacillation. One *c,* double *l.*

vacuity, vacuousness. *Vacuity* is more common.

vacuous ends in *-uous.*

vacuum. One *c,* double *u.*

vacuum cleaner. Two words.

vacuum-packed. Hyphened.

vade mecum, vade mecums. Two words.

vagary ends in *-ary.*

vague ends in *-gue.*

vain, vane, vein. *Vain* means idle, conceited, *vane* means a weather vane, *vein* means a blood vessel.

vainness. Double *n.* The common word is *vanity.*

valance, valence. Spelled with *-ance* in the sense of drapery, with *-ence* in the chemical sense.

vale, veil. *Vale* means valley, *veil* means netting.

valedictorian, valedictory. *E* after *l.*

valet, valeted, valeting. One *t* in all forms.

valiant. Don't use *valiant* when *brave* will do.

Valkyrie. Capital *V.* Spelled with *y.*

valley, valleys.

valor ends in *-or.*

vamoose is slang. Spelled with double *o.*

van. Capitalize *Van* in American personal names, e.g. *Martin Van Buren,* but lowercase *van* in foreign names, e.g. *Ludwig van Beethoven.*

Vandyke. The painter's name is usually spelled like this. A *vandyke beard* is commonly spelled with a small *v.*

vane, vain, vein. *Vane* means a weather vane, *vain* means idle, conceited, *vein* means a blood vessel.

vanilla. One *n,* two *l*'s.

vapor ends in *-or.*

vaporize, vaporizer. Spelled with *z.*

variance, variant end in *-ance, -ant.*

variation. See REPETITION OF WORDS, SYNONYMS.

varicolored. One word.

varied ends in *-ied.*

variegated. *Ie* after *r.*

variety, varieties.

various. Don't use *various* when *several* will do.

varsity. Standard usage.

vaseline ends in *-e.*

vaso-. Compounds are spelled as one word, e.g. *vasoconstriction.*

vaudeville.

vaunt. Don't use *vaunt* when *boast* will do.

veep for *vice president* is listed in Webster's as standard usage.

vehement. Three *e*'s.

vehicle. Don't use *vehicle* when *car* or *truck* will do.

vehicular ends in *-ar.*

veil in the sense of netting is spelled with *ei.*

vein, vain, vane. *Vein* means blood vessel, *vain* means idle, conceited, *vane* means a weather vane.

veld. The common spelling is without final *t.*

velour. Commonly spelled without *s* at the end.

venal, venial. *Venal* means corruptible, *venial* means pardonable.

vend. Don't use *vend* when *sell* will do.

vender, vendor. *Vender* is more common. Don't use *vender* when *seller* will do.

vendible ends in *-ible.*

veneer ends in *-eer.*

venerable ends in *-able.*

venereal ends in *-eal.*

venetian blind. Small *v.*

vengeance ends in *-eance.*

venial, venal. *Venial* means pardonable, *venal* means corruptible.

venireman. One word.

ventilate, ventilation, ventilator. *I* after *t.*

ventriloquism, ventriloquist.

veranda, verandaed. Common spellings. No *h.*

verbal in the sense of spoken has been standard usage since 1591. Jonathan Swift wrote "Mr. Curll immediately proceeded to make a verbal will."

verdant. Don't say *verdant* when *green* will do.

verisimilitude. Don't say *verisimilitude* when *probability* will do.

veritable. Don't say *veritable* when *real* will do.

vermicelli.

vermilion. Commonly spelled with one *l*.

vermouth is spelled with *ou*.

versus. Abbreviated *vs.* in general and *v.* in legal matters.

vertebra, vertebrae.

vertex, vertexes.

vertically ends in *-ally*.

vertigo, vertigoes.

very has been used with the past participle of a verb since 1641, e.g. *very pleased, very tired, very excited.*

Very truly yours. The simpler forms *Sincerely yours* or *Sincerely* are more common.

vessel. Don't use *vessel* when *ship* will do.

vest-pocket (adj.) Hyphened.

vestryman. One word.

vet. Standard abbreviation of *veteran, veterinarian, veterinary.*

veteran. *E* after *t*.

veto, vetoes, vetoed, vetoing.

vexatious ends in *-tious*.

via. Don't say *via* when *by* or *through* will do.

viable. Don't use *viable* when *workable* or *sound* will do.

vial, vile, viol. *Vial* means a small vessel, *vile* means disgusting, *viol* means a musical instrument.

viands. Don't use *viands* when *food* will do.

viaticum, viaticums.

vibes for *vibrations* is listed as standard usage in Webster's.

vibrator ends in *-or*.

vicar ends in *-ar*.

vicar-general, vicars-general. Hyphened.

vice, vise. *Vice* means evil, *vise* is the US spelling of the word for a clamp.

vice-. Most personal titles beginning with *vice* are spelled as two words, e.g. *vice president.* Adjectives beginning with *vice* are usually hyphened.

vice admiral, vice chairman, vice chancellor, vice consul. Two words.

vice-consulate. Hyphened.

vicegerency, vicegerent. One word.

vice governor, vice minister. Two words.

vice-presidency. Hyphened.

vice president. Two words. Capital *V* and *P* when referring to the Vice President of the US or when used as a title preceding a name.

vice-president-elect. Two hyphens.

vice-presidential. Hyphened.

vice rector. Two words.

viceregal. One word.

vice regent. Two words.

vicereine, viceroy, viceroyal, viceroyalty. One word.

vice versa. Two words.

vichyssoise. Small *v.* Spelled with *i,* then *y,* followed by *ss.*

vicinity. Don't write *in the vicinity of* when *about* or *near* will do.

vicious, viscous. *Vicious* means evil, *viscous* means sticky.

vicissitudes. Don't write *vicissitudes* when *ups and downs* will do.

victor ends in *-or.*

victoria. The word meaning a coach is spelled with a small *v.*

victuals, victualed, victualing, victualer. Silent *c, ua,* one *l* in all forms. Don't say *victuals* when *food* will do.

vicuna. The GPO Style Manual leaves out the tilde over the *n.*

vide. Don't use *vide* when *see* will do.

video. Standard usage.

videotape. One word.

vie, vied, vying. Don't use *vie* when *compete* or *rival* will do.

viewfinder. One word.

viewpoint. Standard usage.

vigil. One *l.*

vigilance, vigilant end in *-ance, -ant.*

vigilante, vigilantes. A *vigilante* (with *e*) is a member of a vigilance committee. The plural is *vigilantes.*

vignette ends in *-ette.*

vigor, vigorous are spelled with *or.*

vile, vial, viol. *Vile* means disgusting, *vial* means a small vessel, *viol* means a musical instrument.

vilely ends in *-lely.*

vilification, vilify. *I* after one *l.*

villain, villein. A *villain* is a scoundrel, a *villein* is a serf. Remember "The *villain* lives in a *villa.*"

villainous, villainy. Spelled with *ain.*

-ville as in *dullsville* is listed as standard usage in Webster's.

vinaigrette.

vindicator ends in *-or.*

vindictive. No *a* between *c* and *t.*

vinegar ends in *-ar.*

vineyard. *E* before *y.*

vinyl. First *i,* then *y.*

viol, vial, vile. *Viol* means a musical instrument, *vial* means a small vessel, *vile* means disgusting.

violable ends in *-able.*

violator ends in *-or.*

violence, violent end in *-ence, -ent.*

violin case. Two words.

violoncello. *O* between *l* and *n.* But the common word is *cello.*

VIP, VIPs. No periods. Listed in Webster's as standard usage.

virago, viragoes.

viridescent. Spelled with *sc.*

virtu (art objects). Spelled with *i.* No *e* at the end.

virtue. Don't say *by virtue of* when *by* will do.

virtuoso, virtuosos.

virtuous ends in *-uous.*

virtuousness means full of virtue, *virtuosity* means high skill.

virulence, virulent end in *-ence, -ent.*

virus, viruses. *Virus* in the sense of a disease caused by a virus is standard usage.

visa, visas, (he) **visaes, visaed, visaing.**

vis-à-vis. Spelled with the accent. May mean *face to face with, in relation to, as compared with.*

viscera, visceral. Spelled with *sc.*

viscero-. Compounds are spelled as one word, e.g. *viscerogenic.*

(viscious). Misspelling of *vicious.*

viscount. Silent *s.*

viscous, vicious. *Viscous* means sticky, *vicious* means evil.

vise. US spelling of the word meaning clamp.

(visé). The US word is *visa.*

visibility. Four *i*'s.

visible ends in *-ible.*

visionary ends in *-ary.*

visitor ends in *-or.*

visit with in the sense of chat with is standard usage.

visor ends in *-or.*

visualize. Don't use *visualize* when *see, imagine, think of* will do.

vita, vitae.

vitalize ends in *-ize.*

vitamin. No *e* at the end.

vitiate. Don't use *vitiate* when *spoil* will do.

vitreo-. Compounds are spelled as one word.

vitreous ends in *-eous.*

vitrify. *I* before *f.*

vitriolic. Spelled with *io.*

vituperate, vituperation, vituperative. Don't use *vituperate, vituperation, vituperative* when *abuse, abusive* will do.

vivacious ends in *-acious.*

viva voce. Never hyphened.

viz. Don't use *viz.* when *namely* will do.

vizier.

(vizor). The US spelling is *visor.*

V-neck, V-necked. Capital *V,* hyphen.

vocabulary ends in *-ary.*

vocal cords. No *h* in *cords.*

vocalize ends in *-ize.*

vocation, avocation. *Vocation* means trade or profession, *avocation* means hobby.

voice (verb). Don't use *voice* when *express* will do.

voice box. Two words.

voice-over. Hyphened. Standard usage.

voiceprint. One word.

volcano, volcanoes.

volley, volleys.

volume. Don't use *volume* when *book* will do.

voluptuous ends in *-uous.*

von. Capitalize *Von* in American personal names, e.g. *John Von Neumann,* but lowercase *von* in foreign names, e.g. *Otto von Bismarck.*

voodoo. Two double *o*'s.

voracious ends in *-acious.*

vortex, vortexes.

votable. No *e* before *-able.*

votegetter. One word.

voting machine. Two words.

vouchsafe. Don't use *vouchsafe* when *give* or *grant* will do.

voyeur ends in *-eur*.

vs. Abbreviation of *versus*. (But use *v.* for legal cases.)

vulcanize ends in *-ize*.

vulgar, vulgarity. Spelled with *ar*.

vulgarize ends in *-ize*.

vulnerable ends in *-able*.

-vv-. Rarely used, as in *revving* an engine.

vying. Participle of *vie*. Don't use *vie* when *compete* or *rival* will do.

W

w-. If you can't find the word you're looking for, try *wh.*

wacky. So spelled. Listed in Webster's as standard usage.

waffle in the sense of vacillate is standard usage.

wage earner, wage scale. Two words.

wagon. One *g.*

wagon master, wagon train. Two words.

waif, waifs.

wainscoting. One *t.*

waist, waste. *Waist* means the narrow part of the body, *waste* means refuse.

waist-deep, waist-high. Hyphened.

waistline. One word.

waiting game, waiting list, waiting room. Two words.

waive, wave. *Waive* means give up, *wave* means flutter, move a hand.

waiver, waver. *Waiver* means the act of giving up, *waver* means vacillate.

wake, waked, waked. These are the common verb forms. (*Awake, waken, woke, woken* are rarer.)

walk-. Most compounds are spelled as one word.

walkaway. One word.

walkie-talkie. Hyphened. Standard usage.

walk-in (noun). Hyphened.

walk-on (noun, adj.). Hyphened.

walkout, walkover (noun), **walkup** (noun), **walkway.** One word.

(Walkyrie). The common spelling is *Valkyrie.*

wallboard, walleye, walleyed, wallflower. One word.

wall-less. Hyphened.

wallop, walloped, walloper, walloping. One *p* in all forms.

wallpaper. One word.

wall-to-wall. Two hyphens.

walnut. One *l.*

waltz, waltzer. Spelled with *tz.*

want. Don't use *wish* or *desire* when *want* will do.

wantonness. Double *n.*

war-. Almost all compounds are spelled as one word.

War Between the States. Southern name of the Civil War.

war chest, war cry. Two words.

-ward, -wards. Adjectives before a noun usually end in *-ward,* e.g. *a backward child,* adverbs may end in *-wards,* e.g. *He was moving backwards,* or *-ward,* e.g. *outward bound.*

ward heeler. Two words.

warehouse, warehouseman. One word.

war game. Two words.

warhead, warhorse, warlike, warmaker, warmaking. One word.

warm-blooded, warmed-over. Hyphened.

warmhearted. One word.

warmonger, warmongering. One word.

warmup (noun). One word.

warp and woof. The *warp* runs lengthwise in the loom, the *woof* or *weft* runs crosswise.

warpath, warplane. One word.

warrantee, warrantor, warranty. The *warrantor* gives the *warranty* (or *guarantee*) to the *warrantee.* The *warrantee* is a person, the *warranty* is a contract.

warring, warrior. Double *r.*

warship, wartime. One word.

was, were. The idiom *was* in such expressions as *if I was President* (condition contrary to fact) goes back to 1684. John Bunyan in *Pilgrim's Progress* wrote "as if I was awake." The subjunctive form *were* is more formal. It is always used in the fixed phrase *if I were you.*

(was graduated). The common usage is active, not passive—*he graduated from college.* Don't leave out *from.*

wash-. Almost all compounds are spelled as one word.

wash-and-wear. Hyphened. (Not *'n'.*)

washbasin, washboard, washbowl, washcloth, washday. One word.

washed-out, washed-up. Hyphened.

washhouse. One word.

washing machine. Two words.

washout (noun), **washrag, washroom.** One word.

wash sale. Two words.

washstand, washtub, washup (noun). One word.

wasn't. Common contraction of *was not.*

WASP. All capitals, no periods. Means *White Anglo-Saxon Protestant.* Standard usage.

wassail ends in *-ail.*

Wassermann test. Double *n.*

wastage. Don't use *wastage* when *waste* will do.

wastebasket, wasteland, wastepaper. One word.

watchband, watchcase, watchdog, watchmaker, watchmaking, watchman. One word.

watch spring. Two words.

watchtower, watchword. One word.

water-. Compounds are spelled as one word, as two words or hyphened.

waterbed. One word.

water bottle. Two words.

watercolor. One word.

water cooler. Two words.

waterfall, waterfront. One word.

water gage, water glass, water heater. Two words.

waterhole, waterline, waterlogged, watermark, watermelon. One word.

water meter, water pipe. Two words.

waterpower, waterproof, waterproofed. One word.

water-repellent. Hyphened. Ends in *-ent.*

water-resistant. Hyphened. Ends in *-ant.*

watershed, waterskiing, waterspout, watertight, waterway, waterworks. One word.

wave, waive. *Wave* means flutter, move a hand, *waive* means give up.

wavelength. One word.

waver, waiver. *Waver* means vacillate, *waiver* means the act of giving up.

wavy. No *e.*

wax (verb). Don't use *wax* when *get* or *grow* will do.

wax paper. Two words. The common form.

way in the sense of *away* is commonly spelled without an apostrophe, e.g. *way down, way off.* Standard usage since 1849.

-way. Compounds are spelled as one word, e.g. *stairway, freeway.*

way-. Most compounds are spelled as one word.

waylay, waylaid, waylaying.

we. The pronoun *we,* referring to yourself alone—the editorial *we*—is no longer common usage. When you write of yourself, say *I.*

weak, week. *Weak* means feeble, a *week* means seven days.

weakhearted. One word.

weak-kneed, weak-minded. Hyphened.

wealth is spelled with *ea.*

weapon is spelled with *ea.*

wear and tear. No hyphens.

weariness, wearisome. *I* in the middle.

weather, whether. *Weather* refers to the climate, *whether* means if.

weatherbeaten, weatherbound. One word.

weather gage. Two words.

weatherman. One word.

weather map. Two words.

weatherproof. One word.

weather strip, weather stripping. Two words.

weave. The common forms in the sense of interlace are *wove* and *woven.* In the sense of moving from side to side, write *weaved.*

(weazened). The common spelling is *wizened.*

webfoot. One word.

web-footed. Hyphened.

wed. Don't use *wed* when *marry* will do.

we'd. Common contraction of *we had, we would.*

wedge-shaped. Hyphened.

Wedgwood. Capital *W,* no *e* after *g.*

Wednesday. Don't forget the *d.*

-weed. Compounds are spelled as one word, e.g. *tumbleweed.*

weedkiller, weedkilling. One word.

weekday, weekdays, weekend, weekends, weekender, weeklong, weeknight, weeknights. One word.

(weenie). Spell it *wienie.*

weeny in the sense of tiny is listed in Webster's as standard usage.

weevil, weeviled, weevily. One *l* in all forms.

weigh-in. Hyphened.

weight lifter, weight lifting. Two words.

weight-watcher. Hyphened.

weimaraner is spelled with *ei.*

(weiner, weinie). Misspellings of *wiener, wienie.*

weir is spelled with *ei.*

weird is spelled with *ei.*

weirdie, weirdo, weirdos are listed in Webster's as standard usage.

(welch). The common spelling is *welsh.*

welcome. One *l.*

welder ends in *-er.*

welfare. One *l.*

well. There's a trend towards leaving out the comma after *well* at the beginning of a sentence, e.g. *Well how about that.*

well-. Compound adjectives are commonly hyphened, whether before or after the noun, e.g. *a well-known restaurant, his fears were well-founded.*

we'll. Common contraction of *we will, we shall.*

well-advised, well-appointed, well-being, well-beloved. Hyphened.

wellborn. One word.

well-bred, well-defined, well-disposed, well-favored, well-founded, well-groomed, well-grounded, well-handled. Hyphened.

wellhead. One word.

well-heeled. Listed in Webster's as standard usage.

Wellington. The word meaning a boot is capitalized.

well-intentioned, well-knit, well-known. Hyphened.

well-nigh. Don't say *well-nigh* when *almost* will do.

well-off, well-read, well-rounded, well-spoken. Hyphened.

wellspring. One word.

well-taken, well-thought-of, well-timed, well-to-do, well-wisher, well-wishing, well-worn. Hyphened.

Welsh, welsh. Spelled with *sh* whether referring to people from Wales or meaning going back on a deal.

Welsh corgi. So spelled. Capital *W.*

Welsh rabbit. This form is more common than *Welsh rarebit.*

weltanschauung, weltanschauungs. Small *w.* Underlining (italics) not necessary.

weltschmerz. Small *w.* No *t* before *z.* Underlining (italics) not necessary.

wend one's way. Don't write *wend one's way* when *go, go on* will do.

were, was. The idiom *was* in such expressions as *if I was President* (condition contrary to fact) goes back to 1684. John Bunyan wrote "As if I was awake." The subjunctive form *were* is more formal. It is always used in the fixed phrase *if I were you.*

we're. Common contraction of *we are.*

we remain, at the end of letters, is old-fashioned business jargon. Avoid.

weren't. Common contraction of *were not.*

werewolf, werewolves.

west. Small *w* for the compass direction, capital *W* for the western part of the US or the world, or non-Communist countries in general.

westerly. A westerly wind comes from the west.

westward, westwards. Use *westward* for the adjective, *westwards* for the adverb, e.g. *a westward journey, they traveled westwards.*

wetback. One word. Standard usage, but considered offensive.

wet nurse. Two words.

wet-nurse, wet-nursed, wet-nursing. Hyphened.

we've. Common contraction of *we have.*

(whacky). The common spelling is *wacky.*

whammy, whammies. Listed in Webster's as standard usage.

wharf, wharves.

what. It is standard usage to use *what* with a singular or plural verb, e.g. *What they want is a good lunch.—What they want are promises.*

whatever. One word in all senses.

what have you, what not. Listed in Webster's as standard usage.

what's. Common contraction of *what is.*

whatsoever. Don't use *whatsoever* when *whatever* will do.

what with. Standard usage.

wheelbarrow, wheelbase, wheelchair. One word.

wheeler-dealer. Listed in Webster's as standard usage.

wheelhorse. One word.

when and if. Don't use *when and if* when either *when* or *if* alone will do.

whence, from whence. Don't use *whence* or *from whence* when *from where* or *where . . . from* will do.

where. Don't use *where* when *when* or *if* will do.

whereabouts. Commonly used with *s* at the end and with a plural verb, e.g. *His whereabouts are unknown.*

whereat. Don't use *whereat* when *at which* or *when* will do.

whereby. Don't use *whereby* when *by which* or *so that* will do.

wherefor, wherefore. *Wherefor* means for which, *wherefore* means why. Don't use *wherefor* when *for which* will do. Don't use *wherefore* when *why* will do.

wherefrom. Don't use *wherefrom* when *from which* will do.

wherein. Don't use *wherein* when *in which* will do.

whereinto. Don't use *whereinto* when *into which* will do.

whereof. Don't use *whereof* when *of which* or *of what* will do.

whereon. Don't use *whereon* when *on which* will do.

where's. Common contraction of *where is.*

whereto. Don't use *whereto* when *where* or *to which* will do.

whereunto. Don't use *whereunto* when *where* or *to which* will do.

whereupon. Don't use *whereupon* when *when, on which, after which* will do.

wherewith. Don't use *wherewith* when *with which* will do.

wherewithal. Only one *l.*

whether, weather. *Whether* means if, *weather* refers to the climate.

whether or not. Don't write *whether or not* when *whether* alone will do.

whey, as in *curds and whey,* is spelled with *wh.*

which doesn't necessarily refer back to a noun. Sentences like *the play closed Saturday night, which is too bad* are standard usage.

which, that. When you refer to things rather than persons, use *which* for so-called nonrestrictive—commenting—clauses and *that* for so-called restrictive—defining, limiting—clauses. Put commas around *which* clauses and no commas around *that* clauses. For instance, write *the book, which had 800 pages, kept me up until 2 a.m.* (The *which* clause about the length of the book is just added comment and doesn't tell you what book it was.) But write *the book (that) you gave me for Christmas kept me up until 2 a.m.* (The *that* clause tells what book it was. Note that the word *that* can be left out.)

Don't use *which* when *that* or no pronoun will do. Go on a *which*-hunt.

See also AND WHICH, BUT WHICH.

while in the sense of *but, although, though* or *whereas* has been standard usage since 1588. Shakespeare wrote (Love's Labour's Lost, I, i, 74): "Painfully to pore upon a book To seek the light of truth *while* truth the while Doth falsely blind the eyesight of his look."

whilom is archaic. Write *former* or *formerly.*

whilst. The US word is *while.*

whimsical, whimsically.

whimsy. The spelling without *e* is common.

whiny. No *e.*

whipcord. One word.

whip hand. Two words.

whiplash, whippersnapper. One word.

whipping boy, whipping post. Two words.

whippoorwill. Double *p,* double *o.*

whipsaw, whipsawed. One word.

whir, whirred, whirring. Double *r* in all forms except *whir.*

whirligig. *I* in the middle.

whirlpool, whirlwind. One word.

whirlybird. One word. Listed in Webster's as standard usage.

whisk broom. Two words.

whiskey, whisky. The spelling *whiskey* (plural *whiskeys*) is commonly used for US and Irish products, and *whisky* without *e* (plural *whiskies*) for Scotch and Canadian products.

whiskey sour. Spelled with *-ey.*

whistle. Silent *t.*

whistlestop. One word.

white. Don't capitalize when you refer to race.

white-. Compounds are spelled as one word, two words or hyphened.

whitecap. One word.

white-collar. Hyphened.

white-faced, white-headed, white-hot, white-livered. Hyphened.

white paper, white slave. Two words.

whitewall, whitewash. One word.

whitey ends in *-ey.* Listed as standard, usually used disparagingly, by Webster's.

whither. Don't use *whither* when *where* will do.

whitish. No *e.*

whiz, whizzed, whizzer, whizzing. Double *z* in all forms except *whiz.*

whizbang. One word.

who, whom. *Who* rather than the more formal *whom* has been commonly used since 1400 in such sentences as *who did you talk to?* James Froude wrote "He has a right to choose who he will have for a teacher."—But *whom* rather than the more formal *who* has been commonly used since 1467 in such sentences as *a man whom I thought was my enemy.* Dickens wrote "A strange unearthly figure, whom Gabriel felt at once was no being of this world."

who'd. Common contraction of *who had, who would.*

whodunit. So spelled. Listed as standard usage in Webster's.

whoever, whomever. Spell as one word in all sentences. *Whoever* rather than the more formal *whomever* has been commonly used since 1592. Shakespeare wrote (Henry VIII, II, i, 47) "Whoever the King favours, The cardinal instantly will find employment."

wholehearted. One word.

whole-wheat bread. Hyphened.

wholly. Double *l.*

whom. See WHO, WHOM.

whomever. See WHOEVER, WHOMEVER.

whoop.

whoop-de-do. One *o* at the end. Listed in Webster's as standard usage.

whoopee. Listed in Webster's as standard usage.

whooping cough. Two words.

(whoopla). The common spelling is *hoopla.*

whoosis, whoosises. Double *o.* Listed in Webster's as standard usage.

whop, whopped, whopper, whopping. Double *p* in all forms except *whop.* Listed in Webster's as standard usage.

who're. Common contraction of *who are.*

who's, whose. *Who's* means who is, *whose* means of whom.

whose, referring to things rather than people, has been used since 1382. Shakespeare wrote (Hamlet, I, v, 15) "I could a tale unfold whose lightest word Would harrow up thy soul."

who've. Common contraction of *who have.*

-wide. Compounds are spelled as one word, e.g. *citywide, nationwide.*

wide-. Some compounds are spelled as one word, some are hyphened.

wide-awake, wide-brimmed, wide-eyed, wide-mouthed, wide-open, wide-screen. Hyphened.

widesought, widespread. One word.

widget. Standard usage.

wield is spelled with *ie.*

wiener, wienie. Spelled with *ie.*

wife, wives.

wiggly. No *e.*

wildcat, wildcatted, wildcatter, wildcatting. One word.

wild-eyed. Hyphened.

wildfire. One word.

wild flower, wild oats, wild rice. Two words.

will, shall. In common US usage, *will* rather than *shall* is used to express the simple future, e.g. *I will be there at 10 o'clock.—You will see.*

    Shall is used in first-person questions, e.g. *Shall we go?* and to express command or determination, e.g. *Jack shall go.—They shall not pass.*

willful, willfulness, willfully. The common US spelling is with double *l* in *will.*

willies. Listed as standard usage in Webster's.

will-less. Hyphened.

will-o'-the-wisp. Three hyphens, one apostrophe.

willowware. One word. Double *w.*

willpower. One word.

willy-nilly. Hyphened.

wily, wilier, wiliest, wiliness. *I* in all forms except *wily.*

win (noun) in the sense of victory is standard usage.

wind-. Almost all compounds are spelled as one word.

windbag, windblown, windbreaker, windburn, windchill, windfall, windmill. One word.

window box, window cleaner, window dresser, window dressing, window envelope. Two words.

windowpane. One word.

window-shop, window-shopper. Hyphened.

windowsill. One word.

windpipe, windproof, windscreen, windshield, windsock, windstorm, windswept. One word.

wind tunnel. Two words.

windup (noun, adj.). One word.

windward. No *s* at the end. Means facing the wind.

wine-. Most compounds are spelled as one word.

winebibber. Double *b.*

wine cellar. Two words.

wineglass, winegrower, winepress. One word.

wing-. Some compounds are spelled as one word, some as two, some are hyphened.

wing chair. Two words.

wingding. One word. Listed as standard usage in Webster's.

wing it is listed as standard usage in Webster's.

wingover, wingspan, wingspread. One word.

wino, winos. Listed as standard usage in Webster's.

winter, wintertime. Small *w.*

winterize is spelled with *z*.

wintry. No *e*.

winy. No *e*.

wipeout. One word.

wirecutter, wirecutting, wirehair, wirehaired, wirepuller, wire-pulling, wiretap, wiretapped, wiretapper, wiretapping. One word.

wiry. No *e*.

-wise. Compounds are spelled as one word, e.g. *clockwise, taxwise*.

wiseacre, wisecrack. One word.

wise guy. Two words. Listed in Webster's as standard usage.

wisenheimer. Starts with *wi-*. Standard usage.

wish. Don't use *wish* when *want* will do.

wish to advise, . . . say, . . . state. Usually unnecessary. Avoid.

wishy-washy. Hyphened.

wisteria. The common spelling.

wit, to. Don't use *to wit* when *namely* or *that is* will do.

withal is archaic. Avoid.

with a view to. Don't write *with a view to* when *to* will do.

withhold, withholding. Two *h*'s.

withholding tax. No hyphen.

within. Don't write *within* when *inside* will do.

with-it. Hyphened. Listed in Webster's as standard usage.

without. Don't use *without* instead of *outside* or *unless.*

with reference to, with regard to, with relation to, with respect to. Don't use these compound prepositions when *about* will do.

with the exception of. Don't use *with the exception of* when *except* will do.

with the result that. Don't use *with the result that* when *so that* or *so* will do.

witness-box. Hyphened.

witness stand. Two words.

witticism. Double *t, c*.

wizard.

wizened. The common spelling.

wobbly. No *e*.

woebegone, woeful. Spelled with *oe*.

wok. So spelled. Chinese cooking pan.

wolf, wolves, wolfed, wolfing.

wolfpack. One word.

wolverine ends in *-ine*.

woman, lady. *Woman* is the regular word, as in *a woman in the audience spoke up* or *the room was empty except for a young woman sitting at a table in the back. Lady* is the courteous word, used in salutations or in the presence of the person referred to, as in *Ladies and Gentlemen* or *the lady was here first.*

-woman. Compounds are spelled as one word. e.g. *Congresswoman, madwoman.*

woman-hater, woman-hating. Hyphened.

womanlike. One word.

womb. Silent *b.*

women's lib, women's libber. Standard usage.

wonder. The expression *I shouldn't wonder* is commonly used with a double negative, as in *I shouldn't wonder if it didn't rain.*

wonderland. One word.

wonder-worker, wonder-working. Hyphened.

wondrous. No *e.* Don't use *wondrous* when *wonderful* will do.

wont. Don't use *wont* when *custom, habit* will do.

won't. Common contraction of *will not.*

wonted. Don't use *wonted* when *usual* will do.

-wood. Compounds are spelled as one word, e.g. *oakwood, pinewood.*

wood-. Most compounds are spelled as one word.

woodblock, woodchopper, woodcraft, woodcut, woodcutter, woodcutting. One word.

wood engraver, wood engraving. Two words.

woodenness. Double *n.*

woodland. One word.

wood nymph. Two words.

woodpile, woodshed, woodturner, woodwork, woodworker, woodworking. One word.

woof, warp. The *woof* or *weft* runs crosswise in the loom, the *warp* runs lengthwise.

woolen, woolly. The common US spelling is *woolen* with one *l* and *woolly* with two *l*'s. *Woolen* refers to fabrics, *woolly* may refer to anything, e.g. thoughts.

woolly-headed. Hyphened.

woolpack, woolpacker, woolpacking. One word.

woozy. No *e.* Listed in Webster's as standard usage.

word division. See DIVISION OF WORDS.

wordlist, wordplay. One word.

-work. Compounds are spelled as one word, e.g. *millwork, woodwork.*

work-. Almost all compounds are spelled as one word.

workable ends in *-able.*

workaday. Don't use *workaday* when *everyday* will do.

workaholic. Often used.

workbasket, workbook, workday. One word.

-worker. Compounds are spelled as one word, e.g. *steelworker.*

work force. Two words.

workhorse, workhouse, workingman, workmanlike, workout (noun), **workroom, workshop, worktable, workup** (noun), **workweek.** One word.

worldly. Two *l*'s.

worldwide. One word.

-worm. Compounds are spelled as one word, e.g. *earthworm.*

worm-eaten. Hyphened.

wormhole, wormholed. One word.

worn-out. Hyphened.

worriment, worrisome. *I* in the middle.

worry, worried, worrier, worrying.

worse-. Compounds are hyphened, e.g. *worse-looking.*

worsen. Standard usage.

worship, worshiped, worshiper, worshiping. In standard US spelling, all forms are spelled with one *p.*

worst-. Compounds are hyphened, e.g. *worst-kept secret.*

worsted.

worst to the worst. The idiom is *if the worst comes to the worst.* (Two superlatives.)

-wort. Compounds are spelled as one word, e.g. *liverwort.*

worthwhile. One word.

would, should. In common US usage *should* is used in the sense of *ought to,* e.g. *You should have been there.* Otherwise it is common to say *would* rather than *should,* e.g. *I would think so* rather than *I should think so.* There are also some other standard idiomatic uses, e.g. *if this should happen.*

would appear, would seem, would think. Don't use these phrases if a more straightforward statement will do.

would have. Don't write *would have* twice in such sentences as *If I would have known, I would have been there.* Write *If I had known, I would have been there.*

would like is common US usage in such phrases as *I would like, we would like.*

wouldn't. Common contraction of *would not.*

would rather is standard usage.

would've. Common contraction of *would have*.

wrack, rack. It's spelled *wrack* in *wrack and ruin*, *rack* in *clothes rack, hayrack, rack one's brains*.

wraith. Spelled with silent *w*.

wrangle is spelled with silent *w*.

wrap, wrapped, wrapper, wrapping. Double *p* in all forms except *wrap*.

wraparound (noun, adj.). One word.

(wrapt). Use *rapt* without *w* for *rapt attention*.

wrap-up (noun). Hyphened.

(wrassle). The common word is *wrestle*.

wrath, wrathful. Silent *w*.

wreak, as in *wreak havoc,* is spelled with silent *w*.

wreathe, wreathed, wreathing.

wrestle. Silent *w* and *t*.

wring, wrung, wrung.

wristband, wristlock, wristwatch. One word.

write, wrote, written.

write-down (noun), **write-in** (noun, adj.). Hyphened.

writeoff (noun). One word.

-writer. Compounds are spelled as one word, e.g. *copywriter*.

writeup (noun). One word.

writing desk, writing paper, writing room. Two words.

wrongdoer, wrongdoing, wrongheaded. One word.

wroth, wrathful. *Wroth* is used after the noun, e.g. *He was wroth when he saw what happened.* Don't use *wroth* when *angry* will do.

wrought-up. Hyphened.

wry, wrier, wriest, wryly, wryness. Common US forms.

wunderkind, wunderkinder.

wurst, meaning sausage, is spelled with *u*.

X

X, x. Spell the plural of capital *X, Xs,* but of small *x, x's.*

x, x-ed, x-ing. Hyphen for all verb forms but *x.*

Xanthippe. Spelled with *th.*

xenophobia. One word.

Xerox, Xerox, Xeroxing. Capital initial *X.*

(-xion). In the US, *connection, inflection* and *reflection* are spelled with *-ction.*

Xmas. The abbreviation *Xmas* for *Christmas* has been used since 1551. Standard usage, though taboo at the New York Times and Associated Press.

X-rated. Hyphened. Capital *X.*

X-ray. Hyphened, capital *X* for verb, noun and adjective.

xylophone.

Y

-y. Plurals of words ending in *-y* end in *-ies,* e.g. *lady, ladies.* But the plurals of proper names ending in *-y* end in *-ys,* e.g. *the three Marys, the two Germanys, the two Kansas Citys, the Kennedys.*

yacht is spelled with *cht.*

yachtsman, yachtsmanship. One word.

Yahoo ends in *-oo.*

Yahweh. The common spelling.

yak. No *c.*

-yard. Compounds are spelled as one word, e.g. *backyard.*

yardarm, yardbird, yardman, yardmaster, yardstick. One word.

yarmulke. Common spelling.

yashmak. Common spelling.

yawp. Common spelling. Listed in Webster's as standard usage.

(yclept). Don't use *yclept* when *named* or *called* will do.

yea, yeah. Spell it *yea* for *the yeas have it* and *yeah* for a casual *yes.*

year-end. Hyphened.

yearlong. One word.

year-round. Hyphened.

yegg is listed in Webster's as standard usage.

yellow jack. Two words.

yen, yen. Japanese currency.

yenta is slang.

yeoman. Spelled with *eo.*

yes. The plural is *yeses.* Don't capitalize *yes* or use quotation marks when you aren't actually quoting. Write *he said yes.*

yeshiva, yeshivas. Commonly spelled without *h* at the end.

yes-man. Hyphened.

yet. Don't use *yet* when *but* will do.

yew, you. *Yew* means the tree, *you* means the person addressed.

yield is spelled with *ie*.

yodel, yodeled, yodeler, yodeling. One *l* in all forms.

yoga, yogi. *Yoga* means the system, *yogi* means the practitioner.

yogurt. Commonly spelled without *h*.

yoke, yolk. *Yoke* refers to oxen, *yolk* to eggs.

yokel is standard usage.

yoo-hoo. Hyphened.

yore. Don't use *of yore* when *long ago* will do.

you. The indefinite *you,* meaning *one,* has been standard usage since 1577. John Ruskin wrote "You can talk a mob into anything."

you-all. Hyphened. Used in the South as the plural of *you* or in addressing one person representing a group.

you'd. Common contraction of *you had, you would.*

you'll. Common contraction of *you will, you shall.*

youngster may be offensive. Don't use.

your, you're. *Your* means of yours, *you're* means you are. A common contraction.

your earliest convenience. Don't write *at your earliest convenience* when *soon* will do.

yours. No apostrophe.

yours truly. *Yours sincerely, Sincerely yours* or *Sincerely* are now more common at the end of business letters.

(yous). Nonstandard plural of *you.*

youth. Don't use *youth* when *young man* will do.

youthful. Don't use *youthful* when *young* will do.

you've. Common contraction of *you have.*

yo-yo, yo-yos. Hyphened.

yuan. Currency of China.

Yugoslav, Yugoslavia. Common spellings.

yuletide. One word. Small *y*.

yummy, yummier, yummiest. Listed as standard usage in Webster's.

Z

-z-, -zz-. Words ending in *z* immediately preceded by a single vowel double the *z* before *-ed, -es* etc., e.g. *quiz, quizzed, quizzes, quizzical.*

zany. Standard usage.

zap. Listed in Webster's as standard usage.

(zar). Misspelling of *czar.*

zeal, zealot, zealous. Spelled with *ea.*

zeitgeist. So spelled. Small *z.*

zephyr ends in *-yr.*

zeppelin. Double *p.* Small *z.*

zero, zeros; (he) **zeroes, zeroed, zeroing.** Leave out unnecessary zeros. Instead of *$30.00* write *$30.* Instead of *$5,000,000* write *$5 million.* Instead of *2:00 a.m.* write *2 a.m.*

zero gravity, zero hour. Two words.

zigzag, zigzagged, zigzagging. One word. Double *g* in all forms except *zigzag.*

zilch in the sense of zero is listed in Webster's as standard usage.

zinc, zinced, zincing. Common spelling.

zincky. Common spelling.

zing, zinger, zingy. Standard usage.

zip code. Lower case.

zip gun. Two words.

zippy. Listed in Webster's as standard usage.

zither.

zloty. Currency of Poland.

zoftig ends in *g.* Slang.

zombie ends in *-ie.*

zonked is listed in Webster's as standard usage.

zoo, zoos.

zoological, zoology. Double *o.*

zoom means climb up or move with a humming sound. Don't use
  zoom for moving downwards.
zucchetto is spelled with *cch*.
zucchini is spelled with *cch*. The common plural is *zucchini*.
zwieback is spelled with *ie*.